TROTSKYISM AND MAOISM

THEORY AND PRACTICE
IN
FRANCE AND THE UNITED STATES

TROTSKYISM AND MAOISM

THEORY AND PRACTICE
IN
FRANCE AND THE UNITED STATES

A. BELDEN FIELDS

New York
Westport, Connecticut
London

Library of Congress Cataloging-in-Publication Data

Fields, A. Belden.
  Trotskyism and Maoism.

     "An Autonomedia Book."
     Bibliography: p.
     Includes index.
     1. Communism—France—History—20th century.
     2. Communism—United States—History—20th century.
     3. Communist parties—France—History—20th century.
     4. Communist parties—United States—20th century.
     I. Title
     HX263.F5   1988   324.44'075   83-23042

Autonomedia, Inc.
55 South 11th Street
P.O. Box 568 Williamsburg Station
Brooklyn, New York 11211-0568
USA

Cloth edition published for
Praeger Publishers, Inc.
One Madison Avenue
New York, NY 10010 USA
A division of Greenwood Press, Inc.

ISBN: 0-275-92035-6

Printed in the United States of America

The paper used in this book complies
with the Permanent Paper Standard
issued by the National Information
Standards Organization (Z30.48-1984).

10 9 8 7 6 5 4 3 2 1

Contents

Illustrations follow page 183

For
Jane Ellen Morhaz

ACKNOWLEDGEMENTS

Any work which attempts to open up scholarly enquiry into active social movements which have largely been ignored by scholars is heavily dependent upon the cooperation of precisely the people whom it studies. This work is of that nature and it is no exception to the rule. I regret to say that I am not sure how much reciprocity is involved since the most profound insights of academics are usually nothing that the activists themselves have not considered. At the very least, I hope that I have portrayed accurately and fairly the positions and the actions of the groups with which I have dealt. Since there is always some criticism inherent in analysis, some people who cooperated with me might read some things with which they disagree or which they find offensive. I can only assure them as well as the reading public that such critical analysis is both honest and fallible, that while I do not belong to any of the groups studied I respect the commitment to human emancipation and the dedicated work—often undertaken at considerable personal cost—of those who do, and that I am sincerely grateful for the kindness and the assistance that was so generously extended by a number of individuals affiliated with those groups.

Because there can be political costs attached to talking with writers, some who cooperated with me ask that I not acknowledge their cooperation at all. Others have asked that I acknowledge either only the cooperation of the organization or their personal cooperation without involving the organization. Respecting these requests, I should like to thank the following organizations or the staffs of the following publications in France for their cooperation: *La Cause du Peuple,* Le Centre d'Études et de Recherche sur les Mouvements Trotskystes et Révolutionnaires Internationaux, Les Comités Communistes pour l'Autogestion, *Libération,* La Ligue Communiste Révolutionnaire, Lutte Ouvrière, Le Parti Communiste Marxiste-Léniniste de France, and L'Union des Communistes de France Marxistes Léninistes. Alain Geismar, Alain Krivine, François de Massot, and Michel Raptis were very helpful. I should also like to acknowledge the very kind reception and the extension of privileges by the Fondation Nationale des Sciences Politiques in Paris and its Secretary General, Professor Serge Hertig, as well as by the Centre Universitaire International. Professor Michèle Gibault of the Universite d'Amiens was also very helpful. Special thanks for assistance and kindness go out to H.K.

I also wish to acknowledge the very kind assistance of members of the following organizations in the United States: the Communist Party (Marxist-Leninist), the Revolutionary Communist Party, the Socialist Workers Party and its youth affiliate the Young Socialist Alliance, Spark, the Spartacist League, and Workers World Party. A number of people were kind enough to read and comment on the entire manuscript or on parts of it at various stages of development. For assuming this chore my gratitude goes out to Peter Bock, Berenice Carroll, Walter Feinberg, Richard Kraus, Joseph LaPalombara, Mihailo Markovic, Richard Merritt, Kelley Mickey, Joseph Miller, and Wolf Dieter Narr. Carl Davidson was extremely helpful with the material on U.S. Maoism. Frances Robbins, Judy Gallistel, Judy Holt, Mary Marchal, and Eileen Yoder all did conscientious typing while the late Marsha Smith did equally conscientious proof reading. I am grateful to all of these people. I am also grateful for the institutional support received from the Department of Political Science, the School of Social Sciences, the Office of Western European Studies, and the Research Board of the Graduate School at the University of Illinois in Urbana. I am grateful to Sue Ann Harkey and Christopher Mays of Autonomedia for cover design and index, respectively, and to Mary Alison Farley of the Tamiment Collection at New York University for assistance with archival images.

To three people I wish to express very special appreciation. Without the assistance of Professor Anne Thieulle of the University of Paris VII, assistance which went well beyond what could reasonably be expected out of either friendship or academic courtesy, I could not have kept abreast of the situation in France when I was not immediately on the scene. Her assistance was essential to the project. I am also particularly grateful to Jim Fleming of Autonomedia for the commitment and work which he has devoted to this book. Finally, I am doubly grateful to Jane Mohraz. I am grateful for her skilled editorial assistance. I am even more grateful for her friendship, companionship, and moral support during this entire project.

Despite the good fortune of having all of this assistance, I must assume the sole responsibility for any errors which might appear in the text. I must also assume responsibility for the translations from the French unless otherwise noted.

A.B.F.
Urbana, Illinois

INTRODUCTION

This is a study of political practice and its relationship to both theory and national contextual factors with which those who attempt to implement theory must contend. All political movements claim some relationship to political theories, or at the very least to some maxims derived from theories. The tightness of the relationship between practice and theory by groups active in the political arena manifests itself in a continuum which runs from those groups which view virtually every decision or action as having crucial theoretical implications to those which merely use theory as a legitimizing cover for the pursuit for narrowly conceived self-interest. In the latter case, theory loses all coherence and one is left with moral rationalization.

In focusing on Trotskyist and Maoist groups in this study, we are operating at the tight end of the continuum. At least in their mature years, both Trotsky and Mao subscribed to Marxism-Leninism. Marxism, as understood and elaborated upon by Lenin, conceives of theory and practice as one combined "science," Here the role of theory is neither merely diagnostic, nor simply suggestive, nor primarily prescriptive. Theory is a "scientific" weapon, based on a correct analysis of history and social relations, which gives superior advantage in practice to those who wield it. Conversely, the effect of ignoring theory or of making errors in theory is to doom political practice just as surely as mistakes in deciphering the laws of physics would doom engineering attempts. Marxist-Leninists, in contradistinction to a number of other interpreters and followers of Marxism, accept Engels' modelling of Marxist social theory after theories in the physical and biological sciences. Some, like Mao, have also accepted Engels' extension of the Marxist dialectical method to an understanding of the physical universe—"the dialectics of nature."

When we take a cursory overview of the intended and actual practice—or *praxis* since the activity is intended as a response to Marx's call to transform the social universe in an emancipatory direction—of Marxist-Leninists who operate as opposition currents within capitalist industrialized societies, we can distinguish three levels.

First, there is practice in the form of overthrowing capitalism and instituting socialism. This, of course, has traditionally been the ultimate emancipatory goal of Marxism-Leninism but it has not been accomplished within any capitalist industrialized context. All indigenous revolutionary efforts which have resulted in the acquisition of state power by Marxist-Leninists have occurred within contexts of relatively low industrial development and internal surplus and a low ratio of the proletariat to other more traditional segments of the population.

A second level of practice is the gaining of a mass base of support. The complex structures of industrialized societies are not as congenial to the seizing of power by small vanguard groups as was pre-1917 Russia. Within these contexts, the gaining of mass support is a necessary precondition of goal number one, the institution of socialism. While that latter goal has not been accomplished by Marxist-Leninists in any capitalist industrialized society, both the French and Italian Communist Parties have indeed been able to attract large memberships and significant electoral support. However, in order to maintain their mass support, both the French and Italian parties have had to modify considerably their approach to goal number one. Enter the phenomenon of Eurocommunism, the repudiation of the dictatorship of the proletariat, and the emphasis upon pragmatics at the expense of the science of Marxism-Leninism generally.

A third level of practice is one of surviving over time with sufficient members and resources to both offer a corrective model to Marxism gone astray and to attempt intermittent influence on the larger political universe. Although certainly not by choice, this is the level at which Trotskyist and Maoist formation have been operating. This study examines just how they have gone about attempting to offer an uncorrupted scientific conception of politics within the context of those industrialized societies that Marx and Engels saw as the most fertile terrains for revolutionary change. The specific national contexts in question are France and the United States.

The comparative dimension is extremely important in this endeavor. First, it permits an examination of the impact of different national political characteristics upon movements which subscribe to the same highly specific body of theory. It is interesting to see to what extent such movements "look alike" or "look different" as one moves across national boundaries and political cultures. But, secondly, comparative investigation can also warn against exclusive reliance upon contextual factors. For example, in a discussion of what she regards as the failure of American Trotskyism, Constance Ashton Myers has written that: "An 'all-inclusive' radical party, the kind envisioned by Norman Thomas for the American Socialist Party, was clearly better adapted to American attitudes and traditions."[1] Leaving aside the fact that from 1941 to the present the American Socialist Party has suffered a fate more dismal than that of the Trotskyist Socialist Workers Party, the limited appeal and fragmentation of Trotskyists and Maoists (not only in the United States, but also France, where there exists a strong Marxist tradition and a large and relatively cohesive Communist Party) directs one back to the guiding theories themselves for a full explanation of the characteristics of these movements.

The major proposition of this work is thus that limited appeal, debilitating fragmentation, and the precise lines of cleavage which divide both Trotskyist and Maoist movements in France and the United States are attributable to a *convergence* of (1) the peculiarities of the political culture in which the attempt to apply the theories is made with (2) contradictions which inhere in the guiding theories themselves. Methodologically, this means that the analysis must incorporate both empirical-positivistic explanations based upon external causal factors and a consideration of the internal dialectics of Trotskyism, and Maoism as theoretical structures.

Aside from what it reveals about relationships between political practice, contextual factors, and theory and what it tells us about the problems faced by Marxist-Leninists who attempt a rigorous implementation of their science in capitalist societies, there are additional reasons why a study of this nature is important.

First, as we shall see, these movements played important roles in one of the most significant political phenomena of the 1960s and 1970s in France and the United States. This was the radicalization of young people.

While much of the activity which went on during the late sixties and the early and mid-seventies was spontaneous, Trotskyist and Maoist groups contributed disciplined work of a theoretical, organizational, and propagandistic nature. This work was important in sustaining levels of interest between events and in providing channels for political engagement with greater permanence and direction than demonstrations or street barricades could afford. Trotskyists and Maoists, on their own or in cooperation with others, created wide ranges of sympathizing structures and *ad hoc* support groups devoted to specific struggles. They were thus able to have an impact upon a wider range of the population than their own immediate memberships. Yet this experience goes unrecorded.

Secondly, while in both France and the United States the membership of Trotskyist and Maoist groups has remained well below that of Marxist-Leninist parties with greater sympathy for the Soviet Union, it must be kept in mind that Maoist movements independent of the larger Communist parties are a new historical phenomenon which date from the Sino Soviet split, while Trotskyist movements in France and the United States (as well as on a world-wide level) reached their historical membership peaks in the 1970's. The latter was a rather remarkable achievement on part of Trotskyists. They have survived for over half a century after Trotsky's exile from the USSR without the existence of any regime which could serve as a functioning model or source of support. Yet if this unique variant of Marxism-Leninism does not show any immediate sign of the capability of stimulating or executing a revolution in any capitalist country in the world, neither does it show any sign of disappearing from the scene.

Moreover, the internal discipline and ability to find ways of influencing people outside of their own ranks exhibited by these newly created and juvenated groups, has permitted them to accomplish certain goals. With the near exception of the 1968 French revolt in which *some* Trotskyists and Maoists participated, these accomplishments have fallen short of overthrowing regimes. But they are of intrinsic importance and have affected peoples' lives regardless of whether or not they should prove in the future to have been part of a larger historical revolutionary process.

Despite these considerations, there has been almost no scholarly literature devoted to the dynamics of these groups or the specific content of Trotskyist and Maoist politics. This writer can point to only one article, Jim O'Brien's "American Leninism in the 1970's," which deals with Trotskyist and Maoist movements in the United States.[2] Of the two books produced by American scholars in recent years which deal with Trotskyist movements, one deals with them in the Latin American context while the other deals with the Socialist Workers Party in the United States but only up to the year 1941.[3] There is somewhat more literature in France but most of it is polemical and little has been translated for the benefit of the English language readership.[4]

The absence of published research on this subject matter is an impediment to scholarly understanding. For a concrete example of that, one can consult the review article written by Mario D. Fenyo for the special spring and summer 1977 issue of *Studies in Comparative Communism*. In this special issue devoted to Trotskyism by a major scholarly journal, there is almost no information on contemporary movements. Fenyo, who was charged with the task of reporting on such research, tried. But he came to the conclusion that in the United States there exists a "conspiracy of silence" directed against Trotskyism even by other groups on the Left. His discussion of Trotskyism in Western Europe is very brief because he could not find "any description of the evolution of Trotskyism in the countries of Western Europe, systematic or unsystematic...."[5] This author's experience with both American and Eastern European colleagues, even those who work with socialist systems, has revealed that they know very little about Trotskyism and Maoism as active opposition forces.[6]

But aside from being an impediment to scholarly understanding, the lack of available material of a scholarly or precise nature has been an ad vantage to governments intent upon repressing these movements. In the Soviet Union and the countries of Eastern Europe, including Yugoslavia where accused Trotskyists were put on trial in the early 1970s, the single parties control everything written or said in the media about Trotskyism or Maoism.[7] Either designation is equivalent to "counter-revolutionary." If there are Trotskyists or Maoists in these countries, they can ill afford to make he fact public. In China, Trotskyism is also used as a political charge synonymous with counterrevolutionary.[8] Indeed, it is one of the charges levied against the "Gang of Four."

But repression against Trotskyists and Maoists is not restricted to Marxist regimes. Both French and American governments have also used repressive techniques against Trotskyists and Maoists. However, because of the greater public awareness of their existence in France as well as the greater sympathy for Marxist groups in general, governmental repression usually encounters a public outcry of protest and support for the repressed from other groups and prominent individuals. In the United States, which has developed into a science techniques for obliterating the memory of its own radicals from its school curricula and media, the major problem is certainly not the "conspiracy of silence" perpetrated by other groups on the Left referred to by Fenyo. It is rather the absence of accurate information accessible to the public that has facilitated governmental repression against both Trotskyists and Maoists.

The Trotskyist Socialist Workers Party was the first group to have its leadership tried and convicted under the Smith Act and it was, in the 1960s and 1970s, a major target of the completely illegal COINTELPRO disruption program conducted by the FBI. Aside from the violent aspects of that program itself, much of the effort was devoted to the creation of an image of the SWP as a violent group through the FBI's journalistic contacts and through anonymous letter-writing techniques. The lack of any scholarly or objective media treatment of the SWP meant that there was no possibility of a reality check against the FBI's definition of the party. Once a government is so able to define a group for the few among the general public who are even aware of its existence, the government has a very free hand. More recently, the American government has turned its attention to the Maoist Revolutionary Communist Party. As a result of a January 1979 demonstration against the visit of Premier Teng Hsiao-ping to the United States, the top leaders of that Maoist (and anti present-Chinese leadership) party were indicted on multiple felony charges.

But few people know about either that party or the specific situation and there was hardly a public outcry with which the government had to contend.

The absence of knowledge about these groups has yet another consequence which is also more aggravated in the United States than in France. It encourages chance or uninformed political engagement. Most Americans who initially affiliate with groups outside of the political mainstream do so because of chance encounters with individuals already in the groups. At least at the time of initial engagement, the recruit often has little knowledge of the range of possibilities available. For those who might be inclined toward engagement in Trotskyist or Maoist groups, this book will provide both an overview of the nature of Trotskyism and Maoism and a detailed discussion of the variety of interpretations and kinds of practice which are in existence. If knowledge is better than ignorance for the scholar, it is certainly no less important for the activist the potential activist.

The precise research techniques employed in this study were the collection and examination of documents and textual material, interviews, and participant observation. The research was begun during a sabbatical semester in France in 1972. Additional research trips to France were made in 1975 and again in 1978 after the legislative elections of that year which had such a remarkable impact upon the Left as a whole. An attempt has been made to incorporate all of the national and even some of the regional Trotskyist and Maoist groups operating in both France and the United States. Particularly in the case of Maoism, some tiny and/or purely local groups have been omitted. That was due to the lack of availability of data and access rather than a deliberate attempt to slight any particular groups. While the study focuses on contemporary movements, the importance of the accumulation of past experience for a present identity is recognized. Thus, each of the chapters on the movements begins with an historical treatment going back to their origins.

The work is organized as follows. Chapter 1 first offers a brief and noncritical comparison of Trotsky's basic concepts with those of Mao. In particular, it focuses on two of Trotsky's most important contributions to revolutionary theory, permanent revolution and the Transitional Program, and compares them with Mao's concept of uninterrupted revolution. Even to many scholars who work in related areas, the distinctions between the basic concepts of Trotsky and those of Mao are not clear. Without getting into the more complex problem of theoretical contradiction at this stage, this portion of the chapter is intended to provide such clarification and to provide the reader with some basis for understanding the theoretical inspiration of the movements which are discussed in the main body of the work. The second part of this chapter discusses the similarities and differences between the contexts in which French and American Trotskyists and Maoists attempt to apply their theories in practice.

The body of the work is composed of four chapters dealing with the Trotskyist and Maoist movements in each of the countries through the decade of the 1970s. These chapters discuss the history, patterns of organization, programs, and the strategies and tactics pursued by the variety of groups operating under those banners. Because of the number of groups involved, the frequent splintering and name changes, and the probable lack of prior exposure to this material on the part of most readers, chronological charts of the groups discussed are included at the end of the book, along with the notes and bibliography. The reader might wish to consult these charts to gain an overview before reading each of these chapters.

The sixth chapter attempts a synthetic demonstration of the proposition that the dynamics of Trotskyist and Maoist practice and the configurations which these movements assume within any given national context is determined by the interplay between peculiarities within the specific political culture and contradictions within the guiding theories themselves. The analysis is based upon the data contained in the previous four chapters and a more critical-analytical consideration of the theories than is presented in Chapter 1. The chapter terminates with what, in this author's view, is the major problem facing Marxist-Leninists who attempt to apply uncorrupted, scientistic interpretations of Marxism-Leninism to contemporary industrialized capitalist societies.

As indicated above, during the 1980s there have been some new directions taken by Trotskyists and Maoists in the two countries. An Epilogue has been separately provided to take into account those more recent developments for most of the 1980s, to best accommodate readers whose primary interests are more contemporary.

1
Theories and Contexts

In comparing Trotskyist and Maoist groups claiming reference to a body of theory or a model regime, it will be helpful to accord brief consideration at the outset to some comparisons between the theories of Trotsky and of Mao. While the major concern in this section will be with the differences which exist between these two theories, it should be pointed out that there are indeed similarities.

As indicated in the Introduction, both theorists claimed to be Marxist-Leninists during their mature political years. More concretely that meant that both accepted dialectical materialism as a science, both accepted the concept of a democratic-centralist revolutionary party, and both accepted some interpretation of the dictatorship of the proletariat. Second, both Trotsky and Mao conceptualized the revolutionary process as occurring over time with its own dialectical dynamic. This is incorporated into Trotsky's theory of permanent revolution and into Mao's theory of uninterrupted revolution. Third, both saw their respective countries, which were not the highly industrialized countries in which Marx had anticipated the advent of socialism, as being susceptible to socialist revolution. Fourth, both were highly anti-bureaucratic and critical of the income gaps between political and managerial elites and workers, as well as of gaps within the ranks of workers, which had been permitted to develop in the USSR. Fifth, both were sensitive to the dynamics of intergenerational relationships, Mao attempting to mobilize the younger generation to control the bureaucracy and Trotsky appealing to the younger generation both while his Left Opposition was still operating in the Soviet Union and in his later analysis of the oppressive nature of Stalin's regime. Finally, although this list does not pretend to be exhaustive, Trotsky and Mao agreed that Stalin's tactic of obliging the members of the Chinese Communist Party to scuttle their own structure in order to enter the Kuomintang and work with Chiang Kai-shek in the twenties was an error. Trotsky criticized it at the time, while Mao criticized it openly in retrospect. It was to cost many Chinese Communists their lives when Chiang decided to terminate the relationship by a massacre.

The major differences between the two theorists lie in their respective views of the peasantry and in their conceptions of the nature of the revolutionary process itself. To many readers in the United States, the word "peasantry" has an archaic ring. The question becomes extremely important, however, for any analysis of the possibilities for socialism in the Third World.

Both Trotsky arid Mao knew the peasantry well. Trotsky (then Lev Bronstein) came from an unusual Jewish family which had been able to acquire enough fertile farm land in the Kherson Steppe to hire a number of agricultural workers. Trotsky's view of the peasantry was thus not merely an attempted recapitulation of Marx's views but was based upon his own first-hand experience.

An important part of Trotsky's radicalization was his experience with the plight and submissiveness of farm labor when his father assigned him the task of paymaster on the family farm.[1] Mao also came from the countryside, the Hunan countryside. He was the head of the peasant department of the Chinese Communist Party in the mid-twenties.[2]

Despite their rural, non-Western backgrounds, both Trotsky and Mao were attracted to ideas coming from the West. Mao was attracted to Marxism, a Western body of thought. Trotsky was attracted not only to Marxism but to virtually all of the characteristics of the West except capitalism—technology, science, urbanization, and Western literature, particularly French literature. Mao, however, was able to mold Marxism-Leninism into a body of thought and a model of practice which he felt would enable China to achieve socialism consistent with its special conditions. This is where the Maoist theory of uninterrupted revolution parts company with the Trotskyist theory of permanent revolution.

Marxism is a Western body of thought. It is linear; it is historicist; and it is scientific in the sense of looking for regular laws of social development. All of these are Western characteristics. Moreover, as it was originally formulated by Marx and Engels, it anticipated that the transition from capitalism to socialism would take place once highly productive industrial capitalism had produced both a larger urban proletariat as the agent of its own destruction and an economic surplus which could materially sustain socialism. Redistribution and the new, unalienated socialist person depended upon the absence of both scarcity and the mentality and culture which accompanied pre-industrial scarcity.

In a curious way, Trotsky presented the world with a version of Marxism which remained true to this Western orientation. Curious because Trotsky, from the very early years of the twentieth century, was optimistic about the possibility of revolution in Russia. This was despite the fact that the proletariat was very small in comparison to the peasantry and that the Russian state and foreign investors largely assumed the function which an indigenous capitalist class had assumed in Western Europe and the United States.

The theory of permanent revolution is the key to how a Western-oriented thinker could be one of the earliest to foresee the revolution in the Russian setting. The idea of the permanent revolution was one of combined bourgeois democratic and socialist revolution. While the bourgeois democratic revolution had occurred in the late eighteenth and nineteenth centuries in Western Europe, and thus would be separated from the socialist revolution by a considerable time period, Trotsky thought that the processes could and would be combined into a single process in Russia.

Trotsky thus rejected the idea that a country such as Russia—and after the Russian Revolution he generalized this to what he called the "backward" countries generally—had to pass through a stage of bourgeois democracy like that in the countries of the West. He argued that such a conception of necessary stages would break the revolutionary momentum and turn out to be a counterrevolutionary disaster. Instead of such a "mechanical" application of the European experience, Trotsky advanced the theory of permanent revolution, which involved distinctions, between a "minimum" and a "maximum" program and between the seizure of political power by the workers and socialism.

The peasantry would play an important supportive role in the struggle, to topple the existing, often feudal or neo-feudal, political regimes. There was no doubt that the Russian autocracy was weakened both by its own internal inefficiency and by war. Trotsky's first major formulation of his theory came in *Results and Prospects* (1906), published the year after both Russia's military loss to the Japanese and the 1905 revolution in which Trotsky had been an active participant. Trotsky was convinced that the peasants, who saw themselves as victims of Tsarist oppression, could be counted upon as allies in the struggle to topple the regime so long as the ralying cry was a "minimum program" which emphasized liberal democratic demands.

However, the "maximum program" of the socialists would include collectivism and internationalism.[3] Collectivism, as applied to the agricultural sector by Trotsky, would still leave room for subsistence or semi-subsistence farming of a private nature but would eliminate "small capitalist farming" and the private employment of farm labor. It would thus be opposed by the relatively well-off peasants or kulaks out of individual self-interest. However, Trotsky did not feel that even the poorer peasants or the farm laborers, with whom he had great sympathy, would be capable of understanding or contributing much to the realization of the "maximum program" of the socialists: "But the great predominance of the urban population lies not only in the mass of productive forces that it constitutes, but also in its qualitative personal composition. The town attracts the most energetic, able, and intelligent elements of the countryside."[4]

Trotsky saw no way of changing the consciousness of the peasants short of actually presenting them with socialist structural changes. In the

1906 work, Trotsky clearly stated the dependence of consciousness upon structural change within this context: "If socialism aimed at creating a new human nature within the limits of the old society it would be nothing more than a new edition of the moralistic utopias. Socialism does not aim at creating a socialist psychology as a pre-requisite to socialism but at creating socialist conditions of life as a pre-requisite to socialist psychology."[5]

This being the case, there could be no parity between the proletariat and the peasantry at any point in the revolutionary process as Lenin had suggested in his concept of a "democratic dictatorship of the proletariat and the peasantry." From the very beginning of this process, the proletariat had to secure and maintain political hegemony over the peasantry. In *The Permanent Revolution,* published after he had been exiled from Soviet politics (1929), Trotsky wrote:

> The peasantry can undoubtedly prove to be a
> tremendous force in the service of the revolution;
> but it would be unworthy of a Marxist to believe
> that a peasant party is capable of placing itself at
> the head of a bourgeois revolution and, upon its
> own initiative, liberating the nation's productive
> forces from the archaic fetters that weigh upon
> them. The town is the hegemon in modern society
> and only the town is capable of assuming the role of
> hegemon in the bourgeois revolution.[6]

While Trotsky rejected the notion that the "backward" countries had to pass through a stage of bourgeois democratic revolution in which the peasantry would play a leading role, he also rejected the idea that the maximum socialist program could be implemented as soon as the proletariat assumed political hegemony. This was because of limitations of consciousness within the proletariat itself, because of its numerical inferiority *vis-à-vis* the peasantry, and because such hasty action would invite peasant revolt. Therefore, the minimum program would carry over for some time even after the old regimes had been toppled and the proletariat had secured dominant power over the political structure of the country.

Such securing of political power without attempting to implement the maximum program immediately represents the beginning of the dictatorship of the proletariat for Trotsky. A state in this early phase was referred to by Trotsky as a "workers' state." It is only after the proletariat had very prudently over time instituted the maximum program that Trotsky was willing to use the designation "socialism."

However, Trotsky added another qualification, the most severe in terms of the possibility for socialism in the less industrialized or nonindustrialized world. In *Results and Prospects* (1906) he wrote: "Without the direct State support of the European proletariat the working class of Russia cannot remain in power and convert its temporary domination into a lasting socialist dictatorship."[7] Trotsky fully agreed with Marx that the objective material conditions for socialist revolution resided in the capitalist industrialized world. But in this early stage of his theorizing, he believed that the uniqueness of the Russian situation with its enfeebled political infrastructure would permit the relatively small Russian proletariat to take the lead in at once toppling Tsarism *and* providing a catalytic inspiration which would move the Western European proletariats into revolutionary action. If the latter did not materialize, Trotsky saw no hope for socialism in Eastern Europe or in what we now refer to as the Third World.

This is the element of internationalism in the theory of permanent revolution. Trotsky continued to emphasize this aspect of his theory. In the manifesto which he prepared for the First Congress of the Communist International (1919), Trotsky wrote:

> The workers and peasants not only of Annam,
> Algiers and Bengal, but also of Persia and
> Armenia, will gain their opportunity of indepen-
> dent existence only in that hour when the workers
> of England and France, having overthrown Lloyd
> George and Clemenceau, will have taken state
> power into their own hands.... If capitalist
> Europe has violently dragged the most backward
> sections of the world into the whirlpool of capitalist
> relations, then socialist Europe will come to the aid
> of liberated colonies with her technology, her
> organization and her ideological influence in order
> to facilitate their transition to a planned and
> organized socialist economy.
> Colonial slaves of Africa and Asia! The
> hour of proletarian dictatorship in Europe will
> strike for you as the hour of your emancipation.[8]

The text of *The Permanent Revolution* is just as insistent on this point. There Trotsky wrote: "Whether the dictatorship of the proletariat in Russia leads to socialism or not, and at what tempo and through what stages, will depend upon the fate of European and world capitalism."[9]

And, generalizing the proposition to the nonindustrialized world at large: "Backward countries may, under certain conditions, arrive at the dictatorship of the proletariat sooner than advanced countries, but they will come later than the latter to socialism."[10] Thus if the peasantry in the "backward" areas was incapable of even initiating movement toward its own liberation without the political domination of the indigenous proletariat, that indigenous proletariat was equally incapable of attaining socialism without the support of socialist regimes in at least some of the Western industrialized countries.

This perspective explains why Stalin's notion of "socialism in one country" was an anathema to Trotsky. Trotsky saw this as the major theoretical choice which Marxists had to make and under which everything else had to be subsumed: "Either permanent revolution or socialism in one country--this alternative embraces at the same time the internal problems of the Soviet Union, the prospects of revolution in the East, and finally, the fate of the Communist International as a whole."[11]

For Trotsky, the problem of Stalinism was theoretical misconception, not individual traits of Stalin. In Trotsky's eyes, Stalin erroneously conceived of the revolution as one of discrete stages rather than as a continuous process. Although there were stages within the stages, the two major stages delineated by Stalin were "socialism in one country" and the subsequent stage of "socialism on a world scale."[12] Given Trotsky's theory, there obviously could be no such thing as "socialism in one country," particularly in one country with a low level of development. In Trotsky's view, Stalin's attempt to act as though it were possible led, inevitably, to the Soviet Union becoming a "degenerated workers' state" characterized by bureaucratization, totalitarianism, the cult of personality, income inequalities, and the continued particular oppression of women and the youth.[13] It also determined its international behavior, from the error of forcing the Chinese Communists into the bourgeois Kuomintang only for precious urban cadres to be set up for Chiang Kai-shek's massacre, to Stalin's refusal to encourage the German Communists to join forces with the social democratic left to defeat Nazism. Everything was sacrificed to that impossible goal, the construction of socialism in the Soviet Union all by itself. As a result of Stalin's unquestionable control over the Comintern, Trotsky's hope for a Russian revolution which would touch off a spark in Western Europe where the objective preconditions existed, and whatever hope there was for revolution in the nonindustrialized world, became dimmer and dimmer.

So it was directly to the Western industrialized countries that Trotsky turned his attention in his last major work, *The Transitional Program: The Death Agony of Capitalism and the Tasks of the Fourth International*. This work was written as a strategic guide for the national sections in the Western countries of the Fourth International, the formal Trotskyist international structure created in 1938 to rival the Stalinist Third International or Comintern.

If Trotsky accepted Lenin's explanation that the Russian revolution and revolutionary movement in the nonindustrialized world were results of the uneven development of historical processes tied to capitalism's entry into the stage of imperialism, he had to contend with another manifestation of "uneven development" in the West. This time it was "the contradiction between the maturity of the objective revolutionary conditions and the immaturity of the proletariat and its vanguard."[14]

Because of this contradiction, the distinction between the minimum and maximum programs made in reference to the combined democratic and socialist revolutionary processes within the nonindustrial context was carried over into the Transitional Program. However, while it was to have been a tool of a more highly conscious proletariat in its efforts to muster the support of a backward peasantry in the former instance, in the Transitional Program the distinction becomes a tool at the disposal of Trotskyists in their efforts to raise carefully the consciousness of a lagging proletariat within the capitalist industrialized countries.

The initial demands pressed by the Trotskyists would thus be reformist in nature and congruent with the workers' basically trade unionist consciousness. Among those which Trotsky stipulated were guarantees of full employment, wages tied to prices, reduction in working hours, the right of workers to see the financial accounts of businesses which employ them, worker participation in decision-making in private firms and worker control over public works. If these demands did not bring violent rejection from the capitalists, the further demands—for expropriation of the major industries and the "state-ization" of the banks—would be likely to.[15] There would thus be the need for the arming of the workers. Finally, the culminating point of the Transitional Program would involve the creation of workers' committees in the factories and soviets in the country at large to challenge simultaneously the industrial and political power apparatuses of the bourgeoisie.

At its highest level of development, this confrontation of conflicting sets of structures results in a situation which Trotsky referred to as "dual power."

> Dual power in its turn is the culminating point of
> the transitional period. Two regimes, the bourgeois
> and the proletarian, are irreconcilably opposed to
> each other. Conflict between them is inevitable.
> The fate of society depends on the outcome.
> Should the revolution be defeated, the fascist
> dictatorship of the bourgeoisie will follow. In
> the case of victory, the power of the soviets,
> that is the dictatorship of the proletariat and the
> socialist reconstruction of society will arise.[16]

The Transitional Program was presented by Trotsky as a guideline. It was to serve as a bridge which would apparently obviate the necessity of carrying a minimum program over into the dictatorship of the proletariat as in the case of Russia and the nonindustrialized world. However, Trotsky disclaimed the power to foresee any more precisely the "concrete stages of the revolutionary mobilization of the masses" and he left it to the national sections of the Fourth International to "critically orient themselves at each new stage and advance such slogans as will aid the striving of the workers for independent politics, deepen the class character of these politics, destroy reformist and pacifist illusions, strengthen the connection of the vanguard with the masses, and prepare the revolutionary conquest of power."[17]

Upon the outcome of that struggle within the capitalist industrialized countries lay not only the fate of the indigenous proletariats but also that of the vast majority of humanity which populated the nonindustrialized world. Only approximately two pages of the Transitional Program are devoted to the "backward countries" and they are a summation of the concept of combined revolution. Approximately four pages are criticisms of the Stalinist course in the Soviet Union, and this is a summary repetition of what had already been published in *The Revolution Betrayed*. The real thrust of the direction in which Trotsky was pointing his Fourth International was toward the mobilization of the urbanized, industrial proletariat whose attainment of socialism was a precondition for the attainment of socialism anywhere else in the world.

If Trotsky thus presented the world with a highly Western-oriented version of an already Western-oriented Marxism, Mao presented the polar opposite. Mao bent Marxism to the needs of Chinese society.

To accomplish this task, Mao went to the heart of Marxist philosophy. There is a tension in Marxist thinking and writing between what might be referred to as "scientific" systems theory and philosophy. After the First World War, writers like Georg Lukacs and Karl Korsch attempted to remind Marxist social analysts and strategists that there was indeed a philosophical basis to Marxism.[18] Trotsky, despite the breadth of his work, remained basically a systems theorist and tactician.[19] Mao, on the other hand, touched the philosophical basis of Marxism in at least two of his essays, *On Contradiction* and *On Practice*. And it is in *On Contradiction* that Mao did the preparatory work for his adaptation of Marxism to Chinese conditions:

> When a task, no matter which, has to be perform-
> ed, but there is as yet no guiding line, method, plan
> or policy, the principal and decisive thing is to
> decide on a guiding line, method, plan or policy.
> When the superstructure (politics, culture, etc.)

obstructs the development of the economic base,
political and cultural changes become principal and
decisive. Are we going against materialism when we
say this? No. The reason is that while we recognize
that in the general development of history the
material determines the mental and social being
determines social consciousness, we also--and indeed
must--recognize the reaction of mental on
material things, of social consciousness on social
being and of the superstructure on the economic
base. This does not go against materialism; on the
contrary, it avoids mechanical materialism and
firmly upholds dialectical materialism.[20]

This view of the relationship between structure (the organization of
the mode of production) and superstructure (all other factors including politics
and culture) is very different from Trotsky's insistence, in the theory of
permanent revolution, that in the nonindustrialized world a socialist psychology (read consciousness) must follow the creation of "socialist conditions
of life" (read structure). When this emphasis on the importance of
superstructure is coupled with Mao's epistemological contributions in *On
Practice,* the theoretical structure for the concept of the "mass line" has been
prepared. In that work—in which he attempted to establish the relationship
between "perceptual" and "rational" knowledge, thus specifying the
"epistemology of dialectical materialism"—Mao wrote the following:

Cognition starts with practice and through
practice it reaches the theoretical plane and
then it has to go back into practice.[21]

Translated into revolutionary activity and the mass line, the formulation reads as follows:

In all the practical work of our Party, all correct
leadership is necessarily from the masses, to the
masses. This means: take the ideas of the masses
(scattered and unsystematic ideas) and concentrate
them (through study turn them into concentrated
and systematic ideas), then go to the masses and
propagate and explain these ideas until the masses
embrace them as their own, hold fast to them and
translate them into action, and test the correctness
of these ideas in such action. Then once again con-

> centrate ideas from the masses and once again take
> them to the masses so that the ideas are persevered
> in and carried through. And so on, over and over
> again in an endless spiral, with the ideas becoming
> more correct, more vital and richer each time. Such
> is the Marxist-Leninist theory of knowledge, or
> methodology...[22]

The masses in question are basically the peasantry which comprises the vast majority of the Chinese population. For Mao there was a creativity in the peasantry which was a crucial element in the revolution. And, unlike Trotsky, Mao did not view the peasantry as an ultimately counter-revolutionary force unless it is placed under the tight control of the urban proletariat. At this point, however, a word of caution is required. When Trotsky talked about collectivization, it will be recalled, he was talking about a process which would destroy the ability of individual farmers to engage in market production and to employ wage labor. He claimed not to pose a threat to private subsistence farming. The individual interests thus adversely affected were those of *kulaks,* the relatively well-off peasants.

The ratio of such relatively well-off peasants to poor peasants, tenant farmers, or farm laborers in Russia was undoubtedly much higher than in China. And the Chinese industrial proletariat was proportionately smaller as well. So Mao was relying upon the creativity of a group which was relatively much more important in his society than the equivalent group was in Russian society. Despite this fact, Trotsky was convinced that even the most oppressed of the rural population were poor potential revolutionaries and that the brightest among them would go to the cities.

The document cited above was written in 1943. The theory of the "mass line," with its emphasis upon the particular superstructural conditions of China, thus preceded the 1949 assumption of state power by the Communist Party in China. It was not until approximately a decade after that assumption of power that Mao developed his theory of "uninterrupted revolution," a term sanctioned by Lenin, which, at least on one occasion, Mao referred to as the theory of permanent revolution.[23]

In a 1958 speech to the Supreme State Conference Mao said:

> I stand for the theory of permanent revolution.
> Do not mistake this for Trotsky's theory of
> permanent revolution. In making revolution one
> must strike while the iron is hot—one revolution
> must follow another, the revolution must
> continually advance. The Hunanese often say,
> "Straw sandals have no pattern—they shape

themselves in the making." Trotsky believed that
the socialist revolution should be launched even
before the democratic revolution is complete.
We are not like that. For example after the
Liberation of 1949 came the Land Reform; as
soon as this was completed there followed the
mutual-aid teams, then the low level cooperatives.
After seven years the cooperativization was
completed and productive relationships were
transformed; then came the Rectification. After
Rectification was finished, before things had
cooled down, then came the Technical Revolution.
In the cases of Poland and Yugoslavia, democratic
order had been established for seven or eight years,
and then a rich peasantry emerged. It may not be
necessary to establish a New Democratic
government, but even so, one must still unite
all those forces which can be united.[24]

    Mao's theory differs from Trotsky's in certain fundamental respects. First, it builds upon the theoretical structure which I have previously discussed. It incorporates the epistemological work in *On Practice*, the explication of the role of superstructure in dialectical materialism in *On Contradiction,* and the application of these theoretical underpinnings in the "mass line" which accords such a crucial revolutionary role to the peasantry. Secondly, while Trotsky's theory of permanent revolution does have some lessons for socialists who have assumed state power, it was first developed after the unsuccessful revolution of 1905 and most of it is devoted to a discussion of the process whereby socialists can assume state power. The distinction between minimum and maximum demands, which becomes of paramount importance in the Transitional Program aimed at the transition to socialism in the industrialized countries, loses its significance the closer one comes to the political victory of the proletariat over the bourgeoisie. Mao's theory, on the other hand, is a guide to socialist construction and how to deal with contradictions *after* as well as *before* state power has been secured. Finally, Mao's theory, like Stalin's, conceives of the revolutionary process as one of discrete stages and is more consistent with Stalin's concept of socialism in one country. The heavy emphasis upon the peculiarities of the superstructural situation in a given country plus the faith in the creativity of the peasant masses supported national socialist development within China.

    Mao was critical of Stalin for many of the specific reasons for which Trotsky was critical:

> [W]hen any leader of the Party or the state places himself over and above the Party and the masses instead of in their midst, when he alienates himself from the masses, he ceases to have an all-round, penetrating insight into the affairs of the state. As long as this was the case, even so outstanding a personality as Stalin could not avoid making unrealistic and erroneous decisions on certain important matters....During the latter part of his life, Stalin took more and more pleasure in this cult of the individual and violated the Party's system of democratic centralism and the principle of combining collective leadership with individual responsibility. As a result, he made some serious mistakes: for example, he broadened the scope of the suppression of counter-revolution; he lacked the necessary vigilance on the eve of the anti-fascist war; he failed to pay proper attention to the further development of agriculture and the material welfare of the peasantry; he gave certain wrong advice to the international communist movement, and in particular, made a wrong decision on the question of Yugoslavia. On these issues, Stalin fell victim to subjectivism and one-sidedness and divorced himself from objective reality and from the masses.[25]

and

> Stalin felt that he had made mistakes in dealing with Chinese problems, and they were no small mistakes. We are a great country of several hundred millions, and he opposed our revolution, and our seizure of power.[26]

Mao's ascription of Stalin's errors to subjectivism in this passage is very different from Trotsky's ascription of the same errors to the theoretical misconception of "socialism in one country." For Trotsky, once the commitment to such a theory or concept had been made, Stalin's errors were not "mistakes," as Mao called them, but logical and anticipated consequences of Stalin's theoretical failures.

Shortly after Mao's development of the theory of uninterrupted revolution, and after the confrontation with the Soviet Union had intensified, the world was presented with the "theory of the new democratic revolution." This was presented as Mao's theory, growing out of the Chinese experience with the war against Japanese occupation, the relationship with the Kuomintang, and the victory of the Communist Party in 1949.

However, it seems to have been most often enunciated or explicated by Lin Biao.[27] Lin attempted to link the "theory of the new democratic revolution" with the "theory of uninterrupted revolution."[28] This was the theoretical device by which the Chinese revolution came out to meet the Soviet challenge. The theory of uninterrupted revolution applied only to China and its superstructural peculiarities. The theory of the "new democratic revolution" was a theory which was generalized to the Third World, particularly to the Asian and Latin American contexts. Based first on the United Front to defeat the Japanese and then upon the victory of the socialist forces in 1949, the theory of a new democratic revolution posited a two-stage revolutionary process—a nationalistic patriotic united front to defeat imperialism and, once that "national-democratic" revolution was completed, a socialist revolution.

The two-stage theory presented by the Chinese had long been discussed by Marxist-Leninists and explicitly rejected by Trotsky. Trotsky's theory of permanent revolution was one of a combined democratic bourgeois and socialist revolution, not one of two discrete nationalist-democratic and socialist stages. In any case, just as there is a tension between Trotsky's optimism over the prospects of a successful revolution in Russia and his negative view of the revolutionary potential of the peasantry and strong reliance upon revolution in the industrialized world, so there is a tension between the strong rooting of the theory of uninterrupted revolution in the theoretical works of Mao—which stressed the importance of the particular national superstructural context—and the much broader application of the two-stage theory to the Third World as a whole.

Whereas the major external treats to the construction of socialism in Trotsky's eyes were the capitalist regimes in Western Europe and the United States, in the eyes of the Chinese the major threat to socialism was rapidly becoming the USSR. While Trotsky regarded the Soviet Union as a "degenerated workers' state," Mao and his Chinese compatriots came to view it as a regime of "state capitalism" practicing "social imperialism."

The major responsibility for socialist revolution thus passed to the Third World. The Third World became both the only possible and the inevitable initial setting for the process of world revolution. This inevitability made it possible for the Chinese to assume a very aggressive international policy, of which an essential element was the maintenance of friendly relations with all Third World countries in which the regimes were either hostile to the USSR, or which the Chinese felt that they could influence in that direction. Since these countries would eventually be driven into a socialist direction by "objective" circumstances beyond the control of the present regimes, the Chinese could deal with the most reactionary regimes with equanimity and without attempts to subvert them. They offered only the *model* of the two-stage theory to indigenous revolutionaries. In practice, they worked with existing regimes to counter Soviet influence, sometimes even aiding them in crushing indigenous revolutionary movements if they felt that they were pro-Soviet or Soviet aided or influenced. In this way Mao and the Chinese regime were to have their cake and eat it too, to pursue an extremely aggressive foreign policy but to channel it in directions consistent with the concept of socialism in one country.

Finally, the accumulation of past theories and practice was integrated into still another theory credited to Mao's "creative application of Marxism."[29] This was a global theory first enunciated by Mao in conversations with a Third World leader in February of 1974. It is the "Theory of the Three Worlds." According to this theory, the First World is composed of the capitalist-imperialist United States and the state-capitalist-social-imperialist USSR. These are the "two hegemonist powers," the "common enemies of the people of the world."[30] The Third World is the "main force combating imperialism, colonialism, and hegemonism."[31] The Second World includes the capitalist industrialized countries in Western Europe plus Japan and the industrialized countries in Eastern Europe. They have "dual characters." On the one hand, they share the exploitative character of the countries of the First World under whose hegemony they have been operating. On the other hand, they are struggling to extricate themselves from that hegemony. It is this second characteristic which renders them potential allies of the Third World. French policy is seen as particularly beneficial because of its independence from the United States and construction of an independent nuclear deterrent capability aimed at the USSR. Its Third World intervention is also seen as helpfully anti-Soviet.

Indeed, the most controversial aspect of the theory is the stipulation that within the First World, "of the two imperialist superpowers, the Soviet Union is the more ferocious, the more reckless, the more treacherous, and the most dangerous source of world war."[32]

Four "objective" factors are cited as the reasons for this, along with a disclaimer that the Chinese territorial dispute with the Soviet Union is the real motivating factor on the part of the Chinese. First, because "Soviet social-imperialism" is following on the heels of U.S. imperialism, which has had a good start, it must be more aggressive and adventurous to catch up. Second, because "Soviet social-imperialism" is inferior in economic strength, it must rely upon its military power that much more. Third, because the Soviet ruling clique ("the new tsars") has transformed the dictatorship of the proletariat into a fascist dictatorship, militarization of the economy and state apparatus is facilitated. And, finally, since Soviet imperialism is the result of a degeneration of the first socialist country in the world, it is able to "exploit Lenin's prestige and flaunt the banner of 'socialism' to bluff and deceive people everywhere," whereas U.S. imperialism has been exposed and met with resistance everywhere, including within the U.S. itself.[33]

The entire theory is justified as an acceptable Marxist-Leninist position by "the law of uneven development of imperialism:"[34]

> The emergence of the two superpowers is a new
> phenomenon in the history of the development of
> imperialism. The uneven development of imperi-
> alism inevitably leads to conflicts and wars
> which in turn aggravate this uneven development
> and give rise today to the predominance of imperialist
> superpowers over the run-of-the-mill imperialist
> powers.[35]

> To attain world supremacy, Soviet social-
> imperialism has to try and grab areas under US
> control, just as Germany under Kaiser Wilhelm II
> and under Hitler and the postwar United States had
> to try and grab areas under the control of Britain
> and other old-line imperialists. This is a historical
> law independent of man's will.[36]

Not everyone was convinced by this reading of the "law of uneven development." Within China, opposition to the Theory of the Three Worlds was added to the string of indictments against the "Gang of Four" including Jiang Qing, Mao's widow, whose long list of sins had been associated with Trotskyism and whose behavior had been compared with that of the Trotskyists around the time of Lenin's death.[37]

Moreover, the Theory of the Three Worlds resulted in a wedge being driven between China and China's closest ally, Albania. Only two months after Mao's death, in November 1976, First Secretary of the Central Committee of the Party of Labor of Albania, Enver Hoxha, expressed differences with the Theory of the Three Worlds. On July 7, 1977, the Albanian party published an editorial in its paper and then issued it as a press release. It was a broadside denunciation of the theory. The four central objections are: that the fundamental contradiction between the proletariat and the bourgeoisie has completely gone by the wayside in favor of the distinction based upon level of development and geography; that no distinction is made between revolutionary and reactionary forces in the Third World; that the theory preaches "social peace" and class collaboration within the second world countries and particularly in Western Europe because the struggle against Soviet social imperialism is now more pressing than the struggle against U.S. imperialism; and that at the present time American imperialism and Soviet social-imperialism "are 'the main and biggest enemies of the peoples' today and as such 'they constitute the same danger'."[38]

But even before the Albanians spoke up after Mao's death, this shift in the perception of the major enemy led to a Chinese foreign policy which contemporary Trotskyists find as disastrous as Trotsky found Stalin's foreign policy. From a position of taking an uncompromisingly aggressive attitude toward the capitalist world (at the same time that the Soviets were moving toward accommodation on many fronts), the Chinese have moved toward a virtual alliance position with the United States in many areas where they wish to check Soviet "social-imperialism." The most concrete and visible expression of this posture to date has been in Africa, particularly in Angola and Zaire. However, prior to that, such Chinese policies as support for the government of Sri Lanka (formerly Ceylon) in its suppression of domestic rebels, support for the Pakistani government in the Bangladesh issue (in this case differing with United States policy), the welcoming of President Nixon in China while bombs were still falling on the Vietnamese, and the maintenance of diplomatic relations with the Chilean junta were measures which Trotskyists, as well as almost all other non-Maoists on the Left, found impossible to accept.

For Trotsky, even the Hitler-Stalin Pact and the movement of Soviet troops into Poland and Finland in 1939 did not justify a total desertion of the Soviet Union or its categorization as "state capitalist." However, in the forties some former members of the U.S. Socialist Workers Party who had split off from the SWP did come to the conclusion that the Soviet Union was no longer even a "degenerated workers' state" but one of "state capitalism." This position, advanced three decades before the Chinese accusation, could only be advanced outside the pale of Trotskyism, since Trotsky had specifically repudiated it in *The Revolution Betrayed.*[39]

CONTEXTS OF APPLICATION: FRANCE AND THE U.S.

All political action, including revolutionary politics, must be undertaken within the context of pre-existing institutions and ideologies. The theorist-practitioner cannot hope for a *tabula rasa* on the order of Plato's utopian fantasy. Indeed while it is the function of Marxist practitioners in nonsocialist societies to attempt to transform those institutions and ideologies, as points of departure the latter operate with the force of necessity. If one can posit a chosen future, the structural and ideological present is a given which affects the parameters of action designed to change it in any society.

The contexts of France and the United States, which are the particular national contexts in which the Trotskyists and Maoists which we shall be examining are attempting to operate, offer extremely interesting similarities and differences. First of all, both are capitalist industrialized countries with large working classes and liberal democratic political forms. Unlike the Russian and Chinese contexts in which Trotsky and Mao were obliged to operate, France and the United States conform to the specifications which Marx and Engels felt were necessary for the optimal and least disruptive transition from capitalism to socialism.

Despite the high degree of total wealth which has been generated in the two societies, both preserve severe inequalities in the distribution of that wealth. In France, the inequalities have the harshest impact upon both indigenous and immigrant workers (admittedly upon the latter even more severely than the former), people in certain specific regions such as Brittany and Occitanie, small and tenant farmers, and women. In terms of relative rankings among the European or the capitalist industrialized countries, France is always at or near the the top of the rankings of income and wealth inequality.

While the United States ranks above France in terms of income equality, it still preserves severe disparities in income and wealth distribution and it shows no signs of changing the pattern.[40] Skilled and unionized industrialized workers are better remunerated in the United States than in France. But as in France only approximately a fifth of the work force is unionized, and the non-unionized work force is not so well off. Minority people and women are particularly victimized both by low-paying employment and unemployment. Moreover, those beyond the age of active employment in the United States are severely deprived as a group. They live off of fixed incomes, they are the most susceptible to the effects of inflation, and they are the most likely to require constant nursing care, which has a devastating economic effect in the United States, where a social obligation to provide this care is not recognized. Finally, there are also regional inequalities in the United States. An American variant of Brittany in the west or Occitanie in the south of France would be Appalachia in the southeast of the United States.

In addition to France and the United States both being capitalist industrialized countries which preserve high degrees of inequality internally, they have been the most militarily active of the capitalist industrialized countries in recent years. Since World War II, both countries have engaged in wars against Third World peoples in order to keep them in their economic and political orbits. Until they were defeated at Dien Bien Phu in 1954, the French waged war in Indochina to prevent the Indochinese from throwing off the yoke of French colonial domination. The United States government largely financed that effort, but did not itself become involved in actual combat operations in Indochina until the early 1960s, well after the French defeat. Two years after their defeat in Indochina, the French government became involved in its second major military effort of the post-World War II period. From 1956 until 1962, the French waged war in Algeria to prevent the Algerian Arab majority from liberating itself from French control. France still engages in intermittent military campaigns in West and Central Africa, where it maintains an extensive network of military bases. France has thus spent much of the post-World War II period at war with Third World peoples.

The United States has not been inactive in this regard. As indicated above, it paid for most of the expense of the French Indochinese military campaign. It sent most of the troops and paid for most of the "police action" in Korea from 1950 to 1952. And from the early sixties to 1973, it involved itself in an armed attempt to do what the French proved that they could not do, i.e. determine the political and economic destiny of the Indochinese people. Interspersed between these longer military campaigns were shorter direct military engagements or direct involvement in civil war or regime changes in such countries as Guatemala, Lebanon, Angola, the Congo, Cuba, the Dominican Republic, and Chile.

The French engagement in the Algerian War and the American engagement in the war in Indochina were crucial stimuli in both countries for the production of yet another similarity, the youth radicalization of the 1960s and the early-to-mid 1970s. Because of similar underlying conditions and the rapid transmission of media messages across national boundaries, the youth radicalization spread to most of the other capitalist industrialized countries. But due to the catalytic effects of the Algerian and Indochinese wars, that radicalization developed earlier in France and the United States and had particularly important political and cultural effects in those two countries.

The "youth" involved in both countries were, at least initially, largely students. That is to say that they had a higher than average educational level, they were exposed to social criticism, and they were concentrated in a living and working space in such a way as to greatly facilitate communication and concerted activity. Prior to World War II, the dominant tone within the French university milieu was conservative. Immediately after the war, students who had been involved in the Resistance gained control of the French student union, the *Union Nationale des Éudiants de France* (UNEF) and committed the student union to taking more progressive political positions. UNEF did call for the granting of independence to the Indochinese people, but it did not actually engage in confrontation tactics. Shortly thereafter, the organization came under the control of more conservative students who felt that UNEF should involve itself only with issues concerning the educational system and the quality of life of students *qua* students. It was not until the Algerian War that students with a broader political perspective reasserted control over the organization and turned it into one of the most important anti-war forces in the country.

In the United States, unlike in France, there had been important radical movements within the student milieu (which was much larger than that in France) prior to the Second World War. In the 1930s the Student League for Industrial Democracy (SLID), the Young People's Socialist League (YPSL), and the National Student League (NSL) were left-wing organizations which recruited effectively on American campuses. However, the patriotism associated with the war, the outbreak of the Cold War, the intensification of repression for which Senator Joseph McCarthy was to serve as the national symbol, and the careerist orientation of veterans who only wanted to make up for lost time devoted to war were a heavy obstacle for those who attempted to pursue liberal—not to mention radical—political activities on the campuses in the United States. The first inroads into just liberal politics were made by the civil rights movement. Radical politics made its entry as a result of the war in Indochina. Thus both the French and the U.S. political systems could survive one post-World War II military engagement without paying a great domestic political price. Each system, however, paid a very heavy price for the second try.

In both societies a variety of adult-governed social structures was delegitimized. In both France and the United States, the educational systems came to be viewed mainly as bureaucratic conduits which funneled young people into military bureaucracies in order to fight imperialistic wars and, if one survived or was not subject to the draft because of sex or disability, into capitalist private or public bureaucracies to earn a living as a supportive cog of the system. In France, the student group sponsored by the Catholic Church, *La Jeunesse Étudiante Chrétienne* (JEC), was purged of its leadership by a church hierarchy which refused to accept its protests against the use of torture in Algeria. That experience and the silence of the Church on the war was to pull many a young Catholic away from the Church and to put them into the anti-war movement. In fact, most of the leaders of UNEF during the anti-war period had come through the JEC. In the United States no single religious hierarchy dominates the way the Catholic hierarchy does in France, and some of the most important people in the anti-war movement were associated with various religions.

But in both countries the expressly political structures, mainly the political parties, seem to have been equally delegitimized the way the educational systems were. And the major negative impact was sustained by those groups which were not, in terms of the relative political spectrum in each country, the most conservative forces. In France the main victims of delegitimation in the eyes of the younger people were the major social democratic and communist parties. In terms of their electoral following and their access to public office these parties are strong in France. While barred from national ministries between 1947 and 1981, the Communist Party has consistently elected an important national legislative bloc and controlled an important number of mayoralities and municipal councils. During the entire Fourth Republic, which lasted from the end of the Second World War until 1958, the Socialist Party, then called the *Section Française de l'Internationale Ouvrière* (SFIO), was an important force in the French cabinets as well as in the national legislature. But despite this appeal of the French Left, France continued to remain one of the least egalitarian of the capitalist industrialized societies. The socialists, whose party was blamed for undercutting the revolutionary potential of the 1936 General Strike, were seen as participating in the administration of the bourgeois state and advancing their own career interests at the expense of the working class.

But it was the Algerian War that had the most dramatic negative impact upon the SFIO. For it was under the premiership of a socialist, Guy Mollet, that the Algerian War was begun in earnest. This was the same premier who committed French paratroopers to join with British and Israeli troops in an effort to take the Suez Canal away from Egypt. Thus in the eyes of many younger French people, the SFIO was not content to merely administer an inegalitarian bourgeois state internally, but it was also one of the most aggressively colonialist and imperialist structures in France. It also dealt harshly with those who insisted on attacking the war policy within the party. Nor did the Communist Party come away from the Algerian War with clean hands in the eyes of many of these people. For the representatives of that party continued to vote for the military budget during the war and the Communist Party severely denounced the more militant anti-war movement for what it regarded as adventuristic tactics.

In 1958, the Fourth Republic fell under the threat of a revolt by the professional French military in Algeria and right-wing French nationalistic movements in Algeria and their sympathizers in metropolitan France. This introduced the Gaullist Fifth Republic. The SFIO split, with anti-war dissidents forming a separate party. In 1960, these people merged with dissidents from the Communist Party, the Catholic *Mouvement Républicain Populaire* (MRP) and others to form the *Parti Socialist Unifié* (PSU). This party was virtually the only adult political structure to which the increasingly alienated young people could relate. Most of them, however, did not go into the PSU but worked through UNEF or created other political structures which were clearly under the control of the younger people themselves. The one major but short-term exception to this was the student group of the Communist Party. Between 1963 and 1965, a coalition of Trotskyists, Maoists, and followers of the Italian Communist leader, Palmiro Togliatti, managed to steer the *Union des Étudiants Communistes* in a direction different from that of the party itself. After handling the situation gingerly at first, the party cracked down with expulsions in 1965. After this, a wide variety of Far Left groups independent of any adult structures grew up in France. The events of 1968 created additional impetus for the creation of such groups. That revolt, too, was severely denounced by the Communist Party.

If significant socialist or communist parties are not a part of the U.S. political context, the relations between radicalized youth and the establishment structures—considering both the Socialist and Communist parties in France to be establishment parties in the sense that they work through the established system of politics—have shown remarkable similarities. One can substitute the Democratic Party for the French "Establishment Left" so discredited in the eyes of the newly radicalized French generation. The Democratic Party behaved in Indochina very much like the SFIO had behaved in Algeria, and there were striking similarities in the ways that the two formations treated their internal dissidents. Furthermore, while the student affiliate of the French Communist Party and the French student union (UNEF) were crucial structures in the development of a Far Left which was subsequently to challenge the Establishment Left in France, the Students for a Democratic Society played a very similar role in the United States.

Initially SDS, the youth affiliate of the social democratic League for Industrial Democracy which had been active on campuses in the 1930s, saw the structural solution to political problems in the United States as a "rationalization" of the two-party system which would move the southern conservative Democrats out of the Democratic Party and over into the Republican Party. Where it came into conflict with the adult group was not over this initial innocuous analysis of what needed to be done, but rather over its contention that the United States was at least partly responsible for the development of the Cold War. The older socialists within the League for Industrial Democracy were extremely anti-Communist and anti-Soviet. They were not about to tolerate such an analysis and attempted to bring the SDS back into line. After the imposition of sanctions by the League, SDS completely severed its relationship with the parent group in 1965 and became the major radical organization of young people without any tie to an adult structure in the United States. Initially it went through an "anti-ideological" stage. Then even that orientation evaporated and SDS became a broadly aggregative umbrella under which a multitude of individuals and groups who shared a common desire to fight against the injustices of the existing system operated. It brought together the ideologically relaxed and the ideologically rigid, the counter-cultural types and the strict "politicos" with no time for the counter-culture. Like the French student union and the student affiliate of the French Communist Party when it was under the party's control, SDS was a staging ground for things to come. Numerous other organizations were being created or rejuvenated and were working either within SDS or on its fringes, hoping to recruit people out of it. The reason that SDS rather than the United States National Student Association (USNSA) played this role in the United States is that the American student association had no base of individual membership like the French student union. It was merely a grouping of officers from various American campuses. In 1967, whatever positive image the USNSA had managed to earn for itself by its criticism of U.S. policy in Indochina was shattered by the revelation that the CIA had covertly supplied up to 80 per cent of its yearly budget, and that officers of the organization had performed intelligence functions for the agency.

Another similarity in the contextual situations of the two countries was the use of repressive techniques to deal with the opposition during the war and post-war periods. In both countries, apparently less conservative parties lost power to more conservative ones. In France, the fall of the Fourth Republic meant the exclusion of socialists and relatively progressive Radical Socialists and members of the Catholic MRP from the councils of power. Under the Fifth Republic, the councils of power were shared by Gaullists and conservative Independents. In the United States, opposition to the war policies of Lyndon Johnson caused him not to run again for the presidency. In 1968, Hubert Humphrey was nominated inside the convention hall while the Chicago police were charging demonstrators with their nightsticks and the National Guard, with machine guns mounted on their jeeps, were making sure that the battles were confined to certain areas of the city. The Democrats lost to the extremely conservative ticket of Nixon and Agnew.

In both cases, this transfer of power resulted in a quantum leap in the use of repressive techniques. Under the Gaullists, demonstrations were banned and those who refused to accept the bans were met by charging squadrons of police. The most tragic results of this were the deaths of nine people who were crushed or suffocated to death in a police charge at the Métro Charonne in 1962, only two months before the end of the Algerian War. Nevertheless, the policy of banning demonstrations against government policy and squelching them by force continued after the end of the war. The barricades of 1968 represented a refusal to be driven off any longer. In 1970, largely as a response to 1968, the Gaullist government passed the famous "Anti-Wrecker Law," which held anyone in a demonstration responsible for the acts of anyone else in the demonstration. And the government did not hesitate to prosecute under that law and to send political dissidents to prison under its terms. The government also did not hesitate to prosecute book publishers and newspapers for defamation of the police when they published negative material on police behavior. Organizations were banned and the distribution of printed material under their name prohibited. Finally, the French government got caught in its own version of Watergate when police were called to the offices of the satirically critical newspaper, *Le Canard Enchainé*. The police ran off when they found out that those who had broken into the newspaper's offices during the night were government agents who were in the process of installing listening devices.

In the United States, the level of repression was also intensified once Nixon came into office. In fact, if one studies the political language of the hardliners in the Nixon administration, particularly the language of Attorney General Mitchell, Vice President Agnew, and Nixon himself, one is struck by the similarities between the words with which they characterized their youthful opposition and the characterizations which came out of the mouths of the hardline Gaullists. The one striking difference was that the repression in the United states was more deliberately deadly than that in France. There was nothing in France quite like the systematic elimination of Black Panthers or the deliberate shooting of students at Kent and Jackson State universities. And, at least thus far, no systematic long-term disruption program on the order of the FBI's COINTELPRO has been uncovered in that country. But the fact is that in 1974 the newly installed chiefs of state of both countries—President Giscard d'Estaing, who replaced the deceased Gaullist Pompidou in France, and Gerald Ford, who was appointed by Nixon to assume the office as of his resignation—conceded that civil liberties in their respective countries had been seriously eroded by the preceding governments. They both made public pledges to a greater respect for those liberties.[41]

Thus far we have focused on the similarities of the French and U.S. contexts. We have seen that both are capitalist industrialized societies which preserve internal inequalities and which have engaged in extensive military activity to keep Third World people in their economic and political orbits. This has resulted in both internal and external victims of the dominant systems with whom sensitive and socially conscious young people could empathize. The interpenetration of the military and the educational systems gave students the feeling that they too were the direct victims of bureaucracies which had grown totally insensitive to basic human needs and which treated people as objects for their own instrumental and gruesome ends. And, when the young people declined to be so treated passively and protested, they discovered what Philip Green has referred to as "the iron fist of undeviating authority in the velvet glove of liberal pluralism: Hobbes' ferocious eyes peering out from behind tolerant Madison's skull."[42] What was historically unique about this in both countries is that for the first time the iron fist of state power was being directed against the jaw of a category of people that was largely middle class. Previously it was the working classes and the racial and ethnic minorities who had directly been exposed to the most violently repressive mechanisms of the bureaucratic liberal state.

Thus the perception of internal and external victims of the liberal captitalist system, the obligation to fight in the Third World to defend what its leaders perceived to be the interests of that system, and the direct experience with the internal repressivenesss of the system facilitated an increasingly critical systematic analysis and a rupture of the identity with the interests of the class into which many of the young dissidents were born.[43] They saw themselves as being victimized by that class and its institutions just as workers and minority people were. Thus in France students liked to look upon themselves as "intellectual workers," and in the United States the expression "student as nigger" gained currency.

It was under these conditions that Trotskyism experienced a revitalization and Maoist movements grew into distinct currents of Marxism-Leninism in the two countries. The sensitivity of both these variants of Marxism-Leninism to the problem of bureaucratization in the capitalist Western as well as in the noncapitalist Eastern European industrialized societies, plus the special appeal that both Trotsky and Mao made to youth as particular victims of bureaucratization, could only enhance the attractiveness of Trotskyism and Maoism under the conditions of radicalization on the order of those described here. Thus the similarities in the contextual situations help explain the revitalization of Trotskyism and the appearance of a Maoist movement in both France and the United States.

There are, however, also important differences between the two political contexts. A crucial difference is the strength of the Left in the two countries. Even if there was considerable disenchantment among young people with the SFIO and the Communist Party in France during the 1960s and the early 1970s, those parties continued to maintain substantial membership and voter appeal in the country at large. Moreover, there have been important changes in both parties. With the exception of Mitterrand himself, most of the present leaders of the Socialist Party—including the former General Secretary of the anti-war PSU, Michel Rocard—were not implicated in the Algerian War policies. The Communist Party evolved to a Eurocommunist position, which means that it both rejected the concept of the dictatorship of the proletariat as one appropriate to a pluralistic industrialized society like France, and accorded its own members more latitude in the expression of disagreement with party policy, both internally and externally, than was the case before. Coupled with the absence of a concrete stimulus of a divisive nature, something on the order of the Algerian War, these internal changes in the parties on the Left facilitated much more effective recruiting among the age cohort involved in the 1968 uprising, as well as among the contemporary student population through the mid-seventies. In terms of their over-all appeal, the dominant structures on the French Left missed the taking the presidency in 1974 and control of the legislature in 1978 by only approximately one percent of the vote. Three years later, of course, the Left controlled both.

Moreover, aside from the strong Communist and Socialist parties, there has been a wider range of smaller organizations, movements and publication groups on the Left in France. In order to help people sort these out, a book called *A Guide to France in Struggle* was published in 1974. The book, which extended to over four hundred pages, listed approximately 450 different groupings.[44] There would have been a considerable savings in the cost of paper if such a book had been published in the United States.

Just as there is a plural party system in France, so there are plural labor confederations. The largest, the *Confédération Générale du Travail* (CGT), has a preponderance of Communist Party members at the active cadre level, and half of the membership of its top executive body also belongs to the Communist Party. The second largest labor confederation is the *Confédération Française Démocratique du Travail* (CFDT). It grew out of the Catholic labor movement in the early 1960s. After "deconfessionalizing," it became a more genuinely radical union than the CGT in the eyes of many on the French Left. For example, it was much more supportive of the students during the 1968 uprising than was the CGT, which joined the Communist Party in denouncing the affair and trying to keep a lid on the workers. Since that time the CFDT has moved closer to the Socialist Party. Members of that party are in control of the leadership positions in the smallest of the general labor confederations, the *Confédération Générale du Travail-Force Ouvrière* (CGT-FO). Thus, while there are no formal ties between the labor confederations and the parties in France, there are power relationships within the unions which are related to the party system, and labor is clearly on the Left.

Aside from these structural manifestations of the importance of the Left in France, there is a strong and largely indigenous anarchist-utopian-syndicalist tradition which is deeply rooted in the attitudinal structure of French workers. Sometimes, most notably and on the grandest scale during this century in the 1936 and 1968 general strikes, it is spontaneously acted out in behavior. However, the structures on the French Left have also attempted to respond to this current. The earliest manifestation of this in the 1960s was the demand for worker control over industry (*autogestion*) made by the recently deconfessionalized CFDT. The small PSU immediately responded positively. In the 1970s the Socialist Party, eager for the support of members of the CFDT, also formally adopted the demand. The powerful appeal of this concept in France is best demonstrated by the fact that even the Communist Party, which originally had denounced the concept of *autogestion,* more recently came to accept it.

In the United States, of course, there have been no political structures on the Left anywhere near the magnitude of the French Communist and Socialist parties, nor has there been anything like the array of smaller formations on the Left which has been open to the French. Rather, there are two capitalist parties which contend for political rewards in the system and, with the exception of the Teamsters, the unions have been generally reliable supporters of the Democratic Party. There are a number of explanations for this two-capitalist-party system which has been so inhospitable to the development of parties on the Left. Among them are the long-time use of a single member district electoral system and powerful elected presidency, the ability to offer relatively high wages to skilled craft workers and unionized workers in the basic industries, the effectiveness of political socialization in such institutions as the schools, and the severe repression which has been directed against groups—from the Wobblies to the Panthers—which were perceived as real threats.

Under these conditions, the memories of the labor struggles and the significant radical movements which emerged from them, as well as important past contributions made by Americans to anarchist and utopian thought, have been virtually expunged from post-World War II consciousness in the United States. The very language of politics is so different between the two societies. Even the French conservative who opposes "socialism," "communism," and "Marxism" is not shocked at the mere utterance of the words, any more than a Democrat in the United States would be shocked to hear the name "Republican." But for the vast majority of Americans, those words have a sufficient connotative shock value that anyone who identifies with them is hard pressed to even find an audience which is willing to listen or to consider the substantive content behind them. Indeed, in a number of forums, one would risk physical violence by merely uttering such words in anything but a sense of opprobrium.

Within this context, then, the Communist Party of the United States is quite small, and the Socialist Party of Debs and Thomas—which was already quite small—has splintered into a number of competing groups. The anarchist and utopian tradition has been carried on by only the tiniest of groups and quite ephemeral communal experiments. While there are also some small scattered experiments in operating worker-controlled enterprises, there is certainly nothing like the attraction which syndicalist ideas have for French workers and no national labor federation or brotherhood—with the exception of the tiny Wobbly group which some young people have been trying to revive—calls for worker control the way the CFDT does in France. A virtual ideological monopoly has been imposed on the major arenas of politics and work life in the United States.

A second important difference between France and the United States involves the timing and the structural context of youth radicalization. The high point of the radicalization in the United States coincided with the war in Indochina. After that war was terminated, the level of radicalization declined. In France, although the Algerian war was a crucial stimulus in the radicalization of French young people, that radicalization peaked after, not during, the Algerian conflict. The war ended in 1962, and I would date the high plateau of youth radicalism and militancy in France from 1968 to 1973.[45]

There were several reasons why radicalism and militancy continued to increase after the Algerian War was over. First, the French universities had stagnated pedagogically and the physical working and living conditions of the students had degenerated very severely. In France, with the exception of a small Catholic system of higher education, the universities are all public and are all under a single national ministry of education. The national government is therefore responsible for their condition.

The Gaullist government emerged from the Algerian War with a high degree of hostility toward the student union which had played such an important role in the anti-war movement. It went so far as to try to create a counter student movement. It cut off UNEF's subsidy and it refused to meet with its officers. When UNEF took to the streets to demonstrate against the government's education policies, the Gaullist government responded the way that it had during Algeria. It banned the demonstrations and sent the police in to clear the streets. Thus the cycle of demonstration and repression continued after the war until it brought the entire productive and distributive mechanism of the country to a halt in 1968. In the United States, the universities had not degenerated to the level of those in France and, in any case, under the conditions of the federal system and the much larger network of private universities there is no central point of political responsibility for them. This has been a major inhibiting factor in the creation of a viable national student union in the United States.

Another important factor in the French setting was intellectual unemployment. In the United States, university graduates did not begin to feel the heavy impact of unemployment in the post-World War II period until the mid 1970s. Only then were they truly likely to relate to the "Ode to Higher Education" quoted by Hal Draper from a college journal of the 1930s:

> I sing in praise of college
> Of M.A.s and Ph.D.s
> But in pursuit of knowledge
> We are starving by degrees.[46]

If they had known of its existence, French students would have related very well to Draper's Ode right after the Algerian War. From that time to this day, French university graduates have experienced serious problems in finding employment related to their education. Some social scientists have hypothesized that intellectual employment has a deradicalizing effect on students because they do not want to damage what slight prospects they might have for satisfactory employment. However that relationship will unfold in the long-run in the United States, in France poor employment prospects only added fuel to the process of radicalization in the post-Algerian War period.

Still another interesting difference in the phasing of the radicalization process in the two countries involves its interpenetration with other cultural and social phenomena. From the mid 1960s onward, there was a constant interpenetration between political alienation and cultural alienation and political dissent and manifestations of a youthful counter-culture which challenged aspects of life in the United States which the "Old Left" of the 1930s and its remnants after World War II had left untouched. For the latter, politics was politics and not to be confused with cultural "fads." Politics required discipline and hard work and one's personal life and sensuality came second to it. For the New Left of the 1960s and the early 1970s, life was not so compartmentalized. They saw broader cultural phenomena, personal life, sensuality, and sexuality as being very much related to politics. Then there were even those who thought that these aspects of life were vastly more important than politics, indeed an appropriate substitute for it.

It is true that in France there were some movements that had a broader cultural orientation, such as the Situationists, who tried to turn politics into theater. It is also true that the graphics and the cinema which were done during and after the 1968 revolt were very impressive. Finally, it is true that some of the women participants in the 1968 revolt came to the realization that even the action committees and other experiments which were supposed to be liberating experiences remained quite insensitive to the problem of sexual subordination. However, despite this incipient awakening of the consciousness of some of the women participants and the above-mentioned cultural expressions, there was nothing truly comparable to the scale of the basic challenges to the everyday fabric of American cultural and social existence posed by the counter-culture and the elevation of sexual consciousness within the French context until the mid 1970s. The conception of politics among radicalized French youth in the 1960s and even into the early 1970s was more congruent with the traditional conception of politics in their own culture than was the case in the United States.

The first new direction of politics in the 1970s was toward sexual emancipation. France had not experienced the strong suffrage movements that the United States and Britain had in the late 19th and early 20th centuries. French women did not receive the vote until after the Second World War. Catholicism weighed heavily against the formation of women's political and social consciousness. And the major oppositionist ideology was Marxism, whose male French exponents focused on class oppression and consciousness often to the neglect of the sexual dimension.

However, in the 1970s many of the French women whose political interests had been awakened in 1968 began to mobilize against the highly discriminatory laws concerning abortion, contraception, and divorce. They became critical of the treatment accorded to women in the formations of the Left, which were supposedly attempting to transform the system into a more liberating one. Women formed their own political organizations and attempted to group themselves into caucuses within some of the mixed organizations on the Left. They brought to these organizations and caucuses within the Left the skills and the self-confidence that they had gained in their at least partially successful campaigns against discriminatory legislation. Moreover, these women served as an example to lesbians and gay men who mobilized in the mid 1970s, also after their counterparts in the United States. But the "new issues" of the 1970s for the French were not limited to sexual emancipation. Nuclear power and a host of environmental concerns also became issues around which major political mobilization took place.

Less constructive aspects of the American scene in the 1960s and early 1970s also began to hit France in the middle and late 1970s and early 1980s. During the entire year of 1968, a total of 177 people under the age of thirty-five were arrested by the French police for drug use.[47] From the mid 1970s on, such usage expanded enormously. Along with this increase in drug use there has been the development of a drop-out or fringe culture. In the 1960s there was a sub-culture in France, but it was one of older people. These were the *clochards,* people in their forties, fifties and sixties who slept on cardboard or over ventilators on the sidewalks and who scavenged for food and alcohol. In the 1970s there grew up a sub-culture not unlike that of the hippies of the United States, which the French refer to as *les marginaux.* However, since they are older than most of the hippies were, and have in many cases cut themselves off from future occupational options, they may well turn out to be a more permanent characteristic of French society than the hippies have been in the United States. One also finds a mood of depression among some of these people because their very high expectations of what was possible in 1968 have not been realized.

A final distinction between these two capitalist industrialized societies refers not to their generational dynamics but to their racial and ethnic composition. The United States is a new nation in the Western sense of the term. Its history is that of the displacement of Native American nations by immigrants from other continents. The ideological result of this was a mixed picture. On the one hand there was tremendous pressure on the successive waves of immigrants to become like the "established" citizenry. This often meant adopting the dominant political and economic ideology. On the other hand, immigrant groups and people who were easily differentiated from the White Anglo-Saxon physical and cultural type often felt the need to band together either out of self-defense or in order to preserve their identities and deeply held convictions. From the Jewish Workingmen's Circles to the contemporary Black, Latino, and Asian-American activist groups, associations of this particularistic nature have been important and complicating factors on and for the Left in the United States.

While France had been experiencing the revival of nationalism among the populations of Brittany, Occitanie, and Corsica in the 1970s, it is an old nation even in European terms and has nothing comparable to the racial and ethnic heterogeneity of the United States. However, while the permanent citizenry in France is highly homogeneous, a considerable number of Arab workers from North Africa and a lesser number of Black workers from sub-Saharan Africa have been imported on a temporary basis in the post-World War II boom period to do some of the necessary but least desirable and least renumerated labor. Aside from their unenviable position in the labor force, these workers have been subjected to the same wide array of manifestations of racism that exists in the United States, including not-infrequent physical attacks which periodically result in fatalities. The intensity of racism has increased as the unemployment problem in France has increased, and some of the immigrant workers have fought back. For example, a significant number of immigrant workers conducted a four-year national rent strike to protest the rents and conditions in the residence halls which were specifically constructed to house immigrant workers. The major parties and unions of the Left have not been very supportive of such actions, which they see as having a possible negative back-lash effect upon their own strategies. In spite of their call for equal treatment of immigrant and French workers, these domestic structures view the immigrant worker population as a foreign and transient one and priorities are established on that basis.

This is a considerably different situation from that which exists in the United States, where there is a permanent and integral heterogeneity, where racism and segregation in the country itself rather than in distant colonies has been a major problem throughout American history, where many who were more highly radicalized in the anti-war movement cut their political baby teeth in the liberal civil rights movement of the early 1960s, and where the "Black vote" has become an important political phenomenon. In France, virtually no one paid any attention at all to the plight of the immigrant workers until French Maoists began to do political work with them in the early 1970s.

In sum, while there are similarities, certain structural characteristics differentiate the two political cultures. France has larger and more varied and numerous parties and groups on the Left, an organized labor movement which is also on the Left, an anarcho-syndicalist ideological strain running through its proletariat, and a high degree of racial and ethnic homogeneity among its citizenry. The *phasing* of other phenomena has also been different in the two countries. The Algerian War, the structure and condition of the French university system, and intellectual unemployment led to the creation of a relatively cohesive and radical national student movement in the early 1960s, several years before the radicalization of U.S. students. However, the mobilization of women, gays and lesbians, and environmental and anti-nuclear forces, as well as the creation of a significant counter-culture, came somewhat later in France than in the United States. Even with the earlier entry onto the scene of radical students, traditional political boundaries and issues managed to hang on longer in that old European political culture.

Thus far we have seen that there are elements of Trotskyism and Maoism as bodies of theory, and that there are also contextual similarities between France and the United States, which explain why there was a revitalization of Trotskyist movements and an appearance for the first time of distinctly Maoist movements in both countries during the 1960s and 1970s. As we are going to see, within both countries there is a considerable fragmentation inside each of these currents of Marxism-Leninism.

While there are naturally some similarities between Trotskyism and Maoism in the two contexts, there are also significant differences. Indeed, just the word "Maoism" has different meanings within the two political cultures. The impact of the contextual factors, which are partial explanations of how and why these movements fragment, will be demonstrated as we now turn to an examination of the concrete manifestations of Trotskyism and Maoism in France and the United States.

2
Trotskyism in France

We shall begin our investigation of those concrete manifestations with an examination of French Trotskyism. In this we defer to age since France is an older political community than the United States and Trotskyism is an older current than Maoism. However, age does not always bring serenity. From its beginning, French Trotskyism was a conflict-ridden and fragmented phenomenon. Even Trotsky himself found it impossible to bring harmony to those who were marching under banners bearing his name in France. And there is no more agreement among French Trotskyists today than there was when Trotsky found them so difficult to deal with.

The history of Trotskyism as a distinct current in every country except the Soviet Union dates from the appearance of open disagreement between Trotsky and Stalin in the mid to late 1920s. The first expulsions from the French Communist Party over this split were in 1924, and continued up through 1928 with no unifying structure of the purged former Communist Party members. If those expelled remained politically active, they tended to maintain themselves as tiny groups whose major activity was the publications of newspapers or journals with very small circulations.

In 1929, the year that Trotsky created the bud of a Trotskyist international organization, then called the International Left Opposition, he issued a specific call for the unification of the various French groups. In April of 1930, *La Ligue Communiste* was created and recognized by Trotsky as the official French section of his international following.

The number of followers in most countries, France included, was very small. Of course in the USSR Trotsky's following was considerable but was eliminated, at least in its open manifestation, by the Stalinist repression. In Greece and in Spain, the Trotskyist sections claimed over one thousand members each.[1] But that was exceptional. Yvan Craipeau, one of the earliest Trotskyist leaders in France, estimates that at most there were approximately one hundred Trotskyists in France at the time of the Ligue's creation.[2]

Moreover, there were a number of elements in the situation which differentiated French Trotskyism from Trotskyism in a number of other countries, including the United States. First, while most of the Trotskyists did come from the French Communist Party, most of them were younger militants with very little political experience. Only Alfred Rosmer had experienced leadership positions both within the French Party and at the level of the Comintern, and he left the *Ligue* seven months after its creation.

Without the guidance of older, experienced leaders on the order of James Cannon in the United States, French Trotskyism was immediately afflicted with severe factionalism. Trotsky himself, sometimes calling upon the support of the International and sometimes calling more specifically upon the assistance of the American leaders Cannon and Max Schachtman, attempted personally to fill the experience void.

Initially there were two main tendencies in the French section. The first centered around Rosmer (until his departure), Pierre Naville, and Gérard Rosenthal.[3] Naville was the most important of the three in terms of his impact. He was a member of the Communist Party until his expulsion in 1928. But perhaps even more important, he and Rosenthal were major figures in the surrealist movement of the 1930s. Largely through their influence, the aesthetic aspects of surrealism were to interpenetrate with Trotskyist politics during those years.

Naville's major rival, whom he and Rosmer had tried to remove from his leadership position in the Paris region as early as 1930, was Raymond Molinier. Molinier came from a banking family and was, himself, a businessman. His closest collaborator, still active in contemporary French Trotskyism, was Pierre Frank. Frank was a chemical engineer and an activist in the Chemical Products Union affiliate of the then more radical labor confederation, the *Confédération Générale du Travail Unitaire* (CGTU).[4]

The personal relationships between the supporters of Naville and those of Molinier were extremely acrimonious. As other figures emerged into leadership positions, they too were caught up in the acrimony. Moreover, during the pre-war period of French Trotskyism, it is often difficult to separate out the substantive issues from the personality conflicts—and sometimes difficult to see anything but personality conflicts.

Trotsky himself was sometimes driven to despair over this. In September 1933, two months after he established a brief residency in France, he wrote: "Almost from the very beginning of the existence of the French League its inner life represented a series of crises that never reached the level of principles, but distinguished themselves by extreme bitterness and poisoned the atmosphere of the organization, repelling serious workers despite their sympathy for the ideas of the Opposition."[5] In 1935, after trying to deal with these conflicts, "Trotsky was so appalled that on December 27 he asked the IS (International Secretariat) for a month's leave of absence to free him from the 'disgusting trivia' of the French squabble so that he would be able to accomplish other work."[6]

In the mid 1930s, a major issue for French Trotskyists was how to deal with the Popular Front strategy of the Socialist Party (the SFIO), the Radical Socialists, and the Communist Party. There was a serious fascist threat in France, and Trotsky had been severely critical of Stalin for considering the German social democrats to be such "social fascists" that he refused to permit the German Communist Party to align itself with them in an anti-Nazi workers' front. Now, however, Trotsky felt that the French Communist Party was going to the opposite and equally mistaken extreme of entering into an alliance not only with the socialists but also with the clearly bourgeois Radical Socialist Party of Daladier. Of the three, this party was the strongest in the Chamber of Deputies prior to the 1936 legislative elections but fell behind Léon Blum's socialists in the April-May elections. The Communists ran a poor third but did increase their seats from 10 to 72.

All of the Trotskyist tendencies accepted Trotsky's rejection of Popular Frontism and the substitution of such slogans as "Oust the bourgeois politicians from the People's Front!," "For a Socialist-Communist government!," or "For a workers' and farmers' government!" But the Trotskyists were alone on the Left in rejecting the alliance with the Radical Socialists and, at a time when worker militancy was high and the Left as a whole was making crucial gains, the Trotskyists remained isolated and wracked by internal dissension.

Trotsky himself, in consultation with the International, decided that the best tactic would be for the French Trotskyists to dissolve the *Ligue* and enter the SFIO. The entry into the Socialist Party seemed reasonable from two points of view. First, it would enable the Trotskyists to work against Popular Frontism within a structure that was part of it and that was attracting strong worker support. Secondly, the work within the Socialist Party might just dilute the personal bitterness within the Trotskyist movement. While young Trotskyists had been working in the SFIO's youth section, *La Jeunesse Socialiste,* for about a year previously, the *Ligue* did dissolve itself in August 1934 and its members entered the SFIO. There they constituted themselves as the Bolshevik-Leninist Group (GBL) and continued to publish their own newspaper, *La Vérité* (*The Truth*).

Molinier was enthusiastic about entering the SFIO from the start. His ally Frank initially opposed it, but went along. Naville vehemently opposed the move. He received international support from the American Trotskyist Hugo Gehler who, as we shall see, also opposed entry in the United States a year later. Molinier thought that the entry tactic would finally rid him of Naville, whom he hoped would quit the Trotskyist movement because of his opposition. However, Trotsky used the American leader Cannon to convince Naville not to quit but to enter the SFIO. Molinier complained to Trotsky, still living in France, over the "secret diplomacy carried out here by your representative Cannon in order to bring Naville back to our League, despite himself."[7]

So, in 1934, the Trotskyists, not quite one big happy family, entered the SFIO. A third figure, aside from Naville and Molinier, had been rising in the Trotskyist ranks. It was someone whom Trotsky esteemed more than either Naville or Molinier. This was Jean Rous, four years younger than both Naville and Molinier. Rous rose to the position of national secretary of the Trotskyist faction within the Socialist Party, the GBL, and also sat on the International Secretariat.

The Trotskyists did not remain in the SFIO very long. They entered in August 1934 and were expelled in October 1935. They continued to publish their own papers, to affiliate with the Trotskyist international, and to oppose Popular Frontism. In the adult SFIO they tried to encourage the left-wing non-Trotskyist faction led by Marceau Pivert to maintain a strong anti-Popular Front position. In the youth movement, the *Jeunesse Socialiste*, they were particularly successful in gaining control of the branch in the Seine (Paris region). The branch offices were in the party central headquarters and the adult party resorted to a lock-out to bring the Seine section back into line.[8] When that failed, the Seine youth section was dissolved in July 1935, three months before the GBL was itself expelled.

There was immediate disagreement over how to react to the expulsion. Molinier and Frank, the latter having initial reservations over entering in the first place, wanted to find a way to remain in the SFIO. They wanted to come to a compromise resolution with the SFIO's leadership. Rous, Naville and their followers wanted to remain outside and to reconstitute an independent Trotskyist formation.

Immediately after leaving the SFIO, the factional fight, between Rous and Naville on the one hand and Molinier and Frank on the other, intensified. Molinier wanted to publish a "mass newspaper" but the Central Committee of the GBL refused to agree to it. Molinier, who had been able to collect substantial funds from his business dealings, went ahead and published a paper called *La Commune*. Also, independently of the Central Committee's sanction, he began forming neighborhood Revolutionary Action Groups which would give his paper a mass base.

Rous and Naville were furious. The Political Bureau ordered *La Commune* to cease publication and Molinier's ally, Frank, was removed from his post as editorial secretary for the GBL's official paper, *Révolution*. But at this point Trotsky himself moved against Molinier. At the substantive level, he accused Molinier, who had wanted to stay in the SFIO, of veering toward "centrism," "Popular Frontism," and "capitulation to the social-democratic wave" in order to establish close ties with Pivert.[9]

At the personal level, Trotsky disliked the fact that Molinier's business affairs yielded him funds which provided him the flexibility to establish newspapers and action committees in violation of discipline. Moreover, Trotsky argued that Molinier's elected action committees were a complete misunderstanding of what Trotsky himself meant by "action committees." Molinier's were patterned after what Trotsky thought had been a strategic error on the part of the 1871 Commune, namely the creation of elected action committees *before* power had been effectively seized by revolutionaries.

By the end of 1935, Trotsky was becoming disgusted with Molinier in particular but with the entire French section as well. He insisted upon the expulsion of Molinier, even though Naville was willing to settle for suspension.[10] He used a story concerning Molinier's alleged desertion from the army and use of an insanity plea to indicate that Molinier hardly had the character of a persistent revolutionary and would continue to be a divisive and destabilizing element within the French section. But Trotsky was also put off by Rous and Naville because they refused to print his most critical attacks on Pivert.

After his expulsion, Molinier, with Frank's collaboration, formed his own group. In January of 1936 he formed *Le Comité pour la Quatrième Internationale*. In March the *Comité* constituted itself as a political party, the *Parti Communiste Internationaliste* (PCI). The followers of both the PCI leaders and the GBL leaders were dissatisfied with this organizational split. Thus on May 31-June 1, the Rous-Naville group, the GBL plus its youth affiliate, the *Jeunesse Socialiste Révolutionnaire,* constituted itself as a party as well, the *Parti Ouvrier Révolutionnaire* (POR). On the next day, June 2, the POR fused with the PCI to form a combined party with a compromise name (the PCI had initially been holding out for its name), the *Parti Ouvrier Internationaliste* (POI).

The combination was of short duration. Molinier, who had been admitted as a provisional member, pushed for the creation of a financial commission to seek money for the party. Only the Central Committee, Political Bureau, and Control Commission would know of the commission's activities. This was seen as another attempt by Molinier to use business deals for empire building. The three Molinierists on the Central Committee were suspended. There were charges of falsification of the minutes of the Central Committee meeting. Once again, Trotsky was adamant that Molinier had to go. He was expelled from the combined party, the POI, in July 1936. His followers tried in vain to negotiate his return with Trotsky, who was now living in Norway. Trotsky refused, and in October of 1936, Molinier's PCI resumed its independent existence.

For two years the POI operated as the officially recognized Trotskyist section under the leadership of Rous and Naville, while the PCI continued as a dissident group under Molinier and Frank. The Nazi-fascist threat was growing and neither of the organizations, which claimed to represent 615 members at the founding of the combined party in 1936, was growing. On the contrary, the total Trotskyist membership was declining.

At the end of 1938, Molinier's and Frank's PCI decided on another entry tactic. In that year the socialist Marceau Pivert, who had moderated his criticism of Blum sufficiently to serve as an aide to Blum when the latter became Prémier, left the SFIO to create his own formation, the *Parti Socialiste des Ouvriers et Paysans* (PSOP). The Molinierists, who had always been attracted to work with Pivert, joined the PSOP.

This posed a problem for the POI. On the one hand, Trotsky had been extremely hostile to Pivert, to the point that even the Rous-Naville people refused to publish his most critical statements. Trotsky was to complain about this. On the other hand, Trotsky did not have much confidence in Naville, saw Rous as having come a long way but still learning, and came to the difficult conclusion that the only way to keep the French section alive was to have it follow the example of Molinier's PCI and enter Pivert's PSOP.

This was not a move that the majority of the French section could accept. And it was very badly split. This was shortly after the formal creation of the Fourth International in September 1938. Between that founding and the forced entry of the French section into the PSOP, one group pulled out entirely. This was the *Union Communiste Internationaliste* under the leadership of a Rumanian named Barta. Barta, who initially came to France in transit to the Spanish Civil War, became convinced that Trotsky's criticism of the French section as a whole was correct and that the "trivia" would continue until Trotskyism ceased being a bourgeois debating society and became a true workers movement operating in the factories. That is precisely where Barta sent his followers.

A minority of the POI, under the leadership of Rous and Yvan Craipeau, who had come up through the youth movement which Trotsky thought was doing better work than the adult section, went into the PSOP in February 1939. The majority, including Naville, refused to do so. Trotsky and the International reminded them that international discipline took precedence over majority votes in a national section. In July 1939, Naville and most of his followers submitted and went into Pivert's group. Those who refused were expelled.

At the outbreak of the Second World War Pivert's PSOP simply fell apart. The officially-recognized Trotskyist section, which was the POI, changed its name to the *Comité Français pour la Quatrième Internationale*. Molinier's group changed its name from the PCI to the *Comité Communiste Internationaliste*. While their membership dwindled, particularly during the repression of the Nazi occupation, these two Trotskyist groups, as well as Barta's *Union Communiste Internationaliste,* did operate during the war. However most of the older and better known leaders either fled France or were captured.

The position of all of the Trotskyist groups was that the Communist Party, under Stalin's direction, once again had sold out by uniting with the bourgeois forces in the *Comité National de la Résistance.*

Moreover, it further capitulated to bourgeois national chauvinism by supporting the capitalist Western countries against Nazi Germany. Theoretically, Trotskyists rejected the theory of stages dear to Stalin and Mao which led to the merger of the Chinese Communist Party and the Kuomintang to fight Japanese imperialism. The French situation made such a combination with the bourgeoisie even worse because France had already experienced its bourgeois revolution and France itself was an imperialistic power with a large colonial empire.[11] In the eyes of the Trotskyists, "national patriotism" and combination with the French bourgeoisie in the *Comité National de la Résistance* was a capitulation on the part of the French Communist Party similar to that of the socialist parties, which rallied to the defense of their governments at the outbreak of World War I. For the Molinierists in the CCI, a social revolution was a certainty in Germany and the main enemy was the United States.[12]

The position of the Trotskyists was that resistance had to be international. They did not possess the forces necessary to enter into armed resistance. Moreover, their approach was quite the contrary of sniping at the German occupation forces. Rather they published newspapers and tracts calling upon workers and soldiers of all nationalities to renounce the nationalistic war in favor of socialist revolution and to create a "Workers' Front" without bourgeois participation. They published material in German as well as in French, and tried to organize revolutionary groups among the German soldiers.[13] Needless to say, they became targets for the Germans, the Resistance, and the allies. When Frank escaped to England, he was imprisoned in a camp.

The three Trotskyist groups remained separated until 1944 and still a fourth small group had cropped up during the war. This was the *Groupe Octobre* led by Henri Claude.[14] In 1944 the European Executive Commitee of the Fourth International exerted pressure for unification.[15] In May of 1944, three months before the allies marched into Paris, the former POI and PCI united into a single party which Claude's group also joined. This time the former members of the pre-war PCI succeeded in having the newly combined formation named the PCI, or *Parti Communiste Internationaliste.*

From 1944 to 1952, there were thus two Trotskyist formations in France. There was the PCI, which was an amalgamation and therefore contained a multitude of factions. And there was the group that Barta had formed, the *Union Communiste Internationaliste,* which still refused to have anything to do with the other groups and which continued to lead a largely clandestine existence even after the war. Only the PCI was recognized by the Fourth International.

The international arbitrator who secured agreement among the French groups for the European Executive Committee was Michel Raptis, more commonly known as Pablo, a young Greek who had become the

General Secretary of the Fourth International in 1942. Until 1961, he was to remain the most powerful single individual in the Fourth International.

The new PCI, as well as Barta's group, was active in strikes and plant seizures by workers from just prior to the Liberation through 1947, when the Communist Party was eliminated from the government coalition. But there was still disagreement within the PCI over such questions as the precise nature of the Stalinist bureaucracy and the French Communist Party, the desirability of maintaining an anti-Stalinist democratic centralist party, and even the perpetuation of the Fourth International itself. While Frank and Naville played important roles in these debates, a new group of people assumed prominence as heads of tendencies. People such as Pierre Lambert, David Rousset, Laurent Schwartz, and Gilles Martinet, all subsequently active in a variety of other movements, including Gaullism in the case of Rousset, began to make their impact.[16]

An initial split in 1948 saw Rousset, who was viewed as being on the right-wing of the PCI even then, splitting to create the short-lived *Rassemblement Démocratique Révolutionnaire* with Sartre and Camus. In the same year, Pierre Frank became General Secretary of the PCI. The Communist Party had just been eliminated from the governing coalition and as one of his first acts Frank sent a letter to the Communist Party's General Secretary, Maurice Thorez, proposing a "united front" of the Communist Party and the PCI.[17]

The movement toward the Communist Party was consistent with an analysis being developed by Pablo at the international level. The international office had been moved to Paris immediately after the war and Pablo began to work closely with Frank. Pablo's "conception" was one which he called, "war-revolution."[18] He saw Stalinism as an historically inevitable stage which could only be replaced by a correct form of socialism once there were revolutions in the United States and Western Europe. In the early 1950s, Pablo took United States military superiority, including possession of nuclear weapons, and the U.S. intervention in Korea, as a sign that war between the United States and the Soviet Union was inevitable. The workers would thus be obliged to make their revolution in the Western industrialized countries under these conditions of international warfare. During this combined process of "war-revolution," the Soviet Union would be forced to become more progressive, not because of any internal will but because of the external pressures of its war against imperialism.

During this process, which was viewed as imminent, what happened within the parties which had the greatest attraction for the workers was seen as crucial. In France, this was the Communist Party. Pablo's conclusion was that if the Trotskyists, who had only a tiny following in France in the late 1940s and early 1950s, were to play any role in this at all, they would have to enter the Communist Party and the labor confederation which it dominated, the CGT, and become a progressive motor force within those structures.

However, this time Pablo was obviously not talking about "entrism" in the same sense as it had been practiced in the SFIO or in Pivert's PSOP. In the words of Pablo, this was *entrisme sui generis* appropriate to the analysis of "war-revolution."[19] The Trotskyists would stay in the Communist Party doing hidden and clandestine work until the revolution, whereas entrism into the SFIO was seen as a short-run tactic to accomplish a specific short term purpose, such as the recruitment of militants from a larger pool. Secondly, Pablo was now proposing that the Trotskyists retain an outside organization which would conduct independent work as well as working within the Communist Party.

The majority of the PCI could not accept either the fatalism of "war-revolution" or the compromises and deceptions which they saw as necessary to work within the Communist Party. To them the policy of *entrisme sui generis* meant that there was no real role for a Trotskyist party. In February 1952, the International imposed Pablo's policy on the French section, once again citing the primacy of international discipline over the majority of a national section. The majority, led by Pierre Lambert, refused to accept the discipline and was expelled in July 1952. Lambert and 110 followers formed their own organization, attempting to retain the name of the PCI until 1965, when they took the name *Organisation Communiste Internationaliste* (OCI). Frank and his approximately 35 followers joined the French Communist Party as clandestine entrists.

From 1952 until 1968, French Trotskyism enjoyed only a minimal following. The three major tendencies were the Frankists of the PCI who had entered the Communist Party, the Lambertists of the OCI, and the UCI founded by Barta in 1939. Today these are still the largest Trotskyist formations. The Frankists are now known as *La Ligue Communiste Révolutionnaire* (LCR), the Lambertists in 1982 changed from the OCI back to the PCI, and the decendants of Barta's followers are presently *Lutte Ouvrière*. After 1968, Trotskyism reached its highest point in French history, as it did on a world-wide level. The three major Trotskyist tendencies grew from a total membership of, at best, a few hundred, to a claimed membership of approximately 10,000 members, without counting sympathizers.

LA LIGUE COMMUNISTE RÉVOLUTIONNAIRE (LCR)

Origins of the Ligue

The present Frankist organization has strong historical roots in the 1968 revolt. While the Trotskyists were within the Communist Party, they had a particularly important impact upon the student affiliate, the *Union des*

Étudiants Communistes (UEC). This impact was reinforced by the Frankists' support for the Algerian FLN and the Communist Party's very moderate position and willingness to vote war credits during the Algerian War for independence. As we have seen in Chapter 1, there was such wide-spread dissatisfaction with the Communist Party in its student affiliate that the parent party lost control of its affiliate from 1963 to 1965 to a majority coalition of admirers of the Italian Communist Party (which was asserting independence of Moscow under Togliatti's leadership), Maoists, and Trotskyists.

An extremely important figure in this affair was Alain Krivine. Krivine had entered the youth movement of the Communist Party in 1956, as a "Stalinist," in his own words.[20] During his involvement in anti-war work he was introduced to Trotskyism. In 1960 he joined the PCI group and thereafter acted as an entrist in the UEC. As a student in history at the Sorbonne, Krivine rose to the leadership position in the UEC's Sorbonne section. He played a major role in the "revolt" of both the Sorbonne section and the national organization. The Central Committee of the Communist Party solved the problem of Krivine and the rest of the rebellious Sorbonne students by dissolving the UEC section there, and creating a new one—of carefully screened members—in October 1965. The straw that broke the camel's back for the party was the Trotskyists' open denunciation of Communist support for the 1965 presidential candidacy of François Mitterrand who, at that time, was not running as a candidate of the Socialist Party but of a broader Federation of the Left.

In 1967, a decision was made to create a revolutionary youth group to rival that of the Communist Party. This was the *Jeunesse Communiste Révolutionnaire* (JCR). It was not formally tied to the PCI and Krivine estimates that only about 150 of the approximately 1,000 JCR militants were PCI. But a majority of the top leadership was PCI. The political line, however, was more fluid—more Guevarist than Trotskyist, according to Krivine's own retrospective admission.

The revolt of 1968 occurred only fourteen months after the creation of the JCR. The organization played an extremely important role, both on the barricades and in the organizational maneuvering that went on once the largely spontaneous revolt was under way. Krivine and the other leaders of the JCR allied themselves with both the *22 mars* movement of Daniel Cohn-Bendit on the Nanterre campus and with student union leaders from the *Parti Socialiste Unifié* who dominated the *Union Nationale des Étudiants de France* (UNEF) which tried to give some direction to the spontaneity of 1968.[21] Another purpose of the alliance was to ward off attempts at a take-over of UNEF by the JCR's Trotskyist rivals, affiliated with the OCI, who had denounced the barricades of May and June.

In 1968, both the JCR and the PCI were among many Far Left groups banned after the government reasserted its control. This led to the creation, in the same year, of the *Ligue Communiste*. The creation of the *Ligue* was the creation of a new French section of the United Secretariat of the Fourth International. It brought together in one organization former PCI and JCR members. The name was changed again in 1974 to the *Ligue Communiste Révolutionnaire*, as a result of a second government ban for a 1973 violent clash with a right-wing racist group. I shall simply refer to the organization from 1968 on as the Ligue.

It is always nice to be flattered by one's enemies. In a 1970 secret document circulated among the high command of the French Army, army intelligence offered the following assessment of the Ligue: "The far-left group with the most developed structure throughout France. Dynamic and aggressive...the *Ligue* has for some months been leading a violent anti-militarist campaign...."[22] As if to prove the point, the Ligue demonstrated the capability of obtaining the secret document from the files of the military and published it in its newspaper.

Organization, Membership, and Publications of the *Ligue*

The *Ligue* is the French section of the United Secretariat of the Fourth International, by far the largest of the Trotskyist international organizations. As such, the broad aspects of its internal governance are determined by the statutes of the Fourth International.

Both the United Secretariat and its national sections subscribe to the concept of "democratic centralism." The bottom line of this is that "The decisions of higher bodies are strictly binding on lower bodies."[23] Democratic centralism is also usually interpreted to mean: (1) that debates over basic issues terminate after a decision is made until the decision process, usually a Congress, is renewed; and (2) that criticism and debate are contained within the organization and its internal documents.

In the case of the United Secretariat, the right of factionalism is guaranteed. Moreover, until the winter of 1977--78, there existed a majority and a minority faction, the International Majority Tendency (IMT) and the Leninist-Trotskyist Faction (LTF). The *Ligue* was the largest regular national section of the IMT.[24] While the policies of the IMT prevailed as the policies of the United Secretariat, the minority faction reserved the right to state its position publicly.

The *Ligue's* own internal policy on this as a national section is fluid. There are factions and tendencies within the *Ligue*. At the constituent Congress of the LCR in December 1974 (after the 1973 banning), four different tendencies presented their views for debate. The LCR made these views public along with the vote totals received by each of the resolutions.[25] Formally, all the majority is required by statute to do is recognize the right of factions and tendencies to exist, accord them representation on executive bodies "according to their numerical and political importance," and not obstruct the circulation of viewpoints in internal documents prior to decision-making time.

The Ligue, however, does differ from the OCI and Lutte Ouvrière in that the majority will at times agree to the external publication of internal disagreement even after a majority decision has been reached. Much more than the other two organizations, the Ligue will try to interpret divisive issues as tactical rather than ones of principle, and will permit public venting of divergence in order to keep the losers within the organization.

The Ligue is the largest regular section of the United Secretariat and one of the largest Trotskyist organizations in the world. In 1972, the year before the 1973 governmental ban, it was claiming 5,000 members. But that was a peak and the Ligue began to decline in total membership. It also began to undergo a high rate of membership turnover—largely for personal rather than political reasons, according to the leadership.

Thus the Ligue took the opportunity of the 1973 ban and 1974 reconstitution to do some restructuring. It created two kinds of structures for sympathizers as well as for actual members of the Ligue. First, there were the Red Mole groups (les Taupes Rouges) which were neighborhood and factory committees. Second, there were the Red Committees (les Comités Rouges) which grouped people in other categories, including high school and university students. Still no separate youth affiliate was created during the reconstitution and it would not be until 1978 that the organization would be spurred to move in that direction.

In 1975, the reconstituted Ligue itself claimed approximately 3,000 members but also claimed approximately 2,000 members of factory Red Mole groups, 300 to 400 members of neighborhood Red Mole groups (1,350 people attended the 1975 national convention of Red Mole groups), and 1,000 high school students plus 600 university students in the Red Committees. Keeping in mind that some of these affiliations were over-lapping and that the figures are rough approximations, there was a network of between five and seven thousand people. In 1978, the approximate figure remained relatively constant with 3,300 members of the Ligue itself, 2,200 to 2,500 members of Red Mole groups, plus an additional 2,000 youth and students. A network of six to seven thousand people would not be far off the mark.

In terms of regular members of the Ligue in 1975, 38 per cent were university or high school students, 18 per cent were in the professions, from eight to nine per cent were factory workers (almost all of whom were skilled), and the remaining 35 to 36 per cent were in miscellaneous salaried occupations.[26]

The distribution in age cohorts was as follows: 13 per cent were 18 to 20, 47 per cent were 21 to 25, 27 per cent were 26 to 30, and 13 per cent were over 30. The loss in the turnover phenomenon came largely among older people moving out of the Ligue in response to other pressures in their lives. About 50 per cent of the members in 1975 had been in the *Ligue* only since 1972, and 21 per cent had joined during the previous year (1974). Aside from the loss of older militants, which the less time-consuming sympathizing structures were designed to remedy, the other deficiency was in the participation of women. In 1975, about 30 per cent of the membership was female but, following the typical but not uniquely French pattern of recruitment to leadership positions, only about 16 per cent of the city-level leadership positions were in the hands of women.[27] In 1975 and 1976 women in the *Ligue* began to organize themselves as a self-conscious group and women's commissions were established. In 1977, the women refused to participate in the *Ligue's* Congress unless their representation on the 62-member Central Committee was raised from nine or ten to 20. This was granted, but in the spring of 1978 there was still only one woman on the 12-person Political Bureau, which conducts the business of the *Ligue* between the monthly meetings of the Central Committee.

One of the most impressive aspects of the *Ligue* has been its publications. Trotsky had chided French Trotskyists in the 1930s by holding up the example of the American Socialist Workers Party, which was running a much more extensive press than the French, and with fewer resources. The *Ligue* has remedied this deficiency and has published far more than its French Trotskyist rivals.

Prior to March 15, 1976, the *Ligue* published a weekly paper called *Rouge*. As of June 1975, *Rouge* was run off at 25,000 copies per week. Fourteen to fifteen thousand of these were sold. On March 15, 1976, *Rouge* became a daily paper. That made it the only Trotskyist daily in France. As of 1978, a staff of 80 members was producing the paper, which was selling at 12,000 copies per day.[28] Aside from the daily paper, the *Ligue* also published: *Critiques de l'Economie Politique,* more a journal of economics, which sold at from 2,000 to 5,000 copies; *Cahiers de la Taupe,* a monthly publication designed for factory workers in the Red Mole groups, which sold 5,000 copies; *Cahiers du Féminisme,* a monthly for women which was started in early 1978 and sold from 5,000 to 6,000 copies; and *Barricades,* a monthly selling 5,000 to 6,000 copies, which was distributed among and by groups called *Barricades Circles,* which were the bud of the youth affiliate which the *Ligue* was about to create. In addition, it cooperated with two other groups in the publication of *L'Écho des Casernes,* a publication aimed at soldiers. Finally, the *Ligue,* which formerly relied heavily upon the non-sectarian left-wing publisher, François Maspero, for publication of books, established its own publishing house, *La Brêche.*

The *Ligue's* Program

In 1972, the *Ligue's* Central Committee published a national program under the title *Ce que veut la Ligue Communiste (What the Ligue Communiste Stands For)*. In terms of the basic definition of socialism, that document is more important than subsequent programs issued by the *Ligue* in election years.

The document defines socialism thusly: "Socialism is workers' councils plus automation."[29] For Trotsky, the workers' councils which were dissolved shortly after the Russian Revolution represented the heart of democracy in the new socialist state, and served as the only potentially effective bulwark against the development of a state bureaucracy. For the *Ligue,* the workers have three roles to play in the revolutionary process. First, in the eyes of the *Ligue,* the only way that a successful revolution can take place is through the arming of the workers and the creation, in industrial plants, of workers' militias. The program is extremely critical of the short-lived Allende regime in Chile for not pursuing this path, and points out the complicity of the Chilean Communist Party in the decision not to arm the workers but to rely upon bourgeois legalism for the defense of the socialist government.[30]

Once a revolution supported by armed workers is successful, certain measures must be taken before the workers can exercise complete control over both the state and the factories, both final goals of the *Ligue.* First, the number of work hours must be reduced. "Only inveterate utopians could imagine that the worker, having been submitted all day to this form of oppression, would be able to direct the affairs of state on evenings or Saturdays."[31] The *Ligue* sees a link between control over the work place and control over the state apparatus. "Without freedom in the factory, said the Polish workers who rose up against the bureaucracy in 1956, political democracy is only 'Sunday Freedom' and the workers' state a decoy which is really the prey of the bureaucrats."[32]

However, even after the revolution, the workers do not possess the necessary knowledge to assume sole control over the production process immediately. Early in the post-revolutionary period, the *Ligue* foresees a stage of *cogestion* (participation in decision-making) rather than *autogestion* (complete control over decision-making). The program reads: "[W]orkers, not having the capacity to direct from the beginning a productive process in which they have been assigned only the most menial of tasks and not having been permitted access to information on the more general aspects of the running of the operation, can only look forward to *autogestion* as a middle term prospect, a goal to attain where it is possible."[33] During the period of *cogestion,* work places would be run by committees (*comités d'usine*) which would include workers elected by their peers, a factory director (appointed or elected), and technical staff.

Ultimately, the *Ligue* sees *autogestion* as the only guarantee against the bureaucratization of the state on the order of the USSR and Eastern Europe. But technical innovation which would permit shortening the work hours without declines in productivity must be stressed. Thus the importance of "automation" in the formula of the *Ligue*. Automation is seen as offering to the workers release from overly long and exhausting work hours in order both to learn about the total productive operation and to participate actively in decision-making regarding the operation—something which is regarded as management prerogative under capitalism.

In the *Ligue's* program, labor unions would continue to exist, but there would be a division of function. The unions would not concern themselves with production decisions but would represent the needs of workers as consumers and citizens. The *Ligue* contends that they should pay attention to general working and salary conditions (presumably in contrast to production decisions), social security, paid vacations, and "The participation of workers in all aspects of cultural life."[34] The unions would be guaranteed the right to strike, "[T]he only effective and not purely formal guarantee of the development of working class organizations autonomous of the power of the state."[35]

At the national level, the *Ligue* foresees factory committees and unions all over the country debating elements of national economic plans. Since the *Ligue* sees the proletariat itself as having a multiplicity of specific interests (as did Trotsky), it proposes a plurality of political parties which would aggregate some of these more specific interests and attain greater clarity of the major lines of difference at the national level.

At that level, two kinds of representation would operate. On the one hand, there would be the representatives of the workers in particular industrial sectors. On the other, there would be representatives of political parties with aggregate viewpoints on issues which transcend sectoral affiliation. Due to both constitutional ordering and the fact that everyone involved in a party would also be involved in an industrial or a work sector, there would be constant interaction between parties and workers' organizations. The foreseen system is thus highly pluralistic (within the parameter of complete public ownership of the major means of production) and combines functional representation with a multi-party system. And it must be remembered that Trotskyists view the international systems as being highly integrated. The economy of each country must be a part of a global socialist economic plan.

In insisting that *autogestion* is the only guarantee against bureaucratization on the Soviet model, the *Ligue* quite early developed close relationships with two organizations which pushed the concept well before the Socialist and Communist parties decided to jump on the bandwagon—in the middle and late 1970s, respectively. These are the *Confédération Française Démocratique du Travail* (CFDT) and the *Parti Socialiste Unifié* (PSU). It will be recalled that the CFDT is the second largest labor confederation in France. It was originally Catholic, but the confederation took a syndicalist turn in the early 1960s, and it was the labor confederation most supportive of the uprising in 1968. The PSU, it will also be recalled, was made up largely of dissidents from the Algerian War policies of the SFIO and was also supportive of the 1968 uprising. Aside from housing the Pablist current of French Trotyskyism for a while, the PSU also included such prominent former Trotskyists as Pierre Naville and Yvan Craipeau. At least prior to the mid 1970s, when the CFDT moved closer to the Socialist Party, the *autogestionnaire* PSU and CFDT were both seen by many on the Left as being more truly radical structures than the Communist Party and the CGT.

However, from the very beginning, the *Ligue* maintained a distinction between its position and that of the CFDT and the PSU. That distinction is that the *Ligue* does not see *autogestion* or the decentralized struggle for *autogestion* as being sufficient to topple capitalism and institute socialism. It insists that *autogestion* can only be established after capitalism has been overthrown by a political revolution. The distinction is somewhat similar to that made by Trotsky between his position and Molinier's over the role of workers' committees.

If the *Ligue* sees the institution of *autogestion* as necessary to prevent bureaucratization on the order of the Soviet model, its position regarding that Soviet model and the French Communist Party is not as rigid as those of some other Trotskyist organizations. The *Ligue* still accepts the analysis of one of its members, formulated even before the *Ligue* was formally constituted. In *Mouvement ouvrier, Stalinisme, et bureaucratie,* Henri Weber points to what he calls the "contradictory nature of the Soviet bureaucracy."[36] On the one hand, the Soviet bureaucracy derives its power from the state and the economic and social infrastructure which resulted from the revolution of 1917. The bureaucracy is thus obliged to use its resources to fight off threats to the state and its infrastructures, whether they arise internally, in the form of attempts to restore the bourgeois order of private property and exploitation, or externally, in the form of the military threat and imperialism of the capitalist countries. In these two senses, Weber sees the Soviet bureaucracy as performing a positive function. On the other hand, writes Weber:

> [T]he bureaucracy constitutes a parasitic caste whose
> privileges have not been more widely distributed and
> have been temporarily stabilized because of the
> weakness of the Russian proletariat and the ebbing
> of the revolutionary tide in the world....[I]t must
> maintain internal and external conditions which keep
> the proletariat in an apathetic condition and permit
> its political expropriation.[37]

For Weber, writing in 1966, this contradiction explained the schizoid behavior of the USSR even after "de-Stalinization." At the same time that the Soviet bureaucracy was trying to keep its own proletariat under control, it was having to contend with both capitalist regimes and left-wing revolutionary movements in capitalist countries which frightened it.

Certainly the major left-wing movement in Weber's mind was Trotskyism. And the French Communist Party—one of the most highly Stalinist parties, until the shift to "Eurocommunism"—was seen as the executive arm of the Kremlin bureaucracy in stifling all true revolutionary action in France. For the *Ligue,* Eurocommunism was a kind of "social-democratization." The *Ligue* did not view the program of the Communist Party as a truly revolutionary program. It felt, however, that the Communist Party was in a state of movement in the 1970s, and it doubted that the future of the party would follow historically precedented paths. At the programmatic level, the *Ligue* took a wait-and-see attitude, i.e., that the Communist Party could go in a very positive direction, or that it could wind up with positions even worse than those of Stalin.

Despite the lack of certainty in this regard and its criticism of the party's program, the *Ligue* did see the French party's turn toward Euro-communism as a real break from subservience to the Kremlin bureaucracy. This, plus the open and public display of dissension of those within the party following the loss of the 1978 legislative elections, opened an unprecedented possibility of a dialogue with certain well-known people and officials within the Communist Party. The invitation extended to a Trot-skyist to speak at the Eurocommunistic Spanish Communist Party's 1978 Congress was truly remarkable. But the participation of three prominent French Communist Party members in the panels and debates of the *Ligue's* 1978 festival was just as remarkable.[38]

The question of *autogestion* and the nature of both the Soviet system and the French Communist Party are questions which Trotskyists have debated in the past. The French tradition of syndicalism, coupled with Trotsky's interest in workers' councils and the phenomenon of Stalinism enduring from the 1920s through the early 1950s, assured that this would be the case.

But some new issues were raised in the 1960s and the 1970s. And it has been the *Ligue's* posture toward these "new" issues which has given it a generation differential and a "New Left" look which the other major Trotskyist organizations in France lack.

The *Ligue's* focus on youth, its championing of the cause of women's equality, its defense of the rights of homosexuals, and its opposition to nuclear power contribute to this blend of new and old Left which the French sometimes refer to as *Gauchiste.*[39]

The *Ligue* has gone further in seeing youth as a revolutionary vanguard than have other French Trotskyist groups—or any other Marxist group in France. When the PCI merged with the JCR, the older members of the tiny Trotskyist party were swamped by the members of the youth group. They all were in one organization, without age distinction, and the younger people—like Alain Krivine and Daniel Ben-Said—assumed the leadership positions. Both its attraction within the student milieu and its heavy investment in a campaign to organize recruits in the military—a campaign which, as we have seen, was viewed as a serious threat by the military—have been part of this "youth as a vanguard" aspect of the *Ligue*.

While the youth orientation characterized the *Ligue* from its beginning, the issues of women, homosexuality, and nuclear power are of more recent vintage. Despite the fact that the *Ligue* had demonstrated a theoretical appreciation for the works of Wilhelm Reich, and had included a section on women in its 1972 program, the organization had remained complacent about the fuller appreciation of the situation of women and homosexuals in the society at large, as well as in the organization itself. Beginning in 1976, women and homosexuals in the *Ligue* began to organize and "come out." This resulted in both structural changes within the organization to facilitate expression of women's and homosexuals' concerns as well as more elaborate public analyses and firmer organizational commitments to their struggles. Of the "mixed" organizations on the French Left, the *Ligue*, the PSU, and the *Organisation Communiste des Travailleurs* (OCT)[40] have been the most militant on the question of women, the most willing to permit separate structures for women within their own organizations, and the most supportive of autonomous women's groups.[41] The same is true of their posture *vis-à-vis* lesbians and gay men.

The question of nuclear energy is also of relatively recent vintage. It has been brought to public attention by demonstrations of peasants against the installation of nuclear reactors in their regions and on their farmland. These demonstrations have received international support and, indeed, some of these breeder reactors are multinational operations. The nuclear energy question has also been placed into prominence by the ecology movement, which made a very strong showing in the 1977 municipal elections. The *Ligue's* position is that the power generating capacity of nuclear plants has been oversold to the public, and that the environmental and safety problems attached to it render the government's extensive reliance upon it unacceptable.[42] More than any other French Trotskyist group, the *Ligue* has attempted to work with the larger environmental and anti-nuclear movement.

While each of the above positions distinguish the *Ligue* from one or the other or both of its major Trotskyist rivals in France, the *Ligue's* position on Third World revolutionary movements, which was accepted by the majority of the United Secretariat of the Fourth International, has distinguished it from both of the other French Trotskyist groups and from the minority faction, including the American SWP, within its own international structure.

First, consistent with Pablo's Third World orientation and particular involvement with the Algerian struggle for national liberation[43] as well as the strong Guevarist orientation of the JCR before it merged with the PCI to form the *Ligue*, the *Ligue* has been the most Third World oriented of the major French Trotskyist groups. Unlike the other groups, it made a heavy commitment to support the Vietnamese fighting against the Americans. Prior to 1968, the JCR had been active in a support group called the *Comité Vietnam National*.[44] After the creation of the *Ligue*, a new support group called the *Front Solidarité Indochine* (FSI) was initiated. It was intimately tied to the *Ligue* and a very important part of the *Ligue's* work during the war. In its organization of demonstrations and rallies and its extensive publication of material, it was the most significant anti-war group in France.

Despite the fact that the programs of the Vietnamese Communist Party, the Provisional Revolutionary Government, and the National Liberation Front were not Trotskyist programs, the *Ligue* went further than any other French Trotskyist group and than its American counterpart not only in supporting the armed struggle but in justifying the program of the Vietnamese Communist Party.

Pierre Rousset, son of David Rousset, the former Trotskyist who created the RGR with Sartre and Camus before becoming a Gaullist deputy, was the major *Ligue* theorist on this question.[45] Rousset characterized the *Ligue's* support as "radical, committed, and unconditional, but not uncritical."[46] The two problems were that (1) the programs of the Vietnamese groups fighting the Americans did not call for a complete conversion from capitalism to socialism in the South, and (2) the struggle was predominantly a peasant struggle coordinated by centralized organizations, rather than a struggle enjoying the support of decentralized workers' soviets.

But, Rousset and the *Ligue* argued, these programmatic and structural (bureaucratic) deformations in both the North and the South were due to unique circumstances: colonization, the war, underdevelopment, the international situation, and the "Asiatic tradition of state centralism."[47]

Given the necessity to adjust to these special circumstances, the Vietnamese Communist Party has become an "empirical revolutionary party."[48] This is about as close to the Maoist emphasis upon superstructural characteristics as one is likely to find coming from the pen of a contemporary Trotskyist. Rousset had no doubt that the Vietnamese party had a solid revolutionary vocation and that the end point of its activities would be the creation of a truly socialist society.

In regard to Latin America, the *Ligue* preserved the Guevarist orientation of the JCR by becoming a major supporter of armed guerrilla warfare. None of the other major French Trotskyist groups accepted this, and it also became a primary sore point between the International Majority Tendency and the Leninist-Trotskyist Faction within the United Secretariat.

A problem for the *Ligue* and its majority faction was the withdrawal from the United Secretariat of the Argentinian Revolutionary Workers Party or *PRT-Combatiente*. The armed wing of this party was the well-known ERP, one of the most active guerrilla groups in Latin America. The *PRT-Combatiente* was part of the same majority tendency as the *Ligue*, and the *Ligue* gave it unqualified support. On the other hand, the minority faction in the international organization attacked the militaristic orientation of the Argentinian group and accused it of, among other things, "an erroneous appreciation of Maoism, especially of the theoretical implications of people's war; [and] an apologetic appreciation of Castroism...."[49]

Prior to the 1974 World Congress of the United Secretariat, the *PRT-Combatiente* left the international Trotskyist body and its place was taken by the *Partido Socialista de los Trabajadores* (PST). The PST was an electorally oriented party which did not engage in armed struggle. It affiliated with the minority tendency of the United Secretariat.[50] To make things even sweeter for the *Ligue's* opposition—which saw the PRT's quitting of the Secretariat as a vindication of its criticism that the PRT was not a serious Trotskyist group—the newly affiliated PST was the largest Trotskyist organization in the world. While this was not enough to reverse the majority-minority factional positions,[51] in 1977 the *Ligue* itself began a process of internal criticism over its position and the lack of success of the guerrilla strategy. This was its major concession in the hope of unifying the two factions within the United Secretariat.

The *Ligue's* Tactics

Aside from its extensive publishing and propaganda activity, the *Ligue* has used three other kinds of activities to advance its goals: labor union work, direct action, and electoral activity.

As I have indicated, the *Ligue* has pursued the double strategy of working with its own Red Mole groups in factories as well as working within affiliates of two of the major labor-led confederations. In terms of workers' unions, the *Ligue* has worked and sought office within the largest and second largest labor confederations in France, the Communist party domina-ted CGT and the *autogestionnaire* CFDT. It has not worked within the CGT-FO, a more conservative group, initially created with United States assistance to combat the CGT. While it has more militants within the CGT, it has found it easier to be elected to office in the CFDT. Even though the degree of repressiveness in the CGT in the 1970s lessened somewhat, according to a *Ligue* leader, the CFDT was still a noticeably more open confederation. The teachers in the *Ligue* have been working within the large teachers' federation, the *Fédération de l'Education Nationale* (FEN). They have participated in a current which poses a challenge to the Communists' control over the secondary teachers' affiliate of the FEN.[52]

During the early and mid 1970s, the *Ligue* also engaged extensively in direct action. It is an organization which was built upon a base of 1968 barricade fighters, and it has been known to engage in violent conflict with groups which it regards as fascist or racist. But most of its direct action involved demonstrations in which there was no violence. However, the *Ligue* would not accept what it believed to be illegitimate police bans on its demonstrations. There were occasional battles with the police when the latter attempted to disrupt demonstrations.

The *Ligue* could put more people into the streets for demonstrations than any other Trotskyist of Maoist group. It also had the most highly developed *service d'ordre,* a group of specially designated people with the function of warding off external attacks and maintaining order within the ranks. While the *Ligue* has been viewed as dangerously confrontation-oriented by the Communist Party and by one of the *Ligue's* Trotskyist rivals, the OCI, in the late 1970s the *Ligue* used its own *service d'ordre* to control the violence of a group which claimed to be on the Left. These were the *Autonomes,* a group with a fondness for breaking the property of the state, store windows, and the heads of their political opponents—especially on the Left.[53] After their appearance in 1977, they tried to apply their tactics in demonstrations in which the *Ligue* was a sponsor. The *Ligue* was thus placed in the embarrassing position of being accused by the *Autonomes* and their sympathizers of placing a damper on the most militant forms of confrontation—exactly the same charge which the *Ligue* has always levied against the Communist Party and the CGT.

Finally, the *Ligue* has pursued an electoral strategy—not to win elections but to use the resources available at election time, such as access to national television—to attempt to raise the consciousness of the working class. Krivine, himself twice a candidate for President of the Republic, attempted to justify the strategy in the following terms.

> But one will object to us—is there not something inconsistent in denouncing the idiocy of the parliamentary system, in crying that elections are a betrayal, in advocating a boycott of the referendum [of 1969], and then finally offering a candidate for the presidency of the Republic?
>
> In order to respond to this question it suffices to refer to the history of the workers' movement and to recall what Lenin said: "Revolutionaries are not obliged to reject elections, nor are they obliged to participate in them per se. Everything depends on the political situation."

It is not a position of principle. If the proletariat
is able to feel on its own the nature of the class
domination to which it is subjected, then participation in elections—even on the basis of anti-electoralist themes—will gain nothing and even runs the
risk of lowering political consciousness. But during
periods when the proletariat is not able to experience
this, it would be stupid to confine ourselves to
abstract denunciations of the parliamentary system
when the elections themselves offer the best means
of denouncing it in practice. That is the sense of
Lenin's teaching: use all of the possibilities offered
by the bourgeoisie to topple it.[54]

The *Ligue* ran candidates in the 1969 and 1974 presidential elections, in the 1973 and 1978 legislative elections, and in the 1977 municipal
elections. In 1969, when Krivine first ran for the presidency, he received
239,000 votes.[55] In 1974, the situation became more complicated. First,
Krivine preferred not to run but to join with other Far Left groups, including
the Maoist *Cause du Peuple,* in presenting a common candidate of the Far
Left. Charles Piaget—a CFDT unionist and a leader of the Lip watch factory
strike in Besançon which resulted in workers taking over the plant and
running it along the lines of *autogestion*—was appealed to to become a
candidate. On April 3, 1974, Krivine, Alain Geismar of the *Cause du Peuple,*
and Isaac Joshua of *Révolution* (before it became the OCT) traveled to
Besançon to convince Piaget to run. Piaget, also a member of the PSU,
refused to run because the PSU had decided to support the candidacy of the
Socialist, Mitterrand. Moreover, another Trotskyist group, *Lutte Ouvrière,*
not only refused to be a party to the electoral alliance but announced its own
candidate.

Secondly, the *Ligue* was still under a ban, and if Krivine had run
under the banner of the *Ligue* he would have been liable for arrest. The group
held together under the name of *Rouge,* the *Ligue's* then weekly newspaper.
For purposes of the electoral laws one had to run as the candidate of a party,
not a newspaper. So the *Front Communiste Révolutionnaire* (FCR) was
created. It was the *Ligue* with a legal name.

Krivine used his television time to make a particularly strong pitch
for the rights of those in the armed forces. He called for the recognition of the
right to unionize, to refuse orders contrary to the interests of the workers, for
the recall of officers who bully soldiers or take anti-working class measures,
and for the abolition of all special criminal jurisdiction for the army.[56] In an
April 30 national television address, he appealed to draftees to:

> Refuse to be treated as second class citizens.
> If Mitterrand is elected, we must remain vigi-
> lant toward the reactionary officers who will
> dream of returning to the past....Make them
> know clearly that in no case will you agree to
> march against the people.[57]

Krivine clearly had Chile in mind. The Minister of the Army called a press conference in which he denounced Krivine for "an open appeal for riot and insubordination" in the armed forces and "attempting to undermine the discipline of the army of the Republic."[58]

Krivine also interviewed high school students, militants, and workers on television. When he attempted to interview workers in the FCR, the National Control Commission, which regulates the use of radio and television by candidates, ruled that the FCR was not a nationally recognized party and that its members could not be given media time by Krivine. The PSU, which supported the electoral alliance behind Mitterrand, stepped in and offered its television time to Krivine and the FCR. Krivine interviewed three workers who were identified as PSU, but whom everyone knew to be FCR.[59] Krivine received 93,900 votes, or .36 per cent, on the first round. On the second round the *Ligue* supported Mitterrand's candidacy, but again warned the workers that the bourgeoisie would not permit Mitterrand to carry out the Common Program, as deficient as it was, and that the workers would have to arm themselves to avoid another Chile if he seriously attempted to do so. The armed workers would also, of course, provide additional positive pressure for Mitterrand to pursue a course of transition to socialism in case his own inclinations were less revolutionary.[60]

While the *Ligue* ran Krivine for president in 1969 and 1974 without any kind of formal alliance or common program (although with *Lutte Ouvrière's* support in 1969), it has engaged in electoral alliances in the legislative and municipal elections. In the 1973 legislative elections, the *Ligue* attempted to reach an agreement on the division of electoral districts with *Lutte Ouvrière* and the OCI. *Lutte Ouvrière* went on its own and the OCI offered only a token showing of from six to ten candidates. The *Ligue* ran in 80 parliamentary districts.

In the 1977 municipal elections, the *Ligue* ran on a common list with *Lutte Ouvrière* and the non-Trotskyist OCT. A year later, in the legislative elections of March 1978, the relationship with *Lutte Ouvrière* was once again broken and the *Ligue* engaged in an electoral agreement and common program with the OCT and the *Comité Communistes pour l'Autogestion* (CCA). The latter group is the French affiliate of Pablo's International Marxist-Revolutionary Tendency. When Pablo was expelled from the United Secretariat in 1965, he reconstituted his following and the

French section entered the PSU as a faction, unlike individual Trotskyists or former Trotskyists in the PSU like Naville and Craipeau.[61] In 1977, the CCA left the PSU where they were among the most ardent supporters of *autogestion*. They united with the *Ligue* and the OCT for the first round of the 1978 parliamentary elections. But it is clear that they were also hoping for a merger with the *Ligue*. However, the CCA saw *autogestion* as the key element in the Transitional Program and saw the right to public and permanent factional opposition as a principle for a legitimate Trotskyist Party. While the *Ligue's* majority was willing to grant the right to public opposition to the minority on certain questions, it saw this as a tactical and not a principled question, and would not grant the point to the CCA. In fact, while the CCA's material read as though there were discussions for a merger, the *Ligue* leadership denied this, and simply said that there was an exchange of points of view.

The slogan of the Ligue—OCT-CCA alliance was "Vote Revolutionary on the First Round, Defeat the Right on the Second Round." They thus supported Communists and Socialists—but not the Radical Socialists of the MRG—on the second round. While calling for a vote for Communist and Socialist candidates on the second round to defeat the Right, they attacked the programs of both parties as being deficient.

In sum, the strategy of the *Ligue* has been to open itself to contacts with the Communist Party, to support both Communist and Socialist candidates on the second rounds of elections but to put forward its own program on the first round, and to insist that the Left cannot rely upon bourgeois legalism for defense if it should come to power through electoral means. It has insisted that only the workers who elect the Left could and would defend it. This is why it has called for the arming of the workers after any electoral victory and why it has invested so much energy in organizing within the armed forces. It is convinced that the bourgeoisie will respect its own electoral processes only so long as it is the winner. Chile was only a reminder of that fact. The difference in national context matters very little for, as Chile also demonstrated, the bougeoisie is as internationalist, if not more so, than the proletariat.

L'ORGANISATION COMMUNISTE INTERNATIONALISTE (OCI)

The OCI is rooted in the refusal of the majority of the PCI to accept Pablo's *"entrisme sui generis"* into the Communist Party in the early 1950s. While Pierre Frank led the minority faction into the CP, Pierre Lambert led a majority of approximately 110 followers out of the International Secretariat of the Fourth International. Until 1965, when the name OCI was adopted, both the Frankists and the Lambertists claimed to be legitimate PCI.

At the international level, the OCI joined with the British Socialist Labour League, the Socialist Workers Party of the United States, and a Swiss, a New Zealand, and an exiled Chinese group to form the International Committee of the Fourth International. At the national level, it had its own youth movement, which did not participate in the rebellion within the Communist Party's student movement, the UEC, because the OCI had refused entry. Moreover, it not only did not play a role in the 1968 uprising, but it urged the young people to dismantle the barricades. Ironically, it was banned by the government for participating in the 1968 revolt. It was the only Far Left group to appeal the ban and to win on the appeal. It thus kept its pre-1968 name.

Organization, Membership, and Publications of the OCI

In a number of organizational as well as programmatic aspects, the OCI is much more of an "Old Left" group than is the *Ligue*. While in the *Ligue* the older members of the PCI, such as Pierre Frank, have passed the power over to the rebels of 1968, in the OCI an older and more middle-aged set of leaders still play the leading role. Pierre Lambert, who was born in the early 1920s and is approximately ten years younger than Pierre Frank, is clearly the top leader. There are also a number of people about ten years younger than Lambert who occupy important positions of leadership.

The OCI never permitted itself to be inundated by a wave of younger recruits as the PCI did in unifying with the JCR. The OCI has always tried to recruit heavily among youth and students, but it has also mantained a distinction between the parent organization and the youth and student affiliates.

Moreover, the OCI, through its student affiliate, sought to break the hold of the PSU-JCR alliance over the national student union (UNEF). In the early 1970s, after the PSU-JCR people pulled away from UNEF's politics, OCI students did electoral battle with Communist Party students for control of UNEF. Both sides claimed victory and each appealed to the government and the courts for a favorable ruling. The resolution of the matter was the splitting of UNEF into two, with the OCI's *Alliance de la Jeunesse pour le Socialisme* (AJS) and the CP's *Union des Étudiants Communistes* both claiming to lead the "legitimate" UNEF.

In the OCI itself, however, only about 25 per cent were students in the late 1970s. Approximately 75 per cent of the members were manual workers and professional people. The division between these two categories was about even. Among the professionals, teaching was the most important endeavor. Between 10 per cent and 15 per cent of the members were teachers, from primary schools through university. As close as one high leader of the OCI could come in estimating the percentage of women in the organization was something over 30 per cent, with a possibility of its being close to 50 per cent. There were no precise figures.

The OCI, like the Frankists, has exhibited a remarkable rate of growth since the early 1950s, when Lambert walked out of the PCI with slightly over one hundred members. As late as 1975, the OCI probably had fewer members than the *Ligue* was claiming (without the *Ligue's* sympathizing structures). In 1978, however, the OCI claimed approximately 5,000 members. Indeed, the organization seems to have experienced a spurt of growth in 1977 and 1978.[62] The leadership attributed this to its hard organizational work and to its positions *vis-à-vis* the 1978 legislative elections.

The OCI has had nowhere near the publication output of the *Ligue*. Its regular publications have consisted of a weekly newspaper, *Informations Ouvrières,* and a quarterly journal, *La Vérité*. In 1975, the OCI claimed to sell 16,000 copies of the weekly. The OCI felt that the publication of a daily paper would entail pulling away too many resources which were better devoted to building and solidifying its organizational structure. In addition to the above two publications, the OCI has published a modest number of statements in pamphlet or monograph form on specific issues. These, as well as mimeographed copies of its study courses designed for internal membership education, have been available in its bookstore. Like the *Ligue,* the OCI has maintained a bookstore for the distribution of both its own publications and other books on the Left or on topics of interest to the Left.

The OCI's Program

The OCI views itself as upholding orthodox Trotskyism against the *Ligue's* triflings. It is a stickler for theory, and its members are obliged to go through a rigorous program of schooling in the basic concepts of Marxism, Leninism, and Trotskyism. It claims to abide by the theory of permanent revolution and the Transitional Program, and it has not felt the need to publish extensive programs touching a multitude of specific French problems with little reference to the above theories, the way the *Ligue* has. It is fair to say that the OCI is more theoretical than the *Ligue* and is less willing to change its positions or to adopt new ones. It is less willing to view matters as "tactical" rather than "principled," a distinction which the *Ligue* often uses to justify its flexibility.

On the substantive issues raised in the previous discussion of the *Ligue,* there has been almost total disagreement between the two organizations. The OCI has completely rejected the concept of *autogestion* and has viewed the *Ligue's* program as a capitulation to Pablism. Even before the *Ligue's* 1972 programmatic statement, Jean-Jacques Marie of the OCI accused Ernest Mandel, the Belgian Secretary of the United Secretariat, of:

> replacing the struggle for the overthrow of
> the centralized bourgeois state apparatus by
> the priority demand for "worker control," the

> essential problem hereafter not being "the
> distribution of wealth" but the qualitative
> problem: "who should control machines,
> determine investments, and decide what should
> be produced and how to do it?"[63]

Even though the 1972 statement of the *Ligue* attempted to distinguish between its position and the Pablist position that *autogestion* is the key to the Transitional Program, the OCI felt that the *Ligue* was pandering to *autogestion,* and that such pandering is dangerously counterrevolutionary.

There are two basic sources of the OCI's attitude on this question. First, it is an "Old Left" characteristic of the OCI that it is more attuned to questions of distribution and the structural-political requisites of revolution than to the "qualitative questions" involved in worker control. Workers' committees, such as the soviets after the Russian Revolution, are viewed strictly in structural terms—i.e., as checks on the bureaucracy—rather than as social relationships which are intrinsically good for the full development of the human potentialities of the workers.

Secondly, the OCI views *autogestion* as a social doctrine inspired by the Church to combat Marxism. It sees the logical end point of *autogestion* as the older Church doctrine of corporatism. It is seen as more than just a fad; it is viewed by the OCI as a drug. "It is the miraculous remedy of which the virtues can be compared with the 'opium of the people'."[64]

For the OCI, the notion of *autogestion* creates the image that *decentralized* struggles of workers to control this isolated work environment will solve the problems of the workers. The OCI does not see how such an approach can pose any serious threat to the capitalist economic or political order. It feels that only a centrally organized movement, built upon a mass base of workers' councils and soviets, can lead to revolutionary consciousness among the working class, the overthrow of the bourgeoisie, and the dictatorship of the proletariat.[65] It is not surprising to the OCI that the union which has been pushing *autogestion* the hardest and which has had such an important impact on the PSU and the Socialist Party is a union with Catholic roots which claimed to "deconfessionalize" in the early 1960s. The OCI simply has not accepted the CFDT's radical turn to a form of syndicalism at face value. It sees it as insidiously infecting other organizations of the Left—including the *Ligue,* which it sees as always open to something new and fashionable—with a profoundly counterrevolutionary doctrine.

The OCI also differs with the *Ligue* over the latter's view of the Soviet bureaucracy and the role of the French Communist Party. The OCI is unwilling to accept Henri Weber's point that the Soviet bureaucracy has a contradictory nature, that on the one hand it is suppressing the Soviet proletariat, while on the other it is fighting off attempts to restore the bourgeois order both internally and externally in its battle against imperialism. For the OCI, there is no legitimate role for the bureaucracy to play. Once again Pablo's conceptions, first that the Stalinist bureaucracy is a transition stage between capitalism and socialism which is going to last for some time, and secondly that the Khrushchevian regime was qualitatively different from that of Stalin, are seen to have infected the *Ligue* and diverted it from Trotsky's unqualified denunciation of bureaucracy as an evil which stunts the development of the proletariat.[66]

The OCI's Claude Chisserey first caricatures Weber's position, and then states that of the OCI:

> Thus [according to Weber] the Stalinist apparatus
> is not an agent of the bourgeoisie in the breast of
> the workers' movement! Certainly, we do not con-
> tend that the Stalinist apparatus and the social-
> democratic apparatus are the same. We know that
> the Stalinist apparatus was selected by Stalin and
> is tied to the Stalinist bureaucracy--we know also
> that the bureaucracy is not a class. But the counter-
> revolutionary bureaucracy of the Kremlin is becom-
> ing more and more the instrument of the bourgeoi-
> sie in the USSR and is dictating to the different
> [national] communist parties a policy of support-
> ing the bourgeoisie.[67]

The last sentence is the key to understanding the OCI's attitude toward the French Communist Party. It does not believe that there has been a de-Stalinization and it does not believe that there has been any change in the relationship between the Kremlin and the French CP. It has viewed the apparent conflict between Moscow and the "Eurocommunistic" parties of France, Italy, and Spain as completely phoney and the control of Moscow as strong as it ever was. While the *Ligue* saw the intransigent behavior of the French CP *vis-à-vis* the Socialist Party during the 1978 legislative elections as being motivated by the Communists' concern over their own national position in rapport with the Socialists, the OCI saw it as part of the Kremlin strategy to assure the victory of a bourgeois regime with which it coexists very well.

The "new" issues raised in the 1960s and 1970s which have had such an important impact on the *Ligue* have left the OCI cold. It has never viewed youth as a new revolutionary vanguard. It sympathizes with young people exposed to repression in the military, but it is opposed to the idea of a soldiers' union and the kind of organizing attempt with which the *Ligue* has been involved in the military. It declares its sympathy with specific demands being made by women—such as equal pay for equal qualifications, the right to abortion, and child care facilities—and it claimed in the late 1970s that between 20 and 25 per cent of its Central Committee was composed of women, with a somewhat higher percentage in lower leadership positions. But unlike the *Ligue,* it has issued no specific texts on the question of women, has had no women's commissions or caucuses within the organization, and has made no deliberate attempt to balance its committees and other structures sexually. It feels that it is taking a classical Marxist position in focusing on the specific issues and rejecting temptations to cater to petit-bourgeois tendencies such as sexual separatism, anti-male feminism, or attempts at sexual balance. It claims that its women members have not subjected it to the same sort of internal pressures that the *Ligue* was subjected to. Similarly, it has not felt that homosexuality is a special problem that needs addressing in the organization or in public statements. Finally, it is not opposed to nuclear energy as such—but it is "not not opposed." It is concerned about safety problems faced by the workers in nuclear facilities, but it wishes to be considered neither a proponent nor an opponent on the order of the *Ligue*.

Some of the most intense differences between the *Ligue* and the OCI involve international issues, and particularly the *Ligue's* support of Third World revolutionary movements. In 1969, Krivine wrote the following:

> The impact of the Cuban Revolution and above
> all of the Vietnamese Revolution, has given rise
> and wide diffusion to a new image of socialism, a
> new type of motivation in revolutionary action.
> Socialist revolution appears as the only hope, the
> only path of real emancipation of oppressed people.
> With the revolutionary struggles of the Third World,
> the alternative, "socialism or barbarism" is once
> again becoming evident in the eyes of the new gen-
> erations who reject the capitalist system, exploita-
> tion, repression, the emptiness of the bourgeois
> ideology, the absurdity of public officialidom as
> well as the crimes of imperialism. These young
> people have not yet been demoralized by periods
> of failure and betrayal, they have not yet been
> broken by the capitalist organization of production
> or by the barracks. They do not know what resig-
> nation means and this impatience has not been
> diminished. One year after May 1968, the facts
> have not shown them to be wrong.
> While for their elders the only accessible "so-
> cialist" model remains the workers states under

the control of the Stalinist bureaucracy, the young
people are developing a political consciousness at
the time when the Stalinist monolith is crumbling.
They are making crucial decisions for themselves in
the presence of new aspirations, of a violent rejection
of capitalist "civilization," and of the examples—
worthy of October 1917 and of the Commune—of the
Cuban and Vietnamese revolutions.[68]

The OCI contends that the theory of permanent revolution restates a
basic position of Marx, namely that a successful socialist revolution requires
both a material base and a highly conscious proletariat, both of which are
lacking in Third World countries. Moreover, it contends that the turn to what
it pejoratively calls *Tiers-Mondisme* (Third-Worldism) is not something new
to the generation of 1968. The OCI cites the attraction which Yugoslavia---a
country practicing *autogestion* within the context of a low level of industriali-
zation—Guinea (under Sekou-Touré), and Algeria held for Pablo and Frank
well before the JCR merged with the PCI.[69] Thus youthful romanticism
swept up by Third World "revolutionary movements" merged compatibly
with an already existing current of Trotskyism led by a man who stressed
autogestion and peasant revolution. This makes no sense to the OCI.[70]

While the immediate cause of the OCI's rupture from the Fourth
International was *entrisme sui generis* into the Communist Party, the International Committee of the Fourth International, which the OCI helped to
found, was characterized by its emphasis upon the industrialized counties as
the necessary terrain for successful revolution. However, within the International Committee there were some Latin American sections and
sympathizers.

In 1971, the OCI left the International Committee. The specific
issue was the OCI's defense of the Bolivian Trotskyist *Partido Obrero
Revolucionario* for supporting the Torres government. Gerry Healy, the leader
of the Committee's British section and the most powerful figure in the
International Committee, had condemned the Bolivian party for its behavior.
But it was not so much the specific issue that caused the break, as the OCI's
conviction that Healy was unwilling to discuss issues on an international
basis, and was insisting on formulating himself the positions of the International Committee *vis-à-vis* each national section and each country.

After its departure from the International Committee, the OCI took
the initiative in the creation of another international grouping, *Le Comité
d'Organisation pour la Reconstruction de la Quatrième Internationale*
(CORQI). The OCI was the largest national section, and also housed the
international headquarters. There were approximately eighteen sections in
European and South American countries, as well as in Mexico and Quebec.

There were no sections in the lesser industrialized countries of Asia, Africa, or the Middle East. While the OCI considered the international to be only an organizing committee, and made no claim that it was a "leadership center" or an operation on the order of the United Secretariat, CORQI grew significantly in the late 1970s and occupied increasingly larger segments of the OCI's time and resources.[71]

The OCI's Tactics

As their condemnation of the barricades in '68 suggests, the OCI has been less confrontation-oriented than the *Ligue*. It has relied less upon demonstrations and certainly has not taken to the streets to do battle with the Right.

The OCI has placed great emphasis upon its trade union work. It has been accused of not wanting to work within the Communist-dominated CGT at all at the time of the 1952 split and two contemporary writers omit any reference to the CGT in mentioning the union work of the OCI.[72] They only refer to the OCI's work in the more conservative labor confederation, CGT-FO, and the teacher's confederation, the FEN.

In fact, while the OCI refused entrism into the Communist Party, it differentiated between the party and the labor confederation. But it refused to work within the CGT on Pablo's terms. In 1952, as General Secretary of the Fourth International, Pablo stated, "In order to integrate ourselves into the true mass movement, to work and to remain for example in the mass unions, 'ruses' and 'compromises' are not only permissible but are necessary.[73]

The OCI has worked in the CGT and continues to do so today, but without "ruses" and "compromises." It has claimed that a majority of its unionized non-teachers are in the CGT. Its presence in that confederation has been confirmed to this writer by non-OCI people also working in the CGT.

But it is true that the OCI has found it easier to gain office in the CGT-FO and the FEN. In the CGT-FO, it has worked within a caucus called *Tendance Front Unique Ouvrier*. In the teachers' federation, the FEN, it worked in a large Left caucus, *École Emancipée*. After 1968, the caucus split. Groups which were too *gauchiste* for the taste of the OCI, including the *Ligue*, formed the *École Emancipée Syndicaliste Révolutionnaire*. The OCI formed its own tendency, *École Emancipée-Front Unique Ouvrier*. Thus both the *Ligue* and the OCI have worked within the FEN and the CGT. However, while the *Ligue* has worked within the CFDT, it has refused to work within what it considers to be the counterrevolutionary CGT-FO. On the other hand, the OCI has worked within the CGT-FO, but has refused to work within the CFDT, which it considers to be the carrier of the pernicious clerical doctrine of *autogestion*.

The one union which the OCI, or more properly its youth group, the *Alliance de la Jeunesse pour le Sociatisme* (AJS), controls is the student union, *UNEF-unité syndicale*. That union has nowhere the same significance that UNEF had during the Algerian War or in the mid 1960s.[74] But it still vigorously presents candidates and elects representatives to university bodies and social service boards, such as the student insurance and benefits board.

What is interesting is that while UNEF—in the hands of the PSU leadership supported by the JCR—played the militant political role which it had been accustomed to playing since the Algerian War, once the OCI/AJS gained control they behaved in much the same way that the Communist Party behaves in the CGT. That is to say that under their control the union stressed student benefits narrowly construed, just as the CGT stresses wages without posing a real challenge to management control. The AJS still continues to state the general political positions of the OCI in its newspaper, *Jeune Révolutionnaire,* but the student union's publications reflect none of this. The AJS has thus almost taken its union back to where UNEF was before it became politically engaged during the Algerian War. This position, referred to as "corporatism" by student political activists, has historically been one associated with a Right or conservative political leadership. For the first time, it is now being used tactically by a group on the Left.

The OCI has also taken an approach toward elections very different from the *Ligue.* The 1973 electoral campaign was the only one in that decade in which it offered candidates. Even then it offered only a token showing of no more than ten. Like all of the Far Left groups, the OCI refused to support Mitterrand in the 1965 presidential election. In the 1969 presidential election, it called for support of "any of the working class candidates" on the first ballot, and lost interest in the second ballot because neither the Socialist nor the Communist candidates made that run-off. In the 1974 presidential election—held after the Socialists, Communists, and Radicals of the Left (MRG) had agreed on a common program prior to the 1973 legislative elections—the OCI urged people to vote for Mitterrand on the first and second ballot, despite the appearance of two Trotskyist candidates on the first ballot.

In the 1971 municipal elections, the OCI sat on its hands. In 1977, however, while the *Ligue, Lutte Ouvrière,* and the OCI were running a common list, the OCI urged people to vote for Socialist or Communist party candidates, depending upon who was in a better position in each district.

In the 1978 legislative elections, however, the differences between the OCI and the *Ligue* really crystallized. Once again, while the *Ligue,* the Pablist CCA, and the non-Trotskyist OCT ran in the first round on a short common program, the OCI did not run candidates. Instead it invested its energies in an extensive campaign to force the Communist Party to come to terms with the Socialists in an agreement to defer to the better-placed candidate in the second round. Given the OCI's view of the relationship between the Soviet and French parties, this amounted to an attempt to break the hegemony of the Kremlin over the French party through the exertion of domestic French left-wing pressure.

Unlike the *Ligue,* the OCI placed the blame for the division of the Left squarely upon the shoulders of the Communists. It was very supportive of what it regarded as the Socialist Party's sincere attempts to reach an agreement with Communists. But it balked at the inclusion of the Radicals of the Left (MRG) in any such agreement. This became the second major issue for the OCI. It viewed the inclusion of the Radicals of the Left as a repetition of the mistaken Popular Front strategy of the 1930s, against which Trotsky and the Trotskyists had fought so hard. It criticized the *Ligue* for what it regarded as too narrow a programmatic focus when a major error in the history of the French Left was about to be repeated. The *Ligue* responded that—unlike in the 1930s when Daladier's Radical Socialist Party was stronger than either the Socialists or the Communists prior to the 1936 election—the Radicals of the Left constituted a very small party in 1978 and the program was more important than their inclusion. This did not convince the OCI. It called for a *"Front Unique Ouvrier,"* a "Single Workers' Front" without the inclusion of any bourgeois parties.

While the *Ligue* and *Lutte Ouvrière* do have important differences, they have also maintained relations, participated in common demonstrations, and have openly attended each others festivals where they have openly debated their differences. The OCI has refused this sort of interaction. It feels that since the early 1950s it has preserved the integrity of Trotskyism in France, particularly against Pablist and Frankist revisionism. And it has little respect for *Lutte Ouvrière's* attempts to relate to the Frankists in the *Ligue* or their adoption of the electoral strategy. While historically Barta's followers have been the most isolated current of French Trotskyism, both domestically and internationally, since 1968 it has been the OCI which has consciously chosen domestic isolation from the other Trotskyist currents.

LUTTE OUVRIÈRE

Origins of *Lutte Ouvrière*

Lutte Ouvrière (Workers' Struggle) goes back to the 1939 exit from the POI of the followers of the Rumanian Barta. That group was called the *Union Communiste Internationaliste.* While that name has never been constitutionally changed, the organization has been known to the outside world by the name of its newspaper, called *Voix Ouvrière (Workers' Voice)* until 1968 and *Lutte Ouvrière* after 1968.

Barta and a number of other Eastern Europeans found themselves in France on their way to the Spanish Civil War. They either never made it to Spain or moved back and forth across the border sufficiently to involve themselves in French Trotskyist politics. They brought a background of firsthand contact with Bolsheviks and an experience of clandestine work that the French Trotskyists lacked.

They shared Trotsky's disgust with the behavior of the French Trotskyists. They viewed the French as bourgeois professionals and writers who were too tempted by democratic socialism and could in no sense be considered a serious cadre of professional revolutionaries. To Barta, the whole history of entry into the SFIO or the PSOP was no substitute for Trotskyists going into the factories and recruiting among other workers. Thus while sharing Trotsky's criticism of the French Trotskyists, he took his own group in a different "workerist" direction, also without Trotsky's support.

This created certain problems, because the organization claimed to be a rightful section of the Fourth International, despite the fact that it was not recognized by the International. After the war, in an attempt to secure some sort of reform of the PCI and possible unification with it, it dropped the claim to be a legitimate section of the Fourth International.

Since Barta's followers were not convinced that the post-war PCI was any different from the pre-war Trotskyist formations, particularly in the light of the PCI's refusal to engage in any clandestine activity, the precurser to *Lutte Ouvrière* went it alone.

They claim the major credit for the 1947 Renault strike, and that it was Barta himself and a member who is still in a top leadership position in *Lutte Ouvrière* who led that strike. Their position is that while the Communist Party officially supported the Renault strike, in fact it was against it, and that the CGT leadership, beholden to the Communist Party, tried to stifle it.

Initially Barta's followers were in the CGT. In the face of CGT opposition, they created their own union at Renault, the Renault Democratic Union (SDR). This union existed in only one section of the Renault plant at Billancourt. While they claim that possibly up to three thousand workers adhered to the SDR, there were very few actual militants who were doing the organizational work. Thus despite the wage concessions gained in the 1947 strike, and despite the substantial membership of the SDR, an attempt to show other Trotskyists that they could achieve success within workers' struggles was short-lived. The few militants burned themselves out, many becoming physically ill, and the SDR simply collapsed in 1953. There was a rupture in the organization over the whole meaning of the experience, and for three years it went into a state of dormancy.

In 1956, the organization reappeared under the public name of *Voix Ouvrière*. The thrust of the organization was the circulation of factory bulletins dealing with the problems of workers inside and outside of the factories. Factory groups (*noyeaux*) were created at Renault and in other plants which wrote parts of the bulletins and assured their distribution. Members working inside the plants were assisted by students or workers at other plants who aided in the distribution of literature at the factory gates.

Up to 1968, the production and distribution of these bulletins, plus the publication of a weekly newspaper begun in the mid 1960s, was the only activity of the organization. In that year, it probably did not number more than a couple of hundred people.

In 1968, *Voix Ouvrière* supported the uprising. Although *Voix Ouvrière* was not basically a student organization like the JCR, some of the members mounted the barricades and participated in the university occupations. More, however, played a role in attempting to develop a favorable attitude toward the student uprising within the factories. As a result of this, more university and high school students were attracted to the organization which, because of the governmental ban for its 1968 activities, took the present name of *Lutte Ouvrière*.

Lutte Ouvrière experienced important growth in 1968 and 1969. In 1970, talks began between the leaders of *Lutte Ouvrière* and the *Ligue* for an eventual merger of the two organizations. In January 1971, the leaders signed an agreement for mutual cooperation leading to such a merger. According to this agreement, when the merger was complete the new movement would be the French section of the United Secretariat. The smaller *Lutte Ouvrière* received assurances that the rights of minority factions would be respected and that the policies of the *Ligue* would enjoy a certain degree of autonomy from those of the Secretariat. A single newspaper would replace *Rouge* and *Lutte Ouvrière*.

The merger had obvious advantages for both organizations. For *Lutte Ouvrière,* it afforded the possibility of breaking out of its own national isolation and enjoying international contacts through the United Secretariat. For the *Ligue,* it meant adding to its forces ranks of people who had been concentrating on work within the industrial plants. Between the two of them, the organizations would be operating in from five to six hundred industrial plants. Given the circulation of *Rouge* and *Lutte Ouvrière,* the new combined weekly ought to have had a circulation of approximately 30,000.[75] Although *Lutte Ouvrière* kept its own membership figures secret during the negotiations, *Ligue* leaders were counting on the addition of approximately fifteen hundred people to the French section of the United Secretariat.

By 1974, however, the proposed merger was dead. Given the long-standing hard-line attitude of *Lutte Ouvrière* and its predecessors toward other French Trotskyist organizations, and the recalcitrant programmatic differences, unity was not going to be easy. But, as we shall see, the question of electoral strategy brought the differences to a head and intensified them.

Organization, Membership, and Publications of *Lutte Ouvrière*

There are a number of fundamental differences between *Lutte Ouvrière* as an organization and both the *Ligue* and the OCI. First, *Lutte Ouvrière* conducts both open and clandestine work. Its open face is presented through its weekly paper of the same name which is sold on the streets, a monthly journal entitled *Lutte de Classe* which is not easily obtainable, and its participation in such public events as demonstrations and its yearly festival. Aside from this, however, it publishes almost nothing for general public consumption. It has neither a headquarters where people can go to seek information nor a bookstore for the distribution of literature. All contacts are made either by writing to the postal box of the newspaper or by personal contacts with militants. In this sense, *Lutte Ouvrière* resembles Maoist organizations more than typical Trotskyist organizations of its size.

Second, *Lutte Ouvrière* is the most exacting and highly disciplined of the Trotskyist organizations. At the top there are older people, including the militant who was trained by Barta and played such an active role in the Renault strike, who hold tight reins over the organization. *Lutte Ouvrière* prides itself upon being able to extract work from its militants which the other organizations are not able to extract. If work is not accomplished or if deadlines are not met, there must be explanations. Refusal or inability to perform is reason for expulsion. *Lutte Ouvrière* views the *Ligue* as less than a serious organization, not only because it is overextended but because it has no means of compelling its own militants to perform.

Lutte Ouvrière also sees itself as more rigorous than the OCI. It points out that when it comes to factory work, at least the *Ligue* maintains a presence, however irregular its work, whereas the OCI—which left with the most important factory nucleus in the 1952 split—has not maintained much of an open presence in the plants where *Lutte Ouvrière* operates.

Lutte Ouvrière has also gone further than any other Trotskyist organization in insisting upon the sacrifice of one's personal life to the organization. This is also a trait more characteristic of Maoist than Trotskyist organizations. It used to be that students or former students who entered were placed in factory work. More recently, however *Lutte Ouvrière* has become convinced that it was lacking intellectuals. It thus began to encourage students to finish their studies and to perform intellectual functions for the organization. But it has pointed out that while *Ligue* students would take their three-month holidays like all other students, those in *Lutte Ouvrière* were permitted one month only, and even then they would be expected to participate in such events as training seminars and the caravans that *Lutte Ouvrière* sends into the countryside and villages.

Self-discipline and organizational commitment are primary. There has been strong pressure within the organization not to smoke or to drink. This is viewed as displaying a lack of mastery over oneself. Those who are masters over themselves are able both to perform better and to avoid penetration and provocation by agents of the state. While other organizations serve beer and/or wine at their festivals without a second thought, *Lutte Ouvrière* has made a concession to outsiders but serves such drinks only with food. It has not tolerated drinking and sexual pick-ups at its own events.

Moreover, it has attempted to discourage marriage. Two reasons are given for this. First, it is against marriage because it is against all accommodation with the institutions of the present social system. The members do understand that marriage is viewed by many as offering the only guarantees that women and children have in bourgeois society. And they do not insist that those in the organization who are married must divorce. But the dominant ethos within the organization is that guarantees from marriage are not real guarantees at all, and that people are better off not married. They contend that nonmarital cohabitation is in fact fairly common among the French working class. Second, marital bonds are seen as inhibiting the kind of total flexibility and freedom to do whatever political work the organization asks of its militants.

Finally, while *Lutte Ouvrière* has not been concerned about workers' reactions to its position on marriage, it has been very concerned about workers' reactions to physical appearance. It demands of its members grooming that is not designed to set them off from the standards accepted by most workers. Beards and long hair on men have not been acceptable. Needless to say, the organization has been absolutely against any drug usage, both because it represents a lack of mastery over the self and because it poses security dangers.

Lutte Ouvrière does not release its total membership figure. Estimates given to me by leaders of other organizations on the Left which work in some of the same plants have varied from between 1,000 and 1,500 members and sympathizers to 5,000 members and sympathizers in the late 1970s. In terms of actual members, it is probably smaller than either the OCI or the *Ligue,* but it has a very effective support network in the plants.

In a 1978 interview with the author, a leader of *Lutte Ouvrière* offered the following data on the membership. Wage earners or salaried people comprised 85 per cent of the members. Over 50 per cent were manual workers. Twenty percent were teachers and 15-16 per cent were students. This was the lowest percentage of students of the three major Trotskyist organizations. Moreover, among the students in *Lutte Ouvrière,* those in the *collèges techniques,* or vocational schools, had a particularly heavy representation.

The average age in the organization was between 26 and 28. Those higher up in the hierarchy were older. Women comprised 45 per cent of the membership. While there were no special women's commissions as in the *Ligue,* the leader of *Lutte Ouvrière* insisted that that proportion was also reflected in the governing bodies and has been the normal pattern in the organization. He contended that this was usually voluntarily respected at each level, but that where sexual imbalance did come to the attention of higher bodies there was intervention to correct it.

Lutte Ouvrière's **Program**

Lutte Ouvrière has differentiated itself from the *Ligue* and the OCI not so much on programmatic issues as on its rigor and on the priority given to factory work which it does not see in the other organizations. On the issues which have been discussed in relation to the other two groups, it has been closer to the *Ligue* in some cases and to the OCI in others.

In the case of *autogestion, Lutte Ouvrière* agrees with the OCI that the *Ligue* has been catering to petit-bourgeois notions. But it has not engaged in the kind of open campaign against *autogestion,* which paints it as a clerical counterrevolutionary strategy, the way the OCI has. Nor has it been so hostile to the CFDT. In its view of the Soviet Union, *Lutte Ouvrière* takes the hard-line on the Stalinist bureaucracy that the OCI takes. But while the OCI has not deprived the other Eastern European states of their designation as "deformed workers' states,"[76] *Lutte Ouvrière* does not admit that they are workers' states at all. It considers them bourgeois states.

Like the OCI, *Lutte Ouvrière* thinks that a high level of industrial development is necessary for a socialist revolution. It mistrusts Third World revolutionary movements, and it considers both Cuba and China bourgeois states, just like Eastern Europe. For a while it maintained a relationship with the International Committee of the Fourth International, but it broke all contact in 1966.[77] Unlike the OCI, which made the choice of expanding its international relationships in Europe and Latin America, this reflected a conscious choice of investment of scarce resources. It has maintained contact with two groups composed largely of overseas immigrants in France: one a group of African workers from various countries, and the other a group of workers in and from the French Antilles. The only contact with a genuinely foreign group—a group which does not focus on immigrants in France at all—is with a tiny U.S. group which split off of the Spartacist League and which has been operating only in a couple of cities, particularly in auto plants. They have justified this contact because the U.S. is the most advanced of all the industrial countries and they must keep abreast of what is happening there.

While *Lutte Ouvrière* has shared the OCI's very negative view of the Soviet Union and has taken an even harder line on the other Eastern European countries, it has parted company with the OCI over its view of the French Communist Party. It has taken the position that Eurocommunism is a real phenomenon, and that the French party is going in a revisionist direction. It agreed with the *Ligue* that the Communist Party's hard line *vis-à-vis* the Socialist Party in the 1978 legislative elections was determined by considerations of national political position rather than by an international strategy dictated by Moscow.

On what I have called the "new" issues arising in the 1960s and 1970s, *Lutte Ouvrière* is a mixed bag. It has rejected any conception of youth as a revolutionary vanguard, but unlike the OCI it was involved in the 1968 revolt. Moreover, its position has changed from one of placing little importance upon students and intellectuals—placing them in factories when they did join—to one of greater appreciation for both intellectual work within the organization and students' and teachers' time flexibility. However, it insists that students and youth must adopt the working-class perspective and not see themselves as a separate vanguard. It feels that the *Ligue* has been in error here. It saw the *Ligue's* investment in forming soldiers' committees among the young draftees, while the *Ligue's* implantation in factories still left much to be desired, as an example of mistaken priorities.

Similarly, *Lutte Ouvrière* is against women's separatism, either within or outside its own organization. It is for equality between the sexes, but it insists that a truly revolutionary women's movement must be one united with the working class. It views both the class composition and the nature of the demands of separatist feminism as petit-bourgeois.

Unlike the OCI, however, *Lutte Ouvrière* has admitted that the problem of sexual equality is one which requires conscious attention within the organization. It claims to be attentive to sexual representation on all internal bodies. Moreover, I was assured that attitudes toward sexual equality were systematically discussed before a potential member was accepted, and that the behavior of men toward the women members, with whom they may or may not live and have children, is not regarded as a personal matter but a question of concern to the entire group. There is consciousness of the fact that even men on the Left often use their political engagement as a means of extracting disproportionate domestic servitude from "their" women. *Lutte Ouvrière's* view of marriage also discourages the latter conception. A by-word is "If you see yourself as a socialist, you don't need to be married."

Like the *Ligue, Lutte Ouvrière* is for complete freedom of sexual orientation, but it has not favored a separatist movement based on sexual identity, and it has established no commissions or caucuses based upon this consideration within the organization. It does not accept the argument that gays and lesbians are either (1) a force favoring socialism or (2) subversive because they threaten the family structure. Just as in the case of heterosexuality, *Lutte Ouvrière* insists upon "mastery over oneself" in order that the political work of its militants not be disrupted. Thus, while the organization has encouraged and tolerated sexual norms which are not encouraged or tolerated in the society at large, there is a strong puritanical political work ethic which stigmatizes sensual overindulgence of any sort. One can be what one likes sexually, so long as one respects the equality of others, makes a positive contribution to the work of the organization, and remains "master over oneself."

Finally, *Lutte Ouvrière* has taken a position between the *Ligue's* environmental and safety opposition to nuclear energy and the OCI's position of "neither proponent nor opponent." *Lutte Ouvrière's* position has been that it is against the development of nuclear energy "in the present context." Like the *Ligue,* it participated in popular demonstrations against the installation of nuclear plants where the local people do not want them. But it sees the major problem as capitalism, a system which it sees as more concerned with profits than safety. If safety controls could be exercised over nuclear energy by a non-capitalist system, then *Lutte Ouvrière*—which, like the OCI, places heavy importance upon productivity—would not oppose nuclear energy.

Lutte Ouvrière's Tactics

Lutte Ouvrière's work within factories has been both quantitatively and qualitatively different from that of the *Ligue* and OCI. First, as of 1978 it operated in approximately 300 of the largest plants in France. Even Maoists have been willing to grant the magnitude of the organization's operation in the industrial setting. Second, its major thrust has been the production of weekly bulletins distributed inside or at the gates of the plants.

In 1978, approximately two thousand people participated in the production and distribution of the bulletins. This included both actual members and sympathizers. The bulletin was a single mimeographed sheet. On the front page there is a masthead with the name *Lutte Ouvrière* above the plant name. Below that there appears the same article of general importance in all bulletins throughout France. The article is written at the headquarters. The reverse side, however, is reserved for each plant group. Typically, the groups have used their space for several short articles or notices pertaining to situations arising in the plants as well as general political events.

Lutte Ouvrière also places relatively less emphasis upon trade union work than either the *Ligue* or OCI. It has worked within all three of the largest labor confederations, with over 50 per cent of its unionized militants in the CGT. Where it has refused to work is in the teachers' federation, the FEN. But its work within those labor confederations has been only a part of a larger labor strategy which has emphasized the importance of strike committees outside of the traditional labor union structures. In conflict situations, the bulletin groups have served as nuclei for the formation of such committees. *Lutte Ouvrière* points out that the labor confederations have served to dampen worker militancy and represent no more than approximately 20 per cent of the labor force. That means that 80 per cent of the workers are not represented by the unions. It is imperative to *Lutte Ouvrière* that when these workers strike, they maintain control over their own strikes rather than see them diluted by the encroachment of the present union hierarchies. It argues that this can be done by the more democratic mechanism of the strike committee. It will also be recalled that *Lutte Ouvrière's* disgust with the CGT at Renault in the 1940s and 1950s led it to the step of attempting to create a competitive union, a very drastic move for any group on the Left, and one which none of the other Trotskyist groups has ever made.

As its participation in the 1968 revolt would indicate, *Lutte Ouvrière* has been somewhat more direct-action oriented than the OCI. However, while it has participated in many common demonstrations with the *Ligue,* it has not put nearly the number of people into the streets that the *Ligue* has. So far as this writer knows, there is no record of *Lutte Ouvrière* doing battle with right-wing groups. Direct action tactics in the streets have clearly played a secondary role to the primary one of factory organization.

However, *Lutte Ouvrière* has become more interested in electoral tactics. In the 1969 presidential campaign it supported Krivine on the first ballot and abstained on the second. In the 1971 municipal elections it presented candidates only in Paris' 12th Arrondissement and in a Bordeaux district. In both, it reached an electoral agreement with the *Parti Socialiste Unifié* (PSU).

However, at about this time the organization began to consider a merger with the *Ligue.* It was therefore natural that for the 1973 legislative elections it should consider reaching an agreement with the Trotskyist *Ligue,* which itself was trying to reach an agreement with the OCI, rather than with the PSU. An initial agreement was reached which would have divided the electoral districts up so that the *Ligue* and the OCI each would present candidates in 120 districts, while *Lutte Ouvrière* would try its hand in 80 districts.

The OCI pulled away and presented only a token number of candidates—less than ten. The *Ligue* itself, in a display which confirmed *Lutte Ouvrière's* image of a less than serious organization that cannot get its militants to follow through, could muster only 92 candidates. *Lutte Ouvrière,* which initially was supposed to present only 80 candidates, began to fill in the gaps and wound up presenting 167 candidates. These candidates received about 200,000 votes, while the *Ligue's* candidates received about 100,000.[78]

While *Lutte Ouvrière,* which had not been consulted by the *Ligue* prior to Krivine's 1969 presidential candidacy, supported that candidacy nonetheless, it was not prepared to play second fiddle to the *Ligue* in 1974. After all, it had done twice as well as the *Ligue* in 1973—at the *Ligue's* own game.

In the 1974 presidential elections *Lutte Ouvrière* accepted neither the *Ligue's* strategy of trying to convince PSU member Piaget to become a candidate of the Far Left nor, when that failed, Krivine's candidacy. Instead, before Krivine had announced his candidacy, *Lutte Ouvrière* announced its own 1974 presidential candidate, Arlette Laguiller. Laguiller was a young (34) woman bank employee who had been a strike committee leader in a nation-wide bank strike against *Crédit Lyonnais.*

Lutte Ouvrière was incensed that instead of supporting Laguiller, Krivine would first propose a member of the PSU which was now "tailending the Union on the Left"[79] and, failing in that strategy, would himself run opposing Laguiller. *Lutte Ouvrière* saw a contradiction in seeking out Piaget because he was a well-known strike leader at Lip and then running a graduate from the Sorbonne against their own strike leader, Laguiller.

Once the election campaign was underway, the *Ligue* accused *Lutte Ouvrière* of running an "apolitical," "personalized," and "electoralist" campaign.[80] This meant that *Lutte Ouvrière* had selected a woman worker with broad appeal, particularly among women, who downplayed the more radical aspects of their political program in order to increase their votes. *Lutte Ouvrière* defended its campaign by responding that nothing was being hidden, that the petit-bourgeois *Ligue* could not understand a program directed at the working class and that, unlike Krivine, Laguiller did not need to invite workers to appear on television with her because she was a worker herself. Furthermore, *Lutte Ouvrière* pointed out that Laguiller had consistently stated in the campaign that, "the worker's strength is not in the ballot boxes, but in the factories, " and that this kind of a campaign was a "model of anti-electoralism."[81] Moreover, *Lutte Ouvrière* argued, the number of votes which the working class gives to a revolutionary candidate is of importance not because revolution can be voted in but because it is an indicator of how successfully a group is reaching the working class with its message.[82]

In fact, *Lutte Ouvrière* once again did much better than the *Ligue* on the first round, after which both organizations supported Mitterrand. While Krivine received 93,990 votes or 0.36 per cent of the total cast, Laguiller received over half a million (595,247), or 2.33 per cent of the total. Both organizations would probably have received a somewhat higher total of their combined approximately 700,000 if people between the ages of 18 and 21 had been permitted to vote, as they have been in subsequent elections.

In the 1977 municipal elections, *Lutte Ouvrière* did join the *Ligue* and the *Organisation Communiste des Travailleurs* (OCT) in presenting joint lists. But it refused any cooperation with the *Ligue* and its alliance partners in the 1978 legislative elections. In those elections it ran its own candidates in all of the 474 maninland electoral districts. A related organization, *Combats Ouvriers,* also ran candidates in the overseas territories of Guadeloupe and Martinique. It thus presented more candidates in the first round of the 1978 legislative elections than any other Far Left group, including the PSU's *Front Autogestionnaire.* It also accounted for a disproportionate share of the Far Left's combined vote total of 953,088, or 3.33%.[83]

Unlike the OCI (which ran no candidates at all) and the *Ligue, Lutte Ouvrière* refused to commit itself to urging its supporters before the first round was over to vote for Socialists or Communists on the second round. After the first round, it did urge such votes. In an interview with the author, a leader of *Lutte Ouvrière* explained that there were two reasons for waiting. The first was that the Communist Party had not decided to come to terms with the Socialists until the first round was over. The second was that the organization thought that Arlette Laguiller had a chance to obtain the necessary 12.5 per cent of the vote to stay on the ballot for the second round in Thiers. Had she accomplished this, rather than getting the 8.4 per cent which she actually received, then *Lutte Ouvrière* would have had to negotiate with the larger parties of the Left. A precommitment to support them would have undercut its position.

In fact, in its debate with the *Ligue* before the first round, *Lutte Ouvrière* distinguished itself from both the *Ligue* and the OCI in the very hard line which it took *vis-à-vis* the Socialist and Communist parties. It contended that while in the 1977 municipal elections the choice facing Trotskyists was to unite in a common slate or not have enough candidates to fill the lists, and that the Left's coming to power was not an issue then, in the 1978 elections the circumstances were just the opposite. Here there was a chance for the Socialists and Communists to come to power. While the *Ligue* and the OCI saw this as an opportunity for the working class to exert pressure within parties which they elected, *Lutte Ouvrière* initially took a position closer to Maoist groups—that a victory of the Left would make matters worse:

> Those who vote for the *Lutte Ouvrière* candidates
> will be saying: We distrust the Marchaises[84] and the
> Mitterrands,[85] we have no confidence whatsoever in
> them, we know that if they come to power tomorrow
> the workers will have to struggle just as they had to
> struggle under a Chirac or Barre government to win
> their demands.[86]

This was a position which was easier to maintain so long as there was no agreement between the Communists and the Socialists. But as the election fever spread in France between the two rounds, the internal and external pressures on *Lutte Ouvrière* became too great. Like the other Trotskyist organizations, it wound up urging votes for an overtly social democratic organization and an organization which it was convinced was going from the mistaken path of Stalinism to the equally mistaken path of social democratization *à la* Eurocommunism.

Thus, not even the "workerist" *Lutte Ouvrière*—whose historical vocation has been to teach other Trotskyists how to avoid the pitfalls of petit-bourgeois behavior characteristic of intellectuals and liberal profession-als—could escape the dilemma of French Trotskyism in an age of Eurocommunism. The choice of showing the *Ligue* that it could beat it at its own anti-electoral electoral game involved more than *Lutte Ouvrière* had bargained for.

SUMMARY CONCLUSION

The variety of forms of party organization available within the rubric of French Trotskyism is a virtual microcosm of options available to the French on the Left at large. The *Ligue* and the Pablists have looser forms of organization and share some of the characteristics of the Socialist Party and the PSU, within which the Pablists were nestled until 1977. On the other hand, the OCI, which regards party organization as a highly principled matter, is closer to the stricter organizational pattern of the French Communist Party. *Lutte Ouvrière,* an Eastern European import, represents a unique form which is as close as anything that this writer has seen to the application of Lenin's concept of a clandestine party to a nonabsolutist political context. Indeed, even if the *Ligue* and *Lutte Ouvrière* had not gotten into such difficulty over the question of elections, there is good reason to doubt the potential for unification of two groups with such diverse organizational conceptions.

Within the French context, a number of theoretical or programmatic as well as organizational differences are manifested with particular intensity. The precise nature of the Soviet regime becomes a pressing question for French Trotskyists, because of the strength of the French Communist Party and its actual or possible relationship with the Soviet Union. That party's shift to Eurocommunism and its relationship with the Socialist Party have been difficult and divisive problems for French Trotskyists. The OCI takes the hardest anti-Soviet, anti-French Communist Party position, contending that there are no positive aspects to the Soviet regime and that its hold over the French party is as strong as it ever was. It blames Moscow for sabotaging the party's 1978 alliance with the Socialists. The *Ligue* sees some positive aspects of the Soviet bureaucracy but feels that, in any case, the French party has asserted considerable independence—including its behavior before the 1978 elections. *Lutte Ouvrière* combines the two perspectives. It takes a harder line toward the USSR than the *Ligue*, but parts company with the OCI on its view of the relationship between the USSR and the French party.

Another substantive issue which has proved to be divisive for Trotskyists within the French context is *autogestion,* or worker control over industry. The staunchest promoters of the concept within the world of French Trotskyism are the Pablists, who found the PSU's *autogestionnaire* orientation very compatible. Of the three major groups, the *Ligue* is the most favorable, while the OCI sees the sinister hand of French clericalism behind the CFDT's advocacy of the concept. The OCI's position was similar to the open hostility of the Communist Party until the latter's conversion on the question. *Lutte Ouvrière,* once again, finds itself in a middle position. It thinks that the concept is basically petit-bourgeois, but it does not accord it the same degree of importance that the OCI does and it sees no clerical plot afoot.

While the question of nuclear power has not been terribly divisive among French Trotskyists, another issue which gained saliency in the 1970s has. That is the question of the mobilization of women and homosexuals. The OCI takes a strictly Old Left position on this, arguing that the class basis of politics is crucial and that mobilization in separatist organizations threatens this, while the organization of internal caucuses is a threat to organizational integrity. The *Ligue* and the Pablists take a contrary view on both counts. *Lutte Ouvrière,* once again, offers a completely different orientation, one which claims to have recognized the importance of sexual equality before the question suddenly became salient in France in the 1970s. *Lutte Ouvrière* rejects the bourgeois institution of marriage in practice as well as in theory, and it advocates complete equality for women. However, it distinguishes this from sexual permissiveness, and attempts to impose on both its men and women a staunch revolutionary work ethic which stresses self-control and the refusal to surrender the self to sensuality.

The programmatic differences which have been least affected by peculiarities in the French context are those regarding the Third World. While the Algerian War certainly heightened differences between the Frankists and Lambertists, we shall see that these differences relate much more to elements within Trotskyism itself than to peculiarities within the French context.

At the level of tactics, the posture of French Trotskyists toward elections has become very divisive because of the electoral strategy and strength of the Communist and Socialist parties. The Trotskyists are put in an awkward position of having to respond to the strategies of these parties, which do not meet the standards of Trotskyists but which do command the loyalties of a significant segment of the French working class, by deciding (1) whether or not to run their own candidates on the first ballots and (2) whether or not to support the candidates of the stronger formations on the Left on the second. The next question is how to justify their position, given the fact that they have no faith in the electoral process as an effective mechanism of change. The level of tension which has accompanied French elections, particularly that of 1978, has added to the divisive impact of this phenomenon on French Trotskyists.

Finally, just as the strength of the parties on the Left and the multiple options available in France has impacted upon the Trotskyists, so too has the presence of competing unions on the Left. Each of the three major Trotskyist groups has one labor organization within which it will not work, but in each case the organization is different. The *Ligue* will not work within the social-democratic CGT-FO, the OCI will not work within the *autogestionnaire* CFDT, and *Lutte Ouvrière* will not work within the "intellectualist" teachers' federation, the FEN. *Lutte Ouvrière* is also the least enthusiastic about working within any union structure, since it places almost exclusive reliance upon its own form of plant organization.

If variety is the spice of life, French political life is certainly spicy. The dish, however, has proved to be just a bit too spicy for Trotskyism to digest easily. Each group within the larger French Trotskyist movement has grown considerably since 1968. But what the movement has not been able to do is coalesce. The cleavages on the Left at large have largely been determinant of the lines of cleavage of Trotskyism itself. But at least French Trotskyism matured in the 1960s and 1970s to the stage where the differences are substantive, rather than based upon personality conflicts as in its early years.

Moreover, the inability to coalesce or to challenge the two major formations on the French Left in terms of size has not meant that the French Trotskyists have been completely ineffective. It could be argued that prior to World War II the impact of Trotskyism was largely intellectual and aesthetic. There was, for example, the very interesting interpenetration between Trotskyism and surrealism. After World War II, however, and particularly in the 1960s and 1970s, the Frankist Trotskyists were to play some important explicitly political roles. During the Algerian War, they were active not only in the anti-war movement but in the FLN support networks as well. Six years after that war terminated, the Frankist Trotskyists supported the 1968 revolt and some of its younger members were in leadership positions in one of the most aggressive organizations to mount the barricades, the *Jeunesse Communiste Révolutionnaire*. Shortly after the revolt, the JCR officially merged with the Frankist Trotskyist organization. And it did not take that combination very long to organize and lead the most important support group for the National Liberation Front and the North Vietnamese in their struggle against the Americans. This was part of a world-wide network of support work done by the United Secretariat of the Fourth International to exert pressure on the Americans to leave Indochina. Finally, the Frankist *Ligue* had been conducting a campaign of organization and propaganda within the French armed services, which has caused great concern on the part of the French military and the more conservative segments of the public and the media. This observer has not been able to discern the same kind of reciprocal impact upon the political context on the part of the Lambertist Trotskyists of the OCI or on the part of *Lutte Ouvrière*.

We shall examine the permutations of French Trotskyism in the 1980s separately, in a later chapter. Now we shall turn to an examination of the Maoist heritage in the French national context.

3
Maoism in France

In the last chapter, we saw that the evolution of French Trotskyism over the past half century has led to a point where there are now three major Trotskyist organizations in the country. On a number of dimensions, including the organizational, they represent a continuum. But as the dimension or issue shifts, the organizations do not always occupy the same position on the continuum. For example, while *Lutte Ouvrière* is closer to the OCI than to the *Ligue* on the organizational issue, it is closer to the *Ligue* than to the OCI in its approach to electoralism. This means that there is a certain fluidity in the distinctions between the currents of French Trotskyism which is reflected in their concrete interactions with each other.

In this chapter on French Maoism we are going to see a very different phenomenon. Maoists are fond of saying that things must be divided into two in order to be understood dialectically. At least from 1968 to the mid 1970s the major characteristic of French Maoism was indeed a clear cut dualistic cleavage, with the groups on each side of the cleavage having virtually nothing to do with one another. I shall refer to the two kinds of Maoism reflected in this dichotomy as hierarchical Maoism and anti-hierarchical Maoism.

If French Maoism is divided into two varieties, equal attention is not given to each of them in this chapter. For several reasons, more is given to the anti-hierarchical variety. First, the major movement within this current, the *Gauche Prolétarienne* (Proletarian Left or GP) was, during its heyday, the most dynamic movement on the French Far Left. Second, even during the period that it was outlawed, it felt that the success of its actions depended upon giving them the widest possible publicity. Its openness and its extensive written records and self-criticisms made it possible to collect more data on GP Maoism than on the more cautious hierarchical groups. Third, because there have been only intermittent signs of life on the part of people trying to keep GP Maoism going since 1974, and because much of the written documentation is no longer available, any research and writing on the movement by people who were not themselves participants would be very difficult. I thus see the research which I did on the movement in 1972 as particularly valuable in establishing an historical record, as well as in making possible the analysis of a fascinating current of Maoist expression in France.

This brings me to the last reason for devoting so much attention to this current in France. As we shall see in Chapter 5, there has been nothing like it in the United States. Elements within the French context encouraged the development of this kind of Maoism whereas it was not encouraged in the United States. Although the full dimensions of this will not be spelled out until the Conclusion of this book, the phenomenon of anti-hierarchial Maoism presents us with perhaps the most interesting case of the relationship between aspects of a theory and elements within concrete contexts of application.

Let us now turn to an examination of the history of French Maoism, from its beginning to the point where it experienced the cleavage which we have just been discussing.

FRENCH MAOISM UP TO 1968

Because of the relatively recent nature of the Sino-Soviet split, Maoism as a distinct ideological current has a much shorter history than does Trotskyism. As might be expected, the first stirring of a Maoist current separate from the French Communist Party came within the Franco-Chinese Friendship Association. Prior to the Sino-Soviet split, there was no incompatibility between membership in both the party and the association. However, as the conflict between the Soviet and Chinese parties intensified and the French party began to accept gradually the de-Stalinization decided upon by the Soviet party, some of those in the Friendship Association began to form "Marxist-Leninist Circles." Among these people were the most diehard Stalinists within what was one of the most Stalinist parties in Western Europe.

In 1964, the "Circles" were formally grouped into a national organization, the *Fédération des Cercles Marxistes-Léninistes*. A second group, founded by an expelled former Communist Party member named Claude Beaulieu, was also created in 1964.[1] This was the *Centre Marxiste-Léniniste de France*. It, however, never attained the importance of the first group. It was badly discredited by its support for de Gaulle in the 1965 presidential elections, a support which it justified by de Gaulle's hostility toward American imperialism. It was the only Maoist group not dissolved by decree of the Gaullist government after the 1968 uprising.[2] Beaulieu's group was denounced as the French followers of Liu Shao-shi by the other Maoists, and very negatively viewed by the non-Maoist Left for its support of Gaullism. On the other hand, the Federation, which changed its name to the *Mouvement Communiste Français* (MCF) in 1967, received official recognition as a fraternal organization from the Chinese and Albanian parties.[3]

Both of the above groups came out of the "adult" Communist Party. However, within the student group of that party, the *Union des Étudiants Communistes* (UEC), there was a dynamic taking place which would eventuate in the creation of a different set of Maoist structures. It will be recalled that from 1963 to 1965, the parent party virtually lost control over the UEC. Krivine and his fellow Trotskyists were practicing "entrism" within the UEC. However, the UEC also served as the womb for an important part of the Maoist movement, much the same way that the SDS would serve as a womb for American Maoism.

Perhaps because for the Trotskyists the UEC was a foster home while for the Maoists it was the womb, it was much more difficult for the Maoists to accept a clear break than it was for the Trotskyists. Indeed, in their incipient stage, they were less fully convinced followers of Mao than were those older party members who had split off in 1964. They tended rather to accept the criticisms of theoretical sterility made by Professor Louis Althusser against the party. Althusser, a professor at the *École Normale Supérieure* where this current was initially centered, was a party member who did not make the transition to Maoism the way many of his younger followers within the UEC did.

But they moved more slowly and more cautiously than the Trotskyists because they had no preconceived plan like "entrism." Even though they thought that the Communist Party's support for Mitterrand's 1965 presidential candidacy was an error—perhaps not as great as support for de Gaulle, but an error nonetheless—they did not openly take a hostile position as the Trotskyists did. And they drew a distinction between the "leftist" Trotskyist entrists and "honest militants" in the UEC.[4] They felt that the Trotskyists deserved to be purged, but that in doing so the parent party had also excluded some "honest" militants who were not practicing "entrism" but who were simply expressing different views from the party leadership's. They thus created a structure called the Parisian Collective in which those "honest militants" (mainly themselves) whose cells had been abolished could continue to participate.

The Parisian Collective, however, proved to be a stepping stone to the creation of an organization which was to rival the UEC. In February of 1966, while some of the militants were still in the UEC, they created the *Union des Jeunesses Communistes (marxiste-léniniste),* which is sometimes referred to as the UJC (m-l) but which I shall refer to hereafter simply as the UJCML.[5] In March, Althusser's positions were officially denounced by the Central Committee of the Communist Party.[6] In April, the UJCML retaliated by distributing at the UEC's Ninth Congress a tract entitled "Must We Revise Marxist-Leninist Theory?". This was a direct attack on the position of the Central Committee. The Communist Party had had enough from the UJCML. Members of the UJCML were expelled from the UEC the year after the Trotskyists' expulsion. After that expulsion, the UJCML clearly identified itself as Maoist in ways that it had not previously.[7] It has been estimated that there were approximately 1500 militants in the UJCML at this point.[8]

Aside from Beaulieu's largely discredited group, there were thus two Maoist organizations in France with quite different social compositions prior to the 1968 revolt. The UJCML was almost entirely, if not entirely, composed of students. While there were also some intellectuals in the MCF, the dominant tone was set by older and non-intellectual former members of the Communist Party—the most uncompromisingly Stalinist to boot. They had little patience with the UCML, which they viewed as an elitist organization of young intellectuals who knew nothing about the working class and who placed pseudo-theorizing above practice. The following passage is the conclusion of a document adopted by the Central Committee of the MCF. In this case, it was drafted by an intellectual himself, who had joined the Communist Party in 1940, the year that France was invaded by the Nazis, whom Stalin was to fight.

> It is thus supposed [by the UJCML] that youth
> constitutes the very basis of an independent and
> autonomous organization capable of finding its
> way as an isolated detachment in the capitalist
> world. And, in consequence, priority is here given
> to youth as a class based upon age above that of
> the proletariat as a social class as the carrier of the
> future of the world. Let us add that within youth
> itself it is the students who appear, not only as
> the initiators, but also as the masters of thought,
> as the designated leaders.
> We always come to the same conclusion: we
> must let the students, the intellectuals, constitute
> themselves as an autonomous theoretical detach-
> ment. When they have grasped the truth—acquired
> outside of the workers' experience and verified only
> by "theoretical practice"—they will present them-
> selves before the masses who do not have access
> to the theoretical basics but to a defective transla-
> tion of Marxist theory: the ideology of the workers.[9]

The contention of the MCF was that a youth group can only serve as an appendage of an ongoing party. The UJCML was, however, not about to submit itself to the discipline of an "adult" party. It argued that through a method referred to as the *enquête*—going out to the people and learning from them—the UJCML could come to know and understand not only the workers but also such "secondary categories" as students, the bourgeoisie, and small and tenant farmers. In other words, what the UJCML does not know it must ask. To maintain this kind of openness to input from the masses, the

UJCML contended that the centralized form of organization adopted by the MCF was an impediment. The party was too closed a structure and, in that sense, at least at the present stage of the struggle, the MCF itself was elitist. The creation of a true centralized party would have to be based upon preparatory work such as that being done in the *enquête*.[10] It was, in other words, a long-range goal of the UJCML. Up to that point a more decentralized and fluid movement seeking input from exploited people in various sectors of the population was more appropriate.

While the majority of the MCF and the UJCML were doing battle over the desirability of a centralized party at a given point in time, the leaders of the MCF had to contend with a dissident wing in their group. Largely composed of intellectuals, referred to by their opponents sarcastically as the *"groupe de 'professeurs',"* these dissidents argued against a disciplined party form of organization and for a "grand alliance" of all of the Maoist groups in France, something which the UJCML also favored.

The leadership of the MCF was thus facing precisely the same problem with its intellectuals that the Trotskyists faced after the Second World War. Then, too, a number of intellectuals called for more fluid patterns of interaction, which many viewed as a virtual call for the destruction of the party. The Maoist intellectuals were now doing the same thing, and this general pattern of behavior was not lost on the majority of the MCF:

> This fractional anti-Party group, group of "pro-
> fessors," can be characterized as intellectualist and
> dogmatic. It was rooted in petit-bourgeois ideology
> and seriously believed in its superiority over the
> authentically proletarian elements in the *Mouvement*.[11]

In criticizing the UJCML, a member of the majority of the MCF recalled the words of Lenin:

> On the subject of these elements [the Maoists ex-
> pelled from the UEC], that we in no way view as
> enemies, we simply shall recall what Lenin said in
> *One Step Forward, Two Steps Backward* in regard to
> bourgeois intellectuals who feared proletarian disci-
> pline and organization: "No one would dare deny that
> what, in a general fashion, characterizes the intellec-
> tuals as a particular social stratum in contemporary
> capitalist societies is precisely their individualism
> and inaptitude for discipline and organization."[12]

In late 1967, the anti-party intellectuals were presented with the hard choice. The majority faction of the MCF decided on a formal conversion of the *Mouvement* into a more highly structured party, the *Parti Communiste Marxisie-Léniniste de France* (PCMLF).

The generational and intellectual/non-intellectual cleavages which divided the UJCML and the PCMLF manifested themselves in differences over specific substantive questions. The PCMLF was critical of the decision of the UJCML to hold off criticism of the Communist support of Mitterrand while the UJCML was still part of the Communist student organization. By the spring of 1968, before the massive revolt took place in France, two other fairly clear issues divided the two organizations.

The first involved relations with labor unions. The UJCML had adopted a policy similar to the "entrism" of the Trotskyists (and for which they had been critical of the Trotskyists) but they applied it to the Communist-dominated labor confederation, the CGT, rather than to the Communist Party itself or its student affiliate. The UJCML argued that the CGT is an important confederation (it is the largest in France) in that some sections of it are "revolutionary" despite a "revisionist" national leadership and that, in the minds of most workers, it is the CGT which is associated with the class struggle.

Thus the major strategy of the UJCML was to go into the factories, to join the CGT, and to engage in both open battle against the employers and clandestine political organization. The PCMLF, at this point in time, felt that the CGT was a lost cause. It argued that the Maoists would be purged from the CGT, which was very tightly under the control of the "revisionist" Communist Party-oriented leadership. The PCMLF favored letting their members remain in or join whichever unions they preferred. Its priority was clearly not the penetration of unions, but the construction of a vanguard political party.

A second interesting, if more symbolic, difference developed over support of the struggle of the Vietnamese against the U.S. and the regimes which it sustained in the South. The two organizations had their own NLF support organizations. The PCMLF's organization adopted the slogan, "No new Munichs!" If this meant something to the older members of the PCMLF, it was completely lost on the younger generation for which "Munich" (*i.e.*, the concessions made by the French and British to pacify Hitler) was out of the range of direct experience.[13] By March of 1968, the PCMLF itself recognized the limitations of its slogan and dropped it, contending that it was not understood by the Vietnamese.

Not surprisingly, the PCMLF inherited the Chinese and Albanian recognition from the MCF, and an important element within the UJCML was dissatisfied with the progress of their own organization and began to hope for a merger. Thus in the spring of 1968 the UJCML split, with a group from Lyons taking the initiative in self-criticism. There were admissions that "we persisted in an intellectualist and sectarian attitude," that the UJCML has criticized the MCF "without seeing that our youth could learn from their experience," that the UJCML exhibited "petit-bourgeois sectarianism, our desire to keep ourselves distinct at any price."[14] It was further contended that "while several comrades of the UCML have not been able to rid themselves of a certain petit-bourgeois aestheticism, the PCMLF dares to lead the Marxist-Leninist struggle on the cultural front through its publication, *l'Opposition Artistique.*"[15]

The revolt of May and June thus exploded at a very difficult time for the UJCML. The ideas of the group from Lyons, called the "liquidationist current," found wide-range acceptance within the organization. The current was so named because the logical outcome of these ideas was the liquidation of the UJCML as an organization and the incorporation of its militants within the party structure of the PCMLF.

The UJCML was caught off balance by the revolt. Mainly preoccupied with its own internal problems, it argued against the erection of the barricades in the student district of Paris. On the eve of the battle known as the "Night of the Barricades," May 10, the UJCML took a position similar to that of the Lambertist Trotskyists (the tendency now represented by the OCI and its youth group, the AJS). It argued that a true revolution must be made by the workers and that confrontations without them were meaningless. It urged students to go out to the factories and the working class neighborhoods rather than mounting the barricades in the Latin Quarter. Members of the organization did not participate in the battle that night.

Ironically, the PCMLF, the Maoist organization which had been arguing that youth should not be considered a separate revolutionary class or a group which would give direction to the workers, was more supportive of the students. Some of their members or sympathizers were on the barricades.[16] However, once the labor unions began to demonstrate support for the students and workers began to conduct massive strikes and plan occupations to the point of creating the spontaneous general strike which paralyzed France, then the UJCML joined forces with the broader movement by organizing "long marches" out to the factories in support of the workers.

This attempted reintegration into the broader movement, however, did not save the organization. The pro-discipline party faction argued that the regime survived 1968 because there was not a disciplined party willing and capable of giving any direction to the tremendous energy unleashed by the revolt. By this time they were clearly a majority. The UJCML people who had taken jobs in factories were called out and the majority withdrew from the practical world to seek guidance in the basic texts. It was a massive retreat. The UJCML was put to rest permanently.

The 1968 revolt proved to be a watershed. After it, French Maoist groups proliferated.[17] But they went in one of the two directions indicated in the introduction of this chapter. Those whom I call the hierarchical Maoists accepted the Leninist concept of a centralized and highly disciplined party and attempted to build organizations along those lines. While differing among themselves over specific issues or even theoretical points, they have not offered any terribly new or unorthodox interpretations of Marxism-Leninism-Maoism. As already indicated, the anti-hierarchical Maoists went in a different direction, which was more interesting for comparative purposes. The French signify the distinction between the two currents by referring to the first as *Marxiste-Léniniste* and the second as *les Maoïstes* or simply *les Maos*.

HIERARCHICAL MAOISM

The prototype of hierarchical Maoism is the PCMLF itself. Most of the other hierarchical Maoist organizations have resulted from splits within the PCMLF, which continues to be the officially recognized Chinese organization. Not surprisingly, it defended the position of the Chinese regime right down the line.

Like most of the Far Left organizations, the PCMLF was banned by the government after the 1968 revolt. It became a clandestine organization which made its positions public under the name of its paper, *l'Humanité Rouge* (HR). The party continued to operate, but feared to even permit its Central Committee to meet together in one place. In the summer of 1970, seven or eight of its leaders were arrested for reconstituting a banned organization, and these arrests continued sporadically right up through 1976, when one of their leaders, Roman Le Gal, spent five-and-a-half months in a prison without even being convicted.

Both the caution necessitated by the clandestine posture and repression were having debilitating effects upon the party. Its membership dropped from between two and three thousand to approximately a thousand.[18] Moreover, a group of younger members objected to the clandestine posture, insisted upon meetings of the full Central Committee, and left the party when their demands were refused. They formed a paper called *Le Travailleur* (*The Worker*) in the summer of 1970. They did a self-criticism and were re-admitted back into the party as individuals in 1973. However, a second group of young people, many of them having come from the UJCML, took the same position but did not quit the party. In an attempt to compromise with these people or pacify them, five of their number were given responsibility for editing the paper and were attached to the Central Committee. They used the paper to criticize the party's leadership, and were stripped of their posts. They refused to accept the sanction or to do a self-criticism.

This group was expelled, and it established a paper called *Front Rouge*. It published this paper from the time of its explusion in 1970 to

1974. However, all during this period it refused to recognize the legitimacy of its expulsion. Like the Trotsyists when they were initially expelled from the Communist parties, the people of *Front Rouge* insisted that they were just as legitimately a part of the PCMLF as were those who purged them. This was the only way to make a continued appeal for Chinese and Albanian recognition.

In 1974, they gave up the attempt and formed their own legal party, the *Parti Communiste Révolutionnaire (marxiste-léniniste)* or PCR (m-l). It was a younger party, lacking the older former Communist Party members at the top which the PCMLF had. It was much more open in its activities, since it was not working under the constraint of a ban. And it joined in common demonstrations and other activities with non-Maoist groups on the Far Left, including Trotskyist organizations. In the eyes of the PCMLF, the latter was a particularly serious error and it viewed the PCR (m-l) as an ultraleftist organization attracted to spontaneous action. The PCR (m-l) viewed the PCMLF as a structure ossified by its preoccupation with clandestinity and totally isolated from every other group on the Far Left.

The fortunes of the PCMLF, which had begun to decline in 1970, continued to decline until 1976. The attractiveness of the PCR(m-l), which was growing in size, which was able to publish a daily newspaper just like the PCMLF,[19] and which was much better integrated into the larger Far Left milieu, was not helping the PCMLF.

After 1976, two factors pushed these two largest Maoist French organizations closer together. One was a severe self-criticism which the PCMLF made against itself in 1976.[20] It criticized itself for the following errors made at its 1975 Congress: (1) arbitrarily declaring that a war between the two superpowers was imminent; (2) viewing the French Communist Party as a direct agent of the USSR;[21] (3) focusing exclusively on the superpowers as its target while ignoring the everyday problems of the French working class; (4) veering toward an alliance with the bourgeoisie in defense of French national independence; (5) thusly hesitating to attack the nuclear policy of France, or to side with the peasants protesting the construction of nuclear plants in their regions; (6) thusly seeing the CGT and the Communist Party as the major targets in their factory work; and (7) refusing to support the soldiers in the French armed forces, who were organizing and pressuring just demands, under the pretext that they were led by Trotskyists and used by the revisionist Communist Party.[22] This is the most basic self-criticism that this writer has ever seen any Marxist-Leninist group make of itself. While focusing on specific issues, it basically agreed with the charge of sectarianism levied by the PCR(m-l).

The second factor was the upcoming French legislative elections of 1978. It attests to the tremendous impact which those upcoming elections had upon the entire Left in France that both the PCMLF and the PCR(m-l), neither of which had ever run candidates before, took an electoral turn. The self-criticism of the PCMLF made the PCR(m-l) much more willing not only to enter into a joint electoral pact with the PCMLF but to do so as an act which would be considered a step in the direction of an attempt to actually reunite the two organizations.

In the first Maoist participation in national elections,[23] the two parties ran 114 candidates and received approximately 28,000 votes.[24] While this was a positive experience, some problems still remained in terms of future unification. From the perspective of the PCMLF, there were three problems which had to be resolved before the two groups could unify. First the PCMLF felt that the PCR(m-l) emphasized the concept of the mass line to the point of virtually denying the leadership role of the party. The PCMLF placed its emphasis upon the directive role of the party. This did not concern the internal dynamics of the party, but rather the relationship between the party and the masses.

Secondly, the PCMLF felt that Maoist groups should deal only with each other. The PCR(m-l) entered into discussions with the *Ligue*-OCT-CCA coalition prior to its 1978 electoral agreement with the PCMLF. It was also attracted to the position that Far Left groups should urge their voters to vote for the Communist or Socialist parties on the second round. The PCMLF felt that Maoist groups should not be involved with Trotskyist groups. And it made complete abstention on the second round a condition of its alliance with the PCR(m-l).

Third, while the PCR(m-l) condemned the Gang of Four and criticized the Albanians for their position on the Theory of the Three Worlds,[25] the PCMLF was still not completely at ease with the appreciation which the PCR(m-l) had of that theory and with its response to concrete situations. Shortly after the legislative elections of 1978, when president Giscard d'Estaing felt emboldened to send French paratroopers into Zaire, the two organizations took completely contrary stands. The PCMLF, alone among the French Left, accepted the Chinese position that a Second World country was countering Soviet social-imperialism. The PCR(m-l) took the position that every other group on the Left did, namely that the French were practicing good old-fashioned capitalist imperialism.

During this period of attempted rapprochement, both parties continued their daily work. This involved publishing rather short daily newspapers and selling them either by subscription or through the comprehensive Maoist bookstore, the *Librairie Norman Bethune*. The PCMLF also ran its own bookstore which handled the paper. Both parties were heavily engaged in work within the factories. This work was conducted through the union structures. Like the *Ligue*, they had in the past found it easier to work within the *autogestionnaire* CFDT than within the Communist-dominated CGT. But with the loosening of internal controls within the CGT, the PCMLF developed an increasing taste for working therein. Although not liking its close ties with the Socialist Party since 1974, the PCR(m-l) adopted a more positive view of the CFDT than of any other labor confederation and seemed more content than the PCMLF to make its major investment there. [26]

Neither of the Maoist parties has emphasized youth to the extent that the *Ligue* has. In fact, while the PCMLF contended that between 15 and 20 per cent of its members were teachers in 1978, (mainly at the primary and secondary levels), it readily admitted that as opposed to 1968, a decade later it had almost no students in its ranks.[27] The PCR(m-l), which had a lower average age at both the leadership and general membership level, has made a major attempt at recruiting younger people, including students, through its *Union Communiste de la Jeunesse Révolutionnaire.* This closer similarity in age and student distribution has made it easier for the PCR(m-l) to interact with the rest of the Far Left, while the PCMLF has remained isolated.

Similar to their positions on youth, both of the Maoist parties have expressed concern over the oppression of women, but neither has been willing to go to the extent that the *Ligue* has in terms of organizational commitment or of supporting the autonomous women's movement. For about a year (1974-75) the PCMLF published a little newspaper on women, and at one time they experimented with women's commissions within the party. These attempts were terminated. But this writer was assured that in 1978 much more attention was being devoted to placing women in leadership positions. One leader estimated that while only about ten per cent of the Central Committee was female, about 30 per cent of the emerging leaders coming up through intermediate levels were women. He also estimated that women comprised somewhere between 35 and 40 per cent of the entire party. The party has no position at all on homosexuality, and has been claiming to be concerned uniquely with the effectiveness of its militants' work regardless of their sexual preferences.[28]

Finally, both parties have rejected the nuclear power program of the government and any nuclear power program under capitalism. They thus have shared the views of the Trotskyist OCI and *Lutte Ouvrière,* but do have not accepted the unequivocal rejection of nuclear power by the Trotskyist *Ligue.* As reflected in its 1976 self-criticism, this issue has been a difficult one for PCMLF. Up to 1976, its willingness to support any program which strengthened "Second World" France and thus rendered it less dependent on the United States—including both its own nuclear power program and its own nuclear strike force aimed primarily at the USSR—precluded any critical posture *vis-à-vis* the nuclear policies of the French government. This separated the PCMLF from the growing anti-nuclear movement and from the massive demonstrations against the installation of specific plants which usually displaced farmers in the countryside. In 1976, the PCMLF decided that it could eat its cake and have it, too; that it could support the deployment of nuclear weapons aimed at the Soviet Union but oppose non-military aspects of the nuclear program. That position was questioned by others on the Far Left, including other Maoists.

The Maoist group to raise the sharpest questions about the PCMLF's self-criticism, which it called a "phoney self-criticism,"[29] was the *Groupe pour la Fondation de l'Union des Communistes de France Marxistes Léninistes*. The first five words of the name are usually omitted and the organization is commonly referred to as the UCFML. It is probably the third largest Maoist organization in France.

Most of the Maoist organizations in France have emerged as splits from the PCMLF. This was the origin of the PCR(m-l). The UCFML is an exception. This organization goes back to 1970, when it was founded by Alain Badiou, a philosophy professor at the Faculty of Vincennes (this faculty was itself a concession or an attempt to appease and isolate the Left after 1968), and a leader of the pro-Chinese tendency within the *Parti Socialiste Unifié* (PSU).

The UCFML has made no claim to be a party, as have the other two organizations. In fact, it has not even claimed to be a "union" yet, but a "group" for the formation of a "union." It has readily admitted that it does not yet have a mass base which would entitle it legitimately to refer to itself as a party. It also questions the legitimacy of the PCMLF and the PCR(m-l) so doing.

Despite the fact that it is smaller than the two parties, the UCFML has been a very active group and has exhibited some quite different characteristics from them. A great proportion of its energy has been invested in the support of the struggles of the immigrant workers. In its very first year of existence it directed its efforts at trying to assist the immigrant workers who were still locked into the shantytowns known as *bidonvilies*.[30]

The UCFML has been viewed by the other Maoists as being highly intellectual and theoretical. This is because the organization has insisted upon doing its own independent assessment and analysis of problems which it encounters, and of what is issued as a political line by the Chinese. They have been very blunt in stating that as it has been formulated by the Chinese, the Theory of the Three Worlds is designed to serve the interests of the Chinese state, but that that is not the function of the UCFML. They have been particularly adamant in insisting that the USSR is no more dangerous than the United States, that the NATO alliance must be opposed without equivocation, and that French foreign policy is imperialist and must be strenuously opposed, even if that foreign policy is anti-Soviet and if France does have certain disagreements with the United States. Unlike a tiny group which split off from the PCMLF in 1976, the *Organisation pour la Reconstruction du Parti Communiste de la France*, the UCFML has not raised the

Albanian banner when it has presented its positions. They are very similar, but the UCFML has insisted upon independent analysis and avoided going out of its way to bait the Chinese.

The UCFML has taken a similarly frank but not unnecessarily baiting attitude toward the "Gang of Four," whom both the PCMLF and PCR(m-l) have resoundingly denounced. The UCFML was frank in saying that it found the charges launched against the Gang—charges of Trotskyism, among other things—deficient. Moreover, it found that those levied against Mao's second wife, who was unfavorably compared with his highly sub-servient first wife, contained strong elements of sexism. The UCFML refused to denounce the Gang of Four on the basis of the evidence submitted by the Chinese regime.[31]

Finally, two tactical differences have separated the UCFML from the two Maoist parties. First, while they have had people working within factor-ies, they have been absolutely against working within the unions. They have taken an even harder line on this than the Trotskyist *Lutte Ouvrière,* which has *emphasized* committees outside of the union structures but which still has worked within the unions. The UCFML has worked exclusively through groups which it has created, called the *noyaux communistes ouvriers,* or communist workers' cells. Secondly, while the PCMLF and the PCR(m-l) succumbed to electoralism by running candidates in the 1978 legislative elections, the UCFML retained a strictly non-electoralist posture, and urged people to abstain from those elections.

As was pointed out before this discussion of hierarchical Maoism, despite the differences which have existed among the PCMLF, the PCR(m-l) and the UCFML, none of these organizations or any of the other smaller hierarchical Maoist splinter groups have offered any radically new inter-pretations of Marxism, Leninism, and/or Maoism. For major tactical and theoretical innovations, one must turn to the anti-hierarchical Maoists.

ANTI-HIERARCHICAL MAOISM

In September 1968, while the "liquidationist current" of the UJCML was in seclusion—studying, among other texts, Lenin's *What Is To be Done?*—a current of the non-liquidationists called *Mao-spontex* ("spontex" referring to spontaneity, a very non-Leninist concept) created a new move-ment called *La Gauche Prolétarienne* (The Proletarian Left, or GP). Simul-taneously, a newspaper called *La Cause du Peuple (The Peoples' Cause,* or CDP) was started. The GP was to become the most potent action arm of the anti-hierarchical Maoist movement. The CDP was its public and information arm. The impact of this group was so strong that when in France one said "les Maoïstes", it was usually assumed that one was referring to the GP.

While a very small number of militants created these structures in September (not more than forty started the paper, the CDP), the movement received a shot in the arm when some of the militants from the Nanterre-based *Mouvement du 22 Mars* came in in February and March of 1969. The *22 Mars* played a crucial catalytic role in the 1968 revolt on the Nanterre campus of the University of Paris. Although it was a coalition which included people inclined toward Maoism as well as JCR Trotskyists (like present *Ligue* leader Daniel Ben-Said) and Trotskyist sympathizers, the dominant tone and public image was set by Daniel Cohn-Bendit ("Danny the Red") and his anarchist comrades. Also, some of those who had been fence straddlers in the dispute between the "liquidationists" and the "Mao-spontex" decided to enter. The GP was very careful to screen out those who had taken any kind of leadership position in the "liquidationist" movement so as to avoid bringing the dispute which had destroyed the UJCML into the new organization.

While these people were going into the GP, a second anti-hierarchical Maoist group was being created. This was *Vive la Révolution* (VLR). Nanterre was a stronghold of the VLR and, like the GP, it attracted some of the former *22 Mars* people. But it also attracted some of the "liquidationists" who had gone into the PCMLF and who were very quickly alienated by both the hierarchical nature of the organization and what they perceived to be clandestine caution to the point of inactivity. This anti-hierarchical group led a short life, terminating in the summer of 1971. But it had a significance which transcended its own existence.

Vive la Révolution

VLR was smaller than the *Gauche Prolétarienne*. In 1970, their relative sizes were estimated at "several hundred" and "about fifteen hundred."[32] In social composition they were similar, as might be expected from what has been said about their origin. Like the GP, VLR entered a Parisian automobile plant and attempted to do political work with co-workers.

The special target operation was the Citroën plant in Paris' 15th Arrondissement. They also worked in approximately twenty factories in the Parisian suburbs.[33] Finally, as I have noted, the VLR was similar to the GP in being a non-Leninist and anti-hierarchical organization.

Ideologically, however, the VLR differed from the GP in centering its criticism of bourgeois society around a concept developed by the French Marxist or neo-Marxist sociologist Henri Lefebvre, that of "everyday life."[34] As this concept was developed within the VLR's paper, *Tout,* greater and greater emphasis was placed upon that aspect of everyday life stressed by Wilhelm Reich, the libidinal. *Tout,* which appeared every two weeks during its sixteen number existence, was the first widely distributed, French political publication to stress problems of sex, women's liberation, and gay rights.[35]

Despite the fact that a minority of the total number of articles in

Tout dealt with sexually related topics, the attempt to add this dimension to the revolutionary struggle resulted in the early demise of the organization. Issue number 12 alienated the members of the VLR who were attempting to do factory organizing, other groups on the Far Left, and the government. Two four-page articles, one dealing with women's liberation and the other with homosexuality, resulted in factory organizers declaring the publication useless for distribution to workers, in the Norman Bethune Maoist Bookstore refusing to handle the paper, and in the government banning and seizing the issue--as well as bringing an obscenity charge against Jean-Paul Sartre, who had agreed to serve as the nominal editor of the paper.[36]

The four final issues of *Tout,* which was dissolved in July 1971, engaged in an analysis of the puritanical attitudes of the Far Left, of its inability or unwillingness to see that a truly liberating revolution must break the sexual repressiveness of bourgeois society as well as the economic and hierarchical repressiveness. It was the first group on the French Far Left to make this point. While the VLR itself fell apart, it was helping to set the stage for the entrance of the counter-cultural phenomena which were so visible by the mid 1970s. According to Hess, both the women's liberation movement (the *Mouvement de Libération des Femmes,* MLF) and the gay movement in France (the *Front des Homosexuels Révolutionnaires,* FHR) grew out of the VLR experience, and were initially led by former VLR people.[37]

La Gauche Prolétarienne: Initial Offensives & State Response
The *Gauche Prolétarienne* and its newspaper, *La Cause du Peuple,* continued to thrive and to engage management, the regime, and even the CGT in constantly escalating confrontations. It stole the thunder of the hierarchical PCMLF, which had been leading a very cautious, clandestine existence since its 1968 banning. When the government decided to go after the GP, it was because its dramatic and daring tactics were perceived as a threat to political stability, and not for reasons of sexual morality, as in the case of the VLR.

Most Maoist organizations, indeed most Marxist-Leninist organizations generally, begin with a relatively loose pre-party structure. The party stage represents a tightening up of the hierarchical order. It was quite the opposite in the case of the *Gauche Prolétarienne.* The first two years of the life of GP Maoism, from the fall of 1968 to the fall of 1970, represented the high point of organizational structure of the Mao-spontex current. During this stage there was a committee structure at the national, regional, and local levels. These committees called and coordinated periodic "general assemblies of workers" which were supposed to make the real decisions. While some people came to be known as "leaders," the people within the GP at least told themselves that they were fighting against the importance of distinctions between leaders and non-leaders in the making of decisions. The general assemblies were supposed to maximize political equality. This was a conscious goal, but some people emerged as more influential than others. The influentials were disproportionately male.

The thrust of the GP was to create a new "autonomous" workers' movement by uniting "the anti-authoritarian aspirations as they were expressed and continue to be expressed by youth and the new forms of battle in the working class, anti-despotic forms of battle."[38] The new forms of battle referred to a wide variety of tactics employed by workers during and after 1968, which included occupying plants, holding bosses hostage until they gave into demands, resisting the para-military CRS when it attempted to recapture the plants, and sabotage.

The first step in the implementation of the strategy of developing an autonomous work force was the scrapping of the UJCML's practice of attempting to work within the CGT, the Communist-dominated union. This step was taken early in the game, at a national general assembly of workers which the GP called in January 1969, in an attempt to pull people operating in different plants together so that they could compare notes. This was even a month or two before the people from the *22 Mars* came into the movement. In April, the GP issued the first number of its own review, *Les Cahiers de la Gauche Prolétarienne,* in which the relationship between the "anti-authoritarian revolt" of youth and the proletarian revolution was explicated. The major field of confrontation at this time was the Renault plant at Flins, which again erupted into combat with the police in June 1969. There was also considerable effort placed in the spring of 1969 upon reaching secondary school students.

After confrontations and battles with the police at Flins, a second workers assembly was held. At this assembly ideas were proposed for gaining control over the speed of production lines and directing the battle clearly against oppressive bosses and foremen. There were some experiments with tactics during the summer of 1969, including the introduction of sabotage techniques to interrupt the assembly line in a factory in Roubaix-Tourcoing.

The second issue of *Les Cahiers de la Gauche Prolétarienne,* dated September-October 1969, introduced a new concept which increased the intensity and spread of the battle—"the non-armed but violent battle of the partisans."[39] University and high school students were encouraged to go into the factories, slums, or working class suburbs "to lead the resistance, to lead the violent struggle."[40]

From the very beginning, the Maoists faced opposition within the factories. On the one hand, they had to contend with the militants of the CGT when they entered plants where the CGT had any strength. The CGT did not appreciate the attempts of the Maoists to break their control over the channelling of demands within the work setting. At times, this led to violent confrontations.

On the other hand, engaging in any kind of "political" work in the plants was regarded as grounds for dismissal. In some plants this extended to conversations between workers and to putting political tracts, publications, or clippings on the bulletin boards. In plants such as Renault, the work of the CGT was not considered by management to be "political" and thus was not proscribed. In the sense that the CGT stresses bread and butter demands and tries to accomplish them through accepted channels, it is different from the Maoists, and the Maoists were the first to point out the distinction. In some plants, such as those of Citroën, management deals with even more easily controlled "independent" unions.

However, whether or not the CGT is active in a plant or there is an "independent" union, management has not left it to the unions to enforce discipline within the factories. In many of them there has been a virtual police force under the command of the personnel department charged with patrolling the plant floor and looking for political trouble. The French call these *milices patronales* or the boss' police. And, on top of these people, there have been informants among the immigrant workers who could cause considerable grief upon the immigrants' return home. This was a particularly serious problem for Portuguese workers under the Salazar regime and for Spanish workers under Franco. Deportation for participating in radical action in the French plants could entail very serious consequences.

In March 1970, the French government decided that letting the plant police deal with the militants once they were on the plant floor was too defensive a strategy. There had been some arrests, but not so many that the Maoist movement felt seriously threatened. In March, however, the government decided to strike at the only visible heart of the GP movement. It went after *La Cause du Peuple*. The two editors of the CDP, Le Bris and Le Dantec, were arrested and arraigned for trial. And the police began to seize the newspaper and attack and/or arrest the vendors. It came to a point where simply selling the newspaper could get one a year in prison and perpetual loss of civil rights.

At about the same time, the movement made the decision to go public beyond merely attempting to sell the CDP. It was during that spring that Alain Geismar became the major spokesperson for both the GP and the CDP. Geismar had been a junior faculty member at the Faculty of Science in Paris before the 1968 revolt broke out. He had been active within the university teachers' union affiliated with the large National Federation of Education. By the time the revolt broke out in 1968, he had become the president of the union. Under his leadership, the union was very supportive of the revolt. But Geismar moved well beyond where most of the membership was willing to go politically, and he resigned his union post during the revolt. He was one of the three most prominent personalities involved in the revolt, along with Daniel Cohn-Bendit of the *22 Mars* and Jacques Sauvageot, the Vice-President but actual leader of the student union, UNEF. After the revolt Geismar moved closer to the *22 Mars* and was one of those who merged with the GP in early 1969, Since he was a publicly known figure with considerable public appeal, and since he had already been identified as trouble by the government—which had fired him from his teaching job because of his participation in the 1968 revolt—Geismar seemed like a good person to present the public image of the movement. He certainly could not be slipped into an industrial plant.

Although Le Bris and Le Dantec were arrested in March 1970, Le Dantec did not go to trial until May. Geismar filled the gap at the CDP. Two days before the trial of Le Dantec, Geismar addressed a protest meeting called by a number of groups. He was one of eight speakers. He delivered a very short statement within which included the following message:

> In order to break the manoeuvre of the bourgeoise, to break its attempt to encircle and destroy the pop- ular movement, we must intensify the resistance. For the bourgeoisie May 27 will be the day of the trial of Le Dantec. For all revolutionaries it will be the day of resistance, the beginning of an intensifi- cation of the resistance. There will be no social peace; there will be no social truce....We support all popular initiatives which will take place May 27. We support the meetings and we call upon all those who want to go further, all those who want to make of May 27 a day of resistance, to organize themselves around militants and tomorrow, in each college of the university, meetings will be held in the afternoon to prepare for the organization of the struggle in the streets on May 27.
>
> Because it is in the street that anger will be expressed against the hordes of police which are occupying the streets of Paris. The popular resistance will grow.[41]

Protest demonstrations had been called for the day of the Le Dantec trial. The police banned the demonstrations, a regular practice going back at least as far as the Algerian War, and usually justified on the basis of avoiding traffic disruption.[42] The police charged the demonstrators. Along with the physical injuries inflicted there were approximately 490 arrests in the streets. A police agent with a tape recorder hidden in a brief case had attended the talk given by Geismar two days earlier. On the basis of the portion cited above, Geismar was tracked down and arrested for incitement of the acts for which the demonstrators were charged. While Le Dantec was sentenced to one year in prison for editing the CDP, and Le Bris subsequently to eight months, the state was preparing its case against Geismar.

Like Le Dantec and Le Bris, Geismar underwent a long pre-trial detention. Arrested on June 25th, Geismar waited in prison for this trial until October 20, 1970. Thus—as in the case of Angela Davis in the United States—even if the regime should lose its case in the courts it inflicts some punishment against its adversaries by forcing them to expend resources in their own behalf and by obliging them to remain in prison prior to trial.

From the point of view of both the prosecution and the defense, Geismar's trial was a political trial. The closing argument of the prosecution began as follows:

> The arguments presented before this court have shown the clash of two conceptions of democracy: the classic, positive conception which orients and around which are organized the institutions of most liberal countries such as ours, and the conception of the ex-*Gauche Prolétarienne* which claims to speak for the people but which has no real massive support among the citizentry.
>
> They promise us proletarian dictatorships. They promise us a system favorable to the people, but they ignore the will of the people. Well, our modern conceptions of democracy give a wide place to liberty of expression. Liberty of expression exists. There is a press, there is the possibility of writing, of meeting of speaking. A law almost one hundred years old guarantees a broad freedom of writing and of speech because the infractions, as you know, are extremely limited in this law when it comes to the press and there are all sorts of formal regulations which protect this freedom of the press.
>
> The *Gauche Prolétarienne* declares this system to be formal, esteems that this legal formality does not guarantee real rights, and does not serve at all to defend the cause of certain people.
>
> In truth, it is a question of the interest of tiny groups without any serious popular base.[43]

Like the trial of the Chicago Seven, growing out of the confrontations at the 1968 Democratic Convention, this one raised basic issues. The prosecution in two different breaths argued that Geismar and his group had no popular support and, on the other hand, that, as in the case of the editors of *La Cause du Peuple,* the imprisonment of the Maoists meant the difference between the regime's succumbing or surviving:

> When we tried the case of the *Cause du Peuple*
> here I made the point that to this fundamental
> opposition there must be presented a firm attitude,
> because the fundamental problem is to know if
> we wish to succumb or to survive.[44]

The prosecution further argued that Geismar exerted a particular hold over young students because of his position as a teacher at the Faculty. Geismar responded that the police records themselves show that not even ten per cent of those arrested for protesting the trial of Le Dantec were students. This statistic is interesting not only as a refutation of the proposition of the prosecution but also as some indication of the broadening base of support of the Maoists.

Several other arguments were revealing. The prosecution argued that the fact that Geismar had co-authored a book in 1969 entitled *Vers la Guerre Civile (Toward Civil War)* indicated that freedom of the press was in existence. Geismar responded that the book,written in intellectual terms and selling for quite a bit more than a newspaper, posed no threat at all to the regime. On the other hand, *La Cause du Peuple* was written in language that workers could understand and relate to and, if the worker could afford the price, sold for one franc. If not, it was free. It was thus the distribution and the effectiveness of CDP that frightened the regime, and the lack of effectiveness of the book that permitted the regime to be more libertarian. But even more basically, Geismar argued that bourgeois regimes have never willingly granted rights to their opponents, and that what civil liberties exist in practice have been the result of struggles waged by those who have been oppressed.[45] He portrayed the GP Maoists as continuing that historical struggle.

The prosecution claimed that Geismar's words were responsible for injuries inflicted upon seventy-nine police officers. Yet no medical records were produced to substantiate injuries. The defense asked that Minister of Interior Marcellin be obliged to appear to explain the police complaints. He was not, and the judge ruled that his testimony was not required. The defense asked whether or not the injuries incurred by the police officers could not have been incurred on the unsafe steps of police stations or in the unsafe police wagons. For the police often explained the injuries suffered by people in their custody—particularly by young political dissidents or demonstrators, who claimed that they had been beaten by the police—by declaring that their prisoners had fallen down the stairs in the stations or fallen when they were being transported in the vans. If these explanations were true, the defense argued, the facilities of the police must be terribly unsafe. Thus medical depositions should be submitted to make sure that. the police officers had not fallen victim to the same fate as their prisoners. The judge ruled that such submissions were unnecessary.

Geismar, who had declared that his conviction was a foregone conclusion, was indeed convicted. He was sentenced to and served eighteen months in prison, five of which were spent in solitary confinement. But that was not the only achievement of the government. The *Gauche Prolétarienne* was banned by ministerial decree during the trial and, to continue the spiral of repression, at least three hundred young people who had defied the ban on demonstrations and the show of force (which consisted of 5,000 police officers around the court and in the Latin Quarter) had been arrested by the evening of the first day of Geismar's two-day trial.

Despite the fact that the *Gauche Prolétarienne* was formally banned and that an ever increasing number of its members and leaders were in prison, the movement was not destroyed. On the contrary, it took some dramatic new turns and simply referred to itself as the ex-GP. Those in prison conducted hunger strikes for recognition of their status as political prisoners (regime spokesmen had claimed that there were no political prisoners in France) and for recognition of basic rights of all prisoners. This was coordinated with campaigns for prisoners' rights led on the outside. The *Cause du Peuple* did not cease publication. On the contrary, after Geismar's arrest, following those of Le Dantec and Le Bris, Jean-Paul Sartre assumed the nominal directorship of the CDP. And the publisher, François Maspero, went out on the streets to hawk the paper. This was clearly a challenge to the government to arrest personalities with world-wide reputations and to try them for the same acts for which lesser-known, younger militants had been imprisoned. Maspero was arrested, but charged only with vending without a proper license, a very minor misdemeanor, while no action at all was taken against Sartre.

The Anti-Organization of the Ex-*Gauche Prolétarienne*

The GP militants were convinced that there was an inner dialectic at work so that the movement "naturally" arrived at certain stages at certain points in time. Neither they nor the government could completely control this dialectic. Thus, while committed to a highly voluntaristic conception of the "politics of the act," the movement also had a strong element of non-voluntarism. For example, the reaction to the government's banning of the GP was that the underground stage was the next "natural" one anyway. Even if the government had not banned the GP, this stage would have been dictated by other factors in the environment and the internal, ineluctable dynamics of the movement. The timing of the regime's crack-down was a surprise; they thought they probably had a little more time to operate more openly. But this only meant an acceleration of the timetable.[46]

One militant, a twenty-six-year-old former math major who came from a working-class background and went back into the factories to do political work, clearly demonstrated both the affirmation and the negation in the GP's attitude toward its structure and dynamic:

> It is often said: "Marcellin (the Minister of Interior
> and thus chief police officer of the regime) destroyed
> the *Gauche Prolétarienne*." But no, Marcellin. We
> destroyed the *Gauche Prolétarienne*. It is a glorious
> organization but it has seen its time. Our task is to
> destroy the *Gauche Prolétarienne* or what has replaced
> it and to build the party. The party for me is the capa-
> city to elaborate a consequential revolutionary politics,
> that is to say to tie the particular to the general, the
> immediate to the long-term program, and to truly mo-
> bilize the masses. A party is always a minority. But
> the difference between our party and the other parties
> is that our permanent objective is not only the con-
> struction of the party, it is its destruction. We are
> building the party in order to destroy it.[47]

In fact, the next stage was not one of party construction, not even party construction for party destruction. The theme for 1970-71 became "Widen the Resistance" and emphasis was placed upon action through local, decentralized groups. Some of these groups were already in existence; a number had to be created from scratch.

In the factories there were already the numerous *Comités de Base* (the base committees) which the Maoists had helped to organize but which were not completely Maoist in composition. In the spring of 1971, more militant strike forces called *Groupes Ouvriers Anti-Flics* (GOAF), or anti-cop workers' groups, were created. The primary function of these groups was to deal physically with the attempts to surpress the work of the base committees and to punish individual bosses or management personnel who abused workers.

Secondly, there was a renewed effort made to mobilize young people in the schools, particularly at the secondary or *lycée* level. Third, there were the support groups for the Vietnamese fighting the United States and, more importantly at this stage, for the Palestinians seeking to regain their homeland.

Finally, a wide network of GP support groups was established. There was *Secours Rouge* (Red Assistance), which enjoyed the directorship of the publisher François Maspero and the active support of a number of groups and intellectuals on the Far Left, including Sartre. It was the most important of the GP support groups and its primary function was to come to the aid of those who felt either oppressed by the regime or that their needs were not being met. The gamut of activity went from organizing demonstrations in order to protest political trials to digging mountain towns out of the snow when the government did not respond to appeals. Like another support group, *Les Amis de la Cause du Peuple* (Friends of the CDP) which sold papers and gave other support to the newspaper, *Secours Rouge* would defy the government's legal definitions. A third set of structures, the *Comités Vérité et Justice* (Truth and Justice Committees), did not engage in illegal activity. Their function was to investigate and publicize specific cases in which bourgeois legality was unjustly twisted to the detriment of the deprived and the benefit of the wealthy and powerful. All of these subsidiary groups created by the GP Maoists opened up possibilities of broad contacts for an outlawed movement.

By this time, GP Maoism was indeed beginning to conform more to Kenneth Keniston's definition of a "movement" than to a normal organization. Writing about the young people attending a Vietnam Summer Project in the United States in 1967, Keniston said:

> It is significant that these young men and
> women consider themselves part of a move-
> ment, rather than a party, an organization, a
> bureaucracy, an institution, a cadre, or a faction.
> The term "movement" suggests a spontaneous,
> natural, and non-institutional group; it again
> points to their feeling that they are in motion,
> changing, and developing....Finally, "movement"
> summarizes the radical's perception of the mo-
> dern world, a world itself in flux, unstable, con-
> tinually changing.[48]

Of course the difference between the people Keniston was talking about and the GP Maoists is that the Maoists were moving from a more structured ideological and organizational configuration to a more fluid one, while the American students were still at a very early stage in their radicalization. If those who had passed through the various stages of this current of Maoism from the UJMCL to this decentralized "Widen the Resistance" stage could understand the movement both psychically and politically, it was quite confusing to people on the outside whom the movement was trying to touch. Unless one is part of the inner core, it is not easy to orient oneself to something in a constant state of flux.

This becomes evident in the many testimonies and interviews on record with workers who have at least "sympathized" with what the GP

Maoists were doing in specific situations. There is considerable confusion in the minds of some of these workers as to whether they themselves are "Maoists." But the uncertainly in terms of identification existed on the part of those who were more distant or even hostile to the movement, as well as those who were sympathetic. Some of this confusion is reflected in an interview with three workers who were at least sympathetic with Maoism, however it is understood:

> Patrick (25-year old Maoist militant at Renault):
> When one is a Maoist in a factory, one is made
> responsible for everything that happens at the
> doors, even if it is a completely different group
> which comes and does who knows what. They
> tell me: "Your buddies have distributed a tract,"
> even if they are Trotskyist tracts. Anything that's
> not CP is *gauchiste* [a generic term for the Far
> Left as a whole, by which Patrick means that the
> workers are not getting the distinctions].

> Marcel (44-year old militant coal miner): That is
> a real problem for French Maoism.

> Germain (58-year-old miner, Resistance fighter
> and long-time member of the CP, who explains
> that he was always a Maoist but not of the "1968
> variety" because he does not have long hair): So
> long as the necessary explanatory work has not
> been done, there will be mistrust. Contacts must
> be multiplied; there must be discussion and educa-
> tion. The Maoist spirit must be made to come
> out. There is no concealment among the Maoists.
> On the contrary, all true communists are Maoist;
> but they don't know it yet. There is just a lack of
> information.[49]

Actions and Attractions of the GP and ex-GP

Despite the problems caused by the fluid nature of the movement and its post-1970 outlaw status, the GP Maoists were the most dynamic group on the French Far Left. Their actions were usually dramatic. They were sometimes even the stuff that movies were made of, particularly in the hands of Maoist or Maoist-sympathizing directors such as Jean-Luc Godard, who directed *La Chinoise,* or of Godard and his collaborator Jean Pierre Gorin, who directed the even more widely known film *Tout Va Bien*.[50] Add to this the support of Sartre and Maspero, the personality of Geismar, and the aura of 1968, and one can begin to understand the drama, and not just glamour, which surrounded GP Maoism.

I shall briefly discuss the actions of the GP Maoists, both prior to and after the banning, in four different areas.

(1) The Assault on Renault

The most daring and dangerous of the movement's activities was its factory work. While the GP and then the ex-GP operated in a number of plants and work settings throughout France—including Brandt and Berliet in Lyon, Batignolles in Nantes, the shipyards in Dunkerque, and the coal mines in the North—the Renault automobile plant at Billancourt, right on the perimeter of Paris, was a special target.

First, the GP Maoists wanted to pick up on and generalize the sabotage which was already going on inside the plant, and which was part of an overall increase in worker militancy at that time.[51] Secondly, they wanted to pass from the stage of clandestine sabotage to a more open campaign against what they called "the terrorism of the administration."[52] This brought the Maoists into open and direct conflict with the CGT, which was trying to keep the focus on bread and butter issues. The GP Maoists were thus following in the path of Barta's Trotskyist followers who, in the late 1940s and early 1950s, directly challenged the power and authority of the CGT in its stronghold.

After encouraging the organization of approximately a dozen decentralized *comités de lutte* (committees of struggle, patterned after the 1968 action committees), the Maoists engaged in their first major battle which incurred the wrath of the CGT. In response to an increase in the metro fares, the Maoists organized workers into large groups which jumped over the metro turnstiles and refused to pay any fares. When eight metro police officers attempted to intervene, they were roughed up and chased away. The CGT attacked the Maoists for beating up public employees. The Maoists refused to recognize police of any nature as normal employees with whom they had a proletarian bond. Massive deployments of police were then sent to the station near the plant, and the police sought their own violent revenge.

The Maoists also ran afoul of the CGT in a campaign against an increase in meal prices in the plant restaurant, an increase in which the CGT was directly complicit because it dominated the *Comité d'Établissement* that administered the restaurant. The Maoists distributed tracts against the increase and called for action. Some workers took food without paying in a tactic similar to that applied in the metro. Fights broke out in the canteen between Maoists and CGT militants. The Maoists claimed to enjoy the support of a good number of immigrant workers, and accused the CGT of bringing in members of the Communist youth movement to help them battle the Maoists. While the Maoists won neither the metro nor the meal price issue, they felt that they had unmasked the CGT as a bureaucratic structure which was not looking after the interests of the workers.

After these initial campaigns, the Maoists turned their attention to the work process itself. They adopted a task rotation strategy to challenge pay differentials based upon the hierarchical division of labor. Each worker in a particular unit would teach every other worker how to perform his or her task. When every worker could perform every task, all of the workers demanded the pay of the highest paid among them on the grounds that all were equally qualified.

They also encouraged the direct confrontation of supervisory personnel. Workers began timing themselves rather than accepting the word of the supervisors. Supervisors who complained about the quality of the work were forced into the pits to do the work themselves. And what was regarded as grossly arbitrary behavior toward any worker, or demonstrations of racism toward immigrant workers, was punished violently by the *Groupes Ouvriers Anti-Flics* (the GOAF or Anti-Cop Workers' Groups). Some supervisory personnel were beaten up, and at least one foreman in the painting section had a bucket of paint turned over on his head.

As the violent resistance against the management increased, so did conflict with the CGT. But even one Maoist rival group, the hierarchical UCFML, attacked the GP Maoists for being so indiscriminate in their tactics that on two occasions they attacked anyone who came into range wearing the white smock characteristic of lower management and supervisory personnel in the plant.[53]

More and more plant police were brought into the factory. Firings for political activity, violent or nonviolent, accelerated. Some of the fired workers were handed over to the regular police stationed at the factory gates and were charged with crimes. Others, who were just fired and ejected from the plant, went on a hunger strike. Two important sources of moral support came from Sartre—whom the GP Maoists managed to smuggle into the plant for an inspection trip, but who was quickly ejected by plant police—and from actress Simone Signoret—who paid supportive visits to the hunger strikers.[54]

The confrontations reached their peak in February and March 1972. Pierre Overney, a twenty-three-year-old ex-GP Maoist Renault worker who had been fired along with a number of his politically active comrades, returned to the factory gates on Friday, February 25. He and the others were distributing tracts to the workers as they entered and left the gates. He got into a verbal dispute with one of the heads of the security section at the plant, a M. Tramoni. Tramoni pulled a gun and killed Overney, who was unarmed and standing a good distance from Tramoni.

The next Monday, Renault workers found the plant completely surrounded by the para-military CRS. They checked the papers of all the workers. Seven workers who had known of the killing on Friday and who participated in a demonstration against it were fired.[55] On Tuesday the CRS circled the plant in convoys, and four more workers were fired. On Thursday, eleven workers who had been dismissed before or after the killing managed to get into the plant and issue a public call to resistance. They were attacked by Tramoin's security personnel and turned over to the police. Five were charged under the *Anti-Cassure* ("Anti-Wrecker")Law.

But the Maoists did not rest content with a protest over the killing of one of their own and the firings of their militants and supporters. An ex-GP commando group, the *Groupe Pierre Overney de la Nouvelle Résistance Populaire,* seized and held in an undisclosed location the chief personnel officer at Billancourt, Robert Nogrette. The Maoists had previously engaged in holding bosses prisoner in the plants until they granted concessions (or were freed by the police) and in a plant of a subsidiary of Renault they had "fired" a boss by kicking him out of the plant and obliging him to remain out for several days. But the Nogrette action was one which was perceived as being of a more serious order, serious enough to attract the personal attention and denunciation of President Pompidou.

The commando group demanded, in return for Nogrette's release, that criminal charges be dropped against the workers who had been turned over to the police and that all workers fired after Overney's death (the total had reached about twenty) be reinstated. There was never a threat to kill Nogrette. And, despite the fact that the police were not able to find him and that the concessions were not made, he was released unharmed after approximately forty-eight hours. The Maoists had expected the labor unions, including the CGT and the CFDT, to denounce the action, and they did so. But it is not so clear that they had expected pressure from another source, *i.e.,* the negative reaction of most of the other Far Left groups, which had declared their solidarity with the ex-GP in massive demonstrations after Overney's killing.[56] Even the Trotskyist *Ligue*—the most confrontation-oriented of the Trotskyist organizations, which had good relations with the GP Maoists—joined with most of the other Far Left organizations in publicly criticizing the operation. The *Ligue,* which at the time was a major supporter of guerrilla-warfare tactics in Latin America, felt that the act made no sense given the French political context and the fact that the Maoists clearly had no intention of killing Nogrette if their demands were not met. Indeed, those demands were not met, Nogrette was released unharmed, and it became virtually impossible to do political work at the Renault plant after this affair.

(2) Work with the Immigrants

A major thrust of the work of the GP and ex-GP Maoists was directed at the large immigrant worker population. These workers are dispro-portionately clustered at the lowest job classifications and hence at the lowest wage rates—sometimes at variance with their actual skills or with the tasks which they actually perform. They are also the least able to absorb increases in such costs as metro fares, food prices, and rents. The Maoists thus hoped that their work in protesting the price increases, in adopting the task rotation tactic, and in physically punishing supervisory personnel who exhibited racist behavior against Arab or Black African workers, would garner the support of the immigrant workers and trigger off greater militancy on their part.

An additional tactic—designed to appeal to the Arab workers from Algeria, Morocco, and Tunisia—was the creation of the Palestine Support Committees in the plants. Initially, the GP Maoists gave considerable attention to the war in Indochina. Their own *Comités Vietnam de Base* (Vietnam Committees at the Base) extended uncritical support to the efforts of both the PRG in the South and the government of North Vietnam, while the *Ligue* was critical of some elements of the programs of both of them. Moreover, the Maoists were even more militant in their tactics than the *Ligue*. While the latter concentrated on demonstrations, the Maoists engaged in a number of violent clashes with the police. One occurred after they had taken over the South Vietnamese embassy and had flown the flag of the National Liberation Front over it. However, in the ex-GP stage, these Maoists shifted the emphasis of their work away from Vietnam and to the Palestinian issue. It simply had more appeal to the immigrant worker population that they were trying to reach. Moreover, support for the return of the Palestinian Arabs to their homeland was virtually the only non-French issue to which the ex-GP devoted substantial attention.

However, the Maoists did not limit their attempt to reach the immigrant worker population to agitation within the plants. From its formation in 1968, GP Maoism directed its attention to the plight of immigrant workers who were forced to live in the shantytowns (*bidonvilles*) which were spread across France but which were more numerous in the Parisian region. The word *bidon* means a drum, such as an oil drum, and the huts were made of any such materials which could be stuck together. Heating, sanitation, or running water were luxuries not to be found in these make-shift structures.

The Maoists were active on several fronts in the *bidonvilles*. While denouncing their existence, they insisted that acceptable alternative housing be provided before the *bidonvilles* were destroyed. They thus attempted to avoid urban renewal American-style. The GP Maoists fought this battle particularly strenuously in Argenteuil, a Parisian suburb in which the Communist Party controlled city hall. *Secours Rouge,* the GP support group, attempted to supply services which were supplied inadequately or not at all by public authorities. In one of the more highly publicized actions of a Maoist commando group, the fashionable luxury item and food shop Fauchon was raided and the food was taken out and distributed in the *bidonvilles*. While the hierarchical Maoist UCFML, after its creation in 1970, also worked in the bidonvilles, the GP Maoists were there first. Together they called national and international attention to the existence of these abysmal conditions, and this activity undoubtedly played a major role in the French government's determination to dismantle the *bidonvilles* in a remarkably short period of time. By 1975, almost all of the *bidonvilles* were gone.

The GP and ex-GP Maoists also worked within the regular immigrant ghettos in the larger cities as well as within the residences constructed specifically to house immigrant workers. In the former, they attempted to organize around the issues of police harassment, violent racist attacks by whites, and the irresponsibility of landlords. Particularly favored tactics were rent strikes, resistance to eviction, and squatting in vacant housing.

In 1972, the ex-GP Maoists aided French families in working-class suburbs who were engaging in the same tactics.[57] In the residences constructed for single immigrant workers or those who come to France to spend eleven months out of the year without their families, the GP Maoists encouraged and supported the immigrants' attempts to fight against the racism of some of the residence managers (many of whom were former military people in the colonial service), to gain control over the governance of the houses, to insist upon proper physical maintenance, and to resist the rent increases which were levied against the residents at rather regular intervals. This early work on the part of the GP Maoists—as well as the continuing work of some of its former Arab members and of the UCFML—was an important encouraging and supportive element in a process of conflict which led to a four-year national rent strike within the residences.[58]

(3) Work Outside of the Urban Context

All of the above actions took place within the urban areas. However, the GP and ex-GP Maoists broke out of the urban context to a much greater extent than both the Trotskyists and the hierarchical Maoists. They did so in three ways. First, a year after their creation, the GP Maoists mounted the barricades set up by rural and small-town merchants to protest what they felt to be unfavorable legislation in 1969. Some on the Left, including Sartre, criticized the Maoists for fighting the police alongside petit-bourgeois merchants. The GP was accused of aiding not a progressive movement but a more likely resurgence of right-wing Poujadism.

Secondly, the GP and ex-GP Maoists supported nationalistic movements in two areas of France, Brittany in the West and Occitanie in the South. While in the late 1970s Corsican nationalism attained very violent levels of manifestations, in the early and mid 1970s the strongest expressions of a desire for cultural and political separatism came from the populations of Brittany and Occitanie. While the GP and ex-GP Maoists supported the struggle of these movements against the status quo, the complexities of the question were not any easier for them to handle than the question of racial separatism has been for American Marxists.

After the GP admitted in 1971 that its thoughts on the question of "nationalities" were still in an embryonic state,[59] the following year a GP writer attempted to put the separatist struggle in Occitanie within an acceptably Marxist framework without at the same time attempting to impose upon it any specific form or structure. Stating that the struggle was "for decolonization, against the pillage of material and human resources, and against the deportation of the young," the article then goes on to state, that:

> The question then is not "Occitan nationalism,"
> "European federalism," or "regionalism," but the
> destruction of the French capitalist state and the
> *role of the popular Occitan movement in the de-*
> *struction;* the installation of a new government
> by the proletariat and oppressed people and *the*
> *role that the Occitan popular movement will*
> *play in this:* the abolition of the imperialist sys-
> tem by the international of proletariats and op-
> pressed people and *the place that the popular*
> *Occitan movement will make for itself in this*
> *International.*
> Transcending the structure of traditional nations,
> the present struggles are carving in the world new
> frameworks within which will be exercised the
> power of workers through their control over means
> of production and distribution and over everything
> which is involved with the creativity of peoples and
> individuals. It is not excluded that each framework
> will reflect an ethic reality. It is up to the workers
> then to decide upon their form of organization and
> coordination. This choice will be conditioned more
> by the development of the struggles in the Hexagon
> [France], in Europe, and in the world than by any
> preestablished will. This development being uneven,
> we cannot predict the forms of political organization
> that people will adopt.[60]

The French GP Maoists thus adopted the same kind of flexibility toward separatist movements within France that Mao adopted toward revolutionary movements in countries other than China. Each one will cut its own path.

The most active attempts made by the GP and ex-GP Maoists to reach out beyond the urban environment, however, were two summer campaigns conducted in 1971 and 1972 in the Loire-Atlantique, the Southeastern portion of Brittany. This was an area in which militant farmers had driven their crops into the cities and dumped them in the street, erected barricades on the roads, occupied processing facilities, and, in 1969, even held the visiting Minister of Agriculture captive until he was freed by the police. A number of the above activities entailed physical combat with the police.

While the GP Maoists had made *ad hoc* attempts to establish contacts with the rural population prior to this, in 1970 and 1971 they organized an actual program in which students and other young people from the cities were recruited to go out and live with farming families. There were two very precise political motives. One was to counteract the propaganda campaign that the government had been conducting against the Far Left since 1968. The young revolutionaries wanted a chance to show the farmers that, despite what they saw and heard on television regarding the uprising and the government's enactment of the "Anti-Wrecker Law" in 1970, they were not simply people intent upon delivering havoc upon France. This was a public relations task.

On the other hand, most of the young people were from the cities, and they knew rural life and the rural population as poorly as the farmers knew them. They wanted to come to know that life and the feelings of the farmers first-hand, by living and working with them. Thus, summer programs were also designed to serve the same purpose as the *enquêtes* conducted in the factories. On the basis of this experience, they came to the conclusion that small and tenant farmers had been subjected to tremendous pressures by inflation and the European Common Market. Under the pretended justification of technological efficiency, the capitalists were exerting pressure which was seen as a simple attempt to get the small farmer off of the land and that land into the hands of those who had the wealth to work it more "efficiently." The dominant capitalist economic organization of Western Europe thus was seen as being totally insensitive to the farmer's relationship with the land, and the Maoists strove to demonstrate a respect for that relationship:

> Among the poorest farmers, there are many who
> possess a patch of earth on which they survive
> miserably. And they cling to that earth. There is
> no question of telling them that "property is theft"
> and tearing it away from them. Certain problems
> require time before their resolution. We are told
> that in China, in order to prove the merits of land
> collectivization, those who want to work individ-
> ually are permitted to do so until they see for

themselves that they are wrong. There is no other way of
persuasion.

And then, what endears the earth to the farmer is not primarily money but what the earth represents, the investment
of soul. In the cities, in the factories, work is not humane.
One works for someone else, a boss, in the heat and according
to the pace of the assembly line. One makes a piece of a car,
of a machine. One does not see the result. One does not have
a feeling of control over one's work. The farmer's love of the
earth is also the love for a labor by which one creates something that one controls, something living.

The present battles for survival of the small farmers
are not like the *"selfish demands of the petite bourgeoisie"*
that can be managed by capitalism's offering of higher prices
and represented in Parliament. They are becoming more and
more democratic struggles of a new type turned toward a progressive future, conforming to the development of humanity.
Aiming more and more at the same enemies as the mass of
the people, the farmers, in this epoch of a general wave of
worker contestation, are discovering that they are not alone.[61]

The feeling for the relationship between the farmer and the land and the
generally high value placed upon agricultural life are much more characteristic
of the writing of Rousseau and Proudhon than of Marx or Engels, and certainly of Trotsky. The GP Maoists did not make the distinction between
usufruct and ownership, a distinction which Proudhon took from Rousseau in
the hope of permitting that special relationship with the land to be preserved
under conditions of greater equality. In contradistinction to Proudhon's
attempt to preserve rural individualism through a national credit system
available to small-scale farmers, the GP Maoists did see collectivization, on
the model of the Chinese agricultural communes, as the optimal answer. But
they felt that it was a viable answer only if the landless and small farmers
came to it themselves. They shared the anarchist Proudhon's revulsion at the
thought of bureaucratic compulsion in the form of forced collectivization, and
they rejected Trotsky's pessimism over the capability of the peasantry to
determine their own destiny.

(4) Prisoners' rights

Many of the above actions of GP Maoism involved illegal activity.
Thus, it is not surprising that many of the 1,035 Far Leftists, who Minister
of Interior Marcellin claimed were sentenced to prison between June 1, 1968
and March 20, 1972, as well as others who were held in pre-trial detention
but not convicted, were GP and ex-GP Maoists.[62] The prisons, however,

provided the Maoists with yet another arena for agitation.

The tactic of the Maoists was to claim the status of "political prisoners." Such a status would entitle the Maoists to certain rights under French law. Once their claim was recognized, the Maoists intended to claim that all prisoners should be extended the more humane treatment just by virtue of being human beings. The government was denying that there were any political prisoners in France, and calling the demands a publicity stunt.

The prisoners' claims were supported outside the prison walls by demonstrations organized by *Secours Rouge* and families of the imprisoned militants. In some cases, these demonstrations brought further arrests and confinement. Trials were taken advantage of as forums where parents of people presently detained or former detainees could talk about prison conditions. On September 1, 1970, thirty Maoist prisoners began a hunger strike to demand: recognition of their status as political prisoners; an end to the common practice of putting the Maoists in solitary confinement from the very beginning of their stays; a common location where all of the political prisoners could meet; a more liberal visitation system; and a general improvement in the conditions of detention, including an end to tormenting on the part of prison guards.[63]

As the hunger strike and the supportive demonstrations continued, the government gave in on some of the points in regard to pre-trial detainees. By September 22, all of the strikers in pre-trial detention—except Geismar—were transferred to prison hospitals. And, on September 28, a court accorded the status of political offense to the writing of a slogan on a wall, which had earned its author three months of solitary confinement up to that point. The changes in the treatment of prisoners, however, seem to have been limited to pre-trial detainees, as Geismar himself served more time in solitary after his conviction in October.[64]

The two most important sources of public information on the conditions of prisoners and on their revolt were the Maspero publishing house and *La Cause du Peuple.* Maspero published the pamphlet entitled *The Political Prionsers Speak,* which publicized the hunger strike, and also published extracts from Geismar's testimony at his trial during the following month. The materials received wider distribution than they would have if the Maoists had published and distributed them through their own press, *Éditions Liberté-Presse.* An additional source of publicity for the struggle of the imprisoned Maoist militants was obtained during the September 24 concert of the Rolling Stones in the Palais des Sports in Paris. Before the huge audience the lights were dimmed and the group turned the microphone over to a Maoist militant to explain why the Maoists were in prisons. The Rolling Stones then sang "Street Fighting Man."[65]

Approximately a year after the hunger strike, in the winter of 1971-72, France experienced a surge of general prison revolts. While it is impossible to establish a certain causal relationship between Maoist agitation in the prisons and those revolts, the fact is that the GP Maoists were still circulating through the prisons, and that the movement and its newspaper were supportive of the revolt against the general conditions prevailing in the French prisons which they had come to know so well.[66]

THEORY OR JUST PRACTICE: WHAT WAS GP MAOISM?

At least on the part of some of the militants, considerable thought was given to the direction of the movement. This resulted in three texts which are important for an understanding of the theoretical basis of GP Maoism. The first is the book by Geismar, July, and Morane, *Vers La Guerre civile* (*Toward Civil War*), which was published in 1969 and which served as the early theoretical guide for the movement. The second is a special issue of Sartre's review, *Les Temps Modernes,* which Sartre turned over to the GP Maoists in 1972. The third is *On a raison de se révolter* (*It is Right to Revolt*) which was published in 1974 and which contains transcripts of conversations between GP Maoist leader Pierre Victor, Sartre, and Phillippe Gavi of the Left newspaper *Libération.* Despite the changes over time which are revealed in these texts, there were three constants in GP theory which were its root-definitional characteristics: (1) the emphasis upon action and events; (2) the rejection of hierarchy; and (3) the rejection of dichotomous class conflict.

(1) The emphasis upon action and events

Traditional Marxist-Leninists, regardless of the specific variety, are committed to two propositions. First, Marxism-Leninism must be made to fit the concrete conditions in which one is attempting to apply it as a guide to action. Second, there are limits to the degree of acceptable adaptation to meet those concrete conditions. The disagreements between and among Marxist-Leninists of Maoist, Trotskyist, and Soviet-oriented variety can be seen largely as disagreements over what those limits are. This means that somewhere there is a sacred core which must not be tampered with.

GP Maoism, on the other hand, viewed the relationship between theory and practice as much more reciprocal than traditional Marxist-Leninists. And the balance was tilted toward action. They drew theoretical lessons from actions and events. *Vers La Guerre civile* attempted to draw theoretical-strategic lessons from two events in which the GP Maoists themselves played no role or a minimal role. The violent campaigns in the factories and streets were seen as analogous to the violent resistance of the partisans to Nazism.

But even more important than the Resistance, in which none of the GP Maoists could have participated themselves (it was an "appropriated experience," to use Mannheim's term), was the uprising of May and June 1968. In fact *Vers La Guerre civile* was largely a reflection on the refusal of the UJCML to become involved in the initial conflict. As a result of this experience, this error, the GP Maoist movement felt that it learned several important lessons.

First, it had underrated the importance of fighting in the streets when it urged people to get off of the barricades and to march out to the factories. This reflected too much of a class-versus-class analysis. It failed to recognize the revolutionary potential of students and the lumpenproletariat whose terrain was the streets rather than industrial plants. Revolutionary activity could not be confined to any one terrain.

Second, some of the occupations of the university facilities, and particularly that at the School of Fine Arts in Paris, were seen as models for liberating and creative work. Passive occupations were rejected as contributing little to the spread of revolutionary consciousness. Under such conditions, time was on the side of the regime and such perceived counter-revolutionary forces as the Communist Party and the labor confederation in which it is the dominant force, the CGT. But active and creative occupations like that at the Fine Arts School were seen as prototypes for workers' occupations of plants in which the structure of work had to be changed.

Third, illegal action was crucial. Respect for the bounds of legality was capitulation to the bourgeois capitalistic state without extracting any cost from that state. Illegal action was crucial because it forced the state to demonstrate blatantly its repressiveness and declining legitimacy. Creative illegality raised the revolutionary consciousness of those who engaged in the action as well as those who observed it. Active participation in such activity was thought of as an example for others, who would either join the immediate action or be potential actors in the future actions. Thus any refusal to capitulate, any act of revolt against the power of the state, whether on the part of merchants, farmers, immigrants, young people, or nationalists, was to be supported and encouraged.

(2) The rejection of hierarchy

The GP's unwillingness to accept the Leninist conception of a vanguard party, or indeed any permanent organization with leadership functions, has already been discussed. This represented not only a difference between GP Maoism and the more hierarchical Maoist organizations in France, but also went well beyond what was preached or practiced by the Chinese Communist Party, even at the height of the Great Cultural Revolution. Moreover, the GP Maoists were bothered by another manifestation of hierarchy which they perceived in China, a cult of the personality surrounding Mao. For a time, *La Cause du Peuple* went so far as to drop the little picture of Mao from its masthead. Geismar explained to me that this was because it was too "foreign" for the workers to relate to. Finally, while the GP Maoists tried, they had difficulty accepting and defending Chinese foreign policy. This was especially true in regard to the war over Bangladesh.[67] In a 1975 interview which I had with Geismar, two years after he himself had left the movement, he reflected, "Maoism was not a religion for us."[68]

What did attract the GP movement to Maoism and led to their self-identification as Maoist was the "mass line." This they saw as the essential ingredient of the Cultural Revolution. While they perceived the masses as being cut off from any role in policy determination in the Soviet Union, where everything was resolved in a top-down fashion within the hierarchical party, they saw Mao as appealing to the masses to take an active role in the direction of society.

This they tried to emulate in France with their resistance to the conception of a permanent structure, and through the heavy reliance upon the *enquête* as the means of coming to know what people in specific contexts were thinking. This is why they also directed their efforts to contexts in which people were already beginning to take action to protest or to change their circumstances. They resented charges that they parachuted people in to initiate conflict. They claimed only to provide skills and shock troops on the side of those who were already in revolt. And they differentiated their own concept of a libertarian revolt (*liberté-révolte*) from that of hierarchical groups which engaged in "revolutionary" action only to seek power for themselves over the workers (*liberté-pouvoir*). They saw as examples of the latter both the Communist-Socialist electoral coalitions of the 1970s and what they perceived to be a "putschist" power grab by the *Parti Socialiste Unifié* (PSU) in 1968. In the GP's eyes, the PSU attempted simply to use the 1968 events, the student union which it controlled (UNEF), as well as the labor union in which it had many many members and supporters (CFDT), to put former Premier Pierre Mendes-France (the "French Kerensky") back in power.[69] And they did not hesitate to attack the Trotskyist *Ligue's* predecessor organization, the *Jeunesse Communiste Révolutionnaire* (JCR), for supporting this attempted seizure of state power (*liberté-pouvoir*).[70]

Another interesting aspect of the GP's attack upon hierarchy is their view of its relationship to division of labor and technology. In *Vers La Guerre civile,* Geismar and his comrades wrote that the basis of hierarchical structure and authority is the division of labor.[71] This position is consistent with that of Marx and Engels in their 1846 essay, *The German Ideology.*

However, unlike *Vive La Révolution,* these GP Maoist writers completely ignored what Marx and Engels pointed to as the earliest manifestation of the division of labor—the sexual act—and the earliest structural manifestation of hierarchical authority and exploitation—the family. Indeed, in the domain of sexual relations the GP Maoists exhibited a blind spot. The leaders who emerged at the national level were overwhelmingly males; the question of sexual relations was not openly examined within the movement; and, according to one woman informant, women within the movement on at least two occasions felt driven to confront the males over what they regarded as improper treatment.[72]

Ignoring the possibilities left open by Marx and Engels' work in *The German Ideology* and Engels' follow-up work on sexual exploitation in *The Origins of The Family, Private Property and the State,* the GP Maoists traced the detrimental effects of the division of labor only back to the gap between manual and intellectual labor.[73] It is this division of labor which they saw as the root cause of hierarchical structure and authority. And it is this gap which they saw as the particular job of revolutionary students to close.

This position, enunciated in 1969 in *Vers La Guerre civile,* is still not a terribly unorthodox position.[74] It served as the basis for much of the Cultural Revolution in China. What is original is that the position was subsequently developed into a broader attack in which capitalism, hierarchy, division of labor, and technology become fused. In an attack on the French labor organization which has pushed the concept of worker self-determination (*autogestion*) the furthest—the *Confédération Française Democratique du Travail* (CFDT)—GP Maoist Philippe Olivier wrote the following in the pages of *Les Temps Modernes* in 1972, three years after the *Vers La Guerre civile* had contented itself with a denunciation of the distinction between mental and physical labor.

> But then the question remains: why does the CFDT say that it is fighting against the structure of authority in the workshops, against hierarchy? You are not doing that at all: the CFDT is fighting against "the methods of governance" in the workshops. The power of the bosses, the authority in the workshop, these are "methods of governance." But no... the power of the bosses does not lie in the methods of governance, it lies in a system of organization of work of which one of the effects are the "method of authoritarian governance."
>
> To fight against "authority" in the workshop is to fight against the capitalist hierarchical system; and, in particular, against one of its ruses, "technology."[75]

Olivier accused both the Trotskyists and the French Communist Party of being insensitive to this dimension of the problem. Criticizing this neglect in the program of the Communist Party, which also then rejected *autogestion,* Olivier wrote:

> The criterion for evaluating the position of the classes is not only or even principally the number of nationalizations in

their program. The crucial criterion is their position on the division of labor, on the kind of "hierarchy" in the enterprise and thus on their general conception of social relationships.[76]

In the view of GP Maoism, Soviet-Eastern European socialism, which GP Maoism like all other variants of Maoism views as a form of "state capitalism," is just as susceptible to this kind of criticism as are the overtly capitalist Western societies. There, too, technology and division of labor are used to stratify and control workers, stratification being merely a control mechanism. It is pretended that some people are more capable than others of performing certain tasks which are more highly remunerative. "Capability" is usually based upon imputed intelligence. "Knowledge" is then rationed according to a predetermined, stratified hierarchical plan. The system of education plays a key role in this rationing pattern. It selectively feeds its students into the other social hierarchies, and it visibly stamps on them the level of knowledge of which they are capable.

Technical knowledge thus becomes a mystification, a technique of control, not a search for truth or human emancipation. What is unusual about the analysis of the GP movement is its tendency to fuse technology with division of labor. Whereas Marx saw technology as the phenomenon which would make possible the release of humanity from the detrimental effects of division of labor, the GP Maoists at least implied that technology and division of labor were necessary correlates which together served as the basis of both inequality and alienation. This analysis came closer to that of some earlier utopian wrtiers, such as Fourier, or to contemporary anti-technological writers such as Jacques Ellul and Theodore Roszak, than to that of any other Marxist group known to this writer.[77]

(3) The rejection of dichotomous class conflict

The analysis and structure of *Vers La Guerre civile* was modeled after two works in which Marx attempted to analyze events in France: *The Class Struggles in France,* dealing with the Revolution of 1848 and its aftermath, and *The Civil War in France,* dealing with the Commune of 1871.

In *Vers La Guerre civile* there is an almost Sorelian insistence on a clear separation between the workers and the bourgeoisie. "Hatred" of the bourgeoisie was a necessity. And when the GP Maoists entered the factories, the line of demarcation was drawn at the lowest management level. Foremen on the shop floor were made examples of. Security personnel and police were not treated as workers—as the unions and the Communist Party were wont to treat then—but as agents of the oppressors who had to assume responsibility for their acts.

But even in this early work, a reflection on the events of 1968 and a theoretical-strategic projection, there was one important and conscious deviation from Marx's position. Marx viewed the "lumpenproletariat"—the unrooted, unskilled, hopeless, and often criminal poor who were not a part of the industrial proletariat—as being thoroughly unreliable and ready recruits as security forces and goons to be used against the industrial proletariat. *Vers La Guerre civile,* however, maintained that at least some of the lumpenproletariat were ripe for revolutionary activity.

These were the young who were under-educated and usually unemployed---the young rebels, to go back to "James Dean" terminology, lacking a conscious cause but spontaneously fighting in the streets against state authority in 1968. Rather than let those people remain on the constant border between restlessness and criminality, the GP Maoists were convinced that their consciousness could be raised and that they could be turned into reliable fighters for the revolutionary cause. The GP Maoists viewed the young people and the immigrant workers—who were given the lowest wages, most unpleasant and dangerous tasks, and the least desirable living conditions—as the most harshly treated victims of France's political structures.

In practice, the GP Maoists deviated even further from a clear dichotomous conflict between the proletariat and the bourgeoisie. In 1969, the very year that *Vers La Guerre civile* was published, they mounted the barricades and fought the authorities side by side with small-town merchants, who were protesting what they felt was disadvantageous government policy. And they did this despite criticism—by Sartre himself in this instance—that the cause they were aiding could hardly be considered progressive.

The defense was adaptation to the superstructure of France to the point of aiding virtually any illegal and violent confrontation with the hierarchical regime. This is also what led them into the rural campaigns in western France, which have been discussed. Until the 1972 strike at Joint Français, they saw little industrial worker militancy in that region. But the farmers were hurting and taking action, and this was giving added impetus to a nationalistic movement. If this was where the people were, if they were prepared to do battle on these fronts, then this was where the Maoists felt that they belonged.

Two events which had a very profound effect upon GP Maoism's conceptualization of the struggle were the 1973 Lip strike and the overthrow of the Allende government in Chile by a brutal right-wing junta. The Lip strike—in which the workers of the Besançon watch factory took over the plant and produced and marketed the watches themselves—convinced most of the older GP Maoists that they were no longer needed within the industrial setting. The workers had demonstrated that they were quite capable of conducting their own battles.

From the Chilean coup they learned a lesson which was just the contrary of that of the *Ligue.* The *Ligue's* analysis was that the Chilean coup proved the necessity of revolutionary governments coming to power without bourgeois participation but with the support of an armed working class.

The GP Maoists, however, were convinced by the coup that the bourgeoisie could not simply be written off as an enemy to be controlled. They concluded from the Chilean experience that unless an important segment of the middle class was included in work for social change, it would destroy any such attempts.

The combined impact of Lip and Chile was the attempt by the older group of militants in the ex-GP and CDP to disband the final semblance of organizational coherence and to cease publishing the paper. They advocated emphasis upon "cultural work" spread very widely across social issues and milieux—from environmental issues, in which engineers and managers would be expected to take an interest, to concern for the problems faced by small shopkeepers.[78]

Thus a "liquidationism," similar to that of the UJCML in 1968, was attempted in 1973 and 1974. While most of the older militants who had formed the movement did disperse themselves, a number of younger militants saw no reason to disband because of Chile or Lip. If the older militants were simply burned out by the intensity of the activity and the repression, some of the younger recruits were not. The latter held together enough to continue publishing and distributing La Cause du Peuple on an irregular basis for at least four years after its founders left the paper.

Those older militants spread a bit all over, in a multitude of national, decentralized, and individual contexts. Some of the more militant and violently inclined among them probably joined with younger people in the formation of the Autonomes, a group devoted to property destruction and street fighting which made its formal appearance in 1977 and which subsequently turned its wrath on other groups on the Left. Some might also have been in the specific commando group which executed Tramoni, the killer of Pierre Overney, after Tramoni had been released from a two-year prison sentence in 1977.

It should be pointed out, however, that when that act was committed, and while it was applauded by La Cause du Peuple,[79] it was an isolated event in direct retaliation for the killing of a comrade. In France during this period, even with the appearance of the street-fighting Autonomes, there was nothing like the systematic killings and maimings that were being conducted by the Red Brigades in Italy or by the less-centralized anarchist groups in Germany.[80] For most of the older militants, the GP and ex-GP experience led them in nonviolent, reflective directions.

Geismar and some of the comrades with whom he was closest started a commune. They seem to have taken to heart the message of the old VLR and began experimenting with changes in family structure and living and work arrangements. They were revising Marx by taking him back in the direction of utopian socialism, particularly of the Fourierist variety.

Further, approximately half of the staff of the Left counter-culture daily newspaper *Libération,* which was begun at the end of 1972 under the omnipresent formal editorship of Sartre (who was also called upon to declare himself editor of *Tout* and *La Cause du Peuple* during periods of severe repression), was composed of former GP and ex-GP militants.[81] Here too, as Remi Hess points out, these people were involved in an endeavor which has a striking similarity to what *Vive la Révolution* attempted in its paper *Tout.*[82] By a different and much more arduous route, these people became part of a much larger counter-culture which the VLR attempted to introduce into France from 1969 to 1971, but which destroyed the group in the process.

Still other former GP Maoists went into the arts, the women's movement, the gay and lesbian movements, the environmental movement, or more nationally or ethnically specific movements. Some of the former Arab members have transferred their efforts to a completely Arab group which worked with immigrant workers, the *Mouvement des Travailleurs Arabes.* Former *CDP* editor Le Dantec has attempted to find a new political orientation in the historical thought and folk-culture of his native Brittany, wherein he believes lies an appropriate blend of concern for the collectivity and respect for the individual.

But the former GP members who soon were to get a brief flurry of publicity in the West were those who belonged to a group referred to as the *Nouveaux Philosophes,* or the "New Philosophers." Former GP Maoists such as André Glucksmann and Michel Le Bris (also a former CDP editor, along with Le Dantec) went from their modifications of traditional Marxism-Leninism as GP activists to more systematic criticisms of Marxism it-self—as intellectuals detached from and reflecting upon their past practice.[83] This, of course, was somewhat infuriating to others on the Left who had long felt that both their theory and practice were wrong in the first place, and that their own sudden realization of this would prove very useful to conservative forces in the Western world. Many came to see this as a vindication of Lenin, and as an ultimate proof of the petit-bourgeois nature of the movement all along. This is certainly one of the few things that Trotskyists, hierarchical Maoists, and the French Communist Party would all agree upon.

But whatever evaluation one might make of the whole phenomenon of GP Maoism, it is striking how distinctively French it was. In its refusal to fetter the workers with a hierarchical political organization, and in its emphasis upon action and clear cleavages within the industrial plant itself, it resembled the thought of the French anarcho-syndicalist theorist Georges Sorel. In the value which it placed upon rural life and the relationship between the land and the people who worked it, it shared the sentiments of the Genevan Rousseau and the French anarchist Proudhon. It shared both Proudhon's distaste for hierarchical authoritarianism and the negative view of the division of labor held by the French utopian thinker Fourier.

Both the various Trotskyist groups and the Marxist-Leninist Maoist groups have been universalistic in their theoretical orientations, and most have attempted to maintain or establish ties with the outside world. The GP movement represented a melange of early Marxism and Maoism with French utopianism and anarchism as well as with the French experience. Even the older generation of contemporary theorists who had an impact upon its origins, development, and termination (Althusser, Sartre, Foucault) were all French. And with the exception of the Chilean coup, all of the events which served as theoretical points of reference as the movement progressed were French. GP Maoism had virtually no ties with the outside world. Even the symbolic tie of the little picture of Mao on the masthead of *La Cause du Peuple* was removed for a while because it was too foreign.

GP Maoism was the most distinctively French movement within the French Far Left. Perhaps that is why it was able to strike the imagination of French people who were not even sure of what it was. It was a synthesis of their own radical heritage presented by a new generation.

CONCLUSION

The most interesting impact of the French political context on the Maoist movement is the one that I have just discussed, i.e., the impact which the non-Marxist radical heritage in France had upon the development of an anti-hierarchical variation of Maoism. This resulted in a dichotomous Maoist movement in France. Aside from contributing to this variant of Maoism and the resultant dichotomy, the French political context has also had important and divisive effects upon the Maoist groups in France in a number of tactical areas.

First, the Maoists have differed among themselves on the question of if and how to relate to the various labor confederations on the Left. Although the PCR(m-l) was tempted to push for second ballot support of the coalition of the Left in the 1978 elections, it backed down from that position when faced with the refusal and the ultimatum of its own coalition partner, the Maoist PCMLF. As of these elections, no Maoist group in France had given support to the major parties on the Left the way Trotskyists have in second ballot run-offs. At least some of the Maoists, however, have differentiated between parties and labor organizations, even if members of certain parties dominate certain unions. And we have seen a variety of attitudes adopted toward these structures. The "officially" (Chinese) recognized PCMLF—which used to write off the Communist-dominated CGT as too difficult to penetrate and not worth the effort—turned around on the issue in 1976, and began attempting to work from within it. The PCR(m-l), on the other hand, preferred to work within the CFDT. The UJCFML has taken an even harder anti-union position than the Trotskyist *Lutte Ouvrière*. Like *Lutte Ouvrière* it has created its own groups within the factories, but unlike the Trotskyist group it has refused to work in the unions at all. The GP, which grew out of an organization which had attempted to work within the CGT, turned against working within the established labor structures, and even engaged CGT militants in physical combat in their strongholds.

The strength of the major parties of the Left and the good possibility that they might win the 1978 elections had a severe impact upon the Maoists' behavior *vis-à-vis* elections. Prior to 1978, one could have contended that, with one minor regional exception, a defining characteristic of French Maoists, whether they were hierarchical or anti-hierarchical, was their total lack of interest in elections. But the attention and the level of excitement which was commanded by the prospect of the Communist and Socialist parties coming to power made it impossible for the two largest Maoist organizations to resist entry into the electoral fray. While the UJCFML refused to become involved in the political processes so attractive to the bourgeois parties, and to what it and the other Maoists viewed as revisionist parties on the Left, the PCMLF and the PCR(m-l) dove right in.

Finally, the tactic of violence and the emphasis upon illegality of the *Gauche Prolétarienne* was clearly influenced by the revolutionary heritage of France. The GP was, after all, born out of the latest of those major upheavals, the 1968 revolt. It seemed to feel a special responsibility to make up for the Maoist UJCML's refusal to participate in the revolt. Its actions were considerably more violent than those of Maoists who did not feel that they had to live down the fact that they had some association or lineal tie with an organization which had opposed the latest event in France's revolutionary heritage.

The orientation toward China has also been very divisive among French Maoists, and France's position as a militarily active power upon which China looks favorably has not made the situation any easier for French Maoists. The PCMLF, having been recognized as an official party of sorts by the Chinese, has given 100 per cent support to whomever is in control of the Chinese regime, and has accepted their position on French foreign policy. The PCR(m-l) has really tried to be loyal to the Chinese, but when the Chinese supported the French invasion of Zaire in 1978, it was just too much for the organization to bear. The UCFML, however, has been forthright in saying that its role is not to support the Chinese regime when it thinks that the regime is wrong. That hierarchical Maoist organization has rejected the Theory of the Three Worlds' contention that the USSR is more dangerous than the United States, has opposed NATO without equivocation, and has denounced French imperialism whether the Chinese approve or not.

The anti-hierarchical GP—which at the international level really only interested itself initially in the war in Indochina, and then shifted its major attention to the Palestinian issue—did derive some inspiration from what it thought were Chinese practices in the Cultural Revolution and in the organization of agriculture and industry. But the GP militants admittedly did not really know very much about China, and they were very eclectic in what they thought might be learned from the Chinese experience. In fact, what the Chinese actually were or were not doing or saying was much less important for the GP Maoists than what they thought might work in France. The Chinese revolution was, at best, "inspirationally suggestive" for them; the major inspiration was the mass line, regardless of whether or not that aspect of Maoism was being stressed in China. Of course, this entire question of orientation toward an actual regime or its external policies is one with which Trotskyists simply do not have to deal.

If French Maoists have been heavily affected by the French context, I would argue that they also have made an impact on that context in two specific areas. First, it was the GP initially and then the UCFML which took the lead in calling national and international attention to the plight of immigrant workers in France and in encouraging and supporting militancy among these workers. Secondly, the short-lived *Vive la Révolution* was in the vanguard in raising the sexual dimension of politics, and it produced militants who persisted in this direction through other feminist and gay structures.

Length of survival is not always a good indicator of the impact of a group. As the anti-hierarchical Maoists were fond of pointing out, their movements were mortal, and what mattered was how they used that scarce resource called time. In their own hyperactive way, they did manage to cram a lot into a relatively short period, and they did leave an imprint.

4
Trotskyism in the United States

The previous two chapters have examined Trotskyist and Maoist movements within the French political context. The first of those chapters focused on the impact of elements within French political culture upon a Trotskyist movement in which three major Trotskyist groups have maintained a relative parity. The second examined the impact of elements within that national political context upon a dichotomous Maoist movement.

The present chapter will investigate the phenomenon of Trotskyism within the political context of the United States. As we have seen in Chapter 1, while France and the United States are similar in that they are both capitalist industrialized societies, there are still considerable differences within the political contexts, or what many Marxists refer to as the political superstructures of those countries. This examination will also reveal a configuration of the movement which we have not seen in the cases of French Trotskyism and French Maoism. Rather than the tripartite parity of French Trotskyism and the dualistic character of French Maoism, a single party has, since its creation, remained the dominant force in U.S. Trotskyism.

Let us now turn to an examination of the historical dynamics which led to the creation of the Socialist Workers Party in the United States.

HISTORY: THE SWP DOES THE SPLITS

U.S. Trotskyism had its origin in 1928, at the Sixth World Congress of the Third International—or Comintern—in the Soviet Union. One of the delegates from the Communist Party of the United States at that Congress was James P. Cannon. Cannon was appointed to the Program Commission of the Congress. In what Cannon attributed to an accident, Trotsky's criticism of the draft program got into the translation hopper at the Congress and Cannon received a copy.[1] He and Maurice Spector, a delegate from the Canadian Communist Party, spent almost all of their time reading Trotsky's ideas. They made a pact with each other that they would go back to their respective countries and fight for these ideas, something which would have been useless at the Congress. Trotsky had already been exiled to Alma Ata, and the position of the Soviet leadership toward Trotsky's program was very clear.

Cannon was placed on the Program Commission largely as a consolation prize. For he was the leader of a faction of the U.S. Communist Party which was not in the majority, and the post which was most important to factional leaders was a seat on the Political Commission. That Commission, and not the Program Commission, would decide on the relative merits of the factional positions within the U.S. party.

Cannon had been one of the founding members of the U.S. Communist Party. Prior to the founding of the Communist Party he had been an organizer for the International Workers of the World, which he joined in 1911, and a member of the Socialist Party, which he joined during World War I. He opposed World War I, supported the Russian Revolution, and joined the faction of the Socialist Party which split off to form the Communist Party.

Within the Communist Party, Cannon was part of that faction which wanted to see a U.S.-born leadership rather than domination by the foreign language federations. He was also in the forefront of the faction which wanted to terminate underground work and convert the party entirely into a legal operation. Along with Charles Ruthenberg and Jay Lovestone, Cannon attempted in the early 1920s to liquidate the underground apparatus. They obtained a slight majority on the central committee of the party and, at the Fourth World Congress in Moscow in 1922, managed to rally the support of Lenin, Trotsky, Radek, and Bukharin for the Liquidators' position. This was the first time that Cannon met Trotsky.

The next year, 1923, Cannon found himself aligned with William Z. Foster against his former allies Lovestone and Ruthenberg. This time the issue was the support of the farm-labor movement. Ruthenberg and Lovestone were for it, but Cannon and Fostor were against an alliance with populism. Cannon claimed that "city boys, young intellectuals without experience in the class struggle," of which "Lovestone was the outstanding example," supported the farm-labor alliance, while the Cannon-Foster faction was backed by the trade unionists in the party (with whom Foster was particularly influential) and those who had been in the movement with Cannon from the beginning.[2]

While they formed alliances over specific issues, each of these leaders came to head factions within the Communist Party. Ruthenberg died in 1927, leaving Foster, Lovestone, and Cannon to develop a balance of power within the party. Cannon came to admit that the three of them fought over ideas that were not completely clear to them. But they did have a clear division of labor. The Lovestone faction, which had a slight majority and the support of the Soviet Union until 1929, ran the party apparatus. The Foster faction took care of trade-union work. The Cannon faction ran the International Labor Defense.

Each faction evolved differently. Cannon was attracted to Trotskyism, and took the initiative in founding the U.S. Trotskyist movement after
being expelled from the Communist Party in 1928. The Lovestone faction
tied its fate to that of Bukharin in the Soviet Union, and participated in the
purge of the Trotskyists while Stalin and Bukharin were still in an alliance.
In 1929, when that alliance was dissolved and Stalin became the unquestioned
leader of the Soviet party, Lovestone and his followers were purged from the
party in the United States. The Lovestone faction formed its own group,
which they sustained for ten years. They supported United States entry into
World War II and their leader, Jay Lovestone, converted to an intensely anti-
Communist Cold War position. Before retiring on June 30, 1975, he served
for many years as the head of the Department of International Affairs of the
AFL-CIO, and was the main foreign policy adviser to George Meany.[3] Foster
survived, was the party's presidential candidate in 1924, 1928, and 1932, and
replaced Earl Browder as general secretary in 1946.

Cannon had met Trotsky in 1922, but at that time Trotsky was part
of the Soviet elite. When Trotsky and Zinoviev were expelled from the
Soviet Communist Party in 1927 and the Russian leadership ordered a world-
wide campaign against Trotskyism, Lovestone and Foster became properly
anti-Trotskyist. Cannon refused to take any part in the dispute, admitting that
he did not understand what Trotskyism really was and what issues were involved. It was not until reading Trotsky's document in Moscow during the
following year that Cannon decided to become a Trotskyist.

Upon his return to the United States, Cannon first confided his commitment to Trotskyism to Rose Karsner. She was his first convert and was
also to become his wife. He then confided in two people with whom he
worked closely in the Communist Party and the International Labor Defense,
Max Shachtman and Martin Abern. These people too accepted the Trotskyist
program. In very short order the conversion of the Cannon faction to the
Trotskyist program came to the notice of the other leaders in the party. Cannon, Shachtman, and Abern were brought before the Central Control Commission of the party on charges of indiscipline. During the hearing they not
only admitted that they supported Trotsky's program but published the first
copy of the Trotskyist newspaper, *The Militant*. On October 27, 1928, the
three were expelled from the party and the International Labor Defense.

For a year the Trotskyists could not even afford an office. Nevertheless, they did succeed in making some converts in New York, Minneapolis,
and Chicago. In February of 1929, they published a platform for the group
they wished to create. In the spring of that year they made contact with Trotsky himself, who was then in Turkey. In May, they held the first National
Conference of the Left Opposition in the United States in Chicago, Illinois.

The words "Left Opposition" are important. For, following the example of the followers of Trotsky in the Soviet Union, the Trotskyists in the

United States refused to recognize the legitimacy of their expulsion from the Communist Party. They thus insisted upon their formal status as a faction within the Communist Party, even though they were powerless to participate in any way in the dynamics of the party.

Attending the Chicago Conference were thirty-one delegates and seventeen alternates from twelve cities. They represented a total membership of approximately one hundred. Thus, almost half of the Trotskyists in the United States were at that meeting.[4] They gave themselves the name the Communist League of America, Left Opposition of the Communist Party. The three major points in the program adopted by the Conference were: (1) that the CLA was a faction of the Communist Party and the Comintern; (2) that the CLA intended to attempt to reform the Soviet Union through the instrumentality of the Communist Party and the Comintern; and (3) that the CLA intended to work through the existing labor-union structure in the United States and would confine attempts at independent unionism only to the unorganized sectors. There was some opposition to the second part of the program among those who thought that the Soviet Union was beyond reform.[5]

Several months after the convention, the organization finally managed to rent a cheap office on New York's Third Avenue, and about a year after it to buy a mimeograph machine. And, despite its impoverishment, it kept putting out *The Militant*. But the years 1929 to 1933 were very difficult for the Trotskyists. This was largely due to the fact that in the Commtern's swing to a further left position—the shift which caused Lovestone to be replaced by Foster on orders of Stalin—the dissatisfaction which the Trotskyists had hoped would cause members of the Communist Party to come over to the Trotskyists was largely abated. The left-wing of the party was satisfied by the shift and the ouster of Lovestone.

Even before the Communist Party's shift to the moderate Popular Front position in 1935, the CLA began to break out of its isolation. In 1933 it began to reach out to labor and the unemployed more successfully than it had in the past. Its leaders participated in meetings of the unemployed. Cannon attended a conference of the Progressive Miners Union in Illinois, and the group played a major role in the 1933 strike of hotel workers. The latter turned out to be a fiasco. But the Trotskyists more than made up for this one by their crucial role in the Minneapolis Teamster strike of 1934.[6] This strike—led by Trotskyist teamsters in Minneapolis who were joined and assisted by Cannon and Shachtman—resulted in a major victory for the Minneapolis teamsters. It was a crucial landmark in the development of a powerful teamsters union in the United States.

While the Trotskyists were engaging in their labor activity, the Rev. A.J. Muste was organizing his Conference for Progressive Labor Action (CPLA) and the American Workers Party (AWP). Working through the

Unemployed League, Muste and his colleagues also successfully led the Auto-Lite strike in Toledo. This militant labor action attracted the Trotskyists, who in 1933-34 were becoming even further estranged from the Communist Party. Trotsky was convinced that the Comintern had completely capitulated in Germany and had permitted Hitler to come to power without resistance.

Max Shachtman was to reflect back upon this period and, in particular, the impact of Trotsky himself on his followers: "No movement that I know of was ever so dependent on a single leader for its ideas, its guidance, and its inspiration, as was the Trotskyist movement."[7] The first major strategic directive which Trotsky gave to the Trotskyist movements in all countries was to acknowledge a clear break with the Comintern and to concentrate on "mass work" independent of the Communist Party and on the establishment of relations with other organizations.

As we have seen, in France this took the form of "entrism" into the French Socialist Party (SFIO), in 1934. Trotsky himself pushed for this particular strategic move, but things evolved somewhat differently in the United States. In 1934, the Trotskyist CLA merged with Muste's AWP and became the Workers Party of the United States. A faction within the Trotskyist movement had opposed the merger. But the majority favored it. The Trotskyists were somewhat more numerous than the Muste people by this time. By 1933, the New York branch of the Trotskyists had attained its maximum allowable size of fifty, and a second New York branch was created.

But the merger with the Muste group really only deferred the issue of "entrism" in the United States. Six months after the merger, in June 1935, the issue was discussed at a plenary meeting of the Workers Party. The issue split the party. Muste opposed entrism, and was joined by two leaders of the old Trotskyist group, Martin Abern and Hugo Oehler. Abern was one of the founders of U.S. Trotskyism, along with Cannon and Shachtman. Oehler had assumed prominence in the Trotskyist group by opposing the merger with the Muste forces and by supporting Naville's opposition to entry into the French SFIO. Oehler now joined with Muste in opposing entry into the American Socialist Party.

Cannon claims that he, Shachtman, and James Burnham, who was a new entrant into the combined organization, simply wanted to leave the question open at the June plenum.[8] Given the events in France and their subsequent actions, it is rather clear that they wanted to leave the question open because they were in the minority. They were able to transform their minority into a majority very quickly. Oehler continued to fight on the issue, and asked for permission to set up an independent faction within the party. Shachtman wrote the position paper on why this request had to be denied. Oehler persisted in his opposition, despite warnings from Muste that they had to accept the majority position. Oehler and his followers were expelled for breaking discipline.

Like Communist parties around the world, the U.S. Communist Party was terminating its ultra-left stance of the "Third Period," during which it characterized all other groups of the Left as "social fascists." While the Communists were moderating their position, there was considerable pressure on the Socialist Party to move to the left. Just as in France, much of the pressure to push the Socialist Party in a revolutionary direction came from the youth group, the Young Peoples' Socialist League (YPSL). Cannon, Shachtman, and Burnham were bothered by the fact that these young people were not coming into the Trotskyist movement but were going into the Socialist Party instead. The same was true of a number of workers. They concluded that, if this newly radicalized generation was not coming into the Workers Party, the Workers Party would have to go to them.

In March 1936, three months after the pro-Roosevelt right-wing of the Socialist Party quit, the Convention of the Workers Party voted to take "the French Turn." The negotiations were facilitated by Professor Sidney Hook, who acted as a mediator and conciliator between the two groups.[9] Muste and Abern still opposed the entrist idea, but they had been badly burned when people whom they had defended against charges of Stalinism quit the Trotskyist movement and went over to the Communist Party. The agreement was that the Trotskyists would go into the Socialist Party as individuals, and that any section of the Socialist Party had the right to refuse membership to anyone it did not want. The Trotskyists also gave up the right to continue their own press. *The Militant* ceased publication. Of course, Trotsky, who was living in France at the time, was overseeing the entire operation, just as he had called the shots on the entry into the SFIO.

A number of very important tasks were accomplished by the Trotskyists while they were within the Socialist Party. The access to a wide segment of liberals, intellectuals, and quasi-radicals permitted them to set up the Trotsky Defense Committee with the philosopher, John Dewey, as chairman. This committee declared Trotsky innocent of the crimes with which he had been charged by Stalin. The Trotskyists were active in the campaign of support for the Spanish republicans during the Spanish Civil War. They supported the maritime strike of 1936-37 and gained some influence in the maritime labor movement as a result. They made gains within the UAW. And—despite the ban on a separate press—they inherited the *Socialist Appeal,* which Albert Goldman was publishing in Chicago, and in California they published *Labor Action,* which was nominally a Socialist Party publication.

In the winter of 1937 they went further. They formally declared themselves to be a faction of the Socialist Party and they called a meeting in Chicago of all those who supported the programs of *Socialist Appeal.* By March of 1937 it was obvious that the leaders of the Socialist Party were ready to move for the expulsion of the Trotskyists. At his urging, Trotsky's followers attempted to remain in the party. Cannon contends that Norman Thomas actually agreed to delay a confrontation. The purge came in stages. First, all internal publications were banned. *Socialist Appeal* and *Labor Action* were thus lost. The Trotskyists instituted a system of circulating mimeographed "personal" letters. The Socialist Party then banned the consideration of resolutions on disputed questions by the local branches. This prevented the Trotskyists from seeking local support against the positions of the national leadership. This provoked the Trotskyists to call a meeting of the "National Committee" of their faction in June 1937 in New York. The response to this was the wholesale expulsion of the Trotskyists from the Socialist Party, starting with the New York group itself.

Cannon defended the strategy of entry into the Socialist Party on the basis of the accomplishments already mentioned plus two others. First, he claimed that the Trotskyists doubled their membership as a result of entry, bringing over to their movement a majority of YPSLs.[10] Shachtman has contended that prior to the merger with Muste's AWP, the Trotskyists were short of five hundred members nationally. He contended further that after the merger there were not quite 1,000 members in the combined organization before entry into the Socialist Party.[11] If both Cannon and Shachtman are correct, the Trotskyists emerged from the period of with something under 2,000 members.

A second justification for the policy of entry was that the Trotskyists left the Socialist Party a shambles. According to Cannon:

> [W]hen the Socialist Party expelled us and when we retaliated
> by forming an independent party of our own, the Socialist
> Party had dealt itself a death blow. Since then the SP has
> progressively disintegrated until it has virtually lost any sem-
> blance of influence in any party [sic] of the labor movement.
> Our work in the Socialist Party contributed to that. Comrade
> Trotsky remarked about that later, when we were talking with
> him about the total result of our entry into the Socialist Party
> and the pitiful state of its organization afterward. He said that
> alone would have justified the entry into the organization even
> if we hadn't gained a single new member.
>
> Partly as a result of our experience in the Socialist Party and
> our fight in there, the Socialist Party was put on the side lines.
> This was a great achievement, because it was an obstacle in the
> path of building a revolutionary party. The problem is not
> merely one of building a revolutionary party, but of clearing
> obstacles from its path. Every other party is a rival. Every
> other party is an obstacle.[12]

Muste saw the situation differently. He had opposed the "French Turn" in the United States because he felt that it "would not be morally justifiable or politically sound."[13] Muste claimed that before the merger of his movement with the Trotskyists, he had expressed this conviction and was assured that there was no thought of applying the tactic to the United States.[14]

Muste added:

> James Cannon, the leading American Trotskyist, told a reporter some years later [after the expulsion] that he remembers telling Trotsky about the weakened condition in which his forces had left the Socialist Party and that "Comrade Trotsky said that that alone would have justified our entry into the organization even if we hadn't gained a single member." To me this statement is one of many proofs that in his later years the brilliant Trotsky almost completely lost touch with reality.[15]

Relating a conversation which Muste himself had with Trotsky in Norway, Muste went on to say: "At the end of our talks, somewhat to my surprise, he [Trotsky] said to me in effect that an American version of the 'French Turn' was not the right tactic, but it had been done and I should not let it drive me out of the party to which I had too much to give."[16]

Trotsky's attempt to convince Muste fell on deaf ears, for Muste not only shared Shachtman's view that Trotsky exerted tremendous power over his followers but had come to judge Trotsky's use of that power very negatively: "Trotsky decided that his followers should join the Socialist Party as a faction which would bore from within. He ordered them to do so, and I say 'ordered' deliberately because I became convinced that though in many respects very different from Stalin, Trotsky was no less a dictator in his own party than Stalin was in his."[17] Needless to say, the expulsion from the Socialist Party terminated the relationship between the Trotskyists and Muste and his followers (Muste, himself, refers to them as "Musteites"[18]) as well as between the Trotskyists and the Socialists.

The Trotskyists immediately began republishing the *Socialist Appeal,* and set up a "National Committee of the Expelled Branches." They held a convention of the expelled branches in Chicago from December 31, 1937 to January 1, 1938. On that New Year's Day, the organization which persists to the present day, the Socialist Workers Party (SWP), was officially born. This was eight months before the September 1938 formation of the Fourth International.

Since the creation of the SWP, several factors have distinguished the history of U.S. Trotskyism from that of French Trotskyism. First, while there was intense factionalism which resulted in periodic splits, Cannon's majority position—which was completely supportive of Trotsky and the international majority until the early 1950s—was never really threatened. Second, despite the splitting off of factions and the formation of non-Trotskyist rival groups in the forties and fifties as well as rival Trotskyist groups in the sixties, the hegemony of the SWP over U.S. Trotskyism was never threatened. There is nothing like the relative parity in size between the French *Ligue,* OCI, and *Lutte Ouvrière* in the United States. Finally, the SWP has been subjected to a severe and relentless repression by those who control the political system, the parallel of which can only be found in France during the World War II Occupation.

There have been four major splits in the party. They occurred in 1939, 1952-53, 1962-63, and 1964-65. The first split occurred after the Hitler-Stalin Pact in 1939, the Soviet intrusion into Poland, and the expected move into Finland, a move which materialized during the dispute. The basic question was whether or not to support the Soviet Union. The position of the majority, represented by Cannon, was to accept Trotsky's position that despite the fact that the Soviet Union was a "degenerated workers' state" it was still the only workers' state in existence, and should still be supported in the hope of eventual rectification. The minority position was presented to the party in the Internal Bulletin of January 1939 in a document entitled "The War and Bureaucratic Conservatism."[19] It argued that the new strategy and actions of the Soviet Union were not defensible. The document went further, charging Cannon and his followers with acting against the minority in a bureaucratic manner, hostility toward the intellectuals in the party, and the institution of a leadership cult. The leader in question was Cannon, not Trotsky, who still managed to inspire awe in the U.S. section even in the face of severe disagreement.

While the signatories represented a numerical minority within the party, they were the most prominent builders of the Trotskyist movement, with the exception of Cannon. The four signers, all members of the Political Committee of the party, were Abern, Shachtman, Burnham, and Bern. The first two of these people, it will be recalled, were Cannon's second and third recruits to Trotskyism after he returned from the Comintern's World Congress in 1928.

Abern had been a thorn in the sides of Cannon and Shachtman going back to his alliance with Muste and Oehler in opposition to entry into the Socialist Party. Along with Muste, however, he had accepted party discipline and avoided expulsion. In this case Shachtman had written the formal motion warning the minority of the possible consequences of breaking discipline and refusing Oehler's request for the creation of an independent faction. At the April 1940 SWP convention, just five years later, Shachtman was to make the very same request.

Burnham was always a problem for Cannon and Shachtman. He was an academic who came into the party at the time of the merger with the Musteites. Cannon and Shachtman had attempted to convince him to devote full time to party matters and to leave his academic position. They obviously admired his talents. But Burnham was torn not only between the tension of two different life-styles—one as dedicated member of a proletarian party and the other as middle-class academic—but also by his attraction to socialism as a body of moral precepts, and by his inability to accept Marxism-Leninism as a "science" with epistemological commitments which ran counter to his own more positive ones.

Moreover, Shachtman began to question his own commitment to Marxism-Leninism. In response to an article which the two of them published, Trotsky himself wrote "A Petty Bourgeois Opposition in the Socialist Workers Party" in December 1939. Here Trotsky attempted to demonstrate that the position which Burnham and Shachtman were taking on the Soviet Union was an error that was rooted in their rejection of the dialectic. Because of this they came to a completely negative definition of the Soviet state: "not a workers' and not a bourgeois state."[20] A month later, in January 1940, Trotsky addressed an open letter more directly to Burnham in which he attempted to explicate in further depth what dialectical reasoning was and where he felt Burnham had gone wrong. Trotsky expressed the hope that they could come to an agreement on "the basis of these principles" and pledged himself to join with Burnham in combatting bureaucratism and conservatism (charges which Burnham had levied against Cannon) wherever they were found.[21]

Burnham replied a month later in his stinging "Science and Style: A Reply to Comrade Trotsky." The work is divided into two parts. The first is a complete rejection of dialectics. He writes:

> [T]here is no sense at all in which dialectics (even if dialectics were not, as it is, scientifically meaningless) is fundamental in politics, none at all. An opinion on dialectics is no more fundamental for politics than an opinion on non-Euclidean geometry or relativity physics.[22]

Burnham thus saw the resort to dialectics as an obfuscation of the concrete situation which was going on in the Soviet Union, Poland, and Finland. The second part of the essay is an attack upon the operation of the SWP. Cannon's majority is referred to as "the rotten clique of Cannon"[23] and it is attacked for its "anti-metropolitan, anti-intellectual prejudices which have exclusively reactionary effects."[24] Trotsky himself is accused by Burnham of an anti-Semitic slur because Trotsky had chastized Shachtman for attempting to conduct the revolution from the Bronx. He explained to Trotsky that Bronx meant "Jew" in the United States and that it was likely to be so read in the party.[25]

The showdown came at the next SWP Convention, held in April 1940. The majority group led by Cannon reaffirmed its commitment to the international program of the Fourth International, a program in support of the Soviet Union. The minority was suspended from the party until it could comply with party discipline. In fact, the minority had already formed a new party, the Workers Party, and had rented quarters for it. They also took with them the SWP's theoretical organ, *New International*. But in the next month—specifically, on May 21, 1941—Burnham declared himself a non-Marxist and someone not cut out for political organizational work, much less leadership.[26] He resigned from the new party and began his evolution to the Far Right. He developed a theory that a new managerial "class" had taken over the Soviet Union and was assuming power in all of the industrial countries. He became a militant anti-Communist, testified against the new party at a Department of Justice hearing on "subversion" in the 1950s, and finally became an editor of *The National Review*.[27] Shachtman himself moved further to the right. He changed the name of the Workers Party to the Independent Socialist League and kept it going until 1958, when he brought it into the Socialist Party. There he joined the right-wing, social democratic League for Industrial Democracy group. He backed both the Bay of Pigs invasion in Cuba and the U.S. military intervention in Vietnam. He was an adviser to the president of the American Federation of Teachers, Albert Shanker, and, like Shanker, fought against local control of schools by minorities in New York City. In 1972, the year of his death, Shachtman supported the Humphrey forces against the McGovern forces within the Democratic Party.[28] This is the kind of posture which is common now among those radicalized in the 1930s, but which is so difficult for those radicalized in the 1960s and 1970s to accept coming from self-proclaimed socialists. It served to discredit the social democratic alternative to the Far Left in the eyes of many among the generation of radicals politicized in the sixties and seventies.

In fact, some of Shachtman's followers were unable to accept his evolution. In 1967, a group of them split with Shachtman and the Socialist Party to create the Independent Socialist Clubs of America. In 1969 the name was changed to International Socialists. This organization—which still exists and which publishes a weekly newspaper, *Workers' Power*—considers itself to be a revolutionary rather than a social democratic organization. It encourages militancy within the trade union movement and works toward the creation of a revolutionary party which would facilitate a workers' revolution without ruling over the workers. It rejects "both capitalism and bureaucratic collectivism (the system of dictatorship in Russia, China, and the other so-called 'Communist' societies)."[29] International Socialists (IS) no longer make any specific reference to Trotsky in identifying themselves or their current of thought. They entered the Students for a Democratic Society and attempted to recruit therein. They participated in the anti-war movement, supporting "popular Revolution" in Vietnam but also urging "the rejection by the masses involved in that revolution of the Communist leadership of the NLF."[30]

In going over the documents and letters written at the time, and Cannon's reflections on the period—as well as the more contemporary accounts published by the SWP—very different pictures of these three people emerge. Only Burnham is credited with original thought. Shachtman is referred to as the "attorney" for other people. He is pictured as only speaking for the theoretical propositions developed by others, first those of Trotsky and Cannon, then those of Burnham. An internal document which has been made public relates: "Shachtman shortly announced his conversion to a caricature of Burnham's view; that is that the Stalinist regime in the Soviet Union represented 'bureaucratic collectivism'. "[31] Of the three, Abern is pictured as the most ideologically and theoretically vacuous. He is pictured as a Machiavellian schemer, whose sole interest was in forming alliances in order to cut away at Cannon's power. Some of his followers, however, in combination with other segments in the Workers Party, came to the conclusion that the Soviet Union represented "state capitalism," an interpretation which would later be advanced by Maoists. Curiously, some of them came back into the SWP as an identifiable tendency within the party in 1947.

The second internal crisis of the SWP occurred in 1952 and 1953. But between the Convention of 1940 and the internal crisis of the fifties, the SWP was subjected to severe repression by the Roosevelt Administration, in collusion with the national Teamster leadership under Daniel J. Tobin. Tobin was supporting Roosevelt's movement toward entry into the Second World War. The Communist Party supported entry into the war, and saw this entry as supportive of the Soviet Union. The Socialist Party opposed American entry. The SWP—in conformity with the anti-war position of the Fourth International, and the refusal of French Trotskyists to enter the Resistance even during the Occupation—opposed American participation in the war. While the SWP was quite willing to support the Soviet and Chinese resistance against what it regarded as fascist aggression, it took the Fourth International position that American participation would not be designed to stamp out fascism but to further the cause of international capitalism and to contain the Soviet Union. The SWP opposed conscription for the war but cautioned its members and supporters against draft resistance. It favored entering the armed forces and insisting upon their rights to advocate their commitments.

Teamster Local 544 in Minneapolis was under Trotskyist leadership. Moreover, the members supported the position of the leadership that they should oppose Roosevelt's movement toward entry into the war. Aside from being the president of the AFL-affiliated Teamsters International Brotherhood, Daniel Tobin had chaired the Labor Division of the National Democratic

Campaign Committee during the elections of 1932, 1936, and 1940 and had served as an Administrative Assistant to FDR from July to October 1940. In fact, Tobin's service to the Democrats went back as far as Woodrow Wilson, another Democratic president under whom the Left was severely repressed.

When Tobin moved to bring Local 544 under control by placing the union in receivership under an appointed leader with virtually unlimited power, the four thousand members held an election (June 9, 1941) and voted to disaffiliate from the AFL Brotherhood and accept a charter from the CIO.[32] Tobin telegraphed Roosevelt for help. Roosevelt's secretary, Stephen Early, related at a press conference several days later that: "When I advised the President of Tobin's representations this morning he asked me to immediately have the government departments and agencies interested in the matter notified."[33]

Approximately two weeks later, FBI agents raided the SWP office in Minneapolis and St. Paul and took away vast quantities of literature. On July 15, a federal grand jury indicted twenty-eight members of Local 544 and the SWP, including James Cannon, on two counts. Count one alleged a "conspiracy to overthrow the government by force and violence."[34] This indictment was based upon an anti-slave-holder statute enacted during the Civil War in 1861. The second count was the first attempt to apply the Smith Act, an act opposed by the AFL, the CIO, and the American Civil Liberties Union. But Roosevelt had signed it during the previous year (1940), and a repressive piece of legislation introduced by the anti-labor and racist Representative Howard W. Smith (D-Va.) was signed by Roosevelt and used to bail his labor leader friend Tobin out of difficulty—as well as to silence opponents of his decision to enter the war.[35]

All of the defendants were acquitted on the first count. But the Smith Act proved to be a more effective weapon. Eighteen of the defendants were convicted, and served prison sentences of from twelve to eighteen months. This was only the beginning of a systematic campaign to both destroy the SWP and clear the labor movement of anyone with political ideas to the left of the Democratic Party.[36]

These were tough times. Because of appeals, the party leaders did not serve their prison sentences until 1944 and 1945. Shortly after they were released, the Cold War began and domestic repression was intensified. The number of people who were willing to stay in and pay the price of the repression dwindled. It was in this atmosphere that the split in 1952 and 1953 came about.

The split which occurred in the fifties is the most difficult to pin down precisely. First, the two sides present different interpretations of what the intentions of the minority really were. Second, the situation was complicated by disagreements which were occurring among the various sections of the Trotskyist movement at the international level.

The interpretation which Cannon and his present followers in the SWP give to the split in the fifties is that the minority faction buckled under the pressure of the repression, and opposed putting up presidential candidates and local candidates if signed petitions were required to get them on the ballot. Viewed through the eyes of Cannon and his supporters, the minority was divided into two distinct factions. First there were the "Cochranites proper," Michigan trade-unionists who were heavily influenced by Bert Cochran. This group—again, in the eyes of the followers of Cannon—simply wanted to get the repression off their backs, and gave no consideration to further ties with the Communist Party which was itself undergoing very severe repression. The New York group, however, was suspected of moving toward closer ties with members of the Communist Party.[37]

It is admitted that the latter group comprised only 30 to 40 per cent of the minority faction. Both groups were viewed as "liquidationists," i.e., as intending to terminate the existence of the SWP as a political party as Cannon and his followers understood it, but the New York group was viewed as especially dangerous.

It will be recalled from our discussion of French Trotskyism that Pablo had used his power in the Fourth International to push the French PCI into a policy of *entrisme* into the French Communist Party in 1952. This was part of an international entrist strategy devised by Pablo, who was then the General Secretary of the Fourth International. The strategy was modelled after the Trotsky-conceived entrism of the thirties. But there was a difference. For Trotsky, the entrism of the thirties was a temporary expedient applied under unusual circumstances. For Pablo, entrism was to be a policy which would last at least through the war between the USSR and the United States which he thought to be inevitable. By entering Stalinist organizations, he hoped that the Trotskyists would have some leverage after the international defeat of capitalism. Many of the national sections which had accepted Trotsky's strategy in the thirties simply could not accept these ideas, and in 1953 the Fourth International was split into two groups, the International Committee of the Fourth International and the International Secretariat of the Fourth International. The International Committee was comprised of only a few national sections, including the French Lambertists (now the OCI), the British Healyite Socialist Labour League, and the SWP. The SWP was not to re-enter the International Secretariat until 1963.

The reason that Cannon took this factional split so seriously is that he was convinced that the New York group was complicit with Pablo, and that what they were up to was a policy of entrism into the Communist Party of the United States.

In the major document produced by the minority, "The Roots of the

Party Crisis—Its Causes and Solution," the faction did not address itself to the problem of entrism *a la* Pablo. It did, however, accuse the majority of "Stalinophobia," which it saw as "essentially a petty bourgeois poison."[38] The more substantive charge was that the strong anti-Stalinist position of the SWP's majority was leading to the isolation of the party. It accused Cannon of turning the party into a group almost solely concerned with internal education. This was what the document termed the "independence of the party school."[39] It argued that this "Stalinophobia" also led to incorrect policy decisions. Among these were: the refusal to side with the left-wing in the United Auto Workers because of the influence of Communist Party members, an initial both-sides-be-damned attitude toward the Korean War, and initial hesitations to come to the defense of Communists who were now being tried by the government, as well as to the defense of the Rosenbergs. The minority also took a somewhat more positive view of the nature of the Soviet Union and its Eastern European neighbors.[40]

The minority argued that instead of investing its resources almost exclusively in the internal education of a leadership cadre of the SWP, the party should look outward more. It argued for an active educational and recruitment campaign directed toward workers, Blacks, students, and members of other parties on the Left. It also argued that while the creation of a more broadly aggregative labor party was part of the SWP's platform, Cannon was only paying periodic lip-service to this essential move.

Finally, the minority threw back the charge of "liquidationist" at the majority. Like the PCI in France, the SWP was dwindling in numbers. It was going nowhere in the labor movement and, despite its constant electoral campaigning, it remained mostly unknown. Under these conditions, argued the minority, it was the majority under Cannon which was effectively liquidating the party. In May of 1953 a final vote was taken at a full meeting of the National Committee. The program of the minority lost, 20 to 80 per cent. The minority then engaged in a number of acts which the majority interpreted as violations of party discipline, and they were expelled.[41] The party continued its decline in membership. It reached a low point of somewhere be-tween 50 and a couple of hundred members during the heyday of McCarthyism.

In 1962, the Socialist Workers Party began its move back into the International Secretariat of the Fourth International. This was culminated in the so-called Re-unification Congress of the Fourth International, held in 1963. Whereas the Cannonist majority had to contend with a minority faction which it regarded as Pablist in 1952 and 1953, a decade later it had to deal with a minority which perceived the Cannonists as having gone over to Pablism. Indeed, in order to bring about the reunification, the differences with the British Socialist Labour League (SLL) and the French Lambertist PCI (soon to become the OCI)—which were members of the International Committee—were not emphasized, and the differences with the Pablist

International Secretariat were minimized.

Playing a crucial role in the reconciliation of the SWP with the International Secretariat of the Fourth International was the issue of Cuba. The International Committee saw little difference between Castroism in Cuba and the other Third World movements which had excited the Pablists over the last decade. The majority within the SWP, however, felt that the Cuban Revolution was substantially different in that it was creating a true workers' state. It was thus not to be scorned. The British SLL (now called the Workers Revolutionary Party), headed by Gerry Healy, came into severe conflict with the SWP over the Cuban issue.

But within the SWP itself there was the Minority Tendency, which opposed the reversion to what it felt was Pablism, i.e., the optimistic view of the Cuban Revolution and the movement toward reconciliation with the International Secretariat. To further subdivide, within the Minority Tendency there were two discernible groups which were to fall out among themselves and subsequently go their separate ways.

First, there was the Revolutionary Tendency. Their interpretation of the Cuban Revolution was that it had resulted in a "deformed workers state which was compelled to embrace that ersatz Marxism which is the necessary ideological reflection of a Stalinist bureaucracy, however newly fledged."[42] This group was expelled from the SWP in 1963. By this time it had fallen out with the other tendency in the minority led by Tim Wohlforth, one of the founders and the first national secretary of the SWP's youth affiliate, the Young Socialist Alliance. The Revolutionary Tendency accused the Wohlforth group of feeding documentation to the leadership of the Majority Tendency which was designed to show that the Revolutionary Tendency was planning to split the SWP. Whether or not this was the case or whether such documentation was a causal factor, the Revolutionary Tendency was indeed expelled, despite its denials of any intention to split the party.[43] That tendency now operates as a separate organization under the name of Spartacist League, which publishes a newspaper called *Workers Vanguard.*

Approximately a year later, the Wohlforth group was expelled for violating discipline. The Spartacists accused Wohlforth of deliberately manipulating his own group's expulsion from the SWP so as to present his followers with a fait accompli in order to minimize opposition to his planned affiliation with the International Committee.[44] Wohlforth's group became known as the Workers League and it publishes a paper called the *Bulletin.*

In fact, both the Sparticist League and the Workers League initially had a sympathizing affiliation with the International Committee. Gerry Healy, who was the head of the British section and the most powerful leader of the Inter-national Committee, encouraged a unification of the two groups. When this failed—because of severe disagreement over Cuba and whether or not Pablism had been definitively "smashed"—Healy expelled the Spartacist

League from the International in 1966. Wohlforth's Workers League had taken positions much closer to Healy's own. But, in the fall of 1974, Healy became convinced that one of Wohlforth's closest friends and collaborators within the Workers League was a CIA agent. When Wohlforth refused to go along with her purging, both he and the accused CIA agent, Nancy Fields,[45] were forced out of the Workers League. Both were accepted back into the SWP.[46]

The Workers League has been even more severe in its criticism of Cuba than have the Spartacists. The Workers League has pointed with derision to Castro's support of the Soviet invasion of Czechoslovakia in 1968. It accused Castro of ignoring both the uprising in France and the severe repression against the Black Panthers in the United States in the same year, as well as of extending compliments to the Mexican government which had slaughtered hundreds of opposition students.[47] And by refusing to consider the Castro government a workers' government in any sense of the term, it has —"more or less shamefacedly," according to the Spartacist League, which sees Cuba as a deformed workers' state[48]—actually urged that Cuba under Castro is still in the capitalist orbit. In the words of Tim Wohlforth:

> The task of the socialist revolution in a backward country is to carry through the tasks of the bourgeois democratic revolution by proletarian methods, going over to socialist measures...
> The central economic task in Cuba is to free that country from its dependence on the one export crop of sugar and developing a more balanced economy through an industrialization programme (*sic*). Such economic plans require the political power of the working class in Cuba, oriented towards an international revolutionary struggle against imperialism. Castro has openly abandoned even an attempt at this, placing even greater emphasis on the sugar crop than Batista. The result is that the living standards of the Cuban people, to the extent that they are not subsidized by the Soviet Union, are completely dependent upon the world price of sugar. This alone shows the dependence of Cuba on world capitalism, a problem qualitatively different from those facing the deformed workers' states, and illustrating once again that the petty-bourgeois nationalists, statism or no, Soviet aid or no, are unable to carry forward the bourgeois democratic revolution. To call Cuba a workers' state is to make a travesty of what we are fighting for— socialism itself.[49]

Wohlforth, writing in 1970 when the pamphlet was first published, saw similarities in the positions of Castro and Ben Bella just before the fall of the latter. Pablo, it will be recalled, supported the Algerian FLN before its victory and served as an economic adviser to Ben Bella after that victory. Thus, despite their differences over how specifically to categorize the Cuban Revolution, both the Spartacist League and the Workers League looked for more immediate change in the industrialized countries and a very long road, at best, for the Third World's transition to socialism.

Healy's role in the purge of Wohlforth, the Workers League's national secretary for over a decade, was remarkable. Within a period of three years, Healy succeeded in both alienating the French OCI and decapitating the Workers League in the United States. While his Workers Revolutionary Party in Britain still had a larger membership than the British affiliate of the United Secretariat, and while he had been able to publish a daily paper with only a brief interruption since October 1969,[50] Healy's international following in the late 1970s dwindled to almost nothing, and the American Workers League was debilitated. In a complete about-face, the International Committee moved from a position of insisting on a high level of industrial development as a prerequisite for a successful revolution—a position which it maintained for over two decades—to a more recent posture of staunch supporter of the Palestine Liberation Organization and ardent defender of the Qadhafi regime in Libya. The latter position has not been particularly helpful to the Workers League in the United States, which was now accused of a reversion to Pablism by the Spartacists. Moreover, aside from the other resources at the disposal of the British Healyites which the American section lacks, it has no resource comparable to actress Vanessa Redgrave to call public attention to its positions.

In addition to the SWP and the Spartacists and Workers Leagues, there is a tiny Trotskyist group in the United States which has an interesting French connection. It was formed in 1971 by defectors from the Spartacist League and people from the civil rights movement. It operates only in Baltimore and Detroit where it publishes a paper called *Spark*. While it is not even a national group in the United States, it does have ties with *Lutte Ouvrière* in France, and it follows the same pattern of organization in the factories. It too simply goes by the name of its paper.

An additional group which deserves some attention is one which resulted from a relatively small number of defections from the SWP. This is the Workers World Party (WWP), which was created in 1959 by Sam Marcy and about a dozen others who had done trade union work within the SWP. Their bases of dissatisfaction were broader than those of the people who were to form the two leagues several years later. They objected to the SWP's initial hesitancy regarding the Cuban Revolution, its negative attitude toward China, its condemnation of the Soviet Union for going into Hungary in 1956, and the initiatives which the SWP was beginning to take to attract young people and particularly students. Despite the latter objection, the WWP would in 1962 create its own youth affiliate, Youth Against War and Fascism (YAWF), one of the most confrontation-oriented of the youth movements of the sixties and the only one to support the Weatherman's 1969 "Days of Rage."

The WWP presents us with an interesting case of political ambiguity over what can and cannot be considered to be "Trotskyist." Although its leaders respond that they consider their organization to be Trotskyist when asked the question point-blank, there is no statement of principles which publicly commits the party to Trotsky's ideas. Among their pamphlets which I have read on issues which would seem to invite reference to Trotsky, I have found a reference to him in only one, and that was a passage which remarked on the identity of viewpoint between Trotsky and Stalin on the need to emphasize productivity in a backward country.[51] When pre-Stalinist Russia is under discussion, reference is made to Lenin and his positions but not to Trotsky. The leaders with whom I have talked explain this by saying that: (1) they do not want to resurrect the old Stalin-Trotsky debates; (2) most people would not understand them anyway; (3) if they publicly proclaim themselves to be Trotskyist, they might be mistaken for the larger and better known SWP; and (4) the internal life of the party is more clearly Trotskyist than its external appearance. However, there is no established educational program in Trotskyism for recruits, and while people are urged to read Trotsky's works, it is not required.

In regard to concrete positions, the WWP takes four positions that none of the groups which clearly fly the banner of Trotskyism in France or the United States take. First, it publicly characterizes the USSR, China, Cuba, Angola, North Korea, and Vietnam as "socialist" states. Second, it views Stalin in the same more favorable light that Mao did, arguing that while Stalin made "mistakes" and "errors"[52] in his repressive behavior and development of a bureaucracy, his centralized rule was better than Khrushchev's attempts at de-Stalinization through decentralization. In its literature on this, the WWP does not go into the theoretical differences which Trotsky drew between permanent revolution and socialism in one country, and it does not argue that Stalin's theoretical misconception led of necessity to the kind of systematic degeneration seen by other Trotskyists. Third, while viewing the post-Stalin regime as less desirable than Stalin's, it nevertheless defends it against Maoist charges of capitalism and imperialism by arguing that the means of production are owned by the workers and that there is a centrally planned rather than a market economy. It applauds the Soviet armed intervention in Hungary in 1965 and in Czechoslovakia in 1968 to smash what it considers to be attempts to restore capitalism. It sees the Soviet regime as having a dual character, but the tilt is very much toward the positive.

Finally, while all of the other Trotskyist groups discussed interpret the international aspect of the theory of permanent revolution and Trotsky's formation of the Fourth International as a mandate to reach out to like-minded Trotskyists in other countries, the WWP does not. Rather, feeling that the Marxist-Leninist world is already too fragmented internationally, it prefers to support, make contact with, and attempt to influence governments in the Third World countries which it refers to as "socialist." It has absolutely no contacts with other Trotskyists and sees no basis for any.

While non-Trotskyist publications on the Left sometimes find it convenient to refer to the Workers World Party as Trotskyist, other Trotskyists find difficulty with that. If one defines a group as Trotskyist by how leaders respond to the point-blank question, then the WWP is clearly Trotskyist. But if a clear public profession is required and if certain bottom-line commitments to the theory of permanent revolution and its terminology, as well as to a theoretical and systematic interpretation of Stalinism are required, it becomes more difficult to classify the organization led by former SWP member Sam Marcy as Trotskyist.

This leaves us with four U.S. groups which openly fly the banner of Trotskyism, and which hold to certain bottom-line commitments the way the French groups which we have considered do. These are the Socialist Workers Party, the Spartacist League, the Workers League, and Spark. The SWP does enjoy an undisputed numerical superiority, and since it maintains a level of organization and activity well above that of any other Trotskyist organizations in the United States, the remainder of this chapter will focus on the SWP, and the positions of the other three groups will be discussed only where they represent significlant divergences from those of the SWP.

SWP: MEMBERSHIP, STRUCTURE, AND PUBLICATIONS

After the splits over Cuba and reunification with the International Secretariat of the Fourth International, the SWP demonstrated an increase in membership but an even more impressive increase in activity. In 1975 approximately 1,600 people, including 250 foreign guests, attended the SWP National Convention. At that time the party itself, not including the YSA, had between 1,200 and 1,500 members. By 1978 it probably numbered around 2,000. Next to the Communist Party, the SWP is certainly the largest Marxist–Leninist formation in the United States, and possibly the largest group to the left of the Democratic Party with the exception of the Communist Party.

One person who worked in the party for a considerable length of time offered estimates on party composition as of the late 1970s: 20 per cent students and 20-25 per cent manual workers, with the rest clerical, white collar, or public sector workers. Although Black and Latino people constantly appear on the party electoral slates in the urban areas, the SWP has not in the past attracted minority people to the extent that the Communist Party and its youth affiliates have. It reported some change in this pattern as a result of its deep involvement in the Boston busing issue. Women, however, have been very well represented and a potent force in the party. The above source estimated that fully 40 per cent of the party activists are women. The SWP candidate for president in the 1972 national elections was Linda Jenness, a 31-year-old woman who was politicized in the sixties and who has been particularly active in the feminist movement. She edited a volume entitled *Feminism and Socialism* for Pathfinder Press, which is run by the party. Women consistently have prominent places on the party electoral slates, either approaching or achieving absolute parity with men.

Membership totals, however, do not give a full picture of the impact of the party. Here a structural difference which exists between the SWP and the French *Ligue* plays an important role. Between 1968 and 1978, the distinction between a youth affiliate and an "adult" party did not exist in the French section. In the United States, however, there has been a clear distinction between the SWP and its youth affiliate, the YSA, since 1960.

Trotsky was particularly concerned with the problems of youth in Soviet society and the impact of the political system upon that youth. He was also extremely concerned over the role of women. These twin concerns were translated into a programmatic commitment in the program which Trotsky wrote for the founding of the Fourth International in 1938, the Transitional Program. In it, Trotsky wrote:

> When a program or an organization wears out, the generation which carried it on its shoulders wears out with it. The movement is revitalized by the youth who are free of responsibility for the past. The Fourth International pays particular attention to the young generation of the proletariat. All of its policies strive to inspire the youth with belief in its own strength and in the future. Only the fresh enthusiasm and aggressive spirit of the youth can guarantee the preliminary successes in the struggle; only these successes can return the best elements of the older generation to the road of revolution. Thus it was, thus it will be.
>
> Opportunist organizations by their very nature concentrate their chief attention on the top layers of the working class and therefore ignore both the youth and the woman worker. The decay of capitalism, however, deals its heaviest blows to woman as a wage earner and and as a housewife. The sections of the Fourth Interna-

> tional should seek bases of support among the
> most exploited layers of the working class, con-
> sequently among the women workers. Here they
> will find inexhaustible stores of devotion, selfless-
> ness, and readiness to sacrifice.[53]

The commitment to women, which was manifested in Trotsky's earliest writings, has been reflected in the high rates of participation of women in
the movement which we have noted. Moreover, the SWP—operating in a
country in which women's consciousness and the movements based upon that
consciousness are more highly developed than in France (where they are still a
more recent phenomena)—has over a five year edge on the French *Ligue* in
consciously attending to the role of women within its own ranks.

The commitment to making contact with youth was a major factor
in the entrism of the 1930s. Trotsky saw that the socialist parties were
attracting a new wave of radicalized youth but that many of these younger
people were not satisfied with the leadership of the party elders. The Trotskyists felt that they had something better to offer these people, and when they
were expelled the American Trotskyists, like their French counterparts, took
an important segment of the socialist youth movement with them.

After World War II and prior to 1960, the SWP had no youth affiliate. During the war the SWP was severely repressed and its membership
reached a low point after the war. However, the decision by Shachtman to
bring his followers into the Socialist Party in 1958 redounded to the benefit
of the SWP and was the beginning of a chain of events which led to the
creation of a new youth affiliate.

The youth group of Shachtman's Independent Socialist League was
called the Young Socialist League (YSL). With the merger it was to be united with the Socialist Party's YPSL. Tim Wohlforth had been a founder of the
campus socialist club at Oberlin College and had affiliated with the YSL.
Wohlforth opposed the merger with the Socialist Party and the YPSL, but
lost out to the YSLers who were loyal to Shachtman, chief among them
being Michael Harrington. In 1957, the year before Shachtman's group
merged with the Socialist Party, Wohlforth left the YSL and came together
with members of the SWP to found a paper called *Young Socialist*.

Three years later, in 1960, a formal youth organization was created
called the Young Socialist Alliance. Wohlforth became its national secretary.
As we have seen, Wohlforth was to split with the SWP a few years later,
form the Workers League, and return to the SWP in 1976 after being purged
from the Workers League by Gerry Healy.

By 1960, the general political climate was changing both nationally
and internationally. On the international scene, the Cuban Revolution was
appealing to many young people in the United States.

Domestically, the grip of the McCarthyist repression was beginning to weaken. This was just at the pre-dawn stage of the generational politicization of the 1960s and 1970s. The Trotskyists anticipated this.

The YSA is a support group, a training school, and a recruiting structure for the party. Its basic purpose is to train people under the age of thirty who think that they might be interested in the party. Most of the education is conducted through party documents, some of which are restricted to party and YSA members, and the books published by the party press, which are available to anyone. If the YSA member lives in a city where there is a party branch, the branch will conduct forums and discussions which will also be a part of the training. However, there are YSA chapters in university towns where there are no party branches. In fact, all YSA chapters which are not located together with branch offices in the cities are found in university communities.

If they are viewed as qualified, YSAers may be accepted into the SWP itself before they are thirty years old. However, the general rule is that affiliation with the YSA must terminate at age thirty. After reaching that age, a member of the YSA who wishes to affiliate with the party must reside in or near a city in which there is a branch, and must participate in a continuing program of education and active work conducted by the branch.

During the Vietnam War years, the SWP also increased its attraction in the radicalized university milieu by assuming leadership, through the vehicle of the YSA, of one of the major anti-Vietnam War groups, the Student Mobilization Committee (SMC). While the membership of the SWP remained under the two thousand level—which was at least a tenfold increase over its low point in the 1950s—both the YSA and the SMC, the latter sometimes acting as a transmission to the former, brought many more young people into contact with the SWP. Kirkpatrick Sale writes of the SMC that "its membership in 1969 climbed to an estimated 20,000 people at more than a thousand schools and colleges."[54] And an internal source within the SWP estimated that in the first decade and a half of its existence, somewhere between fifteen and twenty thousand people had been in the YSA.

The importance of the YSA and the SMC to the SWP was evidenced both by the increase in absolute numbers in the size of the SWP during the radicalization of the sixties and early seventies and by the important party functions assumed by younger people. While some of the old timers who had been associated with Cannon, like George Novack, Evelyn Reed, and Farrell Dobbs remained active writers and activists, the crucial core of the activists in the 1970s were in their twenties and thirties.[55]

While the YSA may well have claimed the affiliation of 15,000 to 20,000 people over a decade and a half, at any given point in time it had nowhere near that number. For example, in 1974 it attracted approximately nine hundred people to its annual convention in St. Louis and 1,250 people to a "Social Activists and Educational Conference" which it sponsored in Oberlin, Ohio in the same year.[56] The total membership might have been slightly in excess of these attendance figures, but not by very much. People can go in and out of the YSA fairly easily because they are not committed to party discipline as SWP members are, but are invited in simply if they are in general agreement with the goals of YSA.

Given the membership level of the SWP, it is obvious that most YSAers have chosen not to enter the more highly disciplined party. Many of the former YSAers have remained generally sympathetic with the party, sub-scribe to its publications, and make financial contributions to it, but for personal or political reasons they do not become party members. The prob-lem has been similar to the turnover problem faced by the *Ligue* in France, which chose not to distinguish between youth and parent group.

The termination of the war in Indochina brought further recruitment difficulties. Of course, the SMC went out of business. To enlarge its influ-ence and membership, the SWP adopted four new organizational measures in the mid-seventies. First, it took the initiative in the creation of single-issue groups on the order of the SMC to deal with the issues of the rights of political dissenters and racial minorities. The Political Rights Defense Fund (PRDF) collected money to finance the SWP's suit against the U. S. govern-ment for its program of illegal spying and disruption (including break-ins and beatings) of the activities of the SWP.[57] The campaign for rights of racial minorities was campus-focused and conducted through the National Student Coalition Against Racism (NSCAR).

Secondly, the SWP intensified its post-war energies in external organizations and causes, particularly those concerned with labor and women. It supported more progressive segments of the steel workers and miners unions and took a very active interest and role in the Coalition of Labor Union Women (CLUW). It also became very active in the fight for the Equal Rights Amendment, for abortion upon demand, for equal rights for people of homosexual preference, and against construction of nuclear power plants. In these activities, however, it has worked through organizations which enjoy greater autonomy from it than did PRDF or NSCAR.[58] It has contributed an important element of political skills and energy without being a dominant force.

Third, the SWP opened offices in many more cities than it had in the past and decentralized its work in cities where it had had offices.[59] In just the two years between March 1975 and April 1977, the SWP increased the number of cities in which it had offices from twenty to forty-seven. More-over, it opened neighborhood offices in New York, Chicago, San Francisco, Detroit, Houston, Minneapolis, St. Louis, Philadelphia, Seattle, and Newark. Most of these offices were easily accessible store-front facilities.

Finally, in perhaps its most drastic measure to increase membership, the SWP began to offer three month "provisional memberships" to those who have not gone through the YSA and who might not be willing to undergo an extensive political education while being kept outside of the party structure. Emphasis upon attempts to recruit workers and people in the age group which had been radicalized in the 1960s came to mean that the party had to recruit more people directly into itself rather than relying so heavily upon YSA when its recruitment efforts were largely concentrated upon the campuses.[60] This was a large step for the SWP, which had been critical of the French *Ligue's* merger of the youth and parent groups because it thought the *Ligue's* party integrity suffered. The SWP's use of "provisional memberships" certainly raised more questions about party integrity than did the *Ligue's* use of sympathizing structures to provide for the participation of the not quite fully committed.

Once a member of the party, a militant might hold down a regular job outside of the party and use part of his or her earnings to support the party financially.[61] Or the militant might work for the party on a full-time basis and earn a meager subsistence salary. The SWP is very demanding in terms of the steady work and support which it expects from its members.

This can be seen in both the quantity and quality of the SWP's publications. Much of the work of the party activists is devoted to the publication and dissemination of written material to the external world. The weekly newspaper of the SWP is still called *The Militant,* just as it was at the inception of the Trotskyist movement. It is a substantial paper, usually running between twenty-five and thirty pages on a tabloid format. Most of the paper is devoted to problems and events in the United States and the activities of the SWP, although there is a special section devoted to foreign news entitled "World Outlook." One of the major activities of the SWP and YSA is to sell *The Militant,* and the paper contains a weekly scoreboard which tells who has done the best job. It was claimed that after an intensive subscription campaign in 1974 there were 33,000 subscribers. This was supplemented by an additional 10,000 street sales. The YSA puts out a monthly tabloid with longer articles entitled *Young Socialist.*

Until the beginning of 1978, the SWP put out another weekly publication of its own. This was *Intercontinental Press,* a magazine format publication which emphasized foreign and international news and longer feature articles. It was the most informative source on the activities and positions of the Left in other countries published in the United States. The SWP's relationship with the United Secretariat of the Fourth International provided it with contacts and sources in other countries which most American movements lack. This was reflected in the reporting and analysis. In fact, *Intercontinental Press* was also a forum for the expression of the point of view of the minority tendency within the International, the Leninist-Trotsky-ist Faction. As a result of the agreement to overcome that factionalism in

1977, there was a merger of the SWP's *Intercontinental Press* with the majority tendency's *Inprecor*. In fact, the publication changed very little. The major difference is that articles of more foreign writers from sections previously belonging to the majority tendency were made available to American readers in English translation.

For many years, the SWP also put out a theoretical monthly journal called *International Socialist Review*. In April 1975, however, the *International Socialist Review* ceased publication as a separate journal and began to appear as a monthly supplement in *The Militant*. While the change was dictated by financial considerations, the party also hoped that the inclusion of the new supplement would help in the constant campaign to increase the circulation of *The Militant*.[62]

Finally, there is the book and pamphlet publishing enterprise which the party runs, Pathfinder Press. Pathfinder, located in New York City, publishes a very extensive list of contemporary and historical publications. Along with International Publishers and Monthly Review Press, it is one of the most important publishers of Marxist literature in the United States. The press is completely run by party members, from the business office to the actual printing process. It carries on a tradition of publishing which Trotsky so admired on the part of the American section, and which he held up as an example for emulation on the part of the French section.

THEORY AND PROGRAMS OF THE SWP

The separate identities of the SWP and YSA and the extensive publication activity of the SWP is indicative of a spirit which differs considerably from that which one encounters in the French *Ligue*. It is more similar to the spirit of the *Ligue's* Trotskyist rival, the *Organisation Communiste Internationaliste*. Both the SWP and the OCI—which were allied in the International Committee until the SWP reaffiliated with the International Secretariat in 1963—insist that action must be based on solid theory. Both have internal education programs of considerable rigor. Both are insistent that it takes young people some time before they can be schooled adequately in theory to assume party responsibility. The SWP, however, seems to turn over the reins of party control to people, once they do enter the party itself, more quickly than the OCI. Thus, the SWP's leadership is younger than the OCI's.

Especially in the early and mid-1970s, the *Ligue* gave greater emphasis to action as opposed to theory than either the SWP or the OCI. As we have seen, there was no separate youth organization for a decade after 1968. The *Ligue* emphasized confrontation tactics and believed that these tactics, in themselves, were educational. The atmosphere which has surrounded the *Ligue* has been much more "exciting" in the sense that one could expect anything to happen anytime. The tone of the SWP and the OCI has been more intellectual and theoretical than that of the *Ligue*.[63]

Aside from the different balance of action and confrontation tactics with theory, there have been important programmatic and tactical differences of a more specific nature between the SWP and the *Ligue*. The SWP has presented its program basically in two ways. First, Pathfinder Press has published the party program, but always along with Trotsky's Transitional Program, and always along with an explanation of how the more recent additions made by the party relate to the original document. Second, during election periods the party has published shorter statements of specific points without the major theoretical discussion. *Ce que veut la Ligue Communiste,* the 171-page program published through Maspero by the *Ligue Communiste* in 1972, contained no discussion of the Transitional Program or how the various aspects of the contemporary program relate to it. On the other hand, it does contain a much more exhaustive treatment of what was needed in the present state of national affairs than have the documents of the SWP. The emphasis on action brings with it a much greater emphasis on the present.

Trotsky wrote the Transitional Program in 1938 for the founding of the Fourth International. Italy and Germany had already gone fascist, and Trotsky thought that the other capitalist countries, including the United States, would follow suit. He saw Boss Hauge's attacks on labor in New Jersey as but the beginning of a more general fascist movement, a view which Max Shachtman attempted to temper. There was thus a certain urgency to the program. Trotskyists today, and particularly the SWP, view it as a program which still contains valid analysis and prescription, although needing supplementation to bring it up to date.

Trotsky defined the function of the Transitional Program as follows:

> The strategic task of the next period—a pre-revolu-
> tionary period of agitation, propaganda, and organiza-
> tion—consists in overcoming the contradiction
> between the maturity of the objective revolutionary
> conditions and the immaturity of the proletariat and
> its vanguard (the confusion and disappointment of the
> older generation, the inexperience of the younger gen-
> eration). It is necessary to help the masses in the
> process of the daily struggle to find the bridge be-
> tween the present demands and the socialist program
> of the revolution. This bridge should include a system
> of transitional demands, stemming from today's condi-
> tions and from today's consciousness of wide layers of
> the working class and unalterably leading to one final
> conclusion: the conquest of power by the proletariat.[64]

Trotsky goes on to explain that the Transitional Program will function as a bridge between the *"minimum program"* of "Classical Social Democracy" (i.e., reforms within the framework of bourgeois society) and the *"maximum program,"* which promised substitution of socialism for capitalism in the indefinite future.[65]

The core demands are the right to employment for all workers, a sliding scale of wages (currently called inflationary escalators), and a sliding scale of working hours so that the available work would be divided among the work force with no cut in total weekly wages. The usual objection to such demands by the capitalists is that they cannot be met—firms cannot afford them. But Trotsky sees inflation and unemployment as problems generated by capitalism for which the workers pay the price. His response is that if capitalism cannot remove this burden from the back of the workers, then it should perish, and the workers will learn this when the capitalists reject their demands.

Thus a process is initiated during this transitional period, a process in which a number of strategies begin to unfold as the workers come to understand better the nature of capitalism and its inability to meet their demands. Factory committees will be formed which will use such militant tactics as the "sitdown" strike or occupation. As a first step in their taking complete control over the management of the productive enterprise, they will demand to be presented with the financial records of the firm. Armed workers' self-defense groups will be created to thwart the attempts of the capitalists and the armed forces they control, both public and private, from reasserting their control over the plants. Private banks would be expropriated, without compensation, and a state system of credit established. Alliances would be made with the farmers, whose small holdings would not be touched, just as the small businesses would be left alone. Pricing policies would be made by committees composed of delegates from factories, unions, cooperatives, farms, and more general consumer interests.

By accepting this program step by step, it is anticipated that the workers will be gradually introduced to the soundness of the final goal, the complete abolition of capitalism. In France, many workers are already so convinced and have engaged in factory occupations in 1936 and in the 1960s and 1970s. There is thus less of a need for the *Ligue* to emphasize the Transitional Program in the more radicalized milieu of the French workers than there is for the SWP in the United States, where the workers are more conservative and where none of the major parties and unions even symbolically advocates socialism.

Also peculiar to the U.S. context has been the tendency to advocate the formation of parties among the most oppressed. This began in 1938, when Trotsky and the leaders of the SWP engaged in extensive discussions regarding the formation of the American Labor Party based upon the trade union movement. This resulted from the recognition that the SWP was very small, was likely to remain so for a considerable period, and that the CIO, created only three years earlier, reflected a strong radical current within the labor movement. The strategy was thus to urge the creation of a labor party which could enable this radicalism to transcend the trade union boundaries and the control devices of union bureaucrats. An obvious problem was that the Trotskyists would have to contend with the attempts of the Communist Party to influence such a party. But they were confident that they could do so, despite the presence of Communist Party members in leadership positions of a considerable number of unions.[66]

Only two additions have appeared in the SWP's publication of the Transitional Program. One is an "extension" of the program adopted by the United Secretariat of the Fourth International in 1969. It is entitled "A Strategy for Revolutionary Youth." It contains an analysis of the radicalization of youth in the sixties. It contends that:

> While the bourgeoisie and their echoers in working-class circles decry the "conflict of generations," the "generational gap," and even "symbolic parricide," the issues posed by the youth in revolt are not primarily generational ones. They clearly reflect the major class conflicts of our time. The fundamental significance of this unprecedented radicalization of the youth is the emergence of new forces, ready, willing, and able to enter the arena of class struggle on the side of the colonial peoples and the working class and to give battle to world imperialism and its accomplices, who falsely claim to speak in the name of the working class and its allies.[67]

The program also presents a list of transitional demands for students and for the control of all levels of their education by minority peoples.[68]

The second addition was also formulated in 1969, but its applicability is limited to the American context. This is "The Transitional Program for Black Liberation" which was adopted by the SWP at its own 1969 National Convention. The program argues for Black control over institutions in the Black community and particularly emphasizes control over education. On many specific points, the program is really an anti-poverty one which has implications for the non-Black poor as well. Even recognizing this, the SWP advocates the creation of a Black political party independent of the Republicans and the Democrats. It thinks that, at the present time, only a Black political party can mobilize the Black community into consciousness and action. The SWP anticipates, however, that such a party would form alliances with "students, poor white people, workers and all other forces interested in radical change. It could play a vanguard role in bringing revolutionary ideas to all sections of the country."[69]

Finally, although the party has not formally added them to the Transitional Program, it has developed analyses and favorable positions toward the movements for equality launched by women, Chicanos and Chicanas, and gays and lesbians. Only in the case of gays and lesbians has this involved a reversal of a previous position. For until 1970 the SWP itself—in an attempt to avoid the appearance of attracting unusual social types who might deter broader recruitment—barred gays and lesbians. French Trotskyists never had any such ban.

Thus far, it is only among labor and Blacks that the SWP has advocated the formation of a separate political party. It has, however, held up an already existing Chicano and Chicana party, La Raza Unida, and particularly its victory in the municipal elections in Crystal City, Texas, as an example which should be followed by Blacks.[70]

On both the question of the Black political party and the support of feminism, the SWP is differentiated from the Trotskyist organizations which resulted from the split over Cuba in the sixties. The Spartacist League and the Workers League reject racial separatism and thus a separate Black political party.[71] The Workers League takes a particularly "hard" line on this. Interestingly, a variation of the SWP's position is offered by Spark, the tiny group of less than two dozen members which operates in only two American cities but which has developed an international relationship with *Lutte Ouvrière*. The result of a merger of former members of the Spartacist League and people in the civil rights movement, Spark advocates the creation of a separate Black political party. However, unlike the SWP, which advocates a more broadly aggregative Black party on the order of the labor party that it also advocates, Spark calls for the creation of a *Trotskyist* Black political party.[72]

The Workers League, which is the most vociferous objector to any kind of racial separatism, also rejects the women's liberation movement. It sees the latter as a similar, if more clearly middle-class, diversion from the real class struggle. The Spartacist League, unlike the Workers League, actively supports the passage of the Equal Rights Amendment but took more care than the SWP to point out that it is a minimal step from which no great progressive advances were to have been expected. While the Spartacist League supports equality for women and even publishes a journal entitled *Women and Revolution,* it denounces "feminism" as a separatist, petit-bourgeois movement which is incompatible with Marxism. It feels that the SWP's encouragement of feminism and its work with exclusively women's organizations is counter-productive to the construction of a unified Marxist movement which should deal with all manifestations of inequality through the rubric of class analysis.

To round out the panorama of U. S. Trotskyist positions on issues which have become most salient in the immediate post-war period, the Spartacist League differs from the Workers League in sharing the SWP's present defense of gay rights. Not only has the Spartacist League, unlike the SWP, never banned gays but in August 1977 an entire gay group, the Los Angeles Red Flag Union, merged with the Spartacists. Secondly, like the *Ligue* in France, the SWP stands alone among Trotskyist organizations in its absolute opposition to nuclear energy on environmental and safety grounds.

Both the SWP and the *Ligue* show marked effects of the youth radicalization of the 1960s and early 1970s. This is clearly seen in the SWP's attitude toward racial separatism, feminism, and the movement for gay and lesbian rights. The SWP, however, has shown a certain resistance to the effects of that radicalization in areas that the *Ligue* has not. This is reflected in the SWP's maintenance of a distinction between parent party and youth group, in its more respectful treatment of electoral processes, and in its avoidance of the kind of confrontational street politics engaged in by the *Ligue*.

A very important additional difference between the SWP and the *Ligue* is the interpretation which has been given to Third World revolutionary movements within the context of the theory of permanent revolution. As I indicated in Chapter 1, Trotsky's theory of permanent revolution cast doubt upon the viability of peasant-based revolutionary attempts. Trotsky thought that such attempts were doomed without supportive successful revolutions in the capitalist industrialized countries. However, after World War II, Pablo and his followers in the Fourth International felt that the anti-colonialist and anti-imperialist struggles in the Third World could not be ignored. More and more, the International Secretariat began to orient itself toward Third World revolutionary struggles which were largely peasant-based. Those sections which felt most strongly that this orientation was contrary to the theory of permanent revolution, and thus to Trotskyism, were in no position to serve as a brake on this movement. Since these were the same national sections (including the SWP) which had broken with the International Secretariat over the issue of entrism, they could only criticize this orientation from their own external organization, the International Committee.

The Cuban Revolution, however, had a tremendous impact upon the SWP. In his 1961 report to the National Committee Plenum, Joseph Hansen referred to Cuba as "the first workers state in the Western Hemisphere. And it's a pretty good-looking one."[73] The document extended praise to the Cuban regime for its agrarian reform, the nationalization of industry and agriculture, the institution of a planned economy with government control over foreign trade, the dismissal of "bourgeois" ministers who were initially in the government, the prosecution of officials of the Batista regime, the attempts to aid revolutionaries in other Latin American countries, and the establishment of relations with the Soviet Bloc![74]

Even though the SWP had little regard for the Soviet Union, it applauded the relations which the Cuban regime had established with the Soviets for two reasons. First, in the eyes of the SWP, it guaranteed some kind of protection against U.S. imperialism. In December 1960, the Political Committee of the SWP drafted a document in which it stated: "Upon nationalization of the key sectors of industry, the new state structure became so committed to a planned economy that only civil war can now restore capitalist property relations. A civil war could not succeed without a counter-revolutionary invasion far bloodier than that engineered by Washington in Guatemala in 1954."[75] Only four months after this statement was drafted, the United States-initiated Bay of Pigs invasion took place. Second, the establishment of relations with the Soviet Bloc, along with the progressive evolution of the rest of the characteristics of the regime cited above, was taken as a sign by the majority within the SWP that—although the Cuban revolutionary regime began as a radical bourgeois movement—it was becoming a serious revolutionary movement aiming toward the creation of a democratic workers' and peasants' regime. There was a dual tendency to the revolution, radical bourgeois and proletarian democratic. By the end of 1960, the SWP majority felt that the latter was overcoming the former.

This, of course, placed the majority at odds with its internal minority and with the International Committee, which continued to view the Cuban Revolution as petit-bourgeois. It accounted for the expulsion of those dissidents who formed the Spartacist and Workers Leagues, the severing of relations with the International Committee, and the SWP's "reunification" with the International Secretariat, then renamed the United Secretariat.

The SWP has continued to view the Cuban revolution as coming as close to a true socialist revolution as one has in the real world. It has criticized the Cuban regime, but it has seen the "errors" of the Cuban revolutionary government—the worst of which are Castro's support of the Soviet invasion of Czechoslovakia in 1968, the repression against political dissidents, and the repression directed against homosexuals—as the result of a dual squeeze to which the Cubans have been subjected. On the one hand, the government of the United States has conducted an economic blockade against the Cubans, making them dependent upon the USSR and, on the other, the SWP sees a purposeful policy on the part of the Soviet Union of doling out assistance to the Cubans very slowly so as to increase the dependency even further.

In 1972, almost a decade after the SWP had first indicated its support for the Cuban Revolution, Harry Ring summed up the SWP's assessment of Cuba. The SWP perceived an increase in repression and in the acceptance of the Soviet foreign policy line. The SWP also thought that the "bureaucratic deformations" had not reached the "qualitative stage existing in a country like the USSR or China, where the totalitarian rule of a privileged bureaucratic caste remains complete."[76] Moreover, the SWP did not expect Cuba to follow the same path as those two countries because "these setbacks occur in the context of a rising world radicalization."[77]

There is every reason for optimism that in the not too distant future there will be revolutionary break-throughs which will help end Cuba's isolation and the difficulties stemming from that isolation.

Further, the Cuban leadership has committed some grievous errors, the importance of which cannot and should not be minimized. But that leadership still includes good revolutionary cadres who have not passed beyond the possibility of responding to a re-vival of the spirit of the Moncada Barrack and the Sierra Maestra.

And, finally, all of present world experience is demonstrating that no country can create a barrier sufficient to guarantee immunity from the ever intensifying international youth radicalization. Cuba will not be exempt from this process. And the radicalization will not bring procapitalist ideas to the youth of Cuba. It will only more deeply im-bue them with a conviction of the need to defend, deepen, straighten out, and extend their revolution.[78]

The SWP and the French *Ligue* had no basic differences over the internal dynamics in Cuba. They did, however, have very different views on whether the guerrilla warfare strategy used by Castro and his comrades to come to power ought to be encouraged in other Latin American countries. As indicated in Chapter II, the Ligue and the majority faction of the United Secretariat faced opposition from the SWP and the Leninist-Trotskyist Faction on this point. The majority attempted to clarify and moderate its position at the United Secretariat's 1974 Congress by making clear that what was at issue was armed struggle and not "terrorism," and that this was a strategy but not the only possible one which could be employed in Latin America.

The SWP and the minority faction were not to be placated by this. They put forward the "long detour" position. This position contended that the period following World War II had witnessed a decrease in the level of class struggle in the Western capitalist countries. This was largely due to the hold of Stalinism over the USSR and the Communist parties in Western coun-tries, as well as the anti-Communist repression which accompanied the Cold War in the West. By the late sixties and early seventies, it was evident that class struggle was on the rise again in the West, and it was accompanied by important movements of young people and women. Thus, the long detour away from the main road of world revolution in the aftermath of World War II was coming to an end."[79] It was pointed out that since the Cuban Revolution there had not been a successful revolution in Latin America.

Taking a more global perspective, the SWP and the Leninist-Trotskyist Faction argued that a serious Leninist-Trotskyist approach, indeed the one dictated by Trotsky's Transitional Program, would necessitate a concentration upon the mobilization of the proletariat in the urban centers and industrial plants of capitalism. This obviously meant taking advantage of and being a factor in the resurgence of class struggle in the most highly industrialized countries; in Latin America and the Third World generally, it meant rejecting peasant-based, armed insurrection as a strategy. The armed and rural-based processes of change in China, Cuba, and Vietnam were seen as rooted in a unique historical period of uneven development. The struggle was now visibly coming back to the capitalist industrialized countries. To the extent that Third World revolutionaries could successfully move their countries in the direction of socialism, they would do so by building parties and concentrating on the urban and proletarianized sectors as the Bolsheviks had done in Russia. It will be recalled that Trotsky had hoped that the Russian Revolution would trigger off a revolutionary response in the West. He saw no hope for socialism anywhere in the world without such a movement in the West. In 1974, the SWP and the Leninist-Trotskyist Faction were quite prepared to admit that rural-based, Third World revolutions which took place after World War II had indeed played a role in stimulating the class struggle and opposition movements that they were observing in the Western industrialized countries. For them, however, this was hardly a sufficient reason to encourage a continuation of such ill-conceived strategies.

If the disagreements between the SWP and the *Ligue* over Cuba involved the issue of rural-based, armed insurrection rather than the nature of the Cuban regime itself, it was quite a different matter when it came to Vietnam. Only two months after the 1974 World Congress at which the Leninist-Trotskyist Faction presented its "long detour" position, the SWP and the *Ligue* made public their differences over Vietnam. We have already seen that the position of the French *Ligue,* which articulated the majority position within the United Secretariat, was that while the Vietnamese were not engaging in a socialist revolution on a Trotskyist model, the deviations therefrom were explicable and justified by the unique traditions and circumstances faced by the Vietnamese. In order to deal with these, the Vietnamese Communist Party became an "empirical revolutionary party."[80] The *Ligue* did not doubt, however, the revolutionary vocation of that party and its final success in constructing a socialist society.

While stopping short of comparing this kind of flexible interpretation based upon particular circumstances and cultural traditions with Maoism —something which surely must have crossed the minds of those arguing the case of the SWP—the SWP rejected this interpretation. It agreed with the *Ligue* that "unconditional support" had to be given to the Vietnamese Communist Party and the Provisional Revolutionary Government in the South in their struggle to free themselves from the yoke of U.S. imperialism. But it argued that in both China and North Vietnam, revolutionaries were successful in spite of, rather than because of, their programs. It was the weakness of capitalism, rather than the strength of the analyses and strategies of the revolutionaries, that enabled them to extricate themselves from Western capitalist control.[81]

The SWP argued that, with the exception of Cuba, not one struggle for self-determination in the Third World had resulted in an end to bourgeois government.[82] For the SWP, Stalinism is a petit-bourgeois perspective tied to a massive and privileged bureaucracy. It is petit-bourgeois in that it accepts characteristics of bourgeois capitalism, such as income and status differentials, in the name of productive efficiency. The SWP contended that both the Vietnamese Communist Party and the Provisional Revolutionary Government exhibited these petit-bourgeois or Stalinist characteristics.

Two of the SWP's specialists on the Vietnamese situation, George Johnson and Fred Feldman, pointed particularly to that portion of the program of the Provisional Revolutionary Government which stated: "Freedom of enterprise for private individuals shall be guaranteed. The national bourgeois shall be encouraged to develop such undertaking[s] as [are] beneficial to the country's economy and people's welfare."[83] They further quoted an article written by an official of the PRG in which the latter contended that the PRG:

> stands for the protection of the legitimate right to landownership of plantation owners, rich peasants, the church, pagodas and temples.
> Conflicts between employers and workers will be settled through negotiations in the spirit of reconciliation so as to boost production and ensure decent living conditions for the working people. [The PRG] always respects the right to private ownership and free enterprise and encourages overseas Vietnamese national's [*sic*] investment in home ventures as a contribution to national reconstruction, it encourages Vietnamese residents abroad and foreign capitalists to make investment in capital and technique.[84]

However, the harshest criticism which the SWP published in the *International Socialist Review* was one written by a dissident member of the

Ligue itself, Louis Couturier. Couturier's article did not content itself with an attack on the program of the PRG but took direct aim at the Communist Party of North Vietnam for its own behavior in the North. Couturier, again in the pages of an SWP publication, accused the North Vietnamese party of permitting government and party officials to enjoy special stores, hospitals, "superlative villas surrounded by woodland and staffed by a number of servants," and other perquisites such as automobiles, chauffeurs, and supplementary food rations.[85] He also accused the "Vietnamese bureaucratic leadership" of abandoning the interests of foreign revolutionaries for its own diplomatic interests. As specific instances of this, Couturier cited the abandonment of the cause of Ceylonese revolutionaries for better relations with the government of Ceylon (now Sri Lanka), support of the Soviet intervention in Czechoslovakia, and "total support to the French CP in 1968" when the French Communist Party was denouncing the young people who were rebelling in the streets of France.[86]

The "long detour" interpretation of the SWP and its position on Vietnam brought the SWP closer once again to the understanding of Trotsky's charge to his followers, held by the International Committee, with which the SWP had split over Cuba. The "long detour" made it possible for the SWP to justify its past support for the Vietnamese revolutionaries and even its present qualified support for Cuba, while focusing its attention almost exclusively once again upon the capitalist industrialized world. This shift did not escape the attention of the French OCI, which viewed the SWP with considerably more favor than it did the French *Ligue*.

The shift was also related to the intensification of the efforts of the SWP within the context of American politics, i.e., the dramatic increase in the number of party branches in American cities and the extensive energy devoted to electoral campaigns since the war. Finally, it brought the SWP back to an interpretation of Trotskyism which was less congenial to the anti-imperialist and Third World orientation characteristic of the radicalization of the 1960s and early 1970s. It thus complemented the SWP's views on organization and electoral politics, which were also less congenial to this radicalization than those of the *Ligue*. Moreover, while the *Ligue* has given in on the encouragement of guerrilla warfare in Latin American in order to eliminate formal factionalism within the United Secretariat, there is no indication that it has accepted the "long detour" position which sees the Third World revolutionary movements of the sixties and seventies as historical anomalies. The *Ligue* has refused to raise the question to the level of general principle or theory, thus preserving total flexibility for the future support of Third World revolutions.

THE ELECTORALISM OF THE SWP

Neither the Spartacist League nor the Workers League is electoralist, and this obviously differentiates them from the SWP. But while both the SWP and its fraternal French counterpart in the United Secretariat engage in electoral activity, there is a discernible difference in their approach.

The French *Ligue* is more convinced of the imminence of a fascist threat in France than the SWP is of such a threat in the United States, is more oriented toward direct action including physical attacks on what it considers to be fascist meetings, and uses the electoral process as a forum from which it attempts to convince French workers that elections are ineffectual as mechanisms of change. It is quite open in this regard. The title of one of Krivine's books is *La Farce électorale.*

The SWP is convinced that American workers are attached to the electoral process and that it would be counter-productive to attack it. Moreover, within the SWP there was considerable criticism of the *Ligue's* behavior during the 1974 presidential elections. It was difficult for the SWP to see consistency in the *Ligue's* actions and positions. On the one hand, the *Ligue* belittled electoral activity and accused *Lutte Ouvrière* of falling into the trap of "electoralism." On the one hand, it insisted upon opposing a Trotskyist woman candidate by presenting Krivine on the first ballot, and it ended up supporting the social democrat Mitterrand, who was in an alliance with the Communist Party, on the second ballot.

However, the fact that the SWP is more publicly respectful of the electoral process in the United States than the *Ligue* is in France does not mean that it thinks that the capitalists would willingly give up power to a socialist government even if it were duly effected. It cites Spain in the 1930s and Chile in the 1970s — in which the United States played a crucial role in the overthrow of the Allende government — as instances in which capitalists overthrew socialist governments based upon constitutional electoral outcomes. The strategy of the SWP is to use the electoral campaign forum as a way of building a base of support for itself so that when it does win in the electoral process — and it believes that someday it will — there will be such strong support within the population that the capitalists would not have sufficient power to snatch the victory away, as in the Spanish and Chilean cases.

This strategy goes back to the early days of the party. During the 1941 trial of twenty-eight Trotskyist leaders who were being prosecuted under the 1861 Conspiracy Act and the Smith Act, the U.S. Trotskyist leader James P. Cannon was obliged by the prosecution to address the question of peaceful change through the ballot as opposed to a violent overthrow of capitalism. A portion of the cross-examination, which is reprinted in its entirety and distributed by the party press, went as follows:

Q: What would you say is the opinion of Marxists as
far as the desirability of a peaceful transition is concerned?

A: The position of the Marxists is that the most eco-
nomical and preferable, the most desirable method of
social transformation, by all means, is to have it done
peacefully.

Q: And in the opinion of the Marxists, is that absolutely excluded?

A: Well, I wouldn't say absolutely excluded. We say
that the lessons of history don't show any important
examples in favor of the idea so that you can count
upon it.

Q: Can you give us examples in American history of
a minority refusing to submit to a majority?

A: I can give you a very important one. The conception of the Marxists is that, even if the transfer of the
political power from the capitalists to the proletariat
is accomplished peacefully — then the minority, the
exploiting capitalist class, will revolt against the new
regime, no matter how legally it is established.

I can give you an example in American history. The
American Civil War resulted from the fact that the
Southern slaveholders couldn't reconcile themselves to
the legal parliamentary victory of Northern capitalism,
the election of President Lincoln.

Q: Can you give us an example outside of America
where a reactionary minority revolted against a majority in office?

A: Yes, in Spain -- the coalition of workers' and liberal parties in Spain got an absolute majority in the
elections and established the People's Front Government. This government was no sooner installed than
it was confronted with an armed rebellion, led by the
reactionary capitalists of Spain.[87]

Q: What attitude does the party take toward the ballot?

A: Our party runs candidates wherever it is able to get
on the ballot. We conduct very energetic campaigns
during the elections, and in general, to the best of our
ability, and to the limit of our resources, we participate
in election campaigns.[88]

Q: What is the purpose of the party in participating in
these electoral campaigns?

> A: The first purpose, I would say, is to make full use
> of the democratic possibility afforded to popularize our
> ideas, to try to get elected wherever possible; and, from
> a long range view, to test out the uttermost possibility
> of advancing the socialist cause by democratic means.[89]

In 1974, the SWP ran candidates in fifteen states and the District of Columbia. Most of the candidates were running for national and state offices. In Oregon and the District of Columbia it ran candidates for municipal posts. In California it contested for the Los Angeles County Sheriff position and in the state of Washington for the King County Prosecuting Attorney post. The number of candidates totalled one hundred and two. Of these, fifty-two have names that clearly indicate that they are women. Another eight names could be either male or female, but with a probability that a majority are female. Thus women comprised at least half of the candidates run by the party. And they were prominent among the candidacies of the highest positions sought. Seven of the eleven gubernatorial candidates had names which clearly indicate that they are women, three had clearly masculine names, and one was named Robin. Of the ten senatorial candidacies, five went to men and five to women. The only mayoral candidate, in Washington, D.C., was a woman.

None of the candidates in 1974 expected to win and none of them did. Of the twenty-four candidacies in four states and the District of Columbia for which *The Militant* was able to secure data, the highest percentage of the votes that any single candidate was able to secure was 3.9 per cent.[90] The party has difficulty obtaining election data since the establishment media do not report totals for the SWP and indeed may not even be given figures by the election officials. Election officials in Illinois even refused to permit the party to appear on the 1974 ballot until the SWP threatened a lawsuit.[91]

What the election permitted the party to do was to put forward a program of highly specific demands. Some of these, such as tying wages to increases in the cost of living, are in the original "Transitional Program" drawn up by Trotsky. Others are found in "A Transitional Program for Black Liberation," which was expanded in the 1974 electoral platform to include Puerto Ricans and Chicanos. There were fourteen planks in the 1974 platform, each having a number of specific demands under them. Among the most important are: (1) setting pension, social security, and unemployment benefits at the level of union rates and also tying them to increases in the cost of living; (2) a full employment program based on a shortening of the work week to thirty hours with no cut in pay; (3) an unconditional right to strike which would entail the repeal of the Taft-Hartley and Landrum-Griffin Acts as well as no-strike clauses in contracts similar to those negotiated by the leadership of the International Brotherhood of Steelworkers; (4) rank and file control over the unions; (5) full support for equal rights in all areas for

Blacks, Chicanos, Puerto Ricans, women, gays and lesbians; (6) nationalization and worker control over the energy industries; (7) free medical and dental care through a system of socialized medicine; (8) decent low-cost federally financed housing for all who need it; (9) free public transportation; (10) the termination of all income taxes on earnings under $15,000 annually and 100 per cent taxation on incomes exceeding $30,000 per year; (11) the closing of all tax loopholes for the rich and the corporations and the elimination of all regressive taxes; (12) repeal of the Smith Act and the destruction of the secret lists and files on political activities kept by the FBI and other government agencies; (13) immediate implementation of open admissions and affirmative action plans in the universities to insure access to minority people and women; (14) stiff pollution control enforcement with penalties of 100 per cent taxation of profits and confiscation, and (15) protection for the rights of prisoners including union wages for all prison labor and an end to pre-trial detention (which really hits the poor), the death penalty, the performing of lobotomies and medical experiments, the censoring of mail and reading material, and the curtailment of the right to vote and other political activities of prisoners.[92]

In the area of foreign policy, the platform called for: (1) elimination of the military budget and the transference of these funds to housing, medical care, education, and other social needs; (2) the termination of financial and military support to "dictatorships like South Vietnam, Chile, and Brazil and to colonial settler states like South Africa and Israel;"[93] (3) acceptance of refugees from "Chile, Haiti and other repressive regimes;"[94] (4) dismantling of US military bases on foreign soil; (5) independence for Puerto Rico; (6) abolition of the CIA and the termination of American influence in the internal affairs of other nations; and (7) the publication of all treaties and an end to "all secret international deals."[95]

There were some shifts in strategy and focus in the 1976 elections. Since 1976 was a presidential election year, there was naturally more of a mobilization of the party at the national level than in 1974. The SWP's presidential and vice-presidential candidates were, respectively, Peter Camejo, a thirty-five year old Venezuelan-American and Willie Mae Reid, a thirty-five year old Black woman. The national campaign program was shortened and framed in terms of "A Bill of Rights for Working People." The eight rights were: (1) a job, (2) an adequate income, (3) free education, (4) free medical care, (5) secure retirement, (6) the truth about economic and political policies that effect our lives, (7) control over their own affairs for oppressed minorities, and (8) the right to decide economic and political policy.[96]

The SWP was on the ballot in more states in 1976 than in 1974. It ran candidates in 15 states and D.C. in 1974, and was on the ballot in 27 states and D.C. in 1976. This also was an increase from the previous two presidential years: 18 states and D.C. in 1968 and 23 states and D.C. in 1972.[97]

While on the ballot in more states in 1976, the SWP ran fewer candidates than in 1974, when it did not have to concentrate resources on the national ticket. In 1976 there were 58 candidates on the ballots and 15 write-in candidates as opposed to the 102 candidates in 1974. In California, Colorado, New Mexico, and Texas, the SWP actively supported La Raza Unida candidates. Of the 73 candidates in 1976, 29 could clearly be identified as women by their names, 37 as men, and 7 could have been either. Consistent with the national focus, over half of the total number of candidates ran for national office in 1976, 32 for the House of Representatives and 12 for the Senate, plus the presidential and vice-presidential candidates. Five of the senatorial candidates were women and 7 were men. Nine of the House candidates had names which clearly indicated that they were women, 19 were clearly men, and 4 had names which could be masculine or feminine.[98]

REPRESSION OF THE SWP

In the discussion of the electoral strategy of the SWP, it was almost as though one were considering Republicans and Democrats. The SWP published platforms, ran candidates, and even appeared on the ballots of some states. But there was a crucial difference. The SWP — against which no legal measures have been taken since the 1941 prosecution of SWP and Minneapolis Teamsters leaders — was a special target of illegal measures on the part of both federal and local agencies which were attempting to destroy the organization. The party constantly had to contend with these measures.

In 1973, after the revelations of widespread illegal government activity following the discovery of the Watergate break-in, the SWP fought back. The SWP and the YSA initiated a $27 million damage suit against the government for its illegal activities and also requested a court injunction against further spying. As part of a pretrial discovery, the judge ordered the FBI to release the file it was keeping on the SWP and YSA to those organizations. The party received 3,138 pages of FBI documents, portions of which were published in *The Militant* and in a book entitled *COINTELPRO: The FBI's Secret War on Political Freedom.*

Four kinds of documents are included in the released information, all of them containing deletions which the FBI explained on the basis of national security. There is, first of all, documentation on the forty-one separate "disruption programs" which pertained to the total program which the FBI referred to as "Cointelpro," an abbreviation for Counterintelligence Program. Second, there are sixty-three "investigative files" on fifteen members of the SWP and YSA. Third, there are twenty-three quarterly "field reports" on the SWP spanning the years 1966 to 1974, and sixteen semi-annual "field reports" on the YSA spanning the same time period. Lastly, there are three ten-year "summary reports" on the SWP. These reports are dated 1944, 1955, and 1965.[99]

A number of facts emerge from reviewing the documentation which the party has made public. First, the FBI was particularly concerned about the SWP because the party pursued an electoral strategy. Second, the FBI was particularly fearful over the development of Black militant movements and used racist tactics to keep Black and White militants separate. Third, the FBI routinely attempted to sow dissension among radical groups by sending anonymous letters with false negative information to both members and non-members of the group. Fourth, the FBI had direct lines to both establishment newspaper columnists and television newscasters and fed anti-SWP material to them to be used against SWP candidates.

The SWP has consistently faced attempts to keep it off the ballot. It is now apparent that a major part of Cointelpro were FBI attempts to frustrate the electoral strategy. This is ironic since the justification advanced for repressing groups such as the Panthers was that they were violent and did not use the electoral process. The opposite justification is used in the case of the SWP, a group which renounces the use of violence. The following is the released portion of the text of the letter dated October 12, 1961, which was sent from J. Edgar Hoover to the FBI's New York Office. It is the letter which initiated Cointelpro against the SWP.

> The Socialist Workers Party (SWP) has, over the past several years, been openly espousing its line on a local and national basis through running candidates for public office and strongly directing and/or supporting such causes as Castro's Cuba and integration problems arising in the south.[100] The SWP has also been in frequent contact with international Trotskyite groups stopping short of open and direct contact with these groups.[101] The youth group of the SWP has also been operating on this basis in connection with SWP policies.
>
> Offices receiving copies of this letter are participating in the Bureau's Communist Party, USA Counterintelligence Program. It is felt that a disruption program along similar lines could be initiated against the SWP on a very selective basis. One of the purposes of this program would be to alert the public to the fact that the SWP is not just another socialist group but follows the revolutionary principles of Marx, Lenin, and Engels as interpreted by Leon Trotsky.
>
> It is pointed out, however, that this program is not intended to be a "crash" program. Only carefully thought-out operations with the widest possible effect and benefit

to the nation should be submitted. It may be desirable
to expand the program after the effects have been eval-
uated. Each office is, therefore, requested to carefully
evaluate such a program and submit their views to the
Bureau regarding initiating a SWP disruption program
on a limited basis.[102]

Another document from Hoover to the New York FBI office, dated
"10/8/69," stated:

The Socialist Workers Party (SWP) is a militant communist splinter organization which is growing rapidly.
Members of the SWP are running for the office of mayor in New York City and Atlanta, Georgia.[103]

The candidate for mayor referred to above was Paul Boutelle, who,
the document pointed out, "is a Negro."[104] Boutelle had criticized the SWP
for what he interpreted as racism within the party. Boutelle was a national
leader of the SWP and made his frank criticism at the SWP National Convention, an event which the FBI always surveilled.[105] This gave the FBI an idea.
The FBI document continued:

NYO [the FBI's New York Office] proposes to exploit this issue by sending an anon [FBIese for anon-
ymous] letter to Boutelle in the expectation that Boutelle, who is quick tempered, will become even more
outspoken on this issue. This will thus create a divisive spirit within the SWP. Such action may well
result in Boutelle's resignation from the SWP along
with other members who support him, thus crippling
the SWP in its march for expansion.[106]

The anonymous letter which the FBI composed and sent to Boutelle
with the implication that it was a fellow SWP member contained examples
of the racist literature which the FBI was spewing all over the place in its
anonymous letters. Example: "Some of us within the party are fed up with
the subversive effect you are having on the party, but since a few see your
presence as an asset (because of your color only) not much can be said
openly."[107] Example: "Why don't you and the rest of your fellow party
monkeys hook up with the Panthers where you'd feel at home?"[108] The same
kind of racism permeates the FBI documents relating to their attempts to
drive wedges between the SWP and Malcolm X, Roy Wilkins, and the
Committee to Aid the Monroe defendants in Monroe, North Carolina.[109]

Black candidates of the SWP were singled out for special treatment by the FBI, which seemed to find it incredible that any party would run a Black person for office. When Clarence Franklin was run by the party in the New York City elections of 1962, Charles McHarry, a *New York Daily News* columnist, was fed and printed information on arrest records which this young Black -- born to a Mississippi sharecropper family and taken to New York when he was ten -- had incurred in his past.[110] And when the SWP ran a Black person, Clifton De Berry, for president in 1964, an FBI memo written in March 1964 stated the aim of the FBI to "seriously cripple SWP efforts to gain influence in the Negro civil rights field. It is noted that this is the number one propaganda effort of the SWP, epitomized by their running CLIFTON DE BERRY, a Negro, as SWP Presidential candidate."[111]

On the west coast, the San Francisco FBI office had its chance to try its hand at the anonymous letter technique against another Black candidate, Sam Jordan, who ran for mayor of San Francisco in 1963. Although he was not a member of SWP, that party supported him. In this case an "anonymous longshoreman" [i.e., the FBI] who supposedly feared reprisal on the waterfront sent a letter to Jordan in an attempt to cause a breach between him and his SWP supporters.[112]

The anonymous letter technique was not confined to Blacks, however. This writer has thus far seen copies of three other "anonymous" works of the FBI, one directed at getting a professor fired from a major university, one directed against school board candidates in Denver, and one anonymous leaflet designed to split the anti-war movement.

The professor in question was Morris Starsky, a tenured assistant professor in the philosophy department of Arizona State University at Tempe. Starsky was the faculty advisor of the campus chapters of the YSA and the Student Mobilization Committee to End the War in Vietnam.

Starsky obtained the FBI documents in his own file independently of the lawsuit filed by the SWP. He requested his own file under the stipulations of federal legislation passed after the Watergate revelations. The Director of the FBI, Clarence Kelley, refused to send the file to Starsky, but Attorney General Saxbe ordered Kelley to comply with Starsky's request.

Some of the documents were withheld and those sent to Starsky were censored, all supposedly for the standard reason, "national security." But those documents supplied, even in their censored forms, tell quite a bit about the FBI's attempt to ruin the academic career of the professor.

On July 1, 1968, the Phoenix FBI office sent a memorandum to Hoover which contained the following:

> Starsky's dismissal from the ASU faculty could be
> expected to disrupt New Left organizations at Ari-
> zona State University and in the Phoenix area gene-

rally. In any event, Phoenix will explore means of as-
suring that (censored) is cognizant of the role which
STARSKY and others in the ASU Philosophy Department play in keeping the New Left alive (censored).[113]

This memo was followed by another one on October 1, 1968 which
contained the following:

> 1. *Potential Counterintelligence Action*
> MORRIS J. STARSKY, by his actions, has contin-
> ued to spotlight himself as a target for counterintel-
> ligence action. He and his wife were both named as
> presidential electors by and for the Socialist Workers
> Party when the SWP in August, 1968, gained a place
> on the ballot in Arizona. In addition, they have signed
> themselves as treasurer and secretary respectively of
> the Arizona SWP.[114]

The university administration pressed charges against Starsky before
the Faculty Committee on Academic Freedom and Tenure. It was at this
point that the FBI office in Phoenix composed and submitted to Washington
for approval an "anonymous" letter which was to be sent to members of the
faculty committee. Approval was sought to send the letter to the members,
Professors Rice, Cochran, Effland, Decker, and Adams, in an AIRTEL communication from the Phoenix office to Hoover on April 7, 1970. Permission
to send the letter was received from Washington FBI on April 24, 1970.[115]
The Director of the FBI felt it necessary to caution his Phoenix agents that
the caption "Anonymous Letter to Members of the Faculty Committee on
Academic Freedom and Tenure, Arizona State University" should be deleted
before they sent the letter.

The letter was sent. It tells a story of how Professor Starsky through
bullying and threats drove a former co-worker to a suicide attempt. The former co-worker supposedly had refused to return "socialist literature" to the professor. The two-paragraph letter, signed "A concerned ASU alumnus," ends:

> Should the ASU student body enjoy the guidance of
> such an instructor? It seems to me that this type of
> activity is something that Himmler or Beria could
> accept with pride. If Starsky did not enjoy the pres-
> tige and sanctuary of his position he would be prop-
> erly punished for such a totalitarian venture. Unfor-
> tunately, Murphy is too terrified to testify against
> Starsky's brand of academic socialism.[116]

The Faculty Committee, obviously ignoring the FBI letter, refused to take action against Starsky. But, as in many cases in the academic hierarchies, Starsky won but he lost. What the Academic Committee refused to do, the Board of Regents did. On June 10, 1970, they fired the professor.

Since this was part of the overall Cointelpro program, it is difficult to believe that this is the only academic case in which the FBI has intervened. To know about others, the concerned individuals would have to make a written request to the FBI for their files. And that agency has revealed that if a file did not exist before the request came in, it would be started upon the receipt of the request.

The school board case involved an "anonymous" FBI letter to the President of the Denver school board. The SWP was running two candidates for the board. Thus "A Concerned Mother" wrote a letter to the President in which "she" said:

> In an article of the Denver Post which I am enclosing for your information, this organization is listed as both subversive and on the Attorney General's list of subversive organizations. The article also hints that Mr. Taplin [the husband of one of the candidates] is a communist.
>
> Being a conscientious voter and mother of school age children, I feel that someone should do something to prevent persons of this sort from being elected to the school board.
>
> Although I am much in favor of publicly opposing these people, I feel it best for my family's sake that I withhold my name and leave this situation in your capable hands.
>
> A Concerned Mother[117]

Perhaps the most interesting case of the "anonymous" message was one used to attempt to divide the anti-war movement. In it the FBI proves that it can draw and talk "dirty." The New York FBI office drew up a leaflet entitled "Fly United?" There is a large picture of two ducks in flight. One duck is labeled NEW MOBE (for the New Mobilization Committee, a coalition of anti-war forces) and the other SWP. The NEW MOBE duck is literally being raped by the SWP duck. Under the picture is the word BALLS! And here is the caption message written by the FBI:

> Dig it. It's time to pull the chain, brothers and sisters. If the peace movement in Amerika is to survive, the crap influence of the Socialist Workers Party and its

bastard youth group — Young Socialist Alliance —
must be flushed from New Mobe once and for all.
Stagnant zeros like Freddie Halstead and Harry Ring,
both members of the SWP Nat'l Committee must be
dumped. Let's get rid of the Carol Lipmans, Gus Ho-
rowitzs and the Joanna Minniks along with other SWP
shits! DEMAND AN END TO SWP BALLING! Write
New Mobe today at Suite 900, 1029 Vermont Ave.,
N.W., Washington, D.C.[118]

On February 13, 1970, the New York FBI office sent a memorandum to Hoover in Washington explaining the purpose of the leaflet:

Enclosed for the Bureau is a copy of an unsigned leaflet entitled "Fly United?", mailed this past week to
some 230 selected individuals and organizations in
New Left and related groups under the COINTELPRO
at New York with prior Bureau authority.

The leaflet is designed to cause disruption in the
peace movement, primarily in the New Mobilization
Committee to End the War in Vietnam, and to minimize the growing influence of the SWP in the movement. It is also designed to cause consternation and
confusion in the SWP itself.

The enclosed has been marked "Obscene" because of
its contents. The copy program of the leaflet has been
written in the jargon of the New Left, necessitating the
use of a certain amount of profanity.

Copies of the leaflet have been mailed to members of
the SWP, its youth group the Young Socialist Alliance,
the Student Mobilization Committee, CP USA, DCA
and other groups.

No tangible results have been detected at this early
date, although one source, (censored), has attributed the
leaflet to dissident elements in the New Mobilization
Committee.

The Bureau will be kept advised of reported results.[119]

The government has contended that the COINTELPRO-SWP disruption program was terminated in 1971. This is disputed by the SWP, and
lawyers for the Political Rights Defense Fund — a fund established largely
through the energies of the SWP to fight repression and sponsored by many
prominent non-SWP people—have documented in court numerous post-1971

incidents of attempted disruption. In one instance, a mail check on the SWP was revealed when a 16-year-old New Jersey high-school student wrote to the party for information for a class paper that she was writing. A file was established on her and her family. This was in 1973.

Moreover, in a number of cities, SWP and YSA offices have been broken into and burgled, and members of the party beaten, by right-wing groups. The specific groups involved in this kind of activity or in intimidation varies city by city. In Chicago it was the Legion of Justice, in Los Angeles a group of right-wing Cuban exiles. In Houston, the Ku Klux Klan has assembled before the offices of the SWP, fully armed, while the police refused to do anything about it.

There is widespread suspicion in France that some of the right-wing paramilitary organizations which have attacked people on the Left were actually working in conjunction with the government. On March 24, 1975, the *Chicago Daily News* carried a headline: "Report Cop Spies Backed a Burglary." In the story, investigative reporters Larry Green and Rob Warren wrote:

> A right-wing paramilitary group broke into the office of theYoung Socialist Alliance in 1969 at the behest of Chicago police undercover agents, an informant has told the *Chicago Daily News*.
>
> The informant said police intelligence agents in unmarked cars waited outside to protect the burglars in the event someone discovered the burglary in progress and reported it.
>
> After the burglary at Young Socialist Alliance headquarters, Canal and Jackson, on November 1, 1969, the informant said, the documents were turned over immediately to a federal intelligence agency working with the local police.[120]

What the *Chicago Daily News* did not report in that story was that a member of the YSA was badly clubbed by the burglars. On April 14, however, the paper ran another article, which indicated the degree of violence involved and directly linked U.S. Army Intelligence with several burglaries and acts of violence which the Legion of Justice had committed against a number of anti-war and left-wing groups. Aside from two raids on the headquarters of the YSA, offices of the American Friends Service Committee, the Independent Voters of Illinois, and Newsreel, an anti-war distributor, were also broken into. The newspaper disclosed:

> An army intelligence unit co-operating with Chicago police helped finance and direct right-wing terrorist

activities in northern Illinois from 1969 through 1971, informants have told the *Daily News*.

The terrorists, who were members of a now-defunct organization known as the Legion of Justice, beat, gassed, and wreaked general havoc on members of groups opposed to the Vietnam war.

The Army unit, headquartered in Evanston and known as the 113th Military Intelligence Group, supplied the Legion of Justice with tear gas, mace and electronic surveillance equipment in addition to money, according to the informants...

In some instances, the informants said Army agents assigned to the 113th recruited young men to join the Legion and either paid them directly or gave Sutton [the leader of the Legion] money to pay their rent and expenses.

The sources added that the recruits were required to sign oaths pledging never to reveal their relationship with military intelligence.[121]

The activity of the 113th and the Legion spread beyond Chicago. The newspaper reported that the Army Intelligence group enlisted members of the Legion to incite violence on the campus of Northern Illinois University in DeKalb where a student referendum on ROTC was being conducted in May 1970. Legion members joined an anti-ROTC demonstration on the campus: "'They were told to be the most violent persons there,' one source said. Later, that informant said, the 113th asked one member of the Legion to enroll at Northern to infiltrate New Left activities."[122]

I think that it is safe to say that in almost every major city in the United States where the SWP and the YSA organized, the local police have been cooperating with the federal government's attempt to destroy the SWP. In some places the police simply have been cruder than in others. For example, after refusing to warn the SWP (the police had prior knowledge) or to offer it any protection against armed Klansmen assembled before their offices, the Houston police decided to have their own crack at the SWP. On March 11, 1975, the Houston police arrested the SWP presidential candidate for 1976, Peter Camejo. They stopped the car in which he was returning to SWP headquarters during his Texas campaign tour. When Camejo asked why the car had been stopped, his arm was twisted behind his back and one of the police officers said, "So you're the Commie who's running for president," revealing that the police knew who was in the car before it was stopped.[123]

Although the police claimed to have stopped the car because they thought that they saw a passenger "shredding something," the only charge levied against Camejo was one of interference with the performance of a police officer. While Camejo was being booked at the station, another officer said to him: "You're the big Commie, aren't you? I'm going to get you when you get out."[124] Camejo was acquitted of the charge by a jury, but this was still disruptive of the activities of the party.

Subsequently Camejo was subjected to harassment in at least two other cities. In Atlanta, Georgia, Camejo attempted to attend one of President Ford's regional "economic conferences." He was stopped at the door and introduced himself to the person stationed there. This individual asked him to wait at the door, informing him that he would see what could be done about getting in. He returned with police, who seized and held Camejo for six hours. In Columbia, South Carolina, Camejo had scheduled a news conference for 11 a.m. The police informed the newspapers that the news conference had been rescheduled for 6 p.m. This was a complete fabrication, simply another attempt to disrupt the campaign.[125]

What is revealing is that the federal government — through its own civilian and military agents and through its influence upon local police departments — used illegal, unconstitutional, and violent methods to destroy a party which eschewed violence and which was attempting to build support through the electoral process. Once again, as in its behavior in Chile, the government seemed determined to validate Cannon's prediction that the capitalist regime would never accept even a legally obtained majority option for socialism. Indeed, the U.S. government apparently decided to see that things never would progress to that stage — and to see to it by whatever means necessary. Watergate was simply the introduction into the "two-party system" of some of the milder tactics which have been used against the SWP and other Left anti-war groups for a very long time.[126]

SUMMARY CONCLUSION

From the very beginning, U.S. Trotskyism demonstrated different characteristics from French Trotskyism. Cannon's hegemony over the SWP was never severely threatened, nor was the SWP's hegemony over U.S. Trotskyism. Indeed, Trotsky pointed to the relatively cohesive U.S. movement as a model for the French to follow, and he prevailed upon Cannon to help him try to deal with the divided and conflict-ridden French Trotskyist movement.

As the U.S. Trotskyist movement developed historically, the impact of the political context upon it became quite obvious. This larger context played an important role in differentiating U.S. Trotskyism from French Trotskyism along a number of organizational, theoretical/programmatic, and strategic/tactical dimensions. In a setting with paucity of viable models on the Left, the differences over the best model for party organization in the United States are minimal. The SWP, the Spartacist League, and the Workers League all maintain similar patterns and structures. They, like the French Lambertists, adhere to the conventional model of communist parties in the Western countries. Only tiny Spark offers a different model, that of *Lutte Ouvrière*. And this is due to the impact of an international meeting at which members of Spark were directly influenced by militants from *Lutte Ouvrière*. Spark's form of organization is thus an international import, just as *Lutte Ouvrière's* pattern of organization was imported from Eastern Europe by Barta. An additional effect of the weakness of structures on the American Left is that American Trotskyists have been led to call for the creation of a separate and broadly aggregative labor party. Such a call would make no sense within the French context, where parties on the Left already enjoy wide support among workers.

The political context also has had an impact on several theoretical or programmatic issues. Trotskyists in the United States place much more stress on the Transitional Program than do French Trotskyists who are appealing to a much more radical working class. Since *autogestion* strikes a responsive chord among those workers, that has become a major issue among French Trotskyists while it has not among U.S. Trotskyists.

On the other hand, how to deal with the phenomenon of racial distinctions had been as divisive a question for American Trotskyists as *autogestion* has been for the French. The SWP and Spark support the creation of a separate Black party, while the Spartacist League and the Workers League are opposed. In France, there is simply not the same kind of permanent racial and ethnic diversity. There are, of course, women in both countries. Just as the United States experienced a rising feminist consciousness before France, so too have U.S. Trotskyists dealt with the issue longer than French Trotskyists, and the antagonism over the issue is greater between U.S. Trotskyist groups than between the French groups. While being less divisive than the question of feminism, the treatment of gays and lesbians and their role within the movement also was raised earlier in the United States than in France. But then no group in France had excluded them the way the SWP had in the United States. However this exclusion — enacted out of fear of political costs associated with social deviance — was also a reflection of the differing political contexts and social attitudes in the two countries.

National contextual differences are also important in determining the international issues upon which Trotskyists focus and disagree. While French Trotskyists are badly divided over the precise nature of the Soviet Union and the relation of the French Communist Party to the USSR, U.S. Trotskyists do not dwell on the question. The lack of power of the American Communist Party would not seem to warrant it. One international issue has proved to be terribly divisive for U.S. Trotskyists: the precise nature of the Cuban regime and the position to adopt toward it. For a considerable period, Cuba was the only self-proclaimed Marxist regime in the Western hemisphere, and the majority of the SWP felt that it had to launch a supportive campaign in the face of attempts of the U.S. government to destroy it. This positive attitude toward the Cuban Revolution was also congruent with the appeal which Cuba and personalities such as Fidel and Ché were having for an increasingly radicalized American youth milieu in the 1960s. But it had a literally shattering effect on the party. The Spartacist League, the Workers League, and Spark all owe their existence as Trotskyist groups independent of the SWP to disagreement over Cuba.

In tactical and strategic areas, there are also important differences. Since U.S. Trotskyists are not faced with left-wing competitive unions as the French are, they do not have to choose and disagree over which to work within. While the youth affiliate of the Workers World Party in the United States has been highly confrontation-oriented, no U.S. group openly proclaiming itself to be Trotskyist has been as confrontation-oriented as the French *Ligue,* which was born with the influx of 1968 barricade fighters into the ranks of French Trotskyism. And this includes the SWP, the *Ligue's* fraternal party in the United States. While the SWP has not openly criticized the *Ligue's* confrontational posture in France, it has tried to temper the *Ligue's* support for what it regards as adventuristic strategies in Latin America.

Furthermore, the attitude toward electoralism exhibited by French Trotskyists and by the SWP, the only U.S. Trotskyist group large enough to engage in it in an extensive manner, is quite different. While the French make use of the electoral mechanisms, they are extremely disparaging of them. The SWP, which feels that workers in the United States accept the electoral process, does not engage in such disparagement but tries to demonstrate that the capitalists will never accept outcomes which pose a basic challenge to their control. In recent times, they have pointed both to Chile and to their own treatment at the hands of repressive forces in the United States when they have tried to engage in electoral activity.

In a number of areas and instances, Trotskyists have exerted a reciprocal impact upon the larger U.S. political context. Trotskyists led the 1939 Minneapolis drivers' strike and played a crucial role in the early organizing which led to the creation of a powerful Teamsters Union. The anti-war work of the Socialist Workers Party and its Young Socialist Alliance during the Vietnam war years provided an important element of disciplined work and organizational skills to a generally fluid movement. The SWP's lawsuit which opened up the COINTELPRO files provided a revelation to the American public in terms of the real behavior of the U.S. government toward dissident groups. That party's publications, including both periodical literature and the books and pamphlets published by Pathfinder Press, are an important source of Marxist perspectives and interpretations within a political culture which does not encourage their development and dissemination. Finally, as in France, the Trotskyist movement in the United States has served as a school for political education for many young people who later went in different political and intellectual directions. It was an important stage for these people because even when the leadership was at its dogmatic peaks, ideas were taken seriously.

Leon Trotsky returned to Russia from the United States in May of 1917 and chaired the Petrograd Soviet during the October Revolution that year. He later became War Commissar and created the Red Army. Following Lenin's death in 1924, Trotsky lost all share in the direction of Soviet policy to Joseph Stalin, who expelled Trotsky from the party in 1927 and deported him in 1929. Trotsky was assassinated in a suburb of Mexico City in August, 1940.

A founding member of the Chinese Communist Party in 1921, Mao ZeDong (Mao Tse-Tung) accepted office as Chairman of the People's Republic of China in Peking in 1949, following the successful revolution against Chiang Kai-shek, the nationalist leader. He led China until his death in 1976.

French students demonstrate with a police effigy in the streets of Paris during the events of May, 1968, when youth protests and workers' strikes combined to support the the most sustained general strike in France's history.

Above, left to right: Alain Geismar, head of the *Syndicat National de l'Enseignement Supérieure,* one of three unions uniting left-wing teachers from radicals to Communists in the *Fédération de l'Éducation Nationale;* Jacques Sauvageot, leader of the militant-controlled *Union Nationale des Étudiants de France;* and Daniel Cohn-Bendit, "Danny the Red," affiliated with the *Mouvement de 22 Mars.* Below, left to right: German radical Rudi Dutschke with Alain Krivine of the *Jeunesse Communiste Révolutionnaire.*

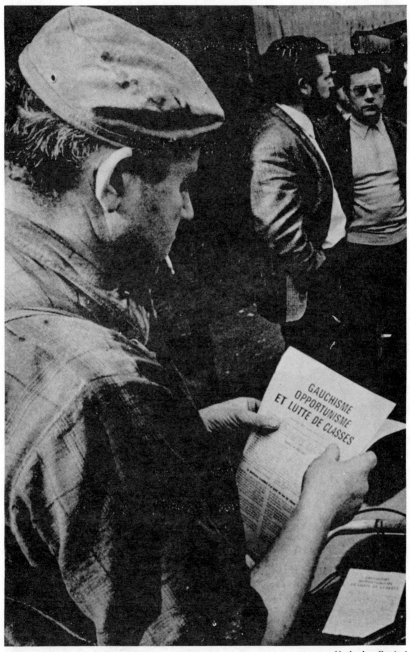

A French worker reads a pamphlet entitled "Leftism, Opportunism and Class
Struggle" during a strike at the Renault auto plant in the spring of 1971.

Joint publication of the French Trotskyist organizations *Ligue Communiste* and *Lutte Ouvrière*, dating from 1971 and promoting working class unity around the issue of equality of wages and salary increases.

la cause du peuple

| 1 F | Boîte Postale 130, Paris-20ᵉ
C.C.P. : N° 3048991 - LA SOURCE | JOURNAL COMMUNISTE
REVOLUTIONNAIRE PROLETARIEN | 3ᵉ ANNEE N° 29
MERCREDI 14 OCTOBRE 1970 |

« Je témoignerai dans la rue. »

Défiant la loi de Marcellin qui prétend interdire les manifestations, liquider la « Cause du Peuple », mettre fin à la liberté de contester, Alain Geismar montre le chemin de l'honneur.

Depuis les barricades de 68, il dit à l'ouvrier :

Pour te défendre, il faut attaquer.

Pour prendre le temps de vivre,

— brise les cadences,

— mate les chefs,

— sabote la production du patron,

— à mauvaise paie, mauvais travail,

— frappe les assassins.

Pour le droit au travail,

— un député, ça peut se lyncher,

— comme un patron, ça peut se séquestrer.

« Organisez-vous » sans attendre le consentement des hommes cravatés qui usent leur pointe bic dans les bureaux du patron.

Union et Résistance !

Pour la liberté d'expression.

Pour le droit de vivre.

Dans l'usine et dans la rue, à notre tour nous témoignerons, les 20, 21, 22 octobre.

Procès Geismar = procès du Peuple.

Patrons et ministres, vous pouvez rugir, lacérer, condamner, retirer droits civiques, droits familiaux, vos barrages ne résisteront pas.

Vous avez semé la haine.

Le 20 octobre, vous récolterez.

JE TEMOIGNERAI DANS LA RUE . 27 mai 70.

ALAIN GEISMAR NOUS MONTRE LE CHEMIN DE L'HONNEUR

TOUS DANS LA RUE LE 20 OCTOBRE

La Cause du peuple, the Maoist journal nominally edited by Jean-Paul Sartre. This issue, from October of 1970, during the third year of its publication, is dedicated to the trial of Alain Geismar. Sartre spoke at large rallies for Geismar, and defied a ban against the periodical by hawking it himself in the streets. Sartre was not arrested, but François Maspero, the book editor, was.

Mexican muralist Diego Rivera's gift to the Communist League of America, featuring Trotsky (center), Engels, Lenin and Marx (full faces behind him), with, among others, Max Shachtman and James Cannon (lower right).

Max Shachtman, who with James P. Cannon and others in the 1920s formed the Communist League of America, Left Opposition of the Communist Party, the earliest Trotskyist party in the United States.

An advertising circular from 1930 announcing a speech by Socialist Workers Party National Secretary James P. Cannon in Boston. Topic: the "collapse of Collective Security, with the working-class of Europe mobilized to die for its respective capitalist class."

MASS MEETING

HEAR *1930*

James P. Cannon

National Secretary of Socialist Workers Party

Cannon has just returned from Europe and was a witness to the collapse of the policy of so-called "Collective-Security." He saw the working-class of Europe mobilized to die for its respective capitalist class.

Workers Center

16 LA GRANGE ST., BOSTON

Sunday, October 30

8.00 p. m.

Auspices:
Socialist Workers Party — 4th International

NEXT SUNDAY: November 6th — MAX SHACHTMAN
"The Russian Revolution and The 4th International"
FORUMS EVERY SUNDAY NIGHT

65

POLITICAL PRISONERS
OF USA FASCISM

Poster for the Black Panther Party, above, with then-imprisoned Panther leaders Bobby Seale and Huey Newton. Right, campaign poster for the Socialist Workers Party of 1968 on the theme of Black and Puerto Rican control of communities.

Black and Puerto Rican Control of Black and Puerto Rican Communities

vote socialist workers
Paul Boutelle for Mayor

No. 4   FALL 1973

Women and Revolution

Journal of the Women's Commission of the Spartacist League   X-523   25¢

Toward a Communist Women's Movement!...2

(Author's collection)

Cover of the Fall 1973 issue of *Women and Revolution,* the journal of the Women's Commission of the Spartacist League of the United States. A twenty-six point program inside called for, among other things, free health care and child care and an end to persecution of prostitutes and homosexuals.

5

Maoism in the United States

Up to this point our study of Trotskyism and Maoism in France and the United States has revealed three different movement configurations. In France there are three major Trotskyist groups with differing positions on organizational patterns, issues, and tactics. On the other hand, a single party has been and continues to be dominant in the world of U.S. Trotskyism, with no other Trotskyist group matching it in size or scope and level of activity.

Until the mid-1970s the French Maoist movement was split between those holding to an anti-hierarchical conception of Maoism and those holding to a hierarchical or more traditionally Leninist conception. By the late seventies, the anti-hierarchical Maoists had just about completely faded from the scene, leaving three dominant hierarchical Maoist groups. The following examination of the Maoist movement in the U.S. reveals that one group dominated in the 1960s but tied its fortunes too closely with those of the Students for a Democratic Society (SDS). It suffered badly as a result of the struggles within SDS, and two new Maoist organizations emerged which, along with the *Guardian* newspaper, became the dominant forces of U.S. Maoism for most of the seventies. We will examine the changes for the 1980s in the Epilogue.

Let us then begin with an examination of the origin and evolution of the first Maoist group in the United States, the Progressive Labor Party.

PROGRESSIVE LABOR

Like the French Maoist movement, the U.S. Maoists can trace the origin of their movement to the early 1960s and the impact which the Sino-Soviet split had upon communist parties in Western capitalist countries.

On June 1, 1962, approximately fifty members and ex-members of the U.S. Communist Party who felt that the Chinese position was correct, and that the Moscow-oriented Communist Party leadership was wrong in supporting the Soviet position, met at the Hotel Diplomat in New York and founded the Progressive Labor Movement.[1]

In its first three years of life the Progressive Labor Movement invested its energies in several activities. It defied the State Department ban on travel to Cuba and sent planeloads of young people there. Upon their return from Cuba these people defied the inquisitorial House UnAmerican Activities Committee. Progressive Labor attempted to organize Black workers in the ghettos. It also attempted to lend support to the miners' strike which broke out in Hazard, Kentucky in 1962 and to the defense of the Black associates of Robert F. Williams in the Monroe, North Carolina kidnapping trial. Finally, the Progressive Labor Movement dominated an anti-war, anti-imperialist group created in May 1964 called the May 2nd Movement (M2M). The M2M adopted the "Out Now!" slogan, which the Trotskyist-dominated Student Mobilization Committee (SMC) used, as opposed to the Communist Party's "Negotiate Now!"

But from the very beginning there were severe recriminations between the SWP and the Progressive Labor Movement (PLM). While both groups adopted the "Out Now!" slogan, the Progressive Labor Movement urged draft resistance while the SWP urged people to go into the armed forces and do political work. Moreover, in both the Hazard, Kentucky and the Monroe, North Carolina actions the SWP accused the PLM of placing its own organizational and publicity interests above the interests of those whom they claimed to be serving. Progressive Labor, on the other hand, lumped both the SWP and the Communist Party in the same "revisionist" camp. Only on the issue of Cuba were they all in agreement for a time. However, Progressive Labor was to completely reverse itself on that issue, as Castro's ties with the Soviet Union and hostility with China increased.[2]

The organization grew rapidly. By 1964 it was claiming six hundred members and in the spring of 1965 eight hundred. The decision was made to transform itself from a movement to a party and at the first party convention, held in the summer of 1965, one observer cites estimates of from one thousand to fourteen hundred members.[3] Almost immediately after the first convention, in February 1966, the tactical decision was made to dissolve the M2M, to tighten organizational discipline, and to enter the Students for a Democratic Society. This again represented a very different strategy from that of the SWP and YSA, which concentrated their attention on the Student Mobilization Committee and remained outside SDS, while criticizing it for insufficient attention to the anti-war effort.

The Progressive Labor Party (PLP) differed from almost every other tendency within SDS in that it was a child of the Old Left and very anti-counter-culture. It was attached to a fixed version of Marxist thought. It felt that if one wished to relate to the workers one had to be like the workers. Counter-cultural generational differences were viewed as middle class phenomena with no relevance to the world of workers. Progressive Labor militants therefore adopted styles and patterns of social behavior which would not appear strange to workers. The men had short haircuts and both men and women dressed "neatly." They refused to use dope, not because of a fear for police action against them—which was the SWP's usually stated reason—but because workers would not respond positively to people who did that kind of thing. Needless to say, they were conspicuous among the more counter-culturally inclined delegates at SDS meetings.

The first political thrust which the PLP attempted within the SDS was a position paper presented in the spring of 1966 advocating a "Student Power" which would connect the efforts to gain student control over universities with those to put an end to war in Vietnam. The presentation of a program by a group with a fixed ideological analysis and program obliged others in SDS, most of whom were still very "anti-ideological," to come up with some kind of coherent statement of where SDS should go. It was at this time that Carl Davidson, an SDS "old-timer" who was later to become a Maoist himself, presented his alternative text "Toward a Student Syndicalist Movement, or University Reform Revisited."

Kirkpatrick Sale stresses the indigenous influence upon Davidson's thinking, "the original syndicalists, the Wobblies--and his own experiences at Penn State and Nebraska."[4] As one who heard Davidson present and discuss the position at a meeting on student power in May 1967, I was struck and continue to be struck by the similarities between the concept of student syndicalism as it was developed by militants within the national student union in France (UNEF) and the proposals of Davidson.[5]

The difference between Davidson's position and that of the PLP was clear. Davidson seemed convinced that (1) the university was the key institution for social change, and (2) students could gain control of the university. The PLP on the other hand felt that one could join the issues of university control, the war, and capitalism but that Davidson's formulation was not supported by any solid theory and would amount to students sticking their heads in the sand of the university. To take over the university (even if one developed a strategy whereby one could do that) is simply not equivalent to taking over the world, the PLP argued.

Shortly after it formed, in March 1963, the Progressive Labor Movement had issued a text of its program entitled "Road to Revolution—I."[6] In December of 1966, approximately eight months after it had offered its "student power" proposals to SDS, the Progressive Labor Party issued a revised "Road to Revolution—II." While the party did not yet completely turn against the NLF in Vietnam, it warned of the dangers incurred by the NLF's acceptance of Soviet assistance and clearly suggested that the Vietnamese refuse to accept the assistance. One of the effects of the new statement was to split the PLP itself. Kirkpatrick Sale contends that most of the people lost to the movement were West Coast and Canadian militants who also comprised the bulk of the non-students in the PLP.[7] I have no data to substantiate the latter assertion, but it is clear that after the 1966 split PLP strength was concentrated on the East Coast and in Chicago.

In any case, by its own admission the PLP was not recruiting well among workers, and if Sale is correct in asserting that it lost most of the non-students it had in 1966, this self-proclaimed vanguard of the working class was in serious trouble. In a summary of a PLP National Committee Meeting in January 1969, one reads the following:

> But because our party may have 50% or 60% or even 90% of
> its members working in trade unions does not necessarily mean
> that we will have become a proletarianized or working class
> party. While we have concluded that the objective conditions
> are certainly ripe and full of class struggle out of which workers
> can be recruited to our party, whom have we been recruiting?
> It is mainly teachers, welfare workers and students, independent
> radicals and professionals. This is good, and should increase.
> But whom have we NOT been recruiting? Industrial workers
> (except in rare instances).[8]

This was particularly serious since the propagated strategy of the PLP at that time was that the revolution would have to be built upon the organization of union caucuses among industrial workers, and that it was particularly the super-exploited Black workers who were the "key revolutionary force."[9] Given the surplus of students and the scarcity of workers in the party, the PLP decided to conduct a "work-in" in the summer of 1967. This was simply an attempt on the part of members of the PLP to secure summer employment in factories and militate among the workers on the order of some of the summer projects of the ex-GP in France.

This project was not much of a success either. In a reassessment of their past strategy, in August of 1969 the party wrote:

> One of the big mistakes we made was to perpetuate the old
> C.P. notion of sending students to work in industry. We
> thought it was only their revisionist politics that made a
> shambles of the "colonization" plan, and that since PL's line
> was correct our students in industry were guaranteed success.
> But we had made only a superficial analysis of the problem.[10]

If the actual attempt to send students to work in the factories was not a success, the PLP claimed a very impressive reception extended to its new newspaper, *Challenge-Desafio*. The party reported that the fortnightly paper, printed in both English and Spanish, had reached a circulation of 100,000 by 1970 and that over half of the purchasers of the paper were "workers on the job."[11]

But selling newspapers and mobilizing workers are two different things. The PLP had tried to shift from a "student power" to a "worker-student alliance" strategy. Its strength, however, was still in the universities, and particularly in the eastern SDS chapters.

Over half of the Harvard SDS chapter was PLP in 1967, and of the approximately two hundred voting delegates at the SDS National Convention in the summer of 1967 approximately forty or fifty were disciplined PLP members.[12] By the fall of 1967, Sale estimates that the party had one thousand members.[13] In terms of a group with a fixed ideology, they were without rivals in SDS.

In that fall of 1967 there was a curious rearrangement of positions. Davidson and the dominant SDS leadership was turning away from the exclusive reliance upon students and gaining control of the universities (students were seen as the "new working class" in the student syndicalist approach of Davidson) and going toward a program of resistance against imperialism on all fronts.

The PLP, however, began assuming a position which some characterized as "right-wing opportunism." It urged students to stick to the question of university complicity, to confine their activities to the campuses, and to avoid confrontations which might alienate both the student body and the community. This was justified by the lesson learned in the summer of 1967, i.e., the necessary groundwork had not been laid for joint student-worker "resistance" to U.S. imperialism, and workers were not prepared to follow students who marched into the factories. The PLP turned its attention to two separate strategies of base-building, one focusing on the campuses and the other on the worker milieu. It advocated the first of these strategies within SDS.[14]

A new configuration of forces within SDS began to emerge. The PLP was forcing prominent people within SDS to develop firmer organizational bonds even if they had no really firm ideological commitments. In the summer of 1968, before the Chicago confrontations, the PLP delivered a stunning defeat to those in control of the National Office (NO) of SDS. With no more than 25 per cent of those attending the convention actually PLP members, the party led the way in defeating both the vague program offered by the NO and attempts of the NO to get a more centralized structure accepted by the convention so that the NO could more effectively combat the PLP.

Frustrated in their attempts, the NO made a very drastic move. One of the problems which the League for Industrial Democracy had with the SDS (while the latter was still the former's youth affiliate) was the non-exclusionist policy of SDS. And this became a cardinal principle for SDS--no one was to be excluded from the organization. At this convention, however, the national officers attempted to convince the delegates that the PLP was an external organization which was attempting to frustrate the SDS's revolutionary efforts. It was clear that the majority of delegates was not agreeable to a move for expulsion, and the national officers did not force the issue to a vote.[15]

Although the PLP was not capturing control of SDS its actions were having very definite effects. It had at least contributed to pushing the whole organization to the left. By the spring of 1968 virtually all of the national leaders considered themselves "revolutionaries." Bernardine Dohrn, elected Inter-Organization Secretary in the spring of 1968, had declared herself to be a "revolutionary communist."[16] She and almost all of the other members of the NO sincerely believed that the PLP's "right-wing opportunism" was obstructing the revolutionary work of SDS.

Virtually all of the NO people, who a couple years before had been ideologically vacuous, were evolving toward either the Weatherman position, as Dohrn was, or toward some non-PLP variant of Maoist ideology.

The other effect was to force the hand of the NO people into taking organizational measures which would be viewed by the non-committed delegates as undemocratic or somehow improper. The first move was the declaration that the PLP was an external group and the seeking of approval by the delegates for greater organizational control. As we have seen, the NO suffered a defeat. The second move of the NO was to advance a slate of candidates for the top three offices in SDS. Again, this violated the norms of the organization. The PLP knew that this would be viewed negatively by the delegates and tactically refused to present a slate of its own. The NO slate won the offices, but only by virtue of lack of competition and at the cost of further offending the sensibilities of the uncommitted delegates.[17]

The confrontations in Chicago during the Democratic National Convention late in the summer drove a further wedge between Progressive Labor and the National Office. At first, the approach of the National Office was to make an appeal to the supporters of Senator Eugene McCarthy to recognize that electoral politics within the two-party system would not result in fundamental change. But when the NO leaders actually saw the turnouts in the streets and in Lincoln Park, they shifted their appeal from the McCarthy supporters to the masses of young people who were there to protest the whole affair. The National Officers became involved in the confrontation politics of the streets. The PLP, on the other hand, reacted to the August confrontation in Chicago in a fashion similar to the reaction of both the Maoist UJCML and the Lambertist Trotskyist OCI to the French uprising earlier in the summer. The PLP claimed, as had the above French groups faced with the barricades of Paris, that the revolution could not be made by students facing off against police but only with the participation of the working class. But the confrontations in Chicago were not followed by anything like the massive workers' strikes in France which then led the French Maoists to go out on "Long Marches" to support the workers occupying their factories.

In 1968 confrontation politics was at its height in most of the Western industrialized countries, and youth groups which opposed it tended to be viewed as traitors to the revolution and to their generation. The verbal, physical, and litigational attacks from the establishment (and in France this included the Communist Party) were becoming very serious, and the tolerance of opposition from young people in "Old Left" groups was diminishing rapidly.

And in the eyes of the NO and many of the rank-and-file SDSers the anti-confrontation, anti-drug, short-haired, highly disciplined PLP people were just as "Old Left" as the Communist Party of which they were originally a dissident faction.

Moreover, the PLP was coming apart at the seams. On the East Coast, and particularly in New York and Philadelphia, some PLP people were quitting and/or being expelled for developing a separate analysis of the working class. At the June 1968 SDS national convention, some of these people from the SDS chapter at Columbia University, who had come under the growing influence of an older former Trotskyist and SWP member named Lyndon LaRouche (alias Lynn Marcus), formed the Labor Committee.[18] While the Labor Committee group was expelled from the Columbia SDS chapter later in the year, its influence spread geographically and it was to evolve into one of the most bizarre formations ever to appear in American politics. The name was changed to the National Caucus of Labor Committees (NCLC).

On the West Coast the PLP's fortunes were also declining. While the organization took over the Berkeley SDS chapter after the former leaders of the chapter led a sit-in to gain university credit which the university was refusing for the course being taught by Eldridge Cleaver—a sit-in which did not accomplish its goal and which resulted in numerous arrests—the PLP found that it had taken over little more than itself. The non-PLP militants in the chapter walked out and formed the Radical Student Union, the first step in the creation of an organization which would replace the PLP as the largest and most vital Maoist group in the United States.

Thus, while the PLP was able to embarrass the National Office at earlier SDS meetings, its proposals at the October 1968 National Council meeting (450 people attended) went down to a resounding two-to-one defeat.[19]

By the National Council meeting of December 1968, the opposition to the PLP had coalesced under the name Revolutionary Youth Movement (RYM). By this time the PLP had reversed itself on a number of positions which drove the wedge in even further. After first supporting the cause of Black nationalism as espoused by the Black Muslims, distinguishing between "revolutionary" nationalism and "reactionary" nationalism, the PLP adopted the position that all nationalism was reactionary. It continued to see Black industrial workers as a key revolutionary force, but it opposed all separatist Black movements. It opposed busing as a Southern plot to drive a wedge against Black and White workers. And it denounced confrontations designed to gain university open admissions, the institution of Black studies programs, and affirmative action programs for the hiring of Black or minority teachers. Its own pet projects at the universities were an anti-ROTC program and the curtailment of university expansion into urban communities, the latter being a particular favorite of its important contingent at Columbia University.

Its position on women was similar to that on Blacks. Women were terribly exploited within the capitalist economy, but it would be a serious mistake to separate the struggle of women from that of the working class as a whole. The object of a revolutionary group should be to hold the working class together, not to separate it into subcategories. The positions of the SWP were thus seen to be completely opportunistic. If there was a separatist movement to be found, be it among Blacks, Latinos, women, or people of homosexual preference, the PLP viewed the SWP as always willing to jump on the bandwagon without any theoretical analysis of how this division of the working class was going to maximize the chances for a successful revolution.

In the international arena, the PLP turned completely against the Cubans and the Vietnamese revolutionary movement. As the Cubans moved closer to the Soviets and as relations with China deteriorated for that reason, the PLP--the first group to send young people down to Cuba in defiance of the State Department ban (the Venceremos Brigade was only created in 1969, seven years after the PLP had sent its first group to Cuba)—designated the regime in Cuba as "bourgeois." On the issues of minorities, women, and Cuba the PLP moved to the positions which had been taken even earlier by the Trotskyist Spartacist and Workers Leagues, which had separated themselves from the SWP. But whereas these Trotskyists had written off the Cuban Castro regime in 1962, the shift in the position of the PLP began about 1966.

Even more difficult for the SDSers to accept was the position on the National Liberation Front in Vietnam. As we have seen, the PLP created an anti-war group, the M2M, which it abolished when the party entered SDS. This abolition was tactical and in no way indicated a negative attitude toward the Vietnamese NLF. As late as March 1969, the Opening Report of the PLP Pre-Convention contained the following passages:

> People's War in Vietnam has proven its invincibility. The Vietnamese people are giving a profound demonstration in revolutionary action. We cannot say too many times how this revolution has inspired and encouraged anti-imperialist and revolutionary developments the world over. We have been in the forefront of compelling the U.S. to get out of Vietnam now, despite all obstacles, and this has shown our class consciousness. Internationalism, the support of the revolutionary process everywhere and the subordination of the local struggle to the over-all class struggle, is a sign of growing maturity. In the final analysis internationalism, the knowledge of the fact that the working class and the oppressed people are united in a common cause and against a common international enemy, gives the working class a great deal of leverage. It enables the revolutionary forces on a world scale

to concentrate their strength against a common enemy as well as to vigorously develop the revolutionary process at home. Obviously our complete support of the people in Vietnam has helped our struggle at home. This struggle has not only raised our own consciousness but also raised the understanding of millions of our people.

We would be foolish to overlook setbacks in the international movement that took place in this period and not try to summarize what they mean. Counter-revolution has scored several significant temporary victories: Indonesia, Algeria, Cuba and the complete transformation of class power in the Soviet Union and in all the eastern European countries except Albania. Additionally, U.S. imperialism has launched attacks in the Mid-East, Latin America and Africa.

Generally speaking, we should view the international revolutionary movement in this way. Because of the importance of the Cultural Revolution in China, and the overwhelming significance of Vietnam, the international movement is strategically stronger. Marxism-Leninism is stronger because it is more thoroughly developed than ever before. The concept of the dictatorship of the proletariat has been clarified and strengthened. People's War has been proven to be a vital contribution to the arsenal of Marxism-Leninism. The understanding of how to fight revisionism in a revolutionary party by clarifying the relationship of the party to the people is invaluable. Three little words--"Serve the people"-- if properly understood and applied, are a weapon for the working class of incalculable force. So, in fact, if the international movement is smaller in numbers than before, its development is higher than ever. Newly emerging revolutionary forces all over the world can benefit enormously from the Thought of Mao Tse-tung. They can avoid the mistakes of Indonesia, the Algerians, and the Arab world, to mention a few.[20]

The statement, of course, reflects the disenchantment of the PLP with Cuba. The rejection of "the Algerians" and the "mistakes of Indonesia" also represent reversals of past support for both the Ben Bella and Boumedienne regimes in Algeria and the Sukarno regime in Indonesia. At this point, all the PLP had left in the international arena were the Vietnamese revolutionaries, China, and China's Eastern European ally, Albania. Of course this was still more than anything that the Trotskyists could offer as models in terms of actual regimes.

However, almost immediately after this statement was issued, the PLP began to turn away from the Vietnamese. In "Program for Black Liberation" published in February 1969—not even a year after the above statement praising the Vietnamese was issued—the PLP drew an analogy between its willingness to support Black separatist movements if the ruling class moved to destroy them physically, even though it thought that they were not revolutionary, and its support for the Vietnamese:

> This is our attitude in regard to Vietnam. Though we no longer
> believe that the Vietnamese leadership is fighting for the dicta-
> torship of the proletariat, we support the efforts of the people
> against imperialism and demand that the U.S. get out now re-
> gardless of what type government the Vietnamese wish to set up.
> We also call upon the Vietnamese workers and peasants to fight
> for the dictatorship of the proletariat as the only way they can
> determine their own destiny.[21]

Six months later the party took a much harder line toward the Viet-namese. In a document entitled "Revolutionaries Must Fight Nationalism," published in August 1969, the PLP contended:

> The Vietnamese leadership, at least in large measure, became en-
> meshed in Soviet "aid." They were passively on the side of the
> Soviets in the China-Soviet struggle. The Vietnamese enthusias-
> tically supported Soviet and other revisionist parties' policies that
> didn't directly involve China. As you recall, the Vietnamese were
> the first to hail Soviet aggression against the Czechs.We have
> always been puzzled by never reading about or seeing any state-
> ment from the South Vietnamese communists. What was the
> communist role in the NLF? We did see the ten-point program
> which was hailed by the Soviets. This program didn't speak of
> socialism. It proclaimed "neutrality" as the aim of the NLF. The
> program was typical nationalist propaganda: vaguely anti-imperi-
> alist, neutralist, and advocating a vague coalition government
> when the U.S. was out of Vietnam.... The ten-point program is a
> variant of the Dimitrov "popular front" theme of the 7th world
> Congress of the Communist International. It envisions the peace-
> ful transition to socialism. The theory is first to win the victory
> of the popular front and then move somehow to socialism. The
> line of peaceful step by step reunification of South and North
> Vietnam through means of negotiations is also variant [*sic*] of the
> peaceful-transition-to-socialist theme. Is it any wonder that the ten-
> point NLF program is everywhere hailed and supported by the revi-
> sionists? How is it possible for revisionists and Marxist-Lenin-
> ists to unite behind the same program? Only by sacrificing the

Dictatorship of the Proletariat, which is the very heart of Marxism-Leninism.[22]

Further along in the document a scathing analogy is drawn between the NLF strategy and that pursued by the communists in Indonesia:

> As Stalin once mentioned, in regard to other national leaders, they run to the imperialist camp when they are threatened by their own people. In other words, when the Indonesian people were getting too close for bourgeois comfort, Sukarno, like other nationalists, betrayed workers to the imperialists. At the moment, Indonesia is tied to the U.S. and Russia. The people are in dire straits. Millions are dead or dying. The masses are learning the hard way the results of "revolutionary" nationalism. When the Indonesian people fight their way back to political power it won't be by relying on the nationalists, no matter how big they talk or even seem to act sometimes. And no fake national program will lead to their rise to political preeminence. NLF-type liberation programs will take radicals right to the graveyard. They will be next to the heroes of Indonesia who have paid a stiff price so others won't make the same mistake.[23]

The previously-referred-to December National Council meeting was extremely bitter, and victories were won by very narrow margins. The PLP's position that racism should be seen as a device at the disposal of the ruling class to divide workers won over the RYM's objection that racism also infected the working class and that Blacks were in the revolutionary vanguard. On the other two issues, RYM won the day. Michael Klonsky, SDS's National Secretary for 1968-69, successfully defended the RYM proposal (whence the name RYM) that SDS try to move out of the student milieu into the larger youth milieu. This offended the PLP's "workerist" orientation. And the RYM position on women, which contended that the oppression of women under male supremacy was even greater than the oppression of working people in general, but which stopped short of urging separatist organizational attempts to combat that supremacy, won over the PLP's contention that the sexual contradiction was secondary to the class contradiction.[24]

The PLP suspected that there would be a move to expel them. Klonsky assured them that that was not the case and indeed no such move was made at the December meeting. But between that meeting and the SDS convention the following June, the PLP attacked the Vietnamese NLF, the Black Panther Party, and the Black student movement.

1969 CONVENTION AND BIRTH OF POST-PLP MAOISM

The convention sealed the fate of both SDS and the PLP. Prior to the convention the anti-PLP forces which had gone under the name RYM split into two groups, RYM I and RYM II. RYM I was what was to become known as Weatherman. RYM II was dominated by people who were more conventionally Marxist-Leninist. In the early days of the convention, however, they remained in an alliance to defeat the PLP. As the ground rules of the convention were being laid, the alliance was defeated by the PLP on two purely procedural points.

The PLP did not have anywhere near a majority of the delegates on the floor. Their victories were a result of their ability to convince uncommitted delegates that their positions were better than those of their adversaries. Nevertheless, the NO panicked and sought assistance from outside the ranks of SDS. The strategy backfired in their faces.[25]

Members of the Puerto Rican Young Lords, the Chicano Brown Berets, and the Black Panthers were all invited to address the convention. The leaders of all of these organizations, as one would expect, attacked the contention of the PLP that all nationalism is reactionary. And things went very well for the NO until Rufus Walls, Minister of Information for the Illinois Black Panther Party, decided to address himself to the question of woman's liberation. He asserted that Panthers believed in having women in the movement; they believed in "pussy power." He also informed the delegates—and the NO people were, of course, quite beside themselves—that "Superman was a punk because he never even tried to fuck Lois Lane." Walls was followed by Panther Jewel Cook who, after hitting at the PLP for not leading any fights on the campus, declared that he too was in favor of "pussy power." And then he repeated a line which Sale attributes first to Stokely Carmichael during the old SNCC days, namely that the position of women in the revolutionary struggle is "prone."[26]

The entire meeting was thrown up for grabs with PLP and the uncommitted delegates shouting "fight male chauvinism" and the NO people huddling, trying to figure out what to do in the face of this disaster. Jared Israel of the PLP took over the microphone and told the delegates that this fiasco illustrated the contrast between the PLP's principled positions and the completely unprincipled and untheoretical politics of the NO. The NO managed to squelch a proposal that there be a full-scale discussion of what had occurred and of the problem of sexism.

The next day the PLP presented their proposal "Less Talk, More Action—Fight Racism" and it was attacked by both RYM factions. That evening Jewel Cook of the Panthers reappeared to read a statement which the Panthers, the Brown Berets, and the Young Lords had all signed and which had the personal approval of Panther Chairman Bobby Seale. Agreement was secured from the floor to turn the microphone over to Cook to read the following statement:

> After a long study and investigation of Students for a Demo-
> cratic Society and the Progressive Labor Party in particular,
> we have come to the conclusion that the Progressive Labor
> Party has deviated from Marxist-Leninist ideology on the
> National Question and the right of self-determination of all
> oppressed people.
> We demand that by the conclusion of the National Conven-
> tion of Students for a Democratic Society that the Progressive
> Labor Party change its position on the right to self-determina-
> tion and stand in concert with the oppressed peoples of the
> world and begin to follow a true Marxist-Leninist ideology...
> If the Progressive Labor Party continues its egocentric
> policies and revisionist behavior, they will be considered as
> counter-revolutionary traitors and will be dealt with as such.
> Students for a Democratic Society will be judged by the
> company they keep and the efficiency and effectiveness with
> which they deal with bourgeois factions in their organization.[27]

Cook then attempted to go into an extemporaneous attack on the PLP. The PLP delegation, however, took up their cries of "Smash redbaiting! Smash redbaiting!", "Read Mao!", and "Bull-shit! Bull-shit!" The NO support-ers retorted with the Panther slogan "Power to the people!" to which the PLP responded "Power to the workers!" Unable to continue, Cook and his Panther cohorts walked out of the hall. Jeff Gordon of PLP then marched to the rostrum with a group of PLPers and announced to the convention that the PLP had no intention of being intimidated out of SDS.[28]

At this point, Bernardine Dohrn, of the RYM I faction, took the microphone—apparently without prior agreement by other NO people—and announced that a decision on whether or not coexistence with the PLP within SDS was possible had to be made. She invited all delegates who wished to discuss the problem to gather in a room adjacent to the main hall. The PLP attempted to get the people to stay in the hall. Sale estimates that of the fifteen hundred delegates, perhaps two hundred gradually filed into the other room while the PLP chanted "Sit down!", "Stay and fight!", and "No split!"[29]

Nothing was decided on that Friday. On Saturday the RYM leaders met with their supporters again. It was apparent to the uncommitted delegates that they had to make a choice of meeting with the PLP—which was now busy carrying out business and passing motions in the absence of the RYM people---or meeting with the RYM group. At this point the organization was *de facto* split. By this time the RYM group had about six hundred supporters while some of the uncommitted and Old Left groups, such as the Spartacist League and International Socialists,[30] stayed with the PLP in the main hall. By an approximately five-to-one majority the RYM group decided to violate both the principle of non-exclusion and the SDS constitution, which stated that expulsions would require a two-thirds vote of the National Council. They then and there voted to expel the Progressive Labor Party.[31]

Dorhn, who was the driving force in the schism, and several other RYM leaders were charged or charged themselves with drawing up the bill of particulars against the PLP.[32] It read as follows:

> The Progressive Labor Party has attacked every revolutionary nationalist struggle of the black and Latin people in the U.S. as being racist and reactionary. For example, they have attacked open admissions, black studies, community control of police and schools, the Black Panther Party and their "breakfast for children" program, and the League of Revolutionary Black Workers.
>
> Progressive Labor Party has attacked Ho Chi Minh, the National Liberation Front of South Vietnam, the revolutionary government of Cuba—all leaders of the people's struggle for freedom against U.S. imperialism.
>
> Progressive Labor Party, because of its positions and practices is objectively racist, anti-communist, and reactionary. PLP has also in principle and practice refused to join the struggle against male supremacy. It has no place in SDS, an organization of revolutionary youth.
>
> For all these reasons, which have manifested themselves in practice all over the country, as well as at this convention, and because the groups we look to around the world for leadership in the fight against U.S. imperialism, including the Black Panther Party and the Brown Berets, urge us to do so, SDS feels it is now necessary to rid ourselves of the burden of allowing the politics of the Progressive Labor Party to exist within our organization.[33]

That Saturday night the PLP agreed to suspend its meetings to hear what the RYM had decided. With the security forces of both groups poised to prevent physical attack, Klonsky, Rudd, and Dohrn mounted the platform and Dohrn took the microphone to recount the misbehavior of the PLP and to inform its members and those who sided with them that they were out of the SDS. She then led the RYM followers out of the Chicago Coliseum where the convention was being held. The next day the PLP continued to hold its convention---which it claimed was the *real* SDS convention—in the

Coliseum, while the RYM people held their convention—which they claimed was the *real* SDS convention—in a church not far from the Coliseum.

The Progressive Labor Party continued to claim for a while that their "Worker-Student Alliance" group was the real SDS. But the organization was effectively isolated from other groups. Moreover, it was unable to accept the shift of the Chinese from an uncompromisingly hostile posture toward the United States to a much more flexible and friendlier policy. In 1971, the PLP decided that China was, in fact, a capitalist country ruled by a "red bourgeoisie."[34] The party continued to operate with a very small membership, in the same position as the Trotskyists in that it had no models in the real world of political regimes.

The demise of the PLP as a force to be reckoned with in the American radical youth movements in no way spelled the end of Maoism in the United States. The irony of the situation is that several Maoist organizations were born out of the attempt to contain the PLP within SDS. Thus what began as a fight against an Old Left Marxist-Leninist group by an amorphous and ideologically vacuous ensemble of New Left forces within SDS ended as a fight between the still-Maoist PLP and a coalition including anti-PLP Maoists and Weathermen.

RYM II, Weatherman's partner in the battle against the PLP, was not completely Maoist. But most of the major figures in it were or were well on their way to becoming Maoist. Michael Klonsky had sharpened his political perspective during his 1968-69 leadership position in SDS and would work within the Maoist Los Angeles Marxist-Leninist Collective after leaving office. RYM II slated Bob Avakian, who had already formed the Maoist Bay Area Radical Union, to replace Klonsky as SDS National Secretary. RYM II's candidate for Educational Secretary was Lynn Wells, a close associate of Klonsky who had worked with the Student Non-violent Coordinating Committee and the Southern Students Organizing Committee, who would lead the Maoist Georgia Communist League after she and Avakian were defeated by Weatherman candidates Mark Rudd and Bill Ayers. Former SDS national officers Clark Kissinger (National Secretary 1964-65) and Carl Davidson (Inter-organizational Secretary 1967-68) also supported RYM II and went on to become important figures in later U.S. Maoism. After his SDS days, Kissinger went on to become a major figure in the U.S.–China People's Friendship Association and a very close associate of Avakian if not actually a member of his party. After his SDS days, Davidson immediately became an editor of the *Guardian,* until 1975, when he joined the group headed by Klonsky. Thus, while having little impact on Trotskyists, the SDS experience was crucial in the development of U.S. Maoism.

OVERVIEW OF U.S. MAOISM IN THE 1970s

After the 1969 confrontation with SDS and the departure of the PLP from the ranks of Maoism, the forces headed by Avakian and Klonsky provided the major organizational thrust of U.S. Maoism. Avakian and Klonsky have been at the helm of the two largest Maoist organizations in the United States, the Revolutionary Communist Party, USA (RCP) and the Communist Party (Marxist-Leninist), or CP (ML) respectively.

While there has not been the fundamental distinction between hierarchical and anti-hierarchical Maoism that we have seen in France, the larger picture of U.S. Maoism has been in some senses even more complex. The three major reasons for the complexity have been the impact of the racial and ethnic issues in the United States, the abstention of the Chinese from taking sides in the conflicts among Maoist groups in the United States until the summer of 1977, and the emphasis upon decentralized city-wide or community political organization that is largely lacking in France but is an important heritage of the 1960s in the United States.

The result was many more groups than found in France. These include the RCP and the CP (ML), which will occupy our attention in the next section, the numerous small groups and collectives spread out all over the country,[35] the U.S.–China People's Friendship Association, and China Books and Periodicals, Inc., with book and literature distribution centers in New York, Chicago, and San Francisco. But the most important Maoist structures in the United States which have no counterparts in France were the racially or ethnically specific groupings and the *Guardian* weekly newspaper.

(1) Racially or Ethnically Specific Groupings

The Third World orientation of Maoism has had as one effect the fortification of Third World identities among Maoists of Third World heritage in the United States. As we shall see in the next section, Maoists attempt to deal with Third World heritage under the rubric of "nationality" rather than that of race or ethnicity. One organizational manifestation of this was the presence of ethnically or racially specific separate organizations, as well as various attempts to group these organizations under umbrella coalitions.

While Klonsky and Avakian found themselves on the same side as the Black Panthers in combatting the PLP in 1969, the Panthers did not claim to be a Maoist organization. And, while the California Communist League (later to become the Communist Labor Party or CLP) was founded in 1968 largely by Black and Puerto Rican former Communist Party members, it was not a completely separatist organization. Rather the origin of Black Maoist organizations was based upon the political evolution of militants in other Black organizations. Among these were the Student Nonviolent Coordinating Committee (SNCC), the Black Workers Caucus movement, and the League of Revolutionary Black Workers which had created the Revolutionary Union Movements. The best known of these movements was the Dodge Revolutionary Union Movement (DRUM) which attempted to organize Black workers within the Dodge automobile factories.[36]

In 1970, former SNCC militants, other radicalized students and former students, and a lesser number of workers formed the Black Workers Congress (BWC), the first clearly Maoist Black political organization in the United States. For two years the League of Revolutionary Black Workers maintained a direct organizational relationship with the BWC. In 1972, a split occurred between the two but some of the League's members transferred affiliation to the Maoist BWC.[37] Approximately two years after that, the BWC itself split apart in four different directions.

Another Black Maoist organization was created in the mid-1970s. This was an outgrowth of the Congress of Afrikan People (CAP), headed by Amiri Baraka (LeRoi Jones). Baraka had begun community organizing in Newark in the mid-1960s. At that time he was a Black cultural nationalist. He was active in the 1970 election campaign of Mayor Kenneth Gibson in Newark. After falling out with Gibson prior to the mayor's 1974 reelection, Baraka moved away from cultural nationalism and over to a Maoist position. Baraka carried over his unique (for American Maoists) electoral orientation by calling for a very broad united front anti-capitalist "national people's convention" to be held in the spring of 1976, a convention which was supposed to select a presidential candidate.[38] Not long after Baraka issued his convention call, the CAP became the Revolutionary Communist League (Marxism–Leninism–Mao Zedong Thought).

Still another Black Maoist organization was the Revolutionary Workers' League (RWL), which grew our of the earlier African Liberation Support Committee. It was part of an umbrella group of "nationally" specific Maoist organizations called the Revolutionary Wing. The Wing was created in 1975 and lasted for about two years. Joining the Black RWL in the Wing were Puerto Rican, Asian-American, and Mexican-American groups.

The Puerto Rican group within the Revolutionary Wing was the Puerto Rican Revolutionary Workers' Organization (PRRWO). Unlike the Black RWL, the PRRWO traced its lineage back to a group which was active in the anti-PLP campaign within the SDS, the Young Lords Party. Before aligning with the RWL in the Revolutionary Wing, the PRRWO had been very close to the Black Workers' Congress. Their shared perspectives included a commitment to the proposition that there are two kinds of nationalism, revolutionary and reactionary, and that the kind that they were advocating respectively for Puerto Rico and the Black Belt South was indeed revolutionary. They also had similar views concerning school busing; it was seen as an integrationist and reformist plot. Finally, they agreed that none of the multinational Maoist groups in the United States gave sufficient recognition to the fact that non-White workers and workers of Third World heritage, who are the victims of both national and class oppression, showed the greatest revolutionary potential. Despite this critical distance from the multinational Maoist groups, the PRRWO and the BWC together had gone through a phase of working relationships, first (in 1972-73), with the RCP's predecessor organization, the Revolutionary Union, and then with the Communist League.[39]

The Chicano and Chicana organization, the August Twenty-Ninth Movement (ATM), participated briefly in the Revolutionary Wing. But on two concrete issues, it parted company with the Black and Puerto Rican affiliates of the Wing. First, it favored compulsory busing in Boston while reserving the right of individual Blacks to choose if they wish to be bused. Second, it supported the struggle for the Equal Rights Amendment while the other affiliates opposed ERA. While the ATM was in the Wing, these differences led critics to argue that it was not a principled coalition. "Instead of ideological struggle, a liberal 'detente' prevail [*sic*] among them."[40]

Two Asian-American organizations did participate in the Wing. One was the San Francisco-based Wei Min She (WMS). It was very close to Avakian's RCP. But WMS did not seem to last much longer than the Wing itself, two years at most. At least some of its militants then went directly into the RCP. Another largely Asian-American group participating in the Wing for only a brief period was the Workers Viewpoint Organization. Led by a former PLP member, it originally was called the Asian Study group.

An Asian-American Maoist group that rejected all ties with the Wing was the New York and San Francisco-based I Wor Kuen (IWK). It had participated in the 1972-73 relationship with the Revolutionary Union, the PRRWO, and the BWC which was called the National Liaison Committee. But it became quite alienated from these groups and thus avoided the Wing, which included some of the same groups. Along with the Chicano and Chicana ATM, which had partcipated in the Wing for a short period. IWK created the League of Revolutionary Struggle (M–L) in 1978. This latter organization was very close to Klonsky's Communist Party (Marxist–Leninist), the great multinational rival of Avakian's Revolutionary Communist Party. IWK thus had been very critical of its Asian-American rival, Wei Min She, for its close ties to Avakian's party. After the demise of Wei Min She, the IWK began to focus its attacks on the Workers Viewpoint Organization, the only one of the Asian-American groups that was truly a national organization.[41]

French Maoists have not had to deal with anything like this terribly complex network of racially or ethnically specific Maoist organizations. Immigrant workers in France have clear national identities and the confusion between race, ethnicity, and nationality is certainly less of a problem, although racism is not. Moreover, although the Trotskyist SWP calls for the creation of a separate Black political party, it is within Maoism and not Trotskyism that such separatist organizations have actually manifested themselves.

Neither the RCP nor the CP(ML) wanted these structures or would think of advocating them like the SWP has. For these "multinational" Maoist parties, such separatist organizations muddied the waters and had a debilitating effect upon their own organizations.

(2) The *Guardian*

The *Guardian* is a weekly newspaper which played an important role in the development of U.S. Maoism. It differs from the French paper *l'Humanité Rouge* in that until the late 1970s the *Guardian* did not attempt to establish any organizational base, whereas *l'Humanité* served as a cover for the PCMLF during its nine years of clandestine activity. Moreover, there is no newspaper without an organizational base which has performed the same quasi-clearinghouse function for Trotskyists as has the *Guardian* for Maoists.

The *Guardian* was originally created to support the presidential campaign of Henry Wallace in 1945. In the 1950s it condemned the prosecution and conviction of the Rosenbergs and denounced the U.S. role in Korea. In the 1960s the paper opposed U.S. policy on Cuba, Vietnam, and the Dominican Republic. It also supported the national claims of the Palestinians.

In 1968 executive editor Irwin Silber succeeded in attracting SDS national leader Carl Davidson to the *Guardian*. Under the leadership of Silber and Davidson, the *Guardian* moved still closer to the Chinese interpretation of Marxism-Leninism and away from what they regarded as the revisionism of the Soviet Union and the various national parties which support it.

In the early 1970s, after the Progressive Labor Party had denounced Mao and before any of the present Maoist parties had declared themselves to be parties, the *Guardian* called for the creation of a "nonrevisionist Marxist-Leninist" party in the U.S. While the pages of the *Guardian* had always been open to a multitude of different groups which wished to express themselves on various subjects, in 1973 the editors turned over its pages to various currents and groups for a discussion of the specific question of party-building.

But the paper itself did not become involved in the actual dynamics of party-building at this time. In its masthead the *Guardian* described itself as an "independent radical newsweekly." It announced that it would continue to remain independent of "one or another tendency in the movements."[42] The editors summed up what they saw as the paper's role at that point in time:

> Seeing the creation of such a party as the historic task of our time is not to suggest that the *Guardian* proposes to organize such a party in the near future. We do not think that a news-paper, by itself, can organize a revolutionary party. Such a party must, of necessity, be rooted in the working class, be multinational in composition and can only come into being out of the collective experience of those directly engaged in

mass struggle.

But the *Guardian* can play an important role in providing
the information and analysis that will help to develop revolutionary consciousness towards the objective of bringing a
party to birth.[43]

Approximately two years after this was written, however, the differences within Maoism were crystallizing and they manifested themselves within the *Guardian*. Initially there were charges that some of Avakian's people
had "infiltrated" the paper, charges denied by Avakian.[44] More importantly,
the relationship between Silber and Davidson was severed. The immediate
catalysts for the split between these two people—who had worked together
for eight years—were the positions which Silber took in the editorial pages
of the *Guardian* on Black nationalism and on Soviet and Cuban support of the
MPLA in Angola. Because both of these issues will be dealt with in greater
depth further on, suffice it to say here that Silber's positions amounted to (1)
a rejection of the idea that the racial question in the United States could be
dealt with in terms of nationality and (2) a defense of Soviet and Cuban
assistance to the Angolan MPLA as a counter to long-standing U.S. involvement there and the more recent South African involvement. This was, of
necessity, coupled with severe criticism of the Chinese position on Angola
which, in Silber's eyes, placed the Chinese in a position of *de facto* ally of
the U.S. and South African governments. Davidson, on the other hand, saw
Silber's defense of the Soviet and Cuban intervention in favor of the MPLA
as encouraging political fragmentation along tribal lines, rather than unity in
Angola. To Davidson, this demonstrated a chauvinistic presumption *vis-à-vis*
a Third World country. Because Silber was backed by a majority of the
Guardian staff, Davidson resigned and went into Klonsky's group.

Since Silber's position on the racial issue, particularly his rejection
of Black Belt nationalism,[45] was closer to that of the Communist Party than
other Maoist groups, and since his position on the international situation
portrayed the Soviet Union more favorably than do the Chinese or Albanian
positions, the *Guardian* was viewed by the other Maoist groups as moving
toward a "revisionist" position, but not yet quite there. That word was
reserved for the Communist Party itself, which has a positive view of Soviet
socialism. The *Guardian* does not go that far. It was thus "centrist."

Nevertheless, this "centrist" position meant isolation from the Maoist groups with which the *Guardian* once had close contacts. This isolation
moved the *Guardian* closer to its own independent initiative at party-building,
a complete reversal of its 1973 role. In a supplement to the June 1, 1977
issue, the *Guardian* enumerated twenty-nine "principles of unity for a new
party" and announced that it was going to establish a national network of
"Guardian Clubs" which would help sustain the paper, engage in local

political action, and become a vehicle for party-building.[46]

But, from the perspective of most of the other self-designated Maoists, such an organization would represent, at best, a current of "ex-Maoism." If this was an appropriate designation for the *Guardian* in the late 1970s, it was not alone in the ranks of ex-Maoism. The Progressive Labor Party, while much smaller and less active than it once was, still continued to exist after its repudiation of Mao. Another such grouping was the Central Organization of U.S. Marxist-Leninists, which had decided that China was on the road to capitalism and that Albania was the last hope for really-existing regimes as role models in the contemporary world.[47] And finally there was the Communist Labor Party which, in one observer's eyes, "floundered ideologically after its founding congress in 1974, and now exists in the general orbit of Communist Party politics, a polite but unwanted left-opposition to the CP."[48]

The *Guardian's* attempt to serve as a vehicle for party building was a failure. But the most impressive aspect of the *Guardian* has always been its performance as a newspaper. Despite the internal conflict to which it was subjected in the 1970s, and its isolation from other Maoist movements with which it formerly had contacts, the *Guardian* in October 1977 had virtually the same circulation that it had in November 1973.[49] It had a wider circulation than the papers of any of the other Maoist organizations and it certainly did a better job of reaching out beyond the ranks of the already committed Maoists or even Marxist-Leninists. It has become an institution on the Left and was read, respected, and relied upon throughout the 1980s as a news source by many who still might not not have accepted its theoretical stance or its specific positions.

RCP AND CP(M-L)

As pointed out in the last section, the Revolutionary Communist Party, USA and the Communist Party (Marxist-Leninist) continue to be the two largest "multinational" Maoist parties or groups to have been founded in the history of the United States. They both go back to the late 1960s, and their founders were involved in the effort to prevent a PLP takeover of SDS. Only the CP(M-L) really had deep roots in SDS, however. The RCP founders intervened in the 1969 convention merely to block the PLP.

The RCP began as the Bay Area Radical Union, centered in the San Francisco Bay area. The group was formed in 1968, intervened in the SDS situation and published the first of its *Red Papers* in 1969, and changed its name to Revolutionary Union (RU) approximately a year later. In 1972 it made two important organizational moves. It came together with the Black Workers Congress and the Puerto Rican Revolutionary Workers oganization in an umbrella group called the National Liaison Committee. This attempt was short-lived. The Committee collapsed in 1973.[50]

More enduring was the creation of a student affiliate called the Attica Brigade, named after the prisoners who had risen up at New York's Attica Prison and many of whom died when Governor Nelson Rockefeller gave the order to quell the rebellion with arms. Together RU and the Attica Brigade engaged in a number of activities, including: uncritical support for the peace proposals of the Vietnamese Provisional Revolutionary Government (as opposed to the SWP's unconditional support for their struggle against American intervention but severe criticism of the PRG's programs and proposals), support for a number of labor strikes and boycotts (including those of the Farah Workers and the United Farm Workers), entrance into work settings to agitate and discredit the union leadership,[51] prisoner support work, a campaign against appearances by Professor William Shockly who propagates a theory of the intellectual inferiority of the Black race, and a "Throw the Bum Out" Nixon impeachment campaign which was careful to tie Nixon in with the capitalist class as a whole and to leave no illusions that Congress or the liberals could be relied upon to do what was necessary.[52]

The most dramatic exploit of the Attica Brigade was the seizure of the Statue of Liberty by twenty of its members on the evening of April 19, 1974. They held it overnight to dramatize the demand that Nixon be impeached and "to expose the fact that Nixon represents the monopoly capitalist ruling class."[53] The Statue was selected because it "represents the patriotic facade which tries to cover the oppressive and exploitative nature of the society in which we live."[54]

The Attica Brigade was heavily concentrated on the East Coast. Two months after the seizure of the Statue of Liberty, in June of 1974, a convention was held in Iowa City to form a new student group which would be spread throughout the country. Approximately four hundred and fifty students from some eighty colleges and universities across the country then launched the Revolutionary Student Brigade (RSB), perhaps the most militant and action-oriented national grouping on U.S. campuses in the 1970s. Among its more notable actions were the organization of the "Off Our Backs" demonstration in Philadelphia in the spring of 1976, participation in the conflict to prevent the destruction of the International Hotel (the I-Hotel, the home of many aged Asian people in San Francisco's Chinatown), and the 1977 confrontations over the decision of the administration of Kent State University to construct a gym on the site of the killing and wounding of anti-war demonstrators by the Ohio National Guard during the Vietnam War.

In 1975, RU became a party, the Revolutionary Communist Party, USA (RCP). It expanded its organizational network further. During the spring 1976 Philadelphia action, it created a web of youth—as opposed to student—organizations, called Youth in Action in most places but Youth United in certain localities. The first major action of this group, as distinct from the

Revolutionary Student Brigade, was an August 1977 demonstration for jobs, on Wall Street. In the fall of 1977, 1,428 people were assembled for the founding of a workers' organization, United Workers Organization. A little later, in November of 1977, approximately 650 people from Youth in Action, the Revolutionary Student Brigade, and some who had not been previously affiliated came together in Champaign-Urbana, Illinois to form a new youth organization combining both students and non-students, the Revolutionary Communist Youth Brigade.[55] Aside from these organizations of its own creation, the RCP played an important but divisive role which resulted in a split in the Vietnam Veterans Against the War.

The Communist Party (Marxist-Leninist) or CP(ML) had its origins in RYM II within SDS. Two years after the defeat of the PLP and the demise of SDS, the Los Angeles Marxist-Leninist Collective, in which national officer of SDS Michael Klonsky was an activist, the Georgia Communist League, and a number of Black, Chicano, and Middle-Eastern groups came together at a conference in Texas. The result of that meeting in May 1971 was the creation of the October League.

The October League was a late bloomer. It was clearly smaller than the RU/RCP, and it was not very visible. It did not have a student affiliate. In late 1975 the organization began to stir with the addition of Carl Davidson to its ranks, and with the creation of a small press, Liberator Press, to publish pamphlets and books. In 1976, it created two other major structures, the Communist Youth Organization and the National Fight Back Organization, which was its "mass organization," i.e., one which people could join if they simply agreed with its general goals. It was deliberately not a workers' organization like the RCP's United Workers Organization. In fact, the CP(ML) attacked the RCP for committing the joint sins of "dual unionism and syndicalism" by setting up an organization designed to pull the most militant workers away from the unions into a workers' organization distinct from the vanguard party.[56]

There were two spin-offs from the National Fight Back Organization. Both were created in 1977. One, the Southern Conference Educational Fund, was simply a southern branch of the National Fight Back Organization. Secondly, there was the Jobs or Income Now Coalition (JOIN), which was initiated by the National Fight Back Organization.

In the summer of 1977, two major events occurred in the life of this organization. Michael Klonsky went on his fourth trip to China. And the October League became the Communist Party (Marxist-Leninist), with Michael Klonsky as chairman of the party, just as Avakian was chairman of the RCP. The trip and the party constitution were not unrelated. For while the Chinese had never shown an open preference for any American Maoist group over another up to that point, the Chinese regime clearly indicated such a preference for Klonsky's group this time, and welcomed it into the network of parties and groups, including the PCMLF in France, to which it gives such recognition.

As will be seen, there were political reasons for the Chinese action but even the SWP's paper, *The Militant,* could not restrain itself from expressing surprise, given the disparity of level of activity and almost certainly of size of the two organizations. However, the CP(ML) undoubtedly tried to use the recognition itself as a resource to keep up the momentum it had developed in 1976 and 1977. It immediately began planning for the establishment of Marxist-Leninist Unity Committees to pull together those unaffiliated, Marxist-Leninist collectives and groups which were scattered over the country. The CP(ML) also turned its attention to organization on the campuses which, up to this point, had been relatively ignored by the party, to the advantage of the RCP's Revolutionary Student Brigade.

The fact that the CP(ML)'s predecessor organization, the October League, was smaller than its counterpart, the Revolutionary Union which became the Revolutionary Communist Party, and that it did not form the organizational network and the liaisons with other groups that the RU and RCP did, does not imply that the organization was totally inactive. In fact, it engaged in some of the same campaigns that the RU/RCP did, but with fewer resources. It was active in the campaign to impeach Nixon, it supported the Farah and United Farm Workers labor actions, it gave its uncritical support to the peace proposals of the Provisional Revolutionary Government in Vietnam. And like the RU it gave at least verbal support to efforts at change within the United Mine Workers Union and the United Steelworkers of America, although it was attacked by the RU for giving such "reformers" as Arnold Miller and Ed Sadlowski "full support" while the RU gave them "critical support."[57] Similarly, it participated in the campaign to prevent the gym from being built on the site of the Kent State shootings. But it did not act in concert with the RSB. As one CP(ML) militant expressed it to me: "We were at the same place." But in at least one action to which the October League made a major commitment, they were not at the same place. That was in Boston, and the campaign in favor of busing, which the RCP rejected. Later, both the CP(ML) and the RCP, as well as virtually every other organization on the Left, turned their attention toward and organized around the high rate of unemployment.

In historical retrospect, Jim O'Brien sees the high point in activity of the RU/RSB as its sustained support for the Farah strike, while that of the October League was its leadership in a less nationally publicized strike in Atlanta, Georgia. This was the 1972 wildcat strike of mainly Black workers who were protesting racial discrimination at the Mead Packaging Corporation. Black OL members initiated the strike, and the elected chairman of the strike committee was an OL member. O'Brien sees this strike as giving the OL the necessary confidence to work in industrial settings. However, the very limited gains won and the lack of support of most of the White workers convinced the OL of the need to work through the unions as well as on the shop floor.[58] The CP(ML)'s attack on the RCP for "dual" unionist" tactics was a logical extension of this commitment.

Internally, there was a moralistic tone to both organizations which is absent in the case of French Maoist organizations or Trotskyist organizations. They seemed to be trying to emulate the natural simplicity, or the asceticism—depending on one's point of view—of the Chinese. The constitution of the RCP required its members to "uphold proletarian morality," while the constitution of the CP(ML) required members to "live a modest and exemplary life, governing private life by the principles of communist morality."[59] The strictest interpretation of this has been applied by the Revolutionary Communist Party. Both people practicing homosexuality and men and women living together outside of legal marriage have been seen as violators of "proletarian morality." The RCP has viewed homosexuality as "bourgeois decadence," and leaders of the RCP have been known to refer to the capitalists as "faggots." In the case of non-marital cohabitation, a member of the RCP explained to me that the tactical question of relating to those outside the party was secondary. Primary were the RCP's opposition to frivolous or exploitative relations among peo-ple, and the legal rights and need for a family of children. The RCP position on this was thus the exact opposite of the French Trotskyist *Lutte Ouvrière's* position against marriage.

The CP(ML) objected to "decadent 'counter-cultural' lifestyles."[60] It too was a defender of the family. The attack on such lifestyles on the part of the CP(ML) was particularly interesting because of this group's roots in the initially very counter-cultural SDS. Its evolution has thus been in the exactly opposite direction of the VLR and GP currents of French Maoism. When this writer pressed some militants in the CP(ML) for a more precise definition of "decadent 'counter-cultural' lifestyles," the response was "homosexuality, free love, rural communes and other forms of escapism." When asked if people who were homosexuals or living together without being married would be barred from membership, the response was was that people would not be asked if they were homosexuals—that would be their business—and that some people live together without being married because of the welfare system. They claimed that they just did not want their members living in a "promiscuous" or "decadent" way. And here the problem of offending working-class people, which was so pressing on the minds of the members of the anti-counter-cultural Progressive Labor Party in the late 1960s, was mentioned as a major concern. And they certainly would not tolerate any of their party members engaging in campaigns in defense of the rights of gays and lesbians on the order of those of the SWP.

Finally, "feminism," aside from being "a petty-bourgeois ideology that serves the interests of imperialism," that directs women's energies toward trying to get a larger slice of the pie for a minority among their ranks, and that attacks men (rather than the capitalists) as a major enemy of women, was also seen as advocating "decadent 'counter-cultural' lifestyles."[61] There was no disagreement between the two American Maoist Parties on this score and, once again, they are differentiated from the Trotskyist SWP and from the French Maoist VLR. Given this definition of "feminism," one could not be a "feminist" and a member of either of these organizations.

Nevertheless, both organizations did claim important contingents of women. Precise membership figures are organizational secrets. The larger organization, the RCP, probably never had over 1,000 members, while the CP(ML) probably had a membership between one-third and one-half that of the RCP.[62] Approximately 50 per cent of CP(ML) was female, and just under 50 per cent of its Central Committee in the late 1970s was female. Eileen Klehr, the Vice-Chairman of the party—and they insisted upon the traditional terminology, arguing that substance is more important than words—is a woman. In the RCP, a bit over 25 per cent of the members were women.

The issue of the role of the women has been a sore point between the two organizations, and this goes back to the CP(ML)'s roots in RYM II within SDS. In 1974, the RCP's predecessor organization attacked the October League, or rather counter-attacked.

> Further, then as now, these opportunists [the leaders of the
> October League] screamed that the RU was "male chauvin-
> ist," because we sharply criticized RYM-2's mechanical po-
> licy that its leadership bodies must have at least 50 percent
> women, and we opposed RYM-2's mockery of the united
> front which reduced it to a gimmick, with positions like
> "women are part of the united front and men must repudiate
> their male privilege in order to join women in the united
> front."[63]

In 1975 and 1977, this writer attended meetings sponsored by RU and RSB which involved panels of speakers. No woman was a participant on either panel, although at the 1975 meeting the people who distributed leaflets and attended to the literature table were almost all females. The women enthusiastically applauded after the men finished their speeches. It is inconceivable that either the SWP or the CP(ML) would have permitted this. On the other hand, of the ten people on the presiding committee of the convention to found the Revolutionary Communist Youth Organization in November 1977, three were women.[64]

As might be surmised from their history, both parties drew from the same age group. Most members of the parties—as distinct from their youth and student groups—were in the 25 to 35 age group. The most prominent leaders in the late 1970s were in their mid-thirties and in the CP(ML) were SDS veterans. But the CP(ML) was very proud of at least three older activists who had been in the battles of the thirties and who ranged in age from sixty to eighty, the latter being the former Black militant within the Communist Party, Harry Haywood, author of the book *Black Bolshevik.*

Finally, something should be said about the physical location and the publications of the organizations. Both parties were headquartered in Chicago, although they both had initial roots in California. The RCP has its roots in the Bay Area Radical Union in the San Francisco–Berkeley area, and the October League was based in the Los Angeles area in its early years. Although both parties rented space for their party activities, the addresses were not public information. People who wished to contact these parties outside of their public meetings or events were obliged to do so either through the post office box numbers of their publications or, in the case of the RCP, through the campus offices of the Revolutionary Student Brigade.

Aside from public meetings and events such as demonstrations, it is precisely those publications which were the parties' major communication link within the parties and with those outside. There were internal documents which were secret to those outside but there was also quite an array of publications for public consumption which was distributed at events, through China Books and Periodicals, Inc., through more general radical bookstores, or through subscription.[65]

Both parties published theoretical journals. The CP(ML) published *Class Struggle.* It was begun in 1975. The RCP started its journal, *The Communist,* in October 1976. However, prior to the appearance of *The Communist,* the RCP (and the RU before it) had issued its theoretical positions in the form of a series of *Red Papers* which go back to 1969.

The CP(ML) also published a newspaper called *The Call.* It was originally a monthly paper, but it became a weekly in 1976, about a year before the formation of the party. The major newspaper of the Revolutionary Communist Party is *Revolution,* a monthly. However, in approximately twenty cities cells of the RCP put out a separate newspaper called *The Worker.* This was an impressive and rather unique enterprise, because the edition was different in each of the cities. It was heavily oriented toward labor problems in the particular area. Certain editions contained special national supplements. And, like virtually all of the Maoist newspapers (the *Guardian* is an exception), each issue contained an English and a Spanish section. Finally, there were two papers geared to students and youth which were associated with the RCP. One was *Fight Back,* the newspaper of the Revolutionary Student Brigade. Prior to 1977 it appeared regularly but by 1977 its appearance was sporadic. In 1977 a paper called *Young Red* also made its appearance. It too was sporadic, appearing four times in 1977. Curiously, *Young Red* seemed to be a paper which was initiated by people in or around some of the Youth in Action groups and over which the party leadership had virtually no control.

The nature of the CP(ML) publications has thus been very different from that of the RCP. The CP(ML) put out fewer publications, but on a more regular basis. Moreover, just as the CP(ML) criticized the RCP for the creation of the United Workers Organization (the charge was dual unionism, syndicalism, and general economism), so the CP(ML) was critical of the RCP for publishing one paper for party cadres and intellectuals and a watered-down trade unionist paper for workers, which is what the CP(ML) considered *The Worker* to be. The CP(ML) was proud that it published the same theoretical journal and weekly paper for everyone.

While neither the RCP nor the CP(ML) had a publishing operation anywhere approaching the SWP's Pathfinder Press, they did have much more modest publishing operations. RCP Publications published a small number of pamphlets. The CP(ML)'s Liberator Press also published a small number of pamphlets, but in addition tried its hand at longer, book-length manuscripts written by party members.

MAJOR DIFFERENCES AMONG U.S. MAOISTS

In the previous section, one major difference between the RCP and the CP(ML) was noted. This was the more negative attitude toward union work and reformist union leaders on the part of the RCP, and its attempt to create a separate workers' organization and a separate network of newspapers aimed specifically at workers. It was because of this that the CP(ML) accused the RCP of dual unionism, syndicalism, and economism. The RCP responded with charges of opportunism for what it regarded as the CP(ML)'s uncritical support of basically reformist leaders within the unions. It will be recalled that despite the difference in context (i.e., influence of the Communist Party and unity or fragmentation of the labor movement), in France both Maoists and Trotskyists differ among themselves on how to relate to the unions. The Maoist UCFML has refused to work within any of the unions, and *Lutte Ouvrière* has engaged in outright attempts to form a competitive union within Renault. The other groups differ over which unions to work within and how much emphasis to place on union work.

In the absence of the anti-hierarchical as opposed to hierarchical division between Maoists which manifested itself in France, there were three other theoretical and/or issue areas over which the RCP and the CP(ML) had serious differences. They were: (1) the international situation, (2) the "national" question, and (3) the Equal Rights Amendment. While the focus of the following discussion of these questions will be on the adversary positions of the RCP and the CP(ML), the positions of others will be included where they round out the variety of Maoist perspectives.

(1) The International Situation

For a considerable length of time now, the international positions of China have not made life easy for Maoists in either France or the United States. Particularly difficult to deal with and justify—both internally and *vis-à-vis* others on the Left—were such Chinese measures as support for the crushing of rebels in Sri Lanka, the reception of President Nixon in China while bombs were still falling on the Vietnamese, support of the Pakistanis during the war over Bangladash, the refusal to sever ties with the Pinochet regime after the coup in Chile, and support for French and U.S. intervention in Africa. Even back in the mid 1960s, one French Maoist group thought that it was practicing good Maoism by supporting the Gaullists. While this group disgraced itself among the Left by jumping the gun and going a bit too far, there was an element of prophecy in its move.

Prior to the clear articulation of the Theory of the Three Worlds, based upon Lenin's concept of the law of uneven development, Maoist organizations had to choose to follow or not to follow Chinese diplomatic positions and moves. But it was a question of loyalty to the Chinese regime for what it had accomplished in China, and supporters were hard put to find adequate theoretical justification.

The Theory of the Three Worlds was an attempt to provide that justification. While it may not have been much of a positive factor conducive to unity among French Maoists, at least it was not very divisive.

Few French Maoists accepted the Albanian criticism of the theory. While the PCR(m-1) could not accept Chinese support for French involvement in Zaire, it granted the theoretical points and attacked the Albanian position. This was a virtual precondition to its negotiations for reunification with the PCML. In the United States, on the other hand, the explicitness of the Theory confronted some people who were capable of overlooking some of China's diplomatic positions, or even rationalizing them, but who simply could not accept the Theory of the Three Worlds. In this case, the Albanian rejection of the Theory greatly encouraged the U.S. opponents.

The most severe criticism of the theory came from Irwin Silber of the *Guardian*. In 1975, Silber had severely criticized the behavior of the Chinese in Angola, where he felt that they had engaged in an "objective" alliance with the United States and South Africa to thwart Soviet and Cuban initiatives. Silber saw these latter initiatives as counters to pre-existing and long-standing U.S. initiatives in Angola. This was the straw that broke the camel's back in terms of the relationship between Silber and Carl Davidson, the latter terminating eight years of work on the *Guardian* and going into the CP(ML)'s predecessor organization, the October League.

In July of 1977, the *Guardian,* under Silber's editorship, took a very clear position on the Theory of the Three Worlds. It rejected the thesis that the Soviet Union and Soviet "social-imperialism" was the main danger to the world.[66] Seven months later Silber attempted to explain the Chinese position, which he continued to reject, on the basis of the conclusions drawn by the Chinese from the Soviet invasion of Czechoslovakia in 1968 and the defeat of the United States military in Vietnam.[67] The first demonstrated the willingness of the USSR to invade a country on its borders. The second demonstrated that there was now a country on its Asian border which, with Soviet assistance, was strong enough to resist even the massive U.S. military might. For the Chinese, the defeat of U.S. imperialism came at the price of an additional presence of Soviet social-imperialism on its very borders. Worse, from the Chinese perspective, this time there was a battle-trained Asian army to back it up. While understanding and attempting to explain the Chinese fear, Silber thought that it was exaggerated, driving the Chinese to untenable positions.

In the July article, the *Guardian* also rejected the Albanian position that both superpowers, the USA and the USSR, were equally enemies of the oppressed peoples of the world and that "it is impermissible to join with one superpower (the US) against the other."[68] The *Guardian* summarized its position:

> We hold that US imperialism is the main enemy of oppressed
> peoples and nations of the world, not both superpowers equally.
> We also believe the Albanian statement underestimates the pro-
> gressive character of the nonaligned movement. At the same
> time, as we have been saying for the past two years, we are
> particularly aware of the danger of class-collaboration of our
> own movement stemming from the thesis of "striking the
> main blow at Soviet social-imperialism."[69]

However, while criticizing the Albanian position on the equally dangerous nature of the two superpowers and its underestimation of the progressive character of the nonaligned movement, Silber did see the positive aspect to the Albanian opposition to the Chinese position:

> The importance of the Albanian position is that it is a drama-
> tic step in opposition to the class-collaborationist consequences
> of the "three worlds" theory. And the Albanians have been unre-
> lenting in their opposition to NATO, the European Common
> Market and the neocolonialist strategy of the US and its West
> European allies. Objectively, therefore, Albania's attack on the
> "three worlds" theory represents a move that will ultimately
> strengthen those who see US imperialism as the main enemy.[70]

The Revolutionary Communist Party's reading of the law of uneven development told it that the Albanian position was correct, that the two super-powers were equally dangerous. Moreover, on one point the Albanian party, the RCP, and the *Guardian* seemed to be in agreement. This was their position that while the competition between the two superpowers posed the threat and the danger of a third world war, such a war was not inevitable.[71] The CP(ML) accepted the Chinese position that such a war was inevitable.[72] It will be recalled that this latter position was one put forward by the Trotsky-ist Pablo as part of his "war-revolution" concept developed during the early period of the "Cold War" between the Soviet Union and the United States.

The RCP added insult to injury to the Chinese by contending that their view of the Soviet Union as the superpower more dangerous to China itself was correct because of "geographical proximity, the defeats inflicted on US imperialism in Asia, China's exposure by propaganda and by example of the New Czar's socialist cover, the USSR's overall position of being on the offensive, etc."[73] In other words China, because of its particular position, was more menaced by the USSR, but this did not justify a universal inter-pretation of the law of uneven development which, by comparison, downplays the menacing nature of U.S. imperialism.

The CP(ML) completely accepted the Chinese position on the theory, and this was largely responsible for the Chinese recognition of the CP(ML) as a fraternal party. This left two areas of agreement between the CP(ML) and the RCP on the international situation. First, there was agree-ment that the Soviet Union is a state capitalist system (not just a degenerated workers state *à la* Trotskyism) practicing social imperialism. Second, there was agreement that the revolutionary vocation had passed to the Third World, and that Maoists were thus placed in a position of doing "revolutionary work in a non-revolutionary situation." The latter position is the exact contrary of that taken by the Trotskyist Spartacist and Workers Leagues, as well as by the Trotskyist SWP since its adoption of the Long Detour analysis. It will be recalled that that analysis—advanced as a minority position which was rejected by the French *Ligue* and the rest of the international majority of the United Secretariat in 1974—contended that there had not been a successful revolutionary movement in the Third World since those of China, Cuba, and Vietnam, and that the revolutionary vocation had come home to the capitalist industrialized societies where the "objective conditions" resided. The estimate of U.S. power by the SWP was also greater than that of the Maoists. And the Third World orientation of the *Ligue* in France helps explain why that section of the United Secretariat could have some relations with Maoists of the GP or even PCR(m-1) variety, while both the RCP and the CP(ML) have had nothing but contempt for the American SWP.

Nevertheless, two very concrete differences emerged out of the differ-ent assessments of the superpowers put forward by the RCP and the CP(ML).

These regard the attitude to take toward Third World revolutionary struggle and the attitude to take toward alliances in the Second World, specifically NATO. The CP(ML) refused to call for the overthrow of any regime in the Third World. It accepted the Chinese premise that the Third World countries, regardless of the nature of their present leadership, are being victimized by both U.S. and Soviet imperialism. That is an "objective" situation in which they find themselves. Neither pro-Soviet nor pro-U.S. leaders can will themselves out of this situation. Ultimately these countries will be forced to unify with each other in an assault against imperialism. By definition, such an assault will be progressive. The moves of the OPEC countries to extract better oil prices from the industrialized countries were seen as part of this inevitable evolution. The CP(ML) held that its responsibility was to call for the overthrow of only one regime in the world and that was the capitalist regime in the United States. It was up to the working people in each of the Third World countries to decide the proper course of action for their own country during the struggle against the two superpowers.

The RCP rejected this position. It, like the *Guardian,* argued that distinctions must be made within the Third World and that revolutionary movements against clearly reactionary regimes should be supported. Even before the Theory of the Three World had been clearly articulated and the two American groups had become parties, this issue had been a sore point between their predecessor organizations, Revolutionary Union and October League. All along, RU/RCP had been a strong supporter of the struggle against the Shah of Iran. When the Shah visited the United States in July of 1973, RU demonstrated opposition in solidarity with anti-Shah Iranian students. The October League (or CP(ML)-to-be) refused to express itself. It saw the Shah as an anti-Soviet force in the Middle East.

The nub of the difficulty to come, once the Theory of the Three Worlds was completely articulated, can be seen in the RU's response to the October League back in 1974:

> Thus, while it is necessary and correct for the People's Republic of China and the Chinese Communist Party to make certain agreements and compromises with imperialist and reactionary states, primarily to make use of contradictions between the two superpowers and in that way strengthen the overall united front and the people's struggle for liberation and socialism, it is not correct for communists in other countries, including the US, to do the same thing.
>
> While the Chinese make certain agreements with the Shah of Iran, it does not follow that the revolutionaries in Iran should let up even in the slightest bit in their efforts to mobilize the people to overthrow the Shah. And revolutionaries

everywhere should not let up the slightest bit in explaining to the workers and oppressed people in their countries who the Shah is, what he represents, why the Iranian people are rising up to overthrow him, and why the exploited and oppressed people of all countries should support the Iranian people's just struggle.

Finally, we want to say categorically that the rightist line OL is beginning to push forward on the international united front is certainly no service to the People's Republic of China. In fact, by using China as a cover for their rightist line, OL is aiding the Trotskyites and revisionists (i.e., the USSR and the supportive Communist Parties) who are vehemently attacking the Chinese and the international and revolutionary united front line the Chinese have been instrumental in developing.[74]

The CP(ML) also took a position on the Second World that the RCP was unable to accept. Like its French counterpart, which took its cues from the Chinese regime, the CP(ML) viewed NATO as a positive anti-Soviet force in Europe and emphasized the "objective" contradiction which exists between the Second World countries and the United States. The Second World countries in Western Europe have this dual character of being at once imperialistic themselves but threatened by the hegemonic United States. Since even that hegemonic power is less dangerous than the Soviet Union, and since the Second World countries in it have a dual character which renders them potential allies of the Third World, the CP(ML) was supportive of the existence of NATO, and adamantly against any attempt to dismantle it unilaterally.

As might be expected, the RCP, which saw both the U.S. and USSR as equally menacing, opposed both NATO and the Warsaw Pact. While the RCP was prepared to admit that there are certain contradictions in the relations between the Western European countries and the United States, it still contended that the Western European members of NATO "are basically in the camp of US imperialism,"[75]—a position taken with even less qualification by the *Guardian*. To make its point that it would not choose sides in any war between what it views as the two equally imperialistic superpowers and their alliance partners, the RCP adopted the slogan "We Won't Fight Another Rich Man's War."[76] This was a slogan of the Second International before World War I, one which was not completely adhered to.

The CP(ML) tried very carefully to accept and follow the foreign policy line in both Maoist and post-Mao China. Its refusal to declare its support for revolutionary struggles elsewhere, which was characterized as rightist by the RU/RCP, had been sanctioned by the Chinese party. This had given the CP(ML) the courage to hurl the charge of "revisionist and Trotsky-

ite political line" back in the teeth of the RCP. In fact, its attacks on the
RCP bore a striking resemblance to the attacks of the Chinese leadership
against the "Gang of Four":

> The RCP would do well to compare its line today with that of
> the Trotskyites in the late 1930's. They too, claimed to "defend"
> the socialist Soviet Union in spite of its "nationalist" errors.
> They too, declared all imperialist powers "equal enemies" and
> opposed the concept of the main blow. They, too, falsely set
> "class struggle" in opposition to the national liberation strug-
> gles in the colonies. They, too, ranted and railed at the parties
> of the Communist International as "social-chauvinists" and
> "class collaborators."
>
> But as long as the RCP continues to pursue its revisionist
> and Trotskyite political line, it will continue to isolate itself
> from the genuine Marxist-Leninists worldwide and oppose the
> actual anti-imperialist and revolutionary struggles of the world's
> people.[77]

The RCP long remained silent on the fate of the "Gang of Four,"
while the CP(ML) joyously celebrated their public humiliation. The RCP
would only concede that it had been "studying the matter."

(2) The "National" Question

As we have seen, the two largest French Maoist organizations have
not done battle with each other over the Theory of the Three Worlds in the
same way that the major U.S. Maoist formations have. And, while regional
national sentiments have been difficult for the French Maoists of the GP
variety to conceptualize, the "national" question in France has had nothing
like the divisive impact upon Maoism that it has had in the United States.

There are two reasons for this. First, racism and the conflict which it
engenders permeate to the very core of American society in a way that French
regional sentiments do not. Secondly, there is the heritage of Comintern intervention on the "national question" in the United States, an intervention
that came about because of the unique importance of this question in the
United States.

In 1928 and 1930, the Comintern adopted resolutions which contended that U.S. Blacks, then referred to as Negroes, constituted an oppressed
nation with their territorial home in the Black Belt South. There was by no
means unanimity on the question within the U.S. Communist Party. But
this was a period during which Stalin was conducting a purge of the Lovestone leadership and other dissidents. Stalin favored the Black Belt position

and was in no mood to tolerate further opposition from the Americans. The Communist Party itself subsequently repudiated the position, but those who followed Stalin's theoretical guidance, like the Maoists, have found it impossible to avoid dealing with the Black Belt Nation thesis.

Without going into detail on Stalin's work on nationality, several points must be made to indicate the origin of much of the present difficulty which Maoists face on this question, to the point that it has been the most serious divisive issue among U.S. Maoists over the longest period of time. It divided Maoists well before the Theory of the Three Worlds entered the scene.

First, Stalin's writings on the national question, particularly *Marxism and the National Question* and *The National Question and Leninism,* are among his most important contributions to the larger body of Marxist- Leninist thought. He engaged in this endeavor largely because of the practical necessity of coming to terms with separatist claims which were being directed to the Soviet party by Jews and Armenians. He specifically rejected the claims of the Jewish Bund for recognition of a "national cultural autonomy" for Jews who were not territorially concentrated.[78] Stalin's definition of a nation was "a historically evolved, stable community of language, territory, economic life, and psychological make-up manifested in a community culture."[79] A deficit of one of these attributes would mean that the people concerned could not qualify as a nation. Since Garveyism was striking a responsive chord with its nationalistic appeal, the Comintern and the CP/USA attempted to offer U.S. Blacks what seemed to them to be a less escapist national option than Garvey's "Back to Africa" national solution. This was the consideration of the states making up the Black Belt, where approximately half of the U.S. Black population was concentrated in 1930, as a Black Nation.

Second, Stalin drew two distinctions which might make sense but which certainly complicate the application of any definition or theory of nationalism. The first is the distinction between nationalism and the more concrete form which it might take. Thus the distinction between "autonomy, federation, or separation" cannot be determined outside of the "concrete historical conditions in which the given nation finds itself."[80] Secondly, there is the distinction between the right of a particular claim to national determination and the interests of the proletariat within the national grouping.[81] One can have a right but be ill-advised to exercise it under certain conditions.

Third, Stalin's theory of nationality became an integral part of two other Stalinist conceptions which were very important for Mao. The first is the conception of revolution in stages, a conception rejected by Trotskyists. The two major stages were socialism in one country, and socialism, or the dictatorship of the proletariat, on a world scale. The second conception was that of "cultural revolution."[82] By the latter he meant a program of education and literacy in peoples' native languages. During the stage of socialism in one country and during the initial period of the stage of socialism on a world scale, national traditions would be taught and equality among nations recognized. Over time, however, and concomitant with the development of a world sociaist economy, Stalin foresaw individual national differences and languages giving way to a common language and international amalgamation.[83] Stalin's theory of nationalism therefore contained important distinctions at each stage of the revolutionary process, as well as distinctions over time. Nationalism which advances the interests of the working class is important at the early stages, but ultimately the universalistic vocation of Marxism–Leninism will render such nationalistic distinctions obsolete.

U.S. Maoists have been caught between the devil and the deep blue sea. They are not yet even at the stage of socialism in one country. So they have a good period of recognition of national distinctions ahead of them. Moreover, despite the fact that the Black population has shown a heavy pattern of outmigration from the Black Belt states to the northern urban areas since 1930, there was indeed a resurgence of Black nationalism in the 1960s and 1970s. If Black dialect could meet the language criterion established by Stalin, how could the question of territory be handled?

There has been a simply incredible variety of responses to the problem. We have already seen the shift of position on the part of the Progressive Labor Party, which first distinguished revolutionary nationalism from reactionary nationalism and declared the nationalism of the Black Muslims to be revolutionary--only to turn around to a position that all nationalism is reactionary and all manifestations of Black separatism detrimental to working-class unity. In the 1970s, there was a wide range of options which were being concurrently offered.

The extremities were represented by Irwin Silber in the *Guardian* and the Communist Labor Party. Silber completely rejected the "Black Belt Nation Thesis." He argued that the Black Belt national concept ignored fifty years of U.S. historical development during which there had been tremendous Black outmigration from the area, as well as "the historically tested Marxist proposition that only 'nations'—not racial groups, tribes, national or ethnic minorities, religious groups, various social substrata, etc.—have not only the right, but the ability to exercise self-determination."[84]

Silber argued that the "scientific" arguments put forward by recent proponents of the Black Belt Nation thesis were a sham and hid the subjective reeasons for their holding on to it. The major "subjective" reason was the "White guilt" of Maoists of New Left origins, whose experience in class struggles had been largely shaped by the civil rights movement and the Vietnam war. He argued that one need go no further than Stalin's definition to see that Black people today do not constitute a "nation."[85]

The Communist Labor Party, formerly the Communist League, outdid even the 1928 and 1930 Comintern positions. Its slogan was "independence for the Negro Nation," leaving no doubt as to the specific form which nationalism was to take. And it extended the territory concerned to all of the thirteen states of the old Confederacy, a territory which exceeds that which is usually referred to as the Black Belt. The citizenship of all the people in these states would be that of "Negro."

Aside from these two positions, virtually every other Maoist group has had a difficult time dealing with the issue. The Black Workers Congress and the Puerto Rican Revolutionary Workers Organization first moved close to the RU/RCP's position in the early 1970s, but then broke with that and moved closer to Communist League, and then broke with them.[86] At its 1973 Congress, the October League took a position on the Black Belt, but warned readers of the resolution that its position did not comprise "a complete analysis of this important question...[but rather] a summation of the experiences and the study of our organization up to that point"[87] This caution is similar to the one issued by the ex-GP Maoists in France regarding their positions on nationalism in Occitanie and Brittany. Finally, RU/RCP has admitted errors and modified its position over time.

The later positions of both the CP(ML), formerly the October League, and the Revolutionary Communist Party (RCP) hung onto the Black Belt notion, at least nominally. The CP(ML) was the less equivocal of the two organizations. It supported the rights of Blacks or Afro-Americans (it used both terms) to secede "to their historic homeland in the Black Belt South."[88] However, the qualifier was added that "Recognition of the right to self-determination does not mean that our Party advocates or supports separation as the solution to the Afro-American national question, nor does it mean that it will give its support to every bourgeois secessionist movement...The CP(ML) supports only those national demands which weaken imperialism and enhance the unity and fighting ability of the [working] class."[89] This position, which distinguishes between reactionary and revolutionary nationalism, stood in contrast with the CP(ML)'s acceptance of the Chinese position that the Third World as a whole, despite regime differences, is a world revolutionary force.

The CP(ML) made two additions to the original Black Belt position of the Comintern. First, it recognized the outmigration of Blacks from the Black Belt into urban areas. Thus, without renouncing its support of the right to self-determination within the Black Belt, the CP(ML) also supported "a policy of regional autonomy which will enable Black people to exercise a high degree of self government and build equality and multi-national unity under the proletarian dictatorship" in Black urban concentrations.[90] Secondly, it extended its support of the right to self-determination to Chicanos, Puerto Ricans, Native Americans, Asian-Americans and the native peoples of Alaska, the Aleutian Islands, the Virgin Islands, Hawaii, and the rest of the U.S.-held Pacific islands.

The RCP claimed to support the right to self-determination in the

Black Belt, but it has certainly been less enthusiastic than the CP(ML). Prior to the formation of the party, Revolutionary Union put forward its position of Black people constituting an "oppressed nation of a new type."

> The heart of our analysis is that on the one hand Black people
> are an oppressed nation of a new type—overwhelmingly work-
> ers, dispersed throughout the US, but concentrated in urban
> industrial areas, with real, but deformed class structure. But on
> the other hand, Black workers, making up the majority of
> Black people, are part of the *single US working class.* And
> further, as we have said consistently in the *Red Papers,* "the
> essential thrust" of the Black people's struggle has not been
> for self-determination in the form of secession, but in the fight
> against discrimination, the denial of democratic rights, violent
> police repression, and against exploitation and oppression as
> members of the working class suffering caste-like oppression
> within the class.[91]

Aside from this rather unique definition of "nationalism" within either a Marxist or a non-Marxist framework, RU was evasive on the Black Belt question at this point in time (1974). It held that those who put forward the right of self-determination as "the essence of the Black liberation strug-gle"[92] were wrong and archaically agrarian, while Blacks within and without the Black Belt were becoming urbanized. As far as RU would go at that point was to contend that: "The RU does not think it is correct to absolutely rule out the possibility of a reconstitution of Black people in the 'Black Belt,' or even the establishment of a separate state there, on the condition, of course, that it was voluntary and not forced."[93]

Approximately one year later, in 1975, a little different presentation appeared in the constitution of the newly formed RCP. Here the words "op-pressed nation of a new type" gave way to "an oppressed nation, but under new conditions, and in different relation to US imperialism than its colonies (and neo-colonies) in other countries."[94] Moreover, the RCP was now pre-pared to declare that "the working class and its Party upholds the right of Black people to return to claim their homeland...The proletariat and its Party in the US upholds the right of Black People to self-determination, the right to secede from the rest of the US and set up a separate state in the general area of the 'Black Belt'."[95]

But here the RCP distinguished between defending a right and advo-cating that it be exercised. The CP(ML) stated that distinction in its program, but did not then go on to oppose the exercise of the right. Not so with the RCP. It contended that "The proletariat and its Party does not advocate this separation for Black people nor favor it under present and foreseeable conditions."[96] Moreover it declared in the same constitution that "the right of nations to self-determination does not apply to Chicanos,"[97] that the proletariat will aid Native Americans in land development "probably in some cases under conditions of regional autonomy,"[98] and that "Hawaii today is part of the US, and the Hawaiian people's struggle is part of the US proletarian revolution."[99]

But the clearest statement of RCP misgivings over nationalism is contained in an article in the Fall / Winter 1977 issue of *The Communist*. There the author writes: "Nationalism, no matter how progressive or revolutionary, in the final analysis ends up by saying my nationality first."[100] And, a little further along: "But a communist must never compromise the stand of his class first and above all, as say opposed to his people first and above all. When all is said and done this is the watershed between Marxism–Leninism and nationalism even of the most refined and progressive sort."[101]

The RCP has been very harsh in its treatment of those who, in its opinion, cross that line and end up on the other side of the watershed. All Maoists hurl such epithets as "metaphysical," "subjective," "mechanical," "empirical," and "petty-bourgeois" or "petty-bourgeois moralizing" at those who take posi-tions which they believe to be "objectively" incorrect. But the RCP has gone even beyond that on the national question. Itself the victim of accusations of "Trotskyism" hurled by the CP(ML) on the Three Worlds question, the RCP has accused such widely divergent organizations as the Progressive Labor Party on the one hand and the Black Workers Congress and Puerto Rican Revolutionary Workers Organization on the other of exhibiting Trotskyism or of taking on "Trotskyite features" in their handling of the national question.[102] The CP(ML) was viewed as completely "opportunistic" on the question, and was accused of using the same methods as the "revisionist" Communist Party and the "Trotskyite" SWP.

Indeed, there are some interesting comparisons to be made between the CP(ML)'s positions and those of the SWP. First, Trotsky himself indicated considerable interest in the Black Belt position.[103] But the closest the SWP has come to taking a position on the issue was its "Freedom Now" Resolution adopted at its 1963 convention. While not specifying the Black Belt, the SWP took the position that if Blacks should opt to be a separate nation, the SWP would support them. Until that time, the SWP would neither advocate nor oppose Black (the Resolution said "Negro") national self-determination. Thus while the Black Belt is not specifically designated, and while the question is not broached in the Transitional Program for Black Liberation, which deals with the creation of a separate Black political party and community control, the "Freedom Now" Resolution is certainly closer to the CP(ML)'s position than to the RCP's highly negative attitude toward Black national self-determination "under present and foreseeable conditions."

Secondly, the "regional autonomy" position in areas of urban concentration brought the CP(ML) close to the SWP's position on community control. In fact, the Los Angeles segment of the CP(ML), which was one of the strongest and from which Klonsky himself came, had been active in the struggle for the separate incorporation of East Los Angeles. The CP(ML) did not insist that forces for community control accept Marxism–Leninism as a precondition for the CP(ML)'s support. But it withheld that support if it felt that the issue was being exploited by minority politicians to enhance their own careers within the system, or if it was designed to enrich a segment of the minority population at the expense of the rest.

Finally, the SWP and the CP(ML)—and the October League before it became the CP(ML)—found themselves on the same side of an issue of major salience to the broader American public: school busing. Both groups not only supported busing in their publications but also were active in the Boston demonstrations in support of busing. Typical of the mode of operation of both groups, the SWP participated in a broader umbrella group in Boston during the 1973 and 1974 demonstrations, while the October League formed its own Fred Hampton Contingent, which was named in honor of the Chicago Black Panther leader slain in his bed by Illinois State's Attorney Hanrahan's police.[104]

The RCP, however, was very far from the SWP's positions in this area. While the RCP denied that its position on Black nationalism resembled that of the Progressive Labor Party during its "all nationalism is reactionary" period, there are similarities. The RCP contended that the PLP took a "one line" position, that it did not "divide things into two." Thus the PLP went from the single-minded, dogmatic position of uncritically supporting the cause of Black nationalism as espoused by the Black Muslims to the exact opposite of denouncing all nationalism. The RCP, on the other hand, claimed to "divide things into two," to attempt to separate out the progressive from the reactionary aspects of any phenomenon. However, as we have seen, the most recent stands taken by the RCP have greatly accentuated the negative on the issue of Black nationalism—or any other nationalism.

Moreover, the RCP, placing itself at odds with virtually every other "multinational" group on the U.S. Left, shared the anti-busing position of the PLP. The headline on the October 1974 issue of *Revolution,* the RCP's monthly newspaper, read: "People Must Unite to Smash Boston Busing Plan."[105] Like the PLP back in the late 1960s, the RCP viewed busing as a divisive issue which was raised by the capitalist establishment to pit Black against White workers. It argued that busing would do nothing to remedy the insufficiency of resources endemic to all of the public schools in Boston. It argued rather for an end to discrimination in housing and better appropriations and facilities for all of the Boston schools. In the eyes of the RCP, the most vicious aspect of groups on the Left supporting busing was that the attacks of these groups were directed against the racism of White workers to the point of calling for action against these "White racists" by the establishment's police forces. The RCP contended that by supporting the establishment politicians' strategy of dividing the White from the Black working classes, those groups were completely separating the struggle over racism or the "national question" from the class struggle. And they were doing so in a way that would prove to be fatal to the latter.

(3) The Equal Rights Amendment

There was no disagreement between the RCP and the CP(ML) on the issue of "feminism." Unlike the SWP, which presented feminism as being perfectly compatible with Marxism-Leninism, and which had recruited an important segment of its membership from women who had originally been politicized by exclusively feminist organizations or around exclusively feminist issues, the RCP and the CP(ML) both denounced feminism as irreconcilable with Marxism–Leninism.

However, on the specific issue of the Equal Rights Amendment there was disagreement between the two Maoist organizations. Once again, the CP(ML) in its support for the ERA found itself on the same side as the SWP on an issue of major salience in American politics. The RCP found itself taking the same position as the Communist Party/USA until 1977, when the CP/USA switched from a con to a pro position on ERA.[106]

The position of the RCP was that the struggle against women's oppression should "center around inequality and discrimination."[107] The major thrust of the demands should be for equal pay for equal work, free child care so that women would not be isolated from production and class struggle, paid maternity leaves with no loss of seniority, an end to forced abortion and sterilization, and the right to safe and voluntary birth control and abortion.[108] But another demand was "Oppose the 'Equal Rights Amendments'—fight to defend protective legislation and extend it to men."[109]

In 1974, the RCP's predecessor organization, Revolutionary Union, launched an attack on the Industrial Welfare Commission of California for using that state's equal rights legislation as an excuse to do away with protective legislation which workers had fought so hard to gain. It contended that "the ruling class, as can be seen by what is happening in California, is using the ERA to step up its attack on protective legislation, as part of its frantic, overall efforts to get out of the crisis it's in by squeezing even more profits out of the working class."[110] While both the CP(ML) and the *Guardian* agreed with the RCP that there was such an attack on protective legislation in California, they argued that the use of equal rights laws for that purpose was a perversion of the intent of those laws, and that there was more to be gained than lost by the adoption of a nationally binding amendment. The RCP, on the other hand, saw the destruction of protective legislation for workers as precisely the intent of "equal rights" laws or amendments when they are adopted by capitalist governments.[111]

Thus, on both the issues of busing and ERA, the RCP saw capitalist plots afoot to divide the working class and to destroy the protective legislation which it fought so hard to gain. On the busing issue, it stood virtually alone among the multi-national or multi-racial groups on the Left. On the issue of ERA it shared the position of the Communist Party until 1977, but was later isolated from it as well as from most of the other Marxist-Leninist and social democratic groups in the United States. To many of these groups, the RCP looked more and more like the PLP which it fought so hard against. Its purist Left analyses brought it into agreement with the ballast of the Right on specific but highly salient issues within the U.S. political context.

SUMMARY CONCLUSION

The most obvious difference to be noted between U.S. Maoism and French Maoism is the absence in the United States of anything like the anti-hierarchical variant which existed in France up to the mid 1970s. U.S. Maoist organizations have all been traditionally Leninist in their mode of organization. Variations within U.S. Maoism have tended to be more sharply focused upon specific issue differences than in France.

Moreover, while the French hierarchical Maoist groups have differed on questions of union strategy and international issues, they have not attacked each other as savagely as the major U.S. Maoist groups have. The PCMLF and the PCR(m-1) have been trying to come together, and managed to run a joint list in the 1978 legislative elections. The UCFML has taken its own positions, but has been conscious of not going out of its way to offend either the Chinese regime or the other Maoist groups in France.

Two factors have encouraged the higher degree of antagonism and fragmentation within the U.S. Maoist movement. First, the two largest French hierarchical Maoist formations, the PCMLF and the PCR(m-1), share the same roots. The PCMLF came out of the French Communist Party and the PCR(m-1) came out of the PCMLF. The reason for the latter rupture was not so much issue specific or even theoretical. It was, rather, that the people who formed the PCR(m-1) felt that the PCMLF had simply become too inactive after it had been banned. The U.S. CP(ML) and RCP, on the other hand, did not come out of the same organization, and their militants never agreed on basic issues. These two U.S. organizations grew out of the New Left of the 1960s, and the only time that they ever acted together was in the attempt to break the power of the Progressive Labor Party within the Students for a Democratic Society. Once they finished that attempt, they presented each other with the same kind of aggressive confrontational posture they had often directed at others.

The second factor which has encouraged antagonism among U.S. Maoists is the salience and intensity of feeling surrounding the specific issues over which they have differed within the U.S. national context. The question of how to deal with racial and ethnic heterogeneity has been no less divisive among U.S. Maoists than it has been of the society at large. It was central to the battles with the Progressive Labor Party in SDS, to the differences between the major Maoist formations which succeeded the Progressive Labor Party, and to the growth of racially and ethnically specific Maoist groups in the United States which could not agree among themselves on how to resolve the "national question."

Another such issue is that of sexual oppression. Within SDS, at the end of 1965, women had begun to press their claims for a greater role and for men to come to grips with the question. By 1968 women's groups and caucuses had formed within and without the organization, and the latter were trying to pull women out of SDS and into directing their energies entirely toward women's liberation. It was in this setting that some of the RYM Maoists fought the PLP's contention that the oppression of women represented a secondary contradiction. And even though the two major successors of PLP in the world of U.S. Maoism both denounced the SWP's encouragement of "feminism" in the form of separatist organizations and different lifestyles, they too differed markedly on how each of them treated women within their own ranks. Although the CP(ML) was headed by a man at the very top—that veteran of so many struggles with PLP in SDS, Michael Klonsky—in the late 1970s the second highest position was held by a woman, and the organization had a strong tradition of sexual parity among the remainder of its leadership positions. For this it has been ridiculed and attacked by the RCP, in which male dominance is much more apparent. Finally, the salience of the issue of the Equal Rights Amendment throughout the late 1970s further widened the gap over the sexual question, both among the two major Maoist formations and even among some of the "national" Maoist groupings.

Further aggravating matters, U.S. Maoists have been particularly affected by the elevation of the USSR to the position of number one world menace within the Theory of the Three Worlds. For U.S. groups, this carried with it a shift of priorities on one's home turf. It has meant, in effect, taking the same positions as those on the anti-Communist Right in supporting U.S. anti-Soviet initiatives. While the RCP was comfortable taking positions (for different reasons, to be sure) on busing and ERA that were the same as those of most of the forces on the Right in the United States, it drew the line at what it regarded as a counter-revolutionary foreign policy. The Chinese regime, which intervened in the context of U.S. Maoism very late compared with its interest in France, complicated life for Maoists who were already trying to operate in a very difficult context.

Despite the intense conflict, U.S. Maoists have had some impact upon the larger political milieu. The Progressive Labor Party did play an important role in pushing the Students for a Democratic Society into a more specifically Marxist and anti-imperialist position. It also was the first U.S. group to send young Americans down to Cuba for a first-hand look at an attempt to build a socialist society. The Revolutionary Union, and then the Revolutionary Communist Party which succeeded the PLP as the largest U.S. Maoist group, has played an extremely important role on the U.S. Left in the post-SDS years. Among Marxist–Leninist groups, its student affiliate and that of the Trotskyist Socialist Workers Party were the most active on campuses across the country. Until the very late 1970s, social-democratic groups were virtually extinct in this setting, and the Communist Party's attention seems to have been concentrated largely in urban areas. In many cases the RCP's Revolutionary Student Brigades and SWP's Young Socialist Alliance were the only organizations present on campuses in a position to provide the organizational and tactical know-how—as well as the dedication and discipline necessary to get work done—when events or issues stimulated desires to respond on the part of a wider segment of student bodies. In terms of specific areas of involvement, James O'Brien points to the RCP's support work for the Farah strikers as its major accomplishment. I would add to that the RCP's steadfast support for the anti-Shah Iranian student move-ment in the United States.

At the very end of the 1970s, a new drama was unfolding within Maoism. In France, the PCR(m-1) joined the "officially" recognized PCMLF in a denunciation of the Gang of Four, and the furthest that UCFML would go was to say that the evidence presented against the Gang was thus far deficient. There was therefore, no real defense of the Gang of Four among the major French Maoist groups. Bob Avaikian and the majority of the Central Committee of the RCP in the United States, however, finally decided to push for a public defense, and charged that China's new leaders were taking China on a revisionist, capitalist road. This position, of course, brought Avakian and his followers one more step along the route taken by the Progressive Labor Party.

Despite the fact that the RCP had been repudiated by the post-Mao Chinese leadership's recognition of Klonsky's CP(ML), a large minority on the RCP's Central Committee could not accept the defense of the Gang and the direct attack on the Chinese leadership. The organization split. The majority faction led by Avakian retained control over the party. But the minority, which became known as the Revolutionary Workers Headquarters, retained control over many of the Revolutionary Student Brigades in the East and Midwest. In 1978, these dissident Brigades issued the following public statement to the Chinese:

Two Octobers ago the Chinese people turned a difficult situation arising from the death of Chairman Mao into an important
victory by defeating the counter-revolutionary Gang of Four.
Aware of the two classes, two lines, and two roads you continue your heroic march down the socialist road. Through
this struggle communists in China and worldwide gained
greater understanding of the tasks of the working class under
socialism. This victory placed the future of China more firmly
into the hands of the Chinese proletariat. Once again the
Chinese people and Party proved capable of conquering all
obstacles.

In the US students and all revolutionary people watched
events unfold closely. China has meant much to the American people. It has year after year proved socialism superior to
capitalism. It was the salvos of the Cultural Revolution that
led to Marxism-Leninism being reborn in the United States.
And once again socialist China was a beacon as the defeat of
the Gang of Four prepared us to remove a counter revolutionary bane in our own ranks. This bane which commanded
a slight majority of the leadership of our party were the US
kissing cousins of the Gang of Four. Their control prevented
us from expressing support for the defeat of the Gang of Four
earlier. It was necessary to break their control of our ranks to
continue to stand with the Chinese revolution.

To turn against China now is to turn against revolution.
This we would never do. Therefore we are determined, even if
apologetically late, to now take the opportunity to express
our warmest congratulations and most militant solidarity.
Today greater than ever before the words of Mao ring loud,
"We have stood up. Our revolution has won the sympathy
and acclaim of the people of all countries. We have friends
all over the world."[112]

The repercussions of this split within the largest Maoist organization in U.S. history, and the continuing developments in all of the major
U.S. Maoist formations in the Reagan years of the 1980s, are explored more
completely in the Epilogue.

6
A Dialectical View of Trotskyism and Maoism

It was explained in the Introduction that an examination of both national contextual factors and the guiding-theories themselves is necessary for a full understanding of the configurations of Trotskyist and Maoist movements. The four preceding chapters attempted to explain how Trotskyist and Maoist movements fragmented in each of the countries. The analysis focused upon the impact of external contextual factors upon the configurations of the movements.

Now we must fill the picture out by going back to the original theories and inspirations of these movements to see why they were so susceptible to fragmentation in the first place. We thus move from a more positivistic analysis to a dialectical one, i.e., to an examination of the internal contradictions of Trotskyism and Maoism as such and their interplay with contextual factors.

THE CONTRADICTIONS OF TROTSKYISM

Trotskyism was born with a major contradiction, namely that the theory of permanent revolution, while calling for the necessity of revolution on a world-wide scale and most importantly in the industrialized countries, was itself directed toward the dynamics of revolution in less-industrialized countries. Prior to the 1905 Revolution, Trotsky was one of the Russian writers and revolutionaries most optimistic about the possibilities for revolution in Russia. Lenin's theory of imperialism and elaboration of the notion of "uneven development" further encouraged Trotsky to debate the issue of revolution within largely peasant contexts, to assert the need for the primacy of the proletariat no matter how small it was in relation to the peasantry.

At the same time that he was arguing that one could not wait for the development of a socialist consciousness or for the material "objective conditions" upon which that consciousness would be based to make a revolution in Russia, Trotsky also argued that the revolution in such a context was doomed unless there were immediate supportive revolutions where the "objective"

231

conditions did prevail. Prior to the 1950s there was unanimous agreement that Trotskyists should concentrate on the implementation of the Transitional Program within the capitalist industrialized setting.

However, once it was clear that the Third World had indeed become the scene of revolutionary activity in the post-World War II period, there was enough flexibility in the theory of permanent revolution to allow Pablo to lead the International Secretariat of the Fourth International in the direction of supporting virtually every manifestation of revolutionary activity in the Third World. Since this revolutionary activity was the only successful revolutionary activity that the younger generation was witnessing, and since a number of ethnic or racial minorities in the United States could relate to these Third World struggles through their heritage, the pressure on the SWP to shift its position became enormous. Because it had made this shift, the party was in a position to take the active role that it did in the anti-war movement during the Indochina conflict. After the war was over, however, it argued that the course of revolutionary activity had come home to the industrialized countries after its "long detour" through the Third World. The Trotskyist French *Ligue* and its majority supporters in the United Secretariat did not make such a clear shift to a position that the main course of world revolution had returned to its true path through the industrialized countries after an aberrant stint in the Third World. At most, the majority faction within the United Secretariat agreed to stop encouraging the tactic of guerrilla warfare in Latin America.

The French *Ligue* thus found itself much closer to the Maoist position on the question of the Third World than did the SWP and the international minority. The *Ligue's* position facilitated good relations with the anti-hierarchical GP movement, as well as with the hierarchical PCR(m-l), whereas there have been no such positive relations between Trotskyists and Maoists in the United States. In fact, the *Organisation Communiste des Travailleurs* (OCT), with which the *Ligue* was allied in the 1978 elections, represented an attempt by former members of the *Ligue* and former Maoists to synthesize what they felt were the most positive elements of the two bodies of theory and practice. Since there has been no positive interaction at all between U.S. Trotskyists and Maoists, there has obviously been little opportunity for such synthetic attempts. But the point is that there is a contradiction within Trotskyism itself on this question of the Third World, so that both the Pablists and the majority of the United Secretariat, on the one hand, and the other organizations which have been discussed, on the other, could at any point in time claim that their interpretations were consistent with Trotsky's theory of permanent revolution.

The same kind of latitude exists on the question of structure. This is an even more complex problem, because Trotsky advocated very different positions depending upon the state of the larger Russian social democratic movement prior to the revolution and the changes in the concrete political conditions in both the pre- and post-revolutionary period. In 1901, he called for a highly centralized and tightly disciplined party which would not recognize the right of factions to exist. In 1903 and 1904, he turned around on the issue and delivered bitter attacks on Lenin for the latter's advocacy of a centralized party led by professional revolutionaries. While accusing Lenin of being another Robespierre, Trotsky advocated an open party controlled by its base committees. There was also emerging in his mind a conception of an organic movement of workers developing its own momentum. In 1904, he explicitly advanced the concept of the general strike, a concept which would become a reality the following year. Just as the central leadership of the party was not to substitute its will for that of the members of the base, so the party as a structure was not to substitute its will for that of the workers engaged in direct revolutionary struggle. Any attempt to do so would inhibit the organic dynamic of the struggle. At this point in time, Trotsky was in the camp of the Mensheviks. His 1904 essay, *Our Political Tasks,* was dedicated to "my dear teacher Paul Borisovitch Axelrod," a major Menshevik opponent of Lenin.[1]

In the 1905 Revolution, Trotsky played a major role in the city-wide soviet elected by the workers who were conducting the St. Petersburg general strike. That revolutionary attempt was crushed by the Tsarist forces and Trotsky was imprisoned. Nevertheless, Trotsky became firmly convinced that the soviet, emerging organically from the activity of the workers themselves, was indeed the proper coordinating and steering mechanism for mass revolutionary upsurge. The references to parties in his work of the following year, *Results and Prospects,* are few and far between. But what there is makes clear that the party no longer had any significant organizational function in Trotsky's thinking. Its role now was limited to consciousness-raising.

It was not until 1917 that Trotsky became a Bolshevik and made the claim that he and Lenin no longer had substantial differences on the party question. Indeed, Trotsky the party administrator took very different positions from Trotsky the revolutionary and theorist out of power. In 1920 and early 1921, when he was first placed in charge of the badly weakened transportation system and then asked to assume broader responsibility in the lagging productive sector, Trotsky went well beyond what even Lenin could accept in arguing that the party had to assert control over recalcitrant labor union leaders who had been elected by the workers. It is not surprising, therefore, that Trotsky went along with Lenin's proposal later in 1921 to ban both non-Bolshevik parties and factions within the single legitimate party. Trotsky the administrator repudiated his own former "fatalistic optimism" and qualitative over-assessment of the unaided revolutionary potential of the proletariat within the Russian context.[2] Against his critics, Trotsky now identified the dictatorship of the proletariat with that of the party. The party, not soviets or unions, was to have the final say on all basic issues. Rosa Luxemburg's

1918 assessment of where the revolution was going under Lenin's and Trotsky's leadership was vindicated.[3]

   After Lenin's death and his own exile by Stalin, Trotsky admitted that some of the measures taken by the government for which he and Lenin bore responsibility were "in conflict with the spirit of Soviet democracy."[4] His retrospective explanation was that the civil war necessitated initial limitations on freedom of political struggle within the soviets, while the enormity of the post-war reconstructive tasks led Lenin and him to see a temporary need for the party's monopolization of power and the strict centralization and discipline which made the toleration of factions impossible. This recourse to the exceptional circumstances justification was not totally consistent with some of the general assertions he had used to defend these measures at the time.

   Trotsky's propensity to blame all of the bureaucratic deformations of the Soviet Union on Stalin and the concept of socialism in one country makes it doubtful that he ever fully admitted to himself the significance and long-term consequences of vesting such power in the party in the first place. However, in the *Transitional Program,* written seventeen years after opposition parties and factions had been banned in the USSR, Trotsky suggested a more constructed role of the parties of his newly created Fourth International in the capitalist industrialized countries. In the pre-revolutionary agitational period, the basic structures confronting the capitalist system and its political apparatus are to be factory committees and elected soviets. During this period, Trotskyist parties would attempt to expose the dangers of the Stalinist and social democratic approaches, offer an alternative revolutionary program to the proletariat, and be instrumental in the development of more militant organizational measures as the struggle intensified — including the creation of an armed workers' militia when the workers recognized the need for that. After the passage from the state of dual power to one of the dictatorship of the proletariat — which is here defined by Trotsky as the power of the soviets and not as the power of a vanguard workers party — a plural system of parties would operate. Although the division of function among the structures is sketchy at best, it is clear that the parties would have to do their representing through elected soviets and that certain representational functions would be reserved for labor unions. This conception is obviously quite at odds with the vanguard — indeed the monopolistic — role played by the Russian party during the period that Trotsky was associated with Lenin.[5]

   The *Transitional Program* does not deal with the internal mode of organization of the party. It is possible to infer, but not a logical necessity, that if the role of the party is less controlling over the revolutionary process then the need for internal centralism is less pressing. However, the Fourth International, for which the *Transitional Program* served as the founding and guiding document, continued to make a commitment to the principle of democratic centralism. But in *The Revolution Betrayed,* written at approximately the same time as the *Transitional Program,* Trotsky contends that the toleration of factions is an important aspect of democratic centralism. At no point in his writing of this period does Trotsky attempt to make theoretically consistent his continued espousal of democratic centralism, on the one hand, and his more constricted view of the party's role and his defense of factionalism, on the other.

It is thus not difficult to appreciate the very conflicting views on these questions which are held by groups claiming to be Trotskyist. In terms of both internal structure and the view of the organization's role in the revolutionary process, the French *Ligue* has been on the "loose" side of the continuum. The distinction between adult revolutionaries steeped in Marxist theory and a youth affiliate of younger potential members who are still learning and being tested in both theory and discipline was dropped when the Frankist PCI merged with and permitted itself to be swamped numerically by the young barricade fighters of the JCR. The emphasis upon continued recruitment of people who had been radicalized during the 1960s and 1970s has militated against the application of strict hierarchical forms. Caucuses representing the interests of women and gays have been permitted to form and to articulate their concerns within the organization. The right to factionalism has been guaranteed. At the international level—i.e., within the United Secretariat—that has been interpreted to include *public* and *permanent* factionalism. While the Pablists of the *Comités Communistes pour l'Autogestion* have argued for a principled adherence to this at the national level as well, the *Ligue* has balked. As on a number of other issues, the *Ligue* has argued that this one is a tactical rather than a principled question. Where issues are deeply felt, and where the suppression of an external venting of views is likely to be organizationally disruptive, such as the diversity of viewpoints on women, then such differences have been made public and factions or caucuses, so highly structured as to suggest permanence, have been permitted.

Similarly, in their orientation toward the revolutionary process and the role of Trotskyist organizations therein, the *Ligue* and the Pablists have been on the "loose" side of the continuum. Both have been very expansive in attempting to reach out to and work with political organizations which are distant from their own ideological configurations. The Pablists participated in the multi-tendency *Parti Socialiste Unifié.* The *Ligue* has continually invited the other Trotskyist organizations to work with it or to attend its festivals and debate the issues. It has worked closely and even run candidates in an agreement with the *Organisation Communiste des Travailleurs,* which included many people who had broken away from the *Ligue.* The *Ligue* has been open to working with Maoists and has been successful in attracting members of the Communist Party to its functions.

The *Ligue* has also been supportive of the more unstructured movements which arose in the late 1960s and 1970s, such as the women's movements, the gay and lesbian movements, the anti-nuclear movement, and the larger environmental movement. This too is a characteristic which it shares with the Pablists. All of the positive positions regarding other structured groups and diffuse movements are consistent with the basic fabric of an organization built upon a base of 1965 barricade fighters. The only major distinctions recognized in May and June of 1965 were those for and those against the revolt. The young people in the JCR celebrated and participated in the spontaneous decentralized action committees wherever they could, while at the national level they worked with the students of the *Parti Socialiste Unifié,* who controlled the national offices of the student union (UNEF), in an attempt to give whatever coordination was possible to the revolt. Frankist Trotskyism in France has thus been rejuvenated by a youth movement and an historical event much more characteristic of Trotsky's 1905 experience and vision of a decentralized mass uprising than by his later apparent conversion to Leninist vanguardism.

From an organizational point of view, the most traditionally Leninist organization within French Trotskyism has been the Lambertist *Organisation Communiste Internationaliste.* While the OCI has also been the most hostile to the Communist Party—which it has continued to view as totally subservient to a still-Stalinist Soviet party—the OCI's conception of the organization and role of a revolutionary organization has sometimes brought it to outlooks and positions very similar to those of the Communist Party. Its attitude toward the 1968 uprising was a case in point. The OCI was critical of that uprising not only because of the crucial role played by young people and students, but because no central soviet or workers' committee was developed to coordinate and guide the affair. While it did not argue for a single party playing the van-guard role, it did reject spontaneity, decentralized activity, and youth acting outside of the theoretical guidance of older revolutionaries. It urged people off of the barricades and verbally attacked the participants almost as severely as the Communist Party did.

The internal organization of the OCI has reflected this more traditional orientation. It is the most centralist of the Trotskyist organizations. Unlike the other Trotskyist organizations, its original founder, Pierre Lambert, has remained at the helm. There has been a clear distinction between the parent organization and the youth affiliate. There has also been a strong emphasis upon theoretical formation, and young people have been obliged to undergo a highly structured educational program before being admitted into the parent organization. There has been no public and permanent factionalism. For the OCI, organizational questions have been viewed as questions of principle, not of tactics. It has viewed the *Ligue* as still suffering from Pablist opportunism which, in its organizational manifestation, was nothing short of liquidationism in the form of *entrisme sui generis*. Lambertist Trotskyism as a separate current was born precisely to counter this threat to Trotskyist revolutionary organization.

Lutte Ouvrière presents us with still a third approach to the organizational question. It has viewed the *Ligue* as being hopelessly lax in its organizational commitment. But it has viewed the OCI's organizational commitment as being a rather formal commitment to centralism which is quite beside the point of successful revolutionary activity. *Lutte Ouvrière* has offered the model of a clandestine organization with a high degree of discipline, whose major activity has been focused upon decentralized work contexts in the major industrial plants. Thus on the one hand *Lutte Ouvrière* could participate in and support the 1968 revolt, which was erupting in all kinds of educational and work contexts, while on the other it could share the OCI's rejection of the youth-as-a-vanguard tendency of the *Ligue*. Its commitment to decentralized revolutionary activity has been indicated both by its relative neglect of labor-union work in favor of extra-syndical groups within the individual plants and by its support of the decentralized eruptions of 1968.

Two shifts in *Lutte Ouvrière's* orientation, however, indicate that the clandestine and "Workerist" model handed down by Barta to his followers might not have been totally suited to the contemporary context. The first is the change of heart on the need for intellectuals to perform intellectual functions for the organization. Second is the massive commitment which *Lutte Ouvrière* has made to electoral politics since the 1974 presidential elections. One element of clandestine work is that the names of party members remain secret. It is one thing to sacrifice the identity of a single person who runs for president and has already become a nationally known strike leader anyway. It is quite another matter to divulge the names of leading members in almost five hundred legislative electoral districts throughout France and some of its overseas possessions—all in the name of anti-electoralism.

The potpourri of alternative political structures available to the French on the Left at large has been replicated in microcosmic form just within the ranks of French Trotskyism. The same general range of organizational options has not been available in the United States, nor have U.S. Trotskyists been faced with anything comparable to the 1968 upheaval which sharpened the differences between the Frankists and the Lambertists over the issue of organizational integrity, as well as that of spontaneity. With the exception of Spark—the tiny group which has been operating in only two cities in the United States, but which has maintained an international fraternal relationship with *Lutte Ouvrière* and tried to follow its organizational pattern —all U.S. Trotskyist organizations have resembled the OCI more than any of the other French Trotskyist groups. This is not strange, since the SWP broke with the policy of the Pablists and Frankists over the issue of *entrisme sui generis* and joined the International Committee of which the OCI was an initiator. On this question of party integrity, the SWP and the OCI stood shoulder to shoulder. When the Spartacists and the Workers League went their separate ways, it was over the issue of Cuba and the Third World. There was no basic disagreement over organizational issues.

Nevertheless, in the 1970s the Socialist Workers Party in the United States reacted to contextual situations in ways which have raised questions about its structural conceptions. The most important of these contextual conditions have been the resurgence of ethnic separatism and the impact of the termination of the war in Indochina.

As we have seen, within the *Transitional Program* Trotsky envisioned a plural party system as a representation mechanism for the soviets after the situation had passed from dual power to the dictatorship of the proletariat. However, within the context of a very weak Left in the United States, the Socialist Workers Party has long called for a plural party system *prior* to the revolution. A joint decision was made by Trotsky and the SWP leaders to call for the creation of a separate labor party in order to break the hold of the two major parties over the U.S. working class. While Trotskyists would obviously attempt to work within this party, it was envisioned as a more broadly aggregative structure. Thus there was already a precedent for the call for the creation of and the support of non-Trotskyist structures in the pre-revolutionary period, when the SWP issued its call for the creation of a separate Black political party and extended its support to the Mexican-American party, *La Raza Unida*. While the Spartacist League and Workers League could accept the call for a separate labor party, they could not accept the later position of the SWP. However, this was not because the SWP was calling for the formation of a plural party system prior to the inception of the dictatorship of the proletariat but rather because, in focusing upon race and ethnicity, the SWP was seen as bowing to petit-bourgeois nationalistic conceptions rather than adhering to the universal concept of class. Spark has tried to have the best of the two conceptions by arguing that a separate Black party would be desirable—on the condition that it is a Black Trotskyist party.

While the above considerations affect the role of a Trotskyist party in the larger revolutionary process, the termination of the war in Indochina posed an internal organizational problem for the SWP. The problem was that a crucial radicalizing stimulus was now missing, and the Young Socialist Alliance was not operating as a recruitment mechanism as effectively as it had been. Moreover, there were a good number of people in their mid-twenties to mid-thirties who had been radicalized but who were not in any national political organization and were not likely to go into a youth group such as the YSA. Thus, after having been critical of the *Ligue* for diluting its organizational integrity by failing to distinguish between a youth group and the parent party, the SWP declared a policy of probational "open" membership to attract people who were not committed Trotskyists.

Finally, the practice of entrism is not one which is clearly consistent with what most people would recognize as Leninism. This tactic was an international one directed by Trotsky himself. The parties entered were either non-centralist social democratic parties or factions which had split off of such parties, such as Pivert's PSOP. The tactic was ultimately justified as a short-term one to gain members and, according to Cannon, to destroy the social democratic parties which were viewed as impediments. However: (1) the Trotskyists did not quit the social democratic parties but were expelled; (2) some Trotskyists (such as Molinier and Frank in France) wanted to challenge the expulsions and reach accommodations in order to remain in the social democratic parties; (3) the Trotskyists at least formally dismantled their own national party structures when they entered the social democratic parties; (4) a good number of former Trotskyists have affiliated with social democratic movements after quitting Trotskyist groups; and, (5) after Trotsky's death, an international strategy of long-term entry into the Communist parties was adopted by the International Secretariat. Given the very limited role reserved for party structures in the *Transitional Program,* these considerations at least give pause to reflect upon whether or not "entrism" as such did not reflect a self-liquidationist tendency, one which is as much a part of the basic fabric of Trotskyism as is its commitment to "Leninism" and "democratic centralism."

Both the substantive content of the Transitional Program and the use of electoral processes also represent contradictions within Trotskyism. The *Transitional Program* is the bridge between the minimum and maximum demands which are to be posed within the context of a highly industrialized capitalist society. The justification for the *Transitional Program* is that the consciousness of the workers in these societies has not kept pace with the "objective" material development. Therefore it is necessary to appeal to workers on the basis of seemingly reformist demands which are understandable at the level of trade unionist consciousness. What the workers will then come to see is that capitalism will not and cannot grant even these demands and will use every resource at its disposal to put down the struggle for their realization.

Given Trotsky's past association with non-Bolshevik political currents and his recruitment to Bolshevism only in 1917, virtually all other Marxist-Leninists view Trotsky's Transitional Program as a manifestation of Menshevism or as social democracy dressed up in Leninist clothing. Just as they see his pessimistic view of the peasantry as being counter-revolutionary within the non-industrialized setting, so they view the Transitional Program and the positing of "minimum demands" as being counter-revolutionary in the capitalist industrialized setting. Virtually every other non-Trotskyist Marxist-Leninist would agree with Carl Davidson's characterization of Trotskyism, "Left in Form, Right in Essence."

Again, the essence is more contradictory. In the first place, the application of the Transitional Program differs because the development of consciousness within the capitalist industrialized world is uneven. In France, there is a much higher degree of radicalization among the workers and the population at large. Thus the *Ligue* in its extensive 1972 program made no direct reference to the Transitional Program, nor have the OCI or *Lutte Ouvrière* pushed it to the fore. Taking advantage of Trotsky's willingness to leave the specific applications to the various national sections of the Fourth International, they have geared their programs to the higher level of radicalization among the French working class and disparaged the moderating tendencies of left-wing parties and union leadership.

Rather than finding trade-union consciousness a problem at the base, French Trotskyists have had greater difficulty dealing with the strong element of syndicalism in French labor, which manifests itself in the concept of worker control or *autogestion*. The difficulty for French Trotskyists has been compounded by Trotsky's own inclusion of worker control as one of the demands of the minimum program, and by his emphasis upon the role of factory committees in the creation of a set of oppositional structures which would challenge the capitalists in their plants as well as at the political level. Trot-sky argued that in the public sectors "workers' control...would be replaced by direct workers' management" and that in such cases "workers' control becomes a school for planned economy."[6] He even singled out the nationalized French weapons industry as illustrative of a situation where "the slogan of workers' control preserves its full strength."[7]

The problem is that the fertility of the French terrain for the slogan of "workers' control" has proved to be greater than Trotsky had anticipated. *Autogestion* has become the key element in the proposals for social change of France's second largest labor confederation (the CFDT) and the *Parti Socialiste Unifié* (PSU) and a key element in the program of the Socialist Party. Even the Communist Party felt obliged to stop its determined opposition to the concept of *autogestion*. Thus Trotsky's attempt to place the question of worker control within the framework of the minimum program runs up against the attraction which *autogestion* itself has as a maximum program.

Since the basic question of hierarchy underlies both issues, the scaling of French Trotskyists on the "tight/loose" continuum in regard to internal party structure is replicated in their view of worker control or *autogestion*. The *Pablist Comités Communistes pour l'Autogestion,* which has the loosest form of internal party structure, has viwed *autogestion* as the key to the Transitional Program. The *Ligue* has been in an intermediate position in both areas, contending that while worker control is desirable in and of itself it must not be seen as a substitute for the political struggle and must be carefully prepared so that productivity does not fall. The OCI and *Lutte Ouvrière,* which have the tightest organizational structures, have completely rejected the concept of *autogestion*. They have viewed it as a distraction from the distributive question and from the major political functions of workers' committees, which are to defend against counter-revolution and the development of bureaucratization along the lines of the USSR. There is indeed enough "play" within Trotsky's work for these differing positions to emerge within the ranks of French Trotskyism. Al-though worker control is less solidly on the agenda in the United States, where it is used as a highly abstract and undefined slogan by the SWP, the social democratic variant of this, "industrial democracy," has been embraced by a number of former Trotskyists and spin-off groups.

The Transitional Program has serveed a somewhat different function for U.S. Trotskyists than it has for French Trotskyists. For French Trotskyists it has been suggestive of ways of trying to liberate a more radical working class from parties and union structures which try to moderate their radicalism. As we have seen, French Trotskyists have disagreed on what the real message is, particularly in regard to how to relate to the strong syndicalist strain in French worker radicalism.

In the United States, the situation is not that of a radical working class with highly developed structures on the Left trying to restrain or channel that radicalism, but rather a working class insulated from radical ideas and the absence of strong structures on the Left. One of the greatest barriers for a Marxist group in the United States is simply the high degree of control which is exercised over political language. Of course, as the treatment accorded over the years to the Socialist Workers Party indicates, there are also more coercive repressive techniques which are brought into play.

It is to this kind of political context—where the distance between the "objective" material conditions and the consciousness of the workers is greatest—that the Transitional Program is really addressed. Here it is not a matter of freeing workers inclined toward radical action from the constraint of left-wing structures, but of trying to communicate with workers who have been bombarded uniquely with pro-capitalist and anti-communist as well as anti-socialist messages by parties, unions, schools, and the media.

Within this context, the SWP has placed a very heavy emphasis upon the minimum program of the Transitional Program. This has been the basic content of all of its electoral programs. Moreover, while the *Ligue,* like the OCI and the CCA, have designated themselves as "communist" organizations in France, the "S" in SWP stands for "Socialist," and the party has referred to itself publicly as a socialist organization. The U.S. Maoist organizations—which have made it a point of principle to refer to themselves as communists—miss no opportunity to insist upon the accuracy of the SWP's nomenclature, if socialist is understood as social democratic, and thus totally inconsistent with Marxism-Leninism.

The electoral behavior of the SWP has also differed from the electoral behavior of French Trotskyists. It will be recalled that the U.S. government was particularly obsessed with the SWP because it engaged in electoral activity. A portion of the prosecution's examination of Cannon on the stand dealt with his attitude toward elections, and the FBI COINTELPRO documents deal extensively with attempts to disrupt the SWP's electoral efforts.

Within the ranks of international Trotskyism, the SWP has been one of the staunchest supporters of the electoral approach. It has argued that, in the United States, workers are very strongly attached to the electoral process and other constitutional provisions and processes which offer at least formal guarantees of political rights, even if the government has acted to infringe upon the exercise of those rights by opposition groups, including the SWP itself. It has opposed the French *Ligue's* position that the major thrust of electoral activity should be to show that elections are a farce, and it has been very distant from the kind of competition which the *Ligue* and *Lutte Ouvrière* have gotten themselves into, to show who can be more electoral while at the same time being more anti-electoralist.

Nor is this completely a question of U.S. exceptionalism. Within the United Secretariat of the Fourth International, it has done battle with the *Ligue* over electoral as opposed to urban guerrilla or violent tactics in Latin America. It has shared the *Ligue's* view that the capitalist interests would not respect electoral outcomes which were not consistent with their interests, and that Chile is a perfect example of this. But it has tried to keep the onus on the capitalists themselves for disregarding both their own electoral rules and their proclaimed concern for human rights.

Fundamentally, the SWP has remained committed to the rationality of its program and to the proposition that, if it is presented in proper terms, there will be a coincidence of an increase in the consciousness of workers and other oppressed sectors of the population and the inherent and structural inability of the capitalist system to meet real human needs. Trotsky argued that the two major problems which would plague capitalism over the long-term were unemployment and inflation. The SWP has been convinced that if it keeps plugging electorally, the objective conditions are such that it will be in a position of having to defend its electoral victories from revolution on the Right—or what is commonly called fascism. The SWP thus has offered the most electoralist, libertarian, and incremental interpretation of the Transitional Program of all of the groups that have been examined.

Finally, there is the contradiction within Trotskyism between a movement which claims to be revolutionary, and thus to be instrumental in bringing about revolution and reconstruction, and the oppositional political posture which Trotskyists have assumed over the past half century. While some Trotskyists have been attracted to certain regimes more than others, no Trotskyist will point to any regime as meeting the criteria of Trotskyism.

This lack of a model in the real world has its advantages. One does not have to make excuses for the actions of regimes. On the other hand, an opposition mentality can develop as a result of constantly playing an oppositional role. In fact, Trotsky and the movements which have followed in his wake have played the role of international superego, critical of both capitalism and those successful revolutions against capitalism which have called themselves socialist. Like most superegos, Trotskyists are little appreciated and much repressed. But the major problem is that Trotskyists set such high and often conflicting political standards for regime behavior that it is difficult to imagine Trotskyists being comfortable in the positive exercise of political power themselves. The very constrained role which Trotsky allows for any "Trotskyist Party" can only reinforce this tendency.

This observation, as well as the ones which have preceded it, should not be taken as a disparagement of Trotskyism. There is a desperate need for informed and intelligent opposition movements. Trotskyists have a long tradition of attracting bright people and of conducting extensive education programs both within and without their own groups. If no one else with a Left perspective could be expected to be critical of a Communist–Socialist governing coalition, Trotskyists could be, and not merely in the service of yet another regime with its own interests.

While Mao theorized extensively on both pre-revolutionary and post-revolutionary practice, the vast majority of Trotsky's political writings are devoted to critiques of both capitalism and Stalinism and strategies for destroying them. Very little is devoted to what the post-revolutionary situation would be like. What there is is very brief and very schematic. Since nowhere have Trotskyists played a major role in the exercise of state power, there has not been the practical necessity to expand upon this aspect of the thought. However, despite the remarkable revitalization of Trotskyism in the 1960s and 1970s, this may have become a circle with no exit. Permanent revolution may have been transformed into permanent opposition.

THE CONTRADICTIONS OF MAOISM

Maoists are quick to jump upon these contradictions within Trotskyism. They argue that the "real" Trotskyism is petit-bourgeois and counter-revolutionary, and that the claim to Marxism–Leninism by Trotskyists is an attempt to gain credibility for their mistaken ideas by using the prestige of Lenin's name. As has been indicated, this writer finds that characterization of Trotskyism an undialectical and a one-sided simplification on the part of people who are usually insistent upon "dividing things into two." Moreover, Maoism contains its own contradictions.

Just as in Trotskyism, there is a tension within Maoism on the question of the role of the party *vis-à-vis* the masses. Like Trotsky, Mao claimed to be a Marxist-Leninist and to offer structural formulations which were consistent with those of Lenin. In *What Is To Be Done?*, written in 1902, Lenin defines the party in the pre-revolutionary phase. Lenin advocates a small party of professional revolutionaries. These revolutionaries would be intellectuals and ex-workers. While students are discussed as potential allies, the peasantry is not referred to even in an allied capacity. Lenin does express concern that he not be understood to say that the party would "do the thinking for all."[8] But if one looks closely at the role which Lenin foresees for the workers as a whole, one finds them distributing literature, participating in demonstrations, and forming ancillary organizations which would have to rely upon the theoretical guidance of the vanguard party. On the function of the party, Lenin wrote:

> [O]ur very first and most imperative duty is to help to train
> working-class revolutionaries who will be on the same level
> in regard to Party activity as intellectual revolutionists (we
> emphasize the words "in regard to party activity," because al-
> though it is necessary, it is not so easy and not so imperative
> to bring the workers up to the level of intellectuals in other
> respects). Therefore, attention must be devoted principally to
> the task of raising the workers to the level of revolutionists,
> but without, in doing so, necessarily degrading ourselves to
> the level of the "laboring masses," as the Economists wish to
> do, or necessarily to the level of the average worker, as Svo-
> boda desires to do.[9]

It was this kind attitude toward the worker which was so offensive to Trotsky in the earlier years. While Lenin was somewhat disturbed by the possibly stifling effect of the party doing the thinking for all, at least disturbed enough to mention it, he saw no alternative to the model of the party and its intellectuals recruiting a limited cadre of gifted workers into its ranks. This party would perform the pedagogical function, as well as the secret work, which would be necessary to raise the workers beyond trade unionist or economist consciousness.

Within Mao's thought, both the party and the revolutionary constituency which it is to serve are altered considerably. On the one hand, Mao retains the formal democratic centralist party structure, sees the party as the vanguard force in making the revolution, and accords it the status of sole legitimate party in the post-revolutionary context. On the other hand, the model of learning and communication which runs from the party to the masses in Lenin shifts in Mao's conception to the model in which the party learns from the masses. The composition of the masses in this case is neither the comparatively backward Russian proletariat portrayed by Lenin nor the more active, capable, and pluralistic proletariat in the Western countries pictured by Trotsky. Rather, in Mao's conception, the revolutionary constituency is composed of the peasant masses. It is the peasant masses who supply the creative inspiration for the party. The party then "systematizes" these ideas and represents them in a constant system of interaction and mutual learning.

Thus while Lenin expressed concern over the possible undersirable consequences of the hierarchical relationship between the masses and the party, a relationship which he felt was nonetheless a necessity, Mao deliberately built in elements of a conflicting model. In the exchange of charges, Trotskyists can certainly respond to Maoist criticisms of lack of party integrity by asking how those who call themselves Marxist-Leninists can assign so much revolutionary creativity to peasants living in a quasi-feudal state when Lenin refused to recognized such capabilities even in the Russian proletariat.

The fact is, there are elements of Maoism which are more utopian or anarchist than Marxist-Leninist. Side by side with dialectical materialism, democratic centralism, and the dictatorship of the proletariat is the recognition —so characteristic of Rousseauist, Proudhonian, and French syndicalist thinking—that no matter how dedicated any structure might be to the general welfare, it will have a tendency to confuse its own corporate well-being with that general welfare. Rousseau, who admitted the need for a single executive structure, argued that the only hope for securing the freedom of a people is to assure that such a structure take direction from the masses and be held accountable to the masses.

The Great Cultural Revolution can be viewed as an attempt by Mao to put Rousseau's principle into practice. In its insistence upon rooting party policy in the "mass line," in its mobilization of the energy of youth to challenge the tread toward bureaucratization on the part of middle-aged elites, in its questioning of the distinction between intellectual and manual labor, and in its insistence that both intellectuals and the cadres go into the fields and workplaces alongside the masses, there is little that resembles Leninism. In place of Trotsky's activist and pluralistic proletariat taking the helm in socialist reconstruction, we have Mao's undifferentiated but creative mass of the peasantry telling the party what its needs are and enforcing accountability.[10]

So long as Mao lived, he was able to manage the reconcilialion of these contradictory aspects of Maoism in Chinese practice — if not with facility, at least well enough to survive politically. But it did not take very long after his death for the contradiction between the anti-hierarchical and the hierarchical Leninist aspects of Maoism to manifest themselves in the form of a power struggle among the surviving leaders. Those presently on top in China argue that hierarchial forms are necessary for efficient socialist reconstruction, and accuse the "Gang of Four" of a Trotskyist opposition to their efforts.

In fact — whatever the views of members of the "Gang of Four" on Trotskyism — the root of this difference can be found in the contradictions within Maoism itself. This was clear within the French context well before the death of Mao. There the anti-hierarchical aspects of Maoism, transmitted particularly through the aura of the Great Cultural Revolution, merged with an indigenous, anti-hierarchical and spontaneous impulse. The *Gauche Prolétarienne* and *Vive la Révolution* represented the anti-hierarchical strain, while the PCMLF, the UCFML, and the PCR (m-l) have represented the more hierarchical and more Leninist strain within Maoism. In the *Gauche Prolétarienne*, we have seen an explicit rejection of Lenin's *What Is To Be Done?*, the use of the *enquête* as a technique for operationalizing the mass line, the contention that a party must be created only to be destroyed, the continual erosion of formal hierarchy within the "movement," the negative view of technology and division of labor which are seen as inherently hierarchical, and the emphasis on action and experimentation on the part of small and decentralized groups. Even within the hierarchical category the PCMLF has called the PCR(m-l) "soft" on the mass line, and thus the party question. The PCR(m-l)'s willingness to talk and act with Trotskyists while the Gang of Four was being accused of Trotskyism added to the PCMLF's suspicions.

Thus in France the major division among Maoists has been of a general ideological nature. This has been recognized in the political language of the French Left. "Les Maos" or "les Maoïstes" are the anti-hierarchical Maoists while "les Marxistes-Leninistes" the hierarchical Maoists. On the other hand, in the United States—where the dominant political culture is issue-oriented, rather than ideological as in France—the differences which have divided Maoists most intensely have been those issues which relate to the specific conditions and politics of the United States. The questions of hierarchy and of party organization have not been central ones in U.S. Maoism, even though they are central to the contradictions of Maoism itself.

This is somewhat curious, because even though the traditional ideological strains which one finds in France are extremely weak in the United States, the youth counter-culture in the 1960s and the early 1970s was characterized by a strong anti-hierarchical orientation. It thus might well have been anticipated that variations of Maoism resembling those of the *Gauche Prolétarienne* and *Vive la Révolution* would have been developed by young people in the United States. Instead, U.S. Maoism has been uniformly hierarchical and an upholder of rigid interpretations of "proletarian morality" quite at odds with the dominant youth culture from which it sprang.

Indeed, U.S. Maoism was a reaction against that youth culture. It was a reaction against those aspects of the counter-culture which met the anti-hierarchical needs of young people in non-political, anti-political, and often highly exploitative ways (e.g., drugs and the commercialization of anti-establishment music). But it was also a reaction against the impact of the youth culture norms on the most important political youth organization of the epoch. In France, the most important such political structure, aside from the student union, was the student affiliate of the Communist Party. That was where French Maoism derived its major impetus. The anti-hierarchical French Maoist groups were a reaction against the hierarchical nature of the Communist Party. While the first U.S. Maoists did come out of the Communist Party as in France, the most important political structure for the development of U.S. Maoism was not that party's youth affiliate but the Students for a Democratic Society. Both of the major U.S. Maoist parties of the 1970s were reactions against SDS's anti-hierarchical norms. Ironically, the most devastating effect of that lack of hierarchy in their eyes was that SDS was rendered virtually defenseless against the attempt at take-over by a hierarchical Maoist organization with an incorrect political line.

While U.S. Maoists — all of whom disapproved of SDS's anti-hierarchical norms — were battling each other, another current was building upon SDS's anti-hierarchical norms. RYM I, or Weatherman, was providing an alternative mode of engagement which appealed to the anti-hierarchical "action" orientation of young people. It did this, however, without the Maoist trappings of the *Gauche Prolétarienne* or *Vive la Révolution*. In the United States, there were no Maoist equivalents of those two French organizations; Weatherman was occupying their political space. The difference in national contexts was thus more determining than a basic contradiction within Maoism itself in this instance.

Nevertheless, there are other contradictions within Maoism which have an effect even upon the more particularistic conflicts between U.S. Maoists. Perhaps the most important of these is the Theory of the Three Worlds. In the area of foreign policy, it posed a problem for both French and U.S. Maoism because its application has amounted to the approval of virtually any anti-Soviet posture or action on the part of capitalist governments in the two countries. Since the governments of both France and the United States are quite active in this area, total support for the Chinese position would place Maoists in the camp of the most reactionary forces in those countries.

At least some Maoists have consciously felt themselves caught in the contradiction between the demands which are made by a body of thought such as Marxism-Leninism on the one hand, and the demands which are made by the leadership of a actual regime which claims to incorporate the principles of that body of thought, on the other. This is precisely contrary to the condition in which Trotskyists have found themselves. They have no regime to which they can point as the embodiment of their theories, and thus no indication that their theories are viable alternatives for the real world. On the other hand, Trotskyists have not been placed in the position of the Maoists in France and the United States, who have had to choose between loyalty to the Chinese regime and siding with the Right in each country on foreign policy issues, or differing with the Chinese regime and participating in a united opposition to what the rest of the Left has clearly seen as imperialistic and reactionary foreign policies.

Maoists have been placed in a situation which is not very different from that in which supporters of the Soviet Union found themselves during the Hitler–Stalin Pact. Perhaps the difficulty in choice facing some Maoists can be better appreciated when it is recalled that not even Stalin's arch enemies, the Trotskyists, were willing to desert the Soviet Union after the signing of the pact and the movement of Soviet troops into Poland and Finland. As critical as they were, the Trotskyists still viewed the Soviet Union as the only workers' state then in existence. Under threat of extinction, it had to be defended. Similarly, in the 1970s most Maoists regarded China as the mainstay of socialism; they felt compelled to react when China believed its existence was being threatened by the state-capitalist Soviet Union. It has simply not been easy for foreign Maoists to "desert" a regime that has transformed a country plagued by foreign domination, economic bondage, and starvation into an independent and militarily strong country which has eliminated starvation.

Trotskyists, who have never had a commitment to a regime, can give "critical support" to revolutionary movements or workers' states under attack even if they consider them to be "deformed." That is at least a positive gesture. But to move from complete support to critical support, no matter how tempered, is likely to be viewed as a wholesale rejection. That it was so viewed by the Chinese regime was indicated in the summer of 1977, by the regime's recognition of the Communist Party (Marxist- Leninist) rather than the Revolutionary Communist Party, which could not accept all aspects of the Theory of the Three Worlds and said so.

But the Theory of the Three Worlds has had an impact on the United States which it has not had in France. This has to do with the role of Third World peoples. The theory postulated that the Third World was in an "objective" revolutionary situation. While asserting this proposition — which is directly contrary to Trotsky's conception of "objective" revolutionary situations — the Maoists in China were able to maintain relations with the most reactionary of Third World regimes. Combined with the concept of socialism in one country, the Theory of the Three Worlds foresaw an inevitable vanguard march toward socialism which would be led by the peoples in each of the Third World countries, and which could not be orchestrated by a foreign power such as China. Therefore China's role in the meantime lay in the sphere of international diplomacy and not of subversion. That role was to encourage the anti-Soviet posture and behavior of Third World governments. For the Chinese, the major threat to true socialist revolution in those countries was not their present reactionary governments but Soviet social-imperialism, which supports revolutionary movements in order to control them. In the Chinese eyes, if the Soviet Union would leave these revolutionary movements alone and practice socialism in one country, then the Third World people themselves would inevitably bring about true socialist revolutions adapted to their particular superstructural situations.

This championing of Third World peoples as the revolutionary vanguard has had a particular impact upon U.S. Maoism. Initially it reinforced the commitment of U.S. Maoists of European heritage to recruit among people of Third World heritage who were seen as the most exploited members of the working class. These people were encouraged to identify with their Third World brothers and sisters who were still in the countries of origin. But then, affected by both the primacy of Third World people in the Theory of the Three Worlds, and racial and ethnic separatism as it intensified in the United States, Black, Asian-American, and Latino Maoists began to assert that they were the revolutionary vanguard within the United States, just as Third World peoples were the revolutionary vanguard in the world at large.

It was one thing to accept a modification of Marxism in the form of a general proposition that the revolutionary vocation in the modern world has passed principally to the peasant masses living under the sometimes semi-feudal conditions of the Third World. Not even the Revolutionary Communist Party took exception to this aspect of the Theory of the Three Worlds. But it was quite another matter to accept the proposition that Third World people within the context of a capitalist industrialized country should be differentiated from the larger proletariat and accorded a higher revolutionary standing. This struck the larger "multi-national" Maoist organization as a separatist and a reactionary nationalistic position which was inconsistent with Marxism-Leninism. The ironic result of this is that Maoists accomplished in fact what the Trotskyist SWP and Spark have been calling for. They formed separate political parties based upon their racial or ethnic identities.

The intrusion of the Comintern under Stalin, Stalin's insistence that racial and ethnic questions within the United States had to be conceptualized as national questions, and the Black Belt Nation thesis posited in the late 1920s, have enormously compounded the difficulties facing U.S. Maoists. On the one hand they have been trying to relate to people of Third World heritage and to recognize their special oppression within a racist society. On the other, they have been attempting to struggle for the unification rather than the division of the working class. This has led not only to disagreement over the Black Belt Nation thesis, which remained at a highly abstract level, but to very bitter disagreements over what position to take on such a hotly contested issue in the United States as was school busing.

Another irony in the situation is that while the Chinese-recognized CP(ML) has taken international positions which placed it in the company of the American Right more often than the RCP has, the situation is reversed when it comes to American domestic issues. The CP(ML) supported the right of Blacks or other minorities to be bused. The RCP saw busing as a capitalist plot to divide the working class. While both parties have rejected "feminism" and sexual separatism, the CP(ML) supported the passage of the Equal Rights Amendment, while the RCP saw it as a threat to the protectionist legislation which the working class as a whole fought so hard to obtain.

By its very nature as a self-proclaimed variant of Marxism designed to meet the superstructural characteristics of Chinese society, Maoism has posed severe problems of readaptation back to the industrialized societies. Ultimately, that contradiction may be the determining one for the future of Maoism in France and the United States. For the pressure on these movements to disregard the political and ideological configurations in their own countries and to support the foreign policy and the internal political line of whoever is in control of the Chinese government has increased enormously. On the face of it, such disregard of superstructure would seem to be decidedly un-Maoist. It could only be justified by a theory or a need of an actual regime which sees the revolutionary vocation of groups within the industrialized countries as at best a very distant one. Under these conditions, the task of maintaining a distinction between a revolutionary party or organization and a friendship association with a largely propaganda function is becoming even more difficult. In France, the confusion of roles has become even greater as the clandestine arch-supporter of China, the PCMLF, has succumbed to the temptations of entering French electoral politics.

CONTRADICTION, SCIENTISM AND
THE THEORY / PRACTICE PROBLEMATIC

Contradiction tends to be negatively viewed in an intellectual milieu dominated by positivistic empiricism. Thus the demonstration that there are contradictions in a body of theory is likely to be understood as a refutation of the validity of the theory. The reader should not conclude that that is this author's view.

Contradiction is endemic in all political theory. Political theory has both an analytic and a prescriptive function. It attempts both to understand the world as it exists and to suggest what a better world might look like. It does this, however, in a world of contradiction and inevitably conflicting values. Theorists are placed in the difficult position of being obliged to struggle to resolve contradiction on the one one hand while realizing the impossibility of completely achieving that task on the other. The theoretical vocation is thus one of a search for better understanding of the present as well as greater insight into the future possibilities of humanity. But because theory is a part of that social universe which it seeks to comprehend, theory cannot completely purge itself of its own internal contradictions.

Dialectical theories, such as Trotskyism and Maoism, consciously recognize the external universe as one of the unfolding of contradiction. But they themselves also reflect this dialectical process. The contradictions of Trotskyism and Maoism as bodies of theory translate themselves into a dialectical dynamic of group political life and interpretation. The present dynamic of Trotskyist and Maoist groups is part of a larger dialectical historical development which included the breaking up of the First International because of the contradiction between Marxist and anarchist strains, the division of Marxism into conflicting social-democratic and Marxist-Leninist interpretations, and the division of Marxism-Leninism into varieties of interpretations, including Trotskyism and Maoism. And within Trotskyism and Maoism there are lines of cleavage which correspond to the contradictory elements within each of these variants of Marxism-Leninism and what are viewed as the exigencies of practice.

To reject the validity of Trotskyism or Maoism because of such internal contradictions and such differing schools of interpretation would logically compel one to reject the validity of every social theory which has ever gained a following. The possibility of multiple interpretation cannot, in itself, invalidate any body of thought. Indeed, it is often a sign of fertility and insightfulness.

On the other hand, two factors render the internal contradictions of Trotskyism and Maoism serious impediments to pushing beyond what we have referred to in the Introduction as the third level of practice, — i.e., a practice involving a very limited number of participants and supporters and capable of at most intermittent impact on the larger body politic. The effect of these factors can be seen in France, where other groups on the Left have been able to build mass bases of support, as well as in the United States, where all groups on the Left are stuck at the third level.

First, as Marxist-Leninists, Trotskyists and Maoists view theory and practice as a combined "science." As pointed out in the Introduction, theory is not merely analytical and suggestive to them but has a one-to-one relationship to practice. When this kind of tightly scientistic approach is taken to theory, the capacity to shelve or skirt the problems posed by contradictions within theory and to get on with practical political tasks is very limited. All major political phenomena or events must be addressed and accounted for by the theory; and correct theory becomes as necessary to proper political practice as physics is to engineering.

The Trotskyist *Ligue Communiste Révolutionnaire* has gone about as far as any of the groups discussed in trying to isolate "tactical" questions from those of "principle" (i.e., theory) and to broaden the scope of the former as much as possible. This approach, however, runs up against the very *raison d'être* of Trotskyist and Maoist movements, as a reaction to Soviet and other Western Marxist-Leninists who have, in the eyes of Trotskyists and Maoists, taken such a pragmatic ("revisionist" or "opportunist") approach. These Marxists have gone too far in viewing the theory-practice problematic as one of a trade-off and in adapting both their theories and their practices to contextual givens. Even though this posture might enable parties which consider themselves to be Marxist to build or maintain a mass following and to paticipate in the administration of the state in certain restricted areas, in the view of Trotskyists and Maoists it in fact fortifies the bourgeois state and makes the ultimate goal of socialist revolution even more difficult to attain for truly revolutionary parties such as their own.

Trotskyists and Maoists thus attempt to provide "principled," "scientific" alternatives to both capitalism and to the Communist parties which they see as having strayed from the correct path. This posture of vigilence against Marxist-Leninist pragmatics — from Trotsky's early criticism of Stalin up through the more contemporary attacks on Eurocommunism — has brought with it the consequence that virtually any serious issue that arises *within* the ranks of Trotskyists and Maoists tends to be viewed as key to the integrity of Marxism-Leninism. It thus becomes potent grounds for disaffection and fragmentation. Students and intellectuals may have greater tolerance for interminable arguments over basic principles before one can make a move in any direction than do more practically-oriented workers, but even within those categories there is a threshold of tolerance. Thus despite the device of the Transitional Program — which is supposed to facilitate the task of Trotskyists in dealing with the contextual givens in the industrialized societies — and Mao's insistence on the importtance of the superstructure for revolutionaries, Trotskyists and Maoists have not been able to rise above the third level of practice — small groups having only intermittent impact on the larger body politic.

It should be reemphasized that they have indeed had that kind of impact. Sometimes acting as part of a larger constellation of forces and sometimes acting in relative isolation from others, Trotskyist and Maoist groups have engaged in practice which transcended their limited ability to recruit members and build support specifically for themselves. It is worth summarizing some of the instances already cited in previous chapters.

It was French Maoist groups which first called national and international attention to the plight of immigrant workers in France by organizing in the shanty towns, the ghettos, and the work places while the Communist Party and Socialists were sitting on the sidelines. When the Algerian War was begun in earnest under a Socialist premier and Communist parliamentarians continued to vote for the military budget, it was the Pablist and Frankist Trotskyists in France who took an active position in support of the FLN during the Algerian war and before there was much of an active anti-war movement, just as the Frankist Trotskyists of the *Ligue* were to organize and lead the major French group in support of the Indochinese fighting U.S. troops several years later. Moreover, the Frankist Trotskyists in the PCI and in leadership positions in the *Jeunesse Communiste Révolutionnaire,* along with the student union and the *Parti Socialiste Unifié's* student affiliate which controlled that union, provided what organizational backbone there was to the 1968 uprising. In more recent years, the French military has obviously been quite worried by the extensive organizational work being done among the draftees by the *Ligue*.

In the United States, both the Trotskyist SWP and the Maoist RCP have played important supportive roles in a number of specific labor disputes, civil rights campaigns, and international solidarity campaigns for victims and opponents of regimes which they regard as oppressive. In the case of the SWP, as in the case of both the *Ligue* and the OCI in France, this has included strong support for civil rights activists in the Soviet Union as well as for victims of such right-wing regimes as those in South Africa, Chile, Argentina, and Iran under the Shah's reign. The anti-war work of the SWP in the 1960s and the early 1970s and the more recent legal suits filed by that Trotskyist party — which revealed extensive illegal and unconstitutional behavior on the part of the FBI and other agencies charged with law enforcement — have undoubtedly had the greatest impact of any of the SWP's initiatives in recent years. The RCP did very significant support work for both the Farah strikers and the anti-Shah Iranian student movement in the United States.

On the campuses, the student affiliates of the Trotskyist SWP and the RCP have played crucial roles in the post-SDS years. As indicated in the chapter on U.S. Maoism, in many cases they alone have been in a position to provide the organizational and tactical know-how when much larger numbers of students attempted to respond to what they regarded as intolerable policies or actions. Finally, the publication of the *Guardian* weekly newspaper and the books, pamphlets, and weekly news digests issued by the SWP have constituted an extremely important portion of the Marxist literature which is available for general reading and academic use in the United States.

Despite these accomplishments, and despite the fact that in the United States Trotskyist and Maoist groups demonstrated more vitality than any of the other organized groups on the Left throughout the decade of the 1970s, Trotskyists and Maoists have thus far not been able to handle their own contradictions well enough to gain a mass following and to prevent very scarce political resources from being dispersed among a number of competing groups ostensibly interested in the same sort of revolutionary transformation in both France and the United States. Their argument that the Communist Party in France has built and retained a mass following on a non-Marxist–Leninist program of system maintenance and participation in the administration of the bourgeois state, rather than upon a revolutionary program and strategy, does indeed illustrate the difficulty facing Marxist-Leninists, who are grappling with the theory-practice problematic in contemporary capitalist industrialized societies. But it does not solve their own problem of attempting a "principled" Marxist-Leninist practice in those societies. If internal contradiction is a characteristic of all theory, it becomes increasingly dysfunctional at the level of practice as the practitioners move away from a suggestive conception of theory and toward a rigidly scientistic conception and a posture of vigilence against all political pragmatics.

The probabilities are that Trotskyists, who for over fifty years since the death of Trotsky have maintained themselves as minority movements, as well as the more recent Maoist movements, will continue to exist and to exert intermittent influence. The opportunities for the exertion of such influence will be heavily dependent upon the contextual situation and external stimuli. The commitment itself, like the participation in the 1968 revolt by some French Trotskyists or support for the Castroist regime in Cuba by the SWP, is likely to be very divisive within the ranks. But for both Trotskyists and Maoists, that is better than exchanging theoretical integrity for a share of the bourgeois pie. Which is to say that in their perspective the second level of practice can be further from the final aim of socialism than the third level. It depends on how it is achieved; it is a qualitative as well as a quantitative question.

7
Epilogue: Developments in the 1980s

This book surveys the whole historical field of Trotskyism and Mao-ism in France and the United States, a path over half-a-century long by the end of the 1980s. The events of the last decade do not alter the basic analysis presented in this work; they confirm the general tendencies outlined here. But because many readers may be primarily interested in the more contemporary situations, in both of the national contexts and in both of the movements, I have chosen to summarize their developments in this separate chapter.

FRENCH TROTSKYISM AND MAOISM IN THE 1980s

In France, there have been several major shifts within the realm of Trotskyism. One of these shifts involved a change of strategy on the part of the *Ligue Communiste Révolutionnaire*. At its 1979 Congress, the United Secretariat of the Fourth International decided that all of its sections, including both the French *Ligue* and the SWP in the United States (which is a sympathizing section because of U.S. law preventing a full, formal affiliation), would concentrate on organizing in basic industry rather than focusing on more broadly-based, single-issue movements. The *Ligue* thus adopted a posture closer to the "workerist" orientation of *Lutte Ouvrière*.

The *Ligue* made two other changes in 1979. First, following up on preparations evident in 1975, it created a youth group distinct from the parent *Ligue*. This youth group was given the name of the 1968 barricade fighters, the *Jeunesse Communiste Révolutionnaire*, which had merged with the older Frankist Trotskyists shortly after that uprising. This represented a reversion to a more traditional form of organization, the absence of which had been the source of considerable criticism from the Lambertist OCI. The reason for the creation of a new JCR was the distancing of the *Ligue* from younger people since its creation in 1969. Once a bastion of students and people who had just left that status, the *Ligue* by 1982 was comprised mainly of salaried working people (85 per cent of the membership, of whom 20 per cent were teachers). In 1982, only fifteen per cent of the *Ligue's* members were students. By 1986, the percentage of students was down to twelve per cent.[1] However, unlike the Lambertists who recruit so heavily among students and control one of the national student unions, the JCR directs its efforts at youth as a whole and particularly working-class youth. That milieu is, of course much more radical in France than it is in the United States, and recruitment within it is much less a distraction from the industrial strategy than recruitment within the student milieu would be.

Second, in shifting its energy and resources to the heavy industry strategy and the building of a youth affiliate, the *Ligue* was forced to discontinue publishing *Rouge* on a daily basis. *The Ligue* thus has lost the distinction of being the only Trotskyist organization to publish a daily newspaper in France. *Rouge* has become a weekly, just like the papers of the other two major Trotskyist organizations.

The 1979 heavy industry strategy represented a compromise within the United Secretariat. It will be recalled that after the end of the war in Indochina, the *Ligue* and the SWP were in two opposing factions within the United Secretariat. The *Ligue* was very Third World oriented and a supporter of guerrilla warfare within the Latin American context, particularly in Argentina. The SWP and the minority faction argued against what it regarded as adventuristic guerrilla tactics in Latin America. It placed its emphasis upon organizational base-building efforts, and, where possible, participation in elections. It also argued forcefully that class struggle and opposition movements had been rekindled in the Western capitalist countries, and that the course of world revolution would henceforth run through the industrialized and proletarianized areas rather than through the rural areas of Latin America and the rest of the Third World.

In 1975, the two factions began a process of negotiation to try to put an end to their factionalism. In late 1976 and 1977, the *Ligue* and the International Majority Tendency engaged in a self-criticism and came to admit that the guerrilla warfare approach did not seem to be bearing fruit anywhere in Latin America. That self-criticism was crucial in putting an end to the major lines of fragmentation in the United Secretariat which pitted the French *Ligue* against the American SWP. By the 1979 Congress, the two major factions in the United Secretariat had been abolished, and the national sections were able to collaborate on strategies. If the old majority tendency agreed to give up its support of the guerrilla warfare strategy in Latin America, the minority tendency emphasized the importance of the industrial working classes in the Middle East, Asia and Africa, as well as in Latin America. Here was an attempt to mediate, within the largest Trotskyist international ogranization, the contradictory pulls within Trotsky's own theory.[2] For the French and

U.S. sections, however, the practical effect of the 1979 turn toward heavy industry was a concentration on organizing within the major plants and unions of their own industrialized countries.

The emphasis on work within the context of French capitalism itself, and the creation of a youth affiliate distinct from the party on the order of the more traditional Trotskyist parties like the OCI, were shifts which would have seemed to provide the basis for more fruitful relations between the *Ligue* and both the OCI and LO. In fact, in 1978 the *Ligue* and the OCI began engaging in talks with the hope of a future fusion. Cuba did remain a stumbling block. Though the OCI now was willing to grant that Cuba was a workers' state, it still regarded it as a Stalinist one badly in need of a political revolution. Even with this residual difference over Cuba, the talks continued. Cuba was an old problem, and both the OCI and the *Ligue* were now focusing on the capitalist industrialized world.

Alas, a Third World revolution was once again to bring out the internal contradictions in Trotskyism, and destroy the attempt at unity. The revolution this time was the Sandinista victory in 1979 over the dictator Somoza in Nicaragua. The dynamics are complex and reflect the fact that while any international grouping or national section can be characterized as "pro-guerrilla warfare," "emphasizing the capitalist industrialized countries," and the like, there is virtually always an internal minority which articulates an aspect of the contradiction which has lost out. Thus, even after the unification of the two major factions in the United Secretariat, there were two minority factions. These two minority factions played a major role in preventing the merger between the *Ligue* and the OCI.

The first of these was the Bolshevik Faction led by the Argentinian, Nahuel Moreno. Moreno, a leader of the Argentinian PST, had been allied with the SWP's faction when it was doing battle both with the *Ligue* and with the majority faction favoring guerrilla warfare. In 1975, as the two factions were trying to negotiate an end to their differences, Moreno became convinced that the SWP's faction was giving too much to the majority. At that point, he created the Bolshevik Faction.

The second minority faction, called the Leninist-Trotskyist Tendency, appeared in 1979, although it had older roots within the *Ligue* itself. These people were mainly members of the *Ligue* who had always been sympathetic to the SWP's position. This minority also thought that the SWP had given in too much to the majority within their own French section.[3]

While Moreno and his faction had opposed guerrilla tactics within the Argentinian context in the early and mid-1970s, they regarded the Nicaraguan situation in 1979 as quite another matter. As opposed to the situation in Argentina, where the Left indeed had been largely destroyed after a segment of it experimented with urban guerrilla warfare, the popular-based revolution in Nicaragua seemed to be succeeding. In the summer of 1979 Moreno's faction,

while still a part of the United Secretariat, sent a brigade of fighters into Nica-
ragua to fight against Somoza. It did not get there until after the fall of the
dictator, but it established itself in the Atlantic coastal town of Bluefields.
Moreno was a severe critic of the Sandinistas' willingness to participate in a
Governing Junta of National Reconstruction, which included people like Al-
fonso Robello (later a *contra* leader) and Violetta Chamorro (widow of slain
La Prensa editor Joaquín Chamorro), who also became an opponent of the
Sandinistas. When Moreno refused to place his forces under the command of
the Sandinistas, they were deported.

In September, the United Secretariat's executive body cited the Bolshevik Faction for lack of discipline because of their intrusion into Nicaragua
and their refusal to submit to Sandinista command.[4] It decided to recommend
further action to the coming Congess of the United Secretariat unless the
Moreno faction changed its behavior. Rather than admitting any wrongdoing,
the Bolshevik Faction denounced the Sandinistas as counter-revolutionary
and, along with French leaders of the Leninist-Trotskyist Tendency, entered
into negotiations with the international grouping dominated by the French
OCI. In 1980, the three tendencies formed a new international Trotskyist
grouping, the *IVe Internationale, Centre de Reconstruction,* which Moreno
was to leave the following year because the OCI refused to denounce the Mitterrand government immediately after it was elected. As a result of this
dispute approximately five hundred members of the French *Ligue* switched
their loyalty to the OCI.

Merger talks between the *Ligue* and the OCI thus led to nothing.
Rather, a revolution in the Third World resulted in tremendous bitterness and
divisiveness within and between national sections and international groupings. In the early 1960s, the issue of Cuba had wracked the U.S. Socialist
Workers Party, causing it to switch its international affiliation from the
International Committee to the United Secretariat and creating such internal
factionalism that two rival U.S. Trotskyist organizations were formed (i.e.
the Spartacist and Workers Leagues). This time the SWP held together in its
support of the Sandinistas, but the *Ligue* paid a high price in terms of
defections and its hopes for a merger with the OCI, a larger organization.
Revolution in the Third World remains as difficult for Trotskyists to agree
upon as it has al-ways been. As has previously been demonstrated, the root of
the problem lies in the theory itself.

The French political context has also continued to pose problems for
those who would like to see a unified Trotskyist movement. Not only does
France have strong political parties on the Left, something which the United
States lacks, but as a result of the elections of 1981, those parties came into
control of the French state for the first half of the decade. Trotskyists thus had
to orient themselves both toward elections and toward policies which could
no longer be blamed entirely on the Right.

The three major Trotskyist organizations assumed very different positions during the 1981 elections which brought the Left to power. In 1981, as in previous elections during the Fifth Republic, there were two rounds. The first round reduced the number of candidates to two; the second determined the winner. As was usual, the OCI did not present candidates in either the presidential or the legislative elections. It urged a first-round vote for Mitterrand in the presidential elections (thereby rejecting the candidacies of both the Trotskyist LO's Arlette Laguiller and the Communist Party's Georges Marchais), and a first-round vote for the candidates of either the Socialist or the Communist parties in the legislative elections. For the second round of the legislative elections, the OCI urged a vote for whichever of the candidates of these two parties survived the first round in a given district. The *Ligue* and LO, which ran their own candidates who presented their parties' programs, viewed the OCI's position as completely opportunist.

As usual, the *Ligue* presented Alain Krivine as its presidential candidate for the first round. The rules, however, had been changed by the conservative government after the 1974 elections. In 1974, candidates needed the signatures of 100 elected local officials to get on the ballot in the first round. A new law stipulated that 500 signatures of such officials had to be secured. Moreover, they had to be secured from officials in at least thirty different *départements,* with no more than 50 of them coming from any single *département.* The *Ligue* did manage to secure 590 signatures for Krivine. However, both the Communist and Socialist parties, which had originally opposed the new law, subsequently pressured their local officials to withdraw their signatures.[5] There were also reports of *préfets* putting pressure on mayors to try to keep local office holders from signing petitions of minor party candidates. As a result of these pressures, 200 of Krivine's signers eventually withdrew their signatures. Thus Krivine, who had been on the first-round ballots in the 1969 and 1974 presidential elections, was kept off in 1981. Nevertheless, he traveled around the country giving speeches; he gave a nationally televised address; and he granted interviews to local papers.

Krivine's message was that it was crucial to vote for the candidates of one of the "workers' parties" (including the PSU and LO as well as the Communist and Socialist parties) to assure the defeat of President Valéry Giscard d'Estaing and to remove the state apparatus from the control of the capitalists.[6] He urged this even though he felt that none of the other candidates of the "workers' parties" was waging a campaign for unity on the Left the way he and the *Ligue* were. The *Ligue* was very upset that the Left was fragmented but, rather than withdrawing from the elections and merely pressuring for mutual cooperation between parties the way thet the OCI did, the *Ligue* tried to use the forums provided by the electoral process itself to urge unified action. After the first round, when Mitterrand and Giscard emerged as the final two candidates, the *Ligue* adopted the electoral slogan: "Now, all together, let's tlirow Giscard out!"[7] It called upon the Communist Party to really put forth an effort to elect Mitterrand, and it called for the formation of a Socialist-Communist government, without any role for the "bourgeois" parties, after the elections. The "bourgeois" ministers that the *Ligue* was trying to keep out of the cabinet were the Radicals of the Left and Left Gaullists. After a few such people were indeed appointed by Mitterrand, the *Ligue* minimized the importance of the matter by contending that they were so few that one could hardly compare this with the fundamental error of the inclusion of the Radicals in the Popular Front of the 1930s.[8]

In the legislative elections, which were held a month after the presidential elections, the *Ligue* presented only 36 candidates.[9] According to Krivine, the reason for the small number of candidates presented by the *Ligue* was financial. In districts where it did not run candidates, the *Ligue* again urged people to vote for candidates of the workers' parties. It also launched a major campaign to get the Socialist and Communist parties to support actively each others' candidates when they survived to confront more conservative candidates in the second round of the legislative elections.

A most remarkable electoral performance was, once again, delivered by *Lutte Ouvrière*. LO managed to gather and keep the requisite number of signatures to keep Arlette Laguiller on the presidential ballot for the first round. Laguiller was one of three women to appear on that ballot. She received as much national television time as any other candidate, and used it to speak bluntly and at a very rapid pace to the French public. During the first round, she received 2.3 per cent of the vote, which placed her sixth out of the ten candidates. Over 668,000 people voted for Laguiller, more than voted for the Gaullist ex-Minister Michel Debré and more than voted for Huguette Bouchardeau of the PSU, subsequently appointed by Mitterrand to a cabinet position.[10]

After Laguiller was eliminated on the first round, LO called for a vote for Mitterrand on the second. Its approach, however, was different from that of both the *Ligue* and the OCI. LO's position has always been that it does not make much difference whether Socialists or Communists — who only pretend to be friends of the workers, or Rightists — who make no such pretences, are in power. It bowed to the slight difference, but without "any illusions," without being specific in its demands on Mitterrand, and without conducting any campaigns in favor of unity between the Socialists and the Communists the way the *Ligue* and the OCI did.

In the 1981 legislative elections, LO ran 158 candidates. This was over four times the number of the *Ligue's* candidates. Just as in 1974, LO was beating the *Ligue* at its own electoral game, and still doing so all in the name of anti-electoralism. As in 1974, there was bitterness engendered by the electoral campaign, with the *Ligue* again accusing LO of opportunistically presenting a watered-down version of its program in order to be more acceptable to the electorate and of refusing to get in there and mobilize the workers to really insure the defeat of Giscard. LO's refusal to engage in such an effort, as well as its refusal until the very last minute to urge a vote for the Left on the second round of the legislative elections, was seen by the *Ligue* as a precious, stand-offish attitude reflective of LO's sectarianism.[11] Thus, while the Nicaraguan situation created bitterness and distance between the *Ligue* and the OCI, the presidential and legislative elections also aggravated relations between Trotskyist organizations, particularly between the *Ligue* and LO.

While the contextually rooted differences between the *Ligue* and the LO in the 1981 elections engendered less intense hostility, the 1983 municipal elections revealed that while the theoretically rooted rupture between the *Ligue* and the OCI over Nicaragua was very deep and would be as difficult to heal as the ruptures among Trotskyists over Cuba. The *Ligue* and LO presented a number of joint lists in the municipal elections, which were conducted according to a modified proportional representation system. Though the *Ligue* and LO could agree to present 80 joint lists, they could not agree on another crucial point. In districts where the two organizations did not present their common lists and in the second rounds where their candidates had been elimi-nated, LO urged voters to abstain from voting. The *Ligue,* on the other hand, urged voters to select other candidates on the Left.[12]

The OCI, which had changed its name to the *Parti Communiste Internationaliste* (PCI) in 1982, refused the invitation to participate in the *Ligue*–LO slates and tried a different approach. This organization, which had almost never presented candidates in past elections, informed Socialist and Communist candidates that unless they accepted demands imposed by the PCI, the latter would run its own candidates. Indeed, the PCI ran candidates but only in districts where the candidates or incumbents of the Sociaist and Communist parties had rejected their demands. This was a fresh approach, that of electoral threat and punishment.

The five years of government by a Socialist president and a legislature with a Socialist majority proved to be a disaster for all of the parties on the Left except the Socialist Party itself. The Socialists retained more voters than any other single party in France. But the Communist Party (which received just under ten per cent of the vote in the 1986 elections), the *Parti Socialiste Unifié* (PSU), and the Trotskyist parties have since declined in both membership and appeal to voters.

As indicated, the OCI did not present candidates in 1981 for either the presidential or legislative elections. It urged a first-round vote for Mitterrand and for either the Socialist or Communist candidates in the legislative elections. The OCI was the most optimistic of all the Trotskyist groups about the possibility of a Socialist government bringing about basic changes. Its main concern was that the "Stalinists," — i.e., the Communist Party — would somehow disrupt the effort.

The Lambertists of the OCI were thus the most deceived of all of the Trotskyist groups when, in their view, the Mitterrand government enacted policies, especially the austerity program, which kept the capitalist system going at the expense of the workers. They could no longer place all of the blame for blocking socialism in France on the Communist Party.

After their disillusionment with the Socialists and approximately two years before the 1986 elections, the Lambertist Trotskyists made a decision to attempt to create a broadly based movement which they hoped would lead to the creation of a third major party on the French Left. They named this attempt the *Mouvement Pour un Parti des Travailleurs* (MPPT). The Lambertist PCI was not dissolved, but the vast majority of its efforts were spent in trying to create this broadly based movement of people dissatisfied with both the Socialist and Communist parties. Because of the shift to proportional representation introduced by the Socialist government, there were many fewer electoral districts in 1986 than there had been in 1981. The MPPT presented a total of 728 candidates in all of the 93 metropolitan legislative districts.[13]

Because the MPPT was supposed to be a broadly based movement, the platform could not be the highly specific Trotskyist one of the Lambertist party. It was a more moderate one, stressing the struggle for true democracy, defense of labor unions against state intrusion, defense of the state social security system, defense of small and medium-sized farmers, equal rights for all immigrant and French workers, and opposition to the decentralization of government services.

The voters' response to the MPPT's offerings was minimal. All of the candidates together only got 183,483 votes (0.68 per cent of the votes cast). While losing its majority in the legislature, the Socialist Party received over 31 per cent of the votes cast, the highest score for any party.

Given the tremendous investment of energy and resources in the MPPT electoral strategy, and the disastrous result, the strains within the Lambertist PCI became too great. Some within the party saw the strategy as a terrible miscarriage which left the PCI with nothing more to offer. They were equally impressed with the Socialist Party's show of electoral strength. Moreover, ties of some of the Lambertist students with the Socialist Party had been strengthened when sections of the Socialist Party's student affiliate had joined together with the student union which the PCI dominated. These links facilitated several hundred party members breaking away from the PCI shortly after the 1986 elections, and negotiating with the Socialist Party for entry therein. The ex-PCI members referred to themselves as *Convergences Socialistes*. They were mainly students and teachers, populations on which the Lambertists have heavily concentrated for many years. The qualitative loss has thus been significant.

The *Ligue* was less enthusiastic about Mitterrand's 1981 candidacy than was the Lambertist organization. Krivine, it will be recalled, had tried to run against Mitterrand on the first round. The *Ligue* also presented some candidates who ran against the Socialists in the legislative elections of that year. On the second round of the 1981 presidential and legistlative elections, the *Ligue* urged a vote for Mitterrand "to defeat the Right" and a vote in the legislative elections for any of the candidates of the "workers' parties." After six months of Mitterrand's government, Krivine was willing to credit it with some positive achievements.[14] However, he warned that if the Socialist and Communist government was really trying to bring about fundamental changes, it would have to be forced to do so by the workers exerting pressure through workers' assemblies and organized labor and political groups.[15] By 1986, the *Ligue's* assessment was completely negative.

The response of the *Ligue* was to try to build an "anti-capitalist alternative." Unlike the Lambertist-driven MPPT, which focused on dissatisfied former voters and members of the Socialist and Communist parties, the *Ligue's* electoral strategy focused on groups which functioned outside of the boundaries of those two parties. The *Ligue* attempted to bring together an electoral coalition that included ecologists, feminists, the anti-racist and anti-imperialist movements, the PSU, the loosely knit *Fédération de la Gauche Alternative* (FGA), the formerly hierarchical Maoist *Parti Pour une Alternative Communiste* (PAC), and two Trotskyist groups, *Lutte Ouvrière* and itself.

The attempt was not a total success. In about a dozen legislative districts, the *Ligue* did run on combined lists with some of these groups, particularly the PSU, the FGA, and the PAC. In 1986, regional elections were held at the same time as the legislative elections. The *Ligue* also joined in combined lists in about fifteen of the regional districts. However, in the legislative elections, the *Ligue* also presented its own lists in districts where it could not work out an alliance. The success was not spectacular. The *Ligue's* candidates received 0.28 per cent of the vote.

The *Ligue* had approached *Lutte Ouvrière* (LO) to join in the broad coalition effort. While the two Trotskyist organizations ran one common list in the legislative and one in the regional elections, LO reacted very negatively to the broad coalition strategy of the *Ligue*. LO felt that there was little common ground between themselves and the ecologists, for example. LO had a political understanding that was based on the theory of permanent revolution and ecologists were very distant from that. They also objected to the inclusion of the PSU because Huguette Bouchardeau from the PSU had served as a minister in the Mitterrand governement.

LO had been the most negative of all the Trotskyist groups toward Mitterrand and the Socialists in 1981, and thus it was the least disillusioned. In 1986, it presented its own candidates in 33 of the legislative districts, as well as in a number of regional elections. With 1.21 per cent of the eligible vote, it was the only Trotskyist organization to break the one per cent barrier in 1986, although it did not do nearly so well as it has when its leader, Arlette Laguiller, occupied a prominent place on the ballot. She has always gotten over two per cent of the vote.[16]

In terms of actual membership, all of the Trotskyist groups have experienced some decline since the early 1980s. In the spring of 1982, the Lambertist PCI was claiming an unprecedented six thousand members. The Ligue had suffered a decline from the middle to the late 1970s, but was up by 1982 to approximately 2,500 core members.[17] The Pablists in the CCA were down to a couple of hundred members.[18]

In 1986, the Lambertist PCI claimed about five thousand members, the *Ligue* claimed two thousand (with an additional 250 in the youth group, the JCR, who were not members of the *Ligue* as well), and the LO claimed approximately two thousand members. It should be pointed out that the PCI's claims were challenged by people in the *Ligue* and LO. While some granted that the MPPT attracted four to five thousand people, they doubted that the PCI itself was much larger than the other two groups. Only LO's membership claims have remained constant. It is probable, however, that their "approximate" figure of two thousand is a bit high as well. The Pablists have split into two; they are now but a handful of militants.

Fewer people mean fewer resources. The PCI invested virtually everything in the MPPT in the two years before the 1986 elections. LO continued its work in the factories, but with the high unemployment in France it was harder to place new militants there. LO also made a heavy investment in the 1986 electoral effort.

The *Ligue* ran the fewest candidates of its own in 1986. It again cited financial constraints. It also had difficulty implementing the heavy industry strategy decided upon by the United Secretariat because of the shortage of jobs in France. But to a greater extent than the PCI and the LO, the *Ligue* invested resources in specific solidarity movements. It played a major role in support of the claims of the indigenous people of New Caledonia for independence from the French. It was a major force in the Nicaraguan solidarity network in France, particularly in the *Comité de Solidarité Avec le Nicaragua*. It sent brigades to Nicaragua, and appeared to be the sole source of information on what was going on in Nicaragua for many other groups on the Far Left, including the LO. It also conducted a campaign in support of the Solidarity labor movement in Poland. Within France, the *Ligue* played an active role in the anti-racist movement, and what remained of the anti-nuclear power and weapons movements in that country. This activity, of course, formed the basis of its hope to reach out to a variety of social movements to offer an anti-capitalist alternative during the 1986 elections.

As fragmented as they were by theoretical differences and by the intrusion of difficult contextual variables, what was remarkable was that the three major Trotskyist parties in France continued to function, to attract and to keep several thousand dedicated militants in a society which has become quite politically conservative, and to serve as the critic and voice of conscience of the two larger parties on the French Left, as well as vociferous critics of the capitalist parties and system.

As difficult as the theoretical contradictions and contextual factors have been for French Trotskyists, they have been much more debilitating for French Maoists. The anti-hierarchical Maoists, of course, have not 'been around since the mid-1970s. Attempts at a merger between the two hierarchical Maoist oganizations, the PCR(m-l) and the Chinese-recognized PCMLF, did not survive the 1978 electoral alliance of the two organizations. The PCR(m-l), which had been viewed with some suspicion by the PCMLF because of its attraction to the "mass line" and its refusal to follow the Chinese foreign policy line to the Nth degree, split into three factions in 1978. Confirming the suspicion of the PCMLF that heavy commitment to the "mass line" entails less of a commitment to a disciplined and centralist party, two of the factions took a liquidationsit position. The third faction was left to try to keep the PCR(m-l) going. In 1979, it was forced to stop publishing its daily newspaper, *Le Quotidien du Peuple*. In the early 1980s, former militants began to publish a new magazine, *Que Faire Aujourd'hui* (*What Is to Be Done Today?*). It was one of the more informative and interesting journals on the Left, but it had no organizational base and did not survive for long.

The PCR(m-l) did not try to present a candidate in the 1981 presidential elections, but it did manage to run 17 candidates in the legislative elections the following month.[19] Its position in 1981, however, was very different from its 1978 position. In 1978, the PCMLF had insisted, as a condition of its electoral alliance with the PCR(m-l), that the latter abstain from supporting the candidates of any of the other parties of the Left. Since there was no alliance between the two organizations in 1981, the PCR(m-l) was free to urge voters in districts where it was not presenting a candidate to vote for Communist, Socialist, *Parti Socialiste Unifié* (PSU), or ecological candidates who had formed an alliance with the PSU.

This gesture to other parties on the Left was part of continuing efforts of the severly weakened PCR(m-l) to establish a wider web of relationships. While it included Communist and Socialist candidates as possibilities for voters where it was not presenting candidates itself, its major effort was to attempt to get other groups together to form a *gauche nouvelle* (New Left) in France.[20] As its electoral endorsements suggest, it focused its efforts on the PSU and the ecologists rather than on Trotskyists or other Maoists. The 1981 elections proved to be the "last hurrah" of the PCR(m-l). The organization dissolved in 1983. It was a fragile compromise between, rather than a strong synthesis of, the *Maoïste* orientation of the *Gauche Prolétarienne* and the pro-Chinese, Marxist-Leninist orientation of the PCMLF.

Part of the problem faced by the PCR(m-l) was also the fact that, at the same time that it was confronted by internal liquidationist currents, its former coalition partner was going through some changes and was now occupying much of the political space that the PCR(m-l) formerly monopolized. In the late 1970s, the PCMLF, which had been legally banned as a result of the 1968 revolt, straightened out its legal status. As is usual in this process, it slightly modified its name. The PCMLF dropped the last word, *Français,* and became the PCML.

By 1983, the PCML's relationship with the Chinese party became somewhat more delicate than it had been. On the one hand, it was still recognized as a fraternal party by the Chinese Communist Party. On concrete international issues, such as the Vietnamese invasion of Cambodia/Kampuchea, the Ethiopean/Eritrean war, and the Soviet invasion of Afghanistan, it stood shoulder to shoulder with the Chinese and against the USSR. It claimed to accept the Theory of the Three Worlds and it issued no criticism of the way in which the post-Mao regime in China treated the "Gang of Four." It also continued to function as a Marxist-Leninist party and to remain immune to the allure of the "mass line."

On the other hand, while it claimed to accept the Theory of the Three Worlds, it also maintained that the Chinese position on it had been misunderstood. The PCML contended that, in fact, the Chinese do not fundamentally distinguish between the two superpowers when they combat their attempts at hegemony.[21] This permitted the PCML to oppose both NATO and the Warsaw Pact in an even-handed way.[22] It thus differentiated itself from the pro-NATO policy of the Mitterrand government and brought itself closer to the position of nearly all the other Far Left organizations in France.

The PCML, however, was not interested in adopting a confrontationist posture *vis-à-vis* either the Socialist or Communist parties. Quite to the contrary. It sought relations with both of these parties. Moves made by the Chinese facilitated this. In 1981, the Chinese Communist Party established relations with the French Socialist Party. The following year, the Chinese Communist Party re-established the relationship with the French Communist Party which had been ruptured during the Sino-Soviet split. In each instance, the PCML established a domestic relationship with a major French party of the Left after the Chinese took the international initiative.

Indeed, in its new posture of calling for a "pluralistic" Left where different approaches need not result in lack of cooperation and contacts, the PCML began taking on the traits of "openness" and lack of sectarianism which were so characterstic of the PCR(m-l). It even did what it used to so strongly attack the PCR(m-l) for doing: it established relations with Trotskyists. In the spring of 1983, leaders of the PCML met with Alain Krivine of the Trotskyist *Ligue* for an exchange of views on the government's austerity program (the views of the two organizations were almost identical) and the implications of the 1983 municipal election results for the Left. A month later, in May 1983, the PCML's monthly journal, *Travailleurs,* published a transcript of a discussion of two PCML leaders with Krivine and with Serge Depaquit of the PSU.[23] Like the PCR(m-l), the PCML was trying to get out of the Maoist ghetto and establish broader ties. But unlike the PCR(m-l), which issued a call for the creation of a New Left on the fringes of the traditional parties of the Left, the PCML attempted to work both on the fringes and with the Socialist and Communist parties.

Its relationship with China became a bit schizoid. The relationship continued to exist and it would be foolish to pretend that it was coincidental that the PCML waited until China made the international move before it reestablished relations with the French Socialist and Communist parties. On the other hand, there were signs of a certain distance. One of the PCML's leaders, Pierre Bauby, publicly stated in 1982: "Even if our positions remain close to those of China, we do not take them anymore as a model. We have given up the idea of reproducing the Chinese model in France."[24] Moreover, what was going on within China was debated and there were different interpretations voiced within the party. The general public position was that there was a tremendous amount of experimentation and trial and error going on there and, under those conditions, it was not appropriate either to applaud or to criticize the present course. The Chinese were finding their own errors and correcting them. The good Maoist argument of separate paths of development was also evoked in defense of a mutual tolerance for different approaches among the Chinese party and parties that were sympathetic to China but which have to operate in their own national contexts. Still, one indication that relations had been somewhat strained was the fact that the PCML could no longer afford to publish the daily newspaper, *l'Humanité Rouge,* because in 1979 the Chinese dropped the number of papers that they were willing to buy daily from 1,000 to 60.[25] The PCML then had to be content with publishing a monthly journal (*Travailleurs*) and a weekly information sheet printed on both sides of the paper (*PCML Flash*).

Paltry resources were also reflected in paltry electoral attempts. After trying unsuccessfully to get Pierre Bauby on the ballot in the first round of the 1981 presidential elections, the PCML ran him as its only candidate in the legislative elections. In the 1983 municipal elections, only a few PCML members and sympathizers were run on combined lists which, varying somewhat by district, included the parties comprising the Union of the Left, i.e., members of the Socialist and Communist parties, the Left Radicals, and the PSU.[26]

In 1985, the PCML formalized some of the positions toward which it had been evolving in the early 1980s. It explicitly rejected sectarianism and attempts of groups on the Left to strive for hegemony in their relations with other groups. It celebrated the plurality of political organizations and social movements and called for mutual respect of differences. It adopted an environmentalist position. As an additional symbolic break with the past, it changed its name to the *Parti Pour une Alternative Communiste* (PAC). At its June 1986 Congress, the PAC broke with democratic centralism and the conception of a vanguard party, the latter being consistent with the positions it had already adopted the year before. In 1986 it used, for the first time, the word *"autogestion."*[27]

In the 1986 elections, the PAC ran candidates in eleven of the legislative and thirteen of the regional districts on the "Alternative" lists, which sometimes included the Trotskyist *Ligue* as well as the other groups mentioned in the discussion above of the *Ligue's* electoral participation. The shift from running on a list which included the Socialist and Communist candidates in 1983 to a list of the smaller, "alternative" groups reflected both an alienation from the policies of the Mitterrand government and the shift to a celebration of a plurality of organizations and movements. Again, the vote totals were low, although one member of the combined regional list was elected in the Maine-et-Loire with 5.31 per cent of the vote. The shift to proportional representation made that possible.

The PAC is the largest of the surviving Maoist groups, but it is still much smaller than the three major Trotskyist organizations. It has only about 300 card-carrying members.[28] The other three Maoist groups which survived the first half-decade of the 1980s are not so much organizations as they are groups of faculty members at specific universities which publish magazines and sometimes sponsor conferences. That is the fate of Alain Badiou's old UCFML. It was abolished in 1984 and a structure called the *Organisation Politique* was declared to take its place. In fact, however, the major functioning group of that tendency of Maoism appears to be the *Association "Les Conferences du Perroquet"* (Association of the Parrot's Lectures). Its members are concentrated at the University of Reims. They publish a bi-weekly called *Le Perroquet* and sponsor conferences on specific topics.

Another group, based at the University of Rennes, is called *Communistes Démocratiques*. This is what is left of the old Brittany-based *Organisation Communiste Française (marxiste-léniniste)* which used to publish the paper *Drapeau Rouge*. The newer group publishes a very slick trimestrial magazine called *Arguments,* which has both a political and a cultural orientation.

A third group, at the University of Bordeau, is called the *Union Marxiste-Léniniste*. It works within the broader federation of diverse little groups on the Left, including anarchists, called the *Fédération de la Gauche Alternative* (FGA). It will be recalled that the FGA was one of the groupings that joined the *Ligue* and the PAC in the 1986 electoral lists.

In addition to the above contemporary Maoist groups, two other organizations which have a relationship to the history of French Maoism might merit some mention. First, there is still a tiny pro-Albanian party in France which publishes a paper called *La Forge*. Second, and of much greater significance and impact on French life, is a group called *Action Directe*. This group, which first came to public attention under that name in 1979, has conducted armed attacks against government offices and personnel, head-quarters of political parties (including both Socialist and conservative), and other targets deemed to be particularly reactionary. The leader of the "nationalist" or most radical tendency in *Action Directe* is a former militant of *La Gauche Prolétarienne* (GP), the major anti-hierarchical Maoist movement of the late 1960s and early 1970s. While some former GP Maoists have moved quite far to the right in France, André Olivier has retained his commitments and is applying the dictum which succeeded in China in 1949, "power comes through the barrel of a gun." Some in *Action Directe* gave that up when the Left came to electoral power in 1981. Olivier persisted and was arrested in the spring of 1986. After the arrest of the 43-year-old to whom *Paris Match* has referred as the *"dernier des Mao"* ("the last of the anti-hierarchical Maoists"), his comrades launched even more audacious armed attacks against the French police.[29]

While theoretical and contextual factors have posed difficulties for French Trotskyists and have kept them divided, the consequences have been much more serious for French Maoist and pro-Chinese forces. Both the PCR(m-l) and the UCFML have passed from the scene. Only the PAC remains as a national organization, with some 300 members. For the PAC to survive, it has had to adopt some of the very same positions that it criticized the PCR(m-l) for taking. It has reached out to a diversity of other parties and groups on the Left after criticizing the PCR(m-l) for doing so. And, it has reinterpreted the Theory of the Three Worlds beyond recognition, so that it is more congruent with the international perspectives of other groups on the French Left. It has gone well beyond the PCR(m-l) in renouncing both the concept of a vanguard party and democratic centralism. While there have been some changes within French Trotskyist groups, one finds nothing like the fundamental transformation of the PCMLF into the PAC. It has really turned into its opposite.

RECENT DEVELOPMENTS
IN U.S. TROTSKYISM AND MAOISM

Theoretical contradictions continue to be divisive among Trotskyist groups, though they have manifested themselves unevenly and in different ways across national contexts. The Nicaraguan issue, which cost the French *Ligue* several hundred members and destroyed attempts at unity between the *Ligue* and the Lambertists in France, has produced some problems for the

SWP, but within the broader framework of the approach to be taken toward Third World revolutions in general and toward solidarity networks in the United States.

The differences between the SWP and the Spartacist League over revolution in the Third World continue to be apparent, but they are sometimes more subtle and always less consequential than the clash between the French *Ligue* and the Lambertists over Nicaragua. In part, this is due to the disparity in size and resources between the SWP and the Spartacist League. Moreover, the Spartacist position on Cuba was not received well within the Left in the United States. Given its meager recruitment and its general image on the Left, the Spartacist League is no longer in a position to use differences over movements or regimes in the Third World, and especially in Latin America, to pull people away from the SWP.

There are differences, but not strong polemics, over both Nicaragua and El Salvador. In regard to Nicaragua, the SWP is supportive of the Sandinista FSLN. It contends that the Sandinista victory has meant that workers and peasants now hold political power in Nicaragua.[30] The Spartacists, like the LO in France, are more critical. They accuse the Sandinista FSLN of following a path of petit-bourgeois nationalism by calling for nonalignment, a mixed economy, and political pluralism which would accommodate the business and professional communities. Nonetheless, the Spartacist League argues that the Nicaraguan revolution must be defended and completed, (the latter involving the elimination of the above petit-bourgeois elements of the program) and that this defense is key to defending both the USSR and Cuba against U.S. imperialism.[31] Given the Spartacist League's very harsh criticism of Cuba, over which it was expelled from the SWP, we have here a notion of interlinked but very deformed revolutions which must nevertheless be defended against the greater evil of U.S. imperialism. The celebratory optimism of the SWP's support is replaced by a critical scepticism and bowing to an imperative.

There are similar differences over El Salvador. The SWP supports the Democratic Revolutionary Front (the FDR) and its military counterpart, the FMLN. It does so noncritically and it specifically supported the FDR's decision to call for an unconditional dialogue with the government of El Salvador.[32] The Spartacists rejected any negotiations and attacked "bourgeois politicians" in the FDR for trying to sell out the revolution through negotiations. The Spartacists called for a military victory for the FMLN.[33] Thus, in both the Nicaraguan and Salvadoran instances, the Spartacists indicated a scepticism toward the forces at work in these revolutions, while the SWP extended noncritical support.

Where the internal contradictions within Trotskyism over revolution in the Third World resulted in particularly strong polemics on the part of the Spartacists was in the case of Iran. Citing the attacks of Khomeini and others in the new regime on U.S. imperialism and the very negative reaction to the Iranian revolution in the West, the SWP initially portrayed the Iranian revolution as progressive. It argued that workers could organize an even more progressive movement under it more effectively than they could under the previous Western-supported regime. It rejected the argument that religion automatically renders a movement regressive because "history has shown that progressive *political movements* often take a *religious form*. Thus the anti-monarchical revolution in seventeenth-century England was fought out under the guise of the Protestant Reformation."[34] At the very beginning of the Iranian revolutionary process, the SWP emphasized what it saw as the crucial role played by the workers in the oil fields. It then shifted to an emphasis on workers' committees in the urban factories rather than the oil-field workers.[35] Unlike any other U.S. Trotskyist group, the SWP had an Iranian counterpart which was trying to be a force in the process.

The Spartacist League, on the other hand, saw nothing but a reactionary, nationalistic, and religiously fundamentalist regime which was not being challenged by any progressive party. It saw the position of the SWP on Iran as a complete sell-out of Trotskyism by the "ex-Trotskyists of the American Socialist Workers Party."[36] The Spartacists further chided the SWP: "When the SWP was faced with a mass-based opposition to the Shah which at times stoned women for not wearing the symbol of medieval oppression, the veil, even these veteran cynics have had to go through some gyrations to claim that black is white, that the *ulema's* Muslim fundamentalism is really 'a step forward.' But they have made the effort, nonetheless, for the *mullahs* have indeed achieved the SWP's one criterion for support: 'mass action in the streets'."[37] The Spartacists went on to argue that the "anti-imperialism" of Khomeini and his followers was only really an "obscurantist hatred for Western culture and modernization."[38] The SWP's position on Iran typified what the Spartacists regarded as the immediate impulse of the SWP to respond enthusiastically to "action" in the Third World, its formal theoretical commitments notwithstanding.

Aside from these Third World situations, the other major disagreement between and SWP and the Spartacists which arose in the 1980s was over the situation in Poland. The SWP supported the Solidarity movement just as it has many of the dissidents within the USSR. The SWP argued that Solidarity was standing up to "the privileged bureaucracy that governs Poland's economy [and] also exercises dictatorial rule over all other aspects of Polish society. For this reason, Solidarity found the struggle for economic democracy led directly to a fight for democracy in the rest of society."[39] It argued further that Solidarity's experience said a lot about "where the American labor movement should be headed."[40] The Spartacists, while also critical of the Polish regime, saw Solidarity as a counter-revolutionary movement, just as they viewed at least some of the Soviet dissidents defended by the

SWP. The Spartacists, who resemble the French Lambertists in viewing religion as a particularly dangerous force capable of deceptively progressive social doctrines, pointed to Solidarity's support within the Church and referred derisively to its "clerical nationalist fervor."[41] Whether it be Islam or Catholicism, the Spartacists see religion as totally incompatible with socialism or any progressive movement toward it.

As the Sparticists were hammering away at the SWP for its stance toward the above movements, the SWP was beginning to face both internal dissention and isolation within the United Secretariat. The first major split involved a critique by a tendency led by the SWP's 1976 presidential candidate, Peter (now also known as Pedro) Camejo. Camejo argued that under the leadership of party chairman Jack Barnes, the turn-toward-industry strategy had become a mechanical "workerist" schema. That is, the party was seen as dissociating itself from both mass movements which were gaining strength around issues such as U.S. intervention in Central America and the nuclear freeze, and from work in unions other than industrial ones such as those of government employees, teachers, and service workers. Camejo argued that within the SWP there was a deep supicion of the generation radicalized by the 1960s, a generation which was influential in both the rising mass movements and unions in the non-heavy industry areas. The workerist and economic determinist position of the SWP, Camejo argued, was cutting the SWP off from the most promising concrete movements in U.S. society. Camejo argued that, given its position, the SWP ought not to be surprised that it had dwindled to just over 1,000 members by 1983. He held up the Australian SWP, which had reached out to the social movements in that country and, he claimed, was experiencing growth, as a non-sectarian model for the U.S. party to emulate.[42]

In 1982, Camejo found himself outside of the SWP. He had gone to live for a while in Venezuela, switched his membership to the Venezuelan section of the United Secretariat, and was refused readmission into the U.S. section when he returned. He then led in the creation of the North Star Network, a California-based group which rejects the appropriateness of a Leninist vanguard party within the present U.S. context.[43] It argues that such a party must grow out of the variety of current oppositionist mass movements rather than attempt to impose itself on them. North Star thus networks with a wide range of groups, most intensively with those involved in Central American solidarity and with the Rainbow Coalition initiated by Jesse Jackson. It is also part of a movement which began in 1986 to form a National Committee for Independent Political Action.

The second split involved Les Evans, long-time activist and former editor of *Intercontinental Press* (the publication of which ceased in 1986). Evans was expelled in 1984. For Evans, the problem was that in the mid-1980s the SWP moved to a position of outright rejection of the theory of permament revolution. In the first article of the first issue of *New International,* a journal of Marxist politics and theory that the SWP launched with the Revolutionary Workers League of Canada, Jack Barnes explicitly declared Trotsky's skepticism toward the peasantry and his rejection of Lenin's formulation of a "democratic dictatorship of the proletariat and peasantry" to have been an error. What convinced the SWP that Trotsky's thinking was erroneous were the "workers' and farmers' governments" in Cuba, Nicaragua, and Grenada (the latter during the New Jewel Movement). The successes of these governments were now to serve the SWP as models for change on a worldwide basis and in the United States. Barnes credited the example of the above governments, along with the proletarianization of the SWP as a result of the turn-toward-industry strategy, with revealing to the SWP that Trotsky's conception of social change was only correct when he brought his thinking into conformity with that of Lenin and the longer Marxist tradition, i.e., during the decade between 1917 and 1927.[44]

Evans refused to reject the theory of permanent revolution as a tool by which to assess regimes and opposition movements.[45] The group he created after his expulsion, Socialist Action, worked actively in the broader Central American solidarity movement to which it attempted to contribute greater theoretical and critical rigor. Unlike Camejo's group, Socialist Action did not deny the present need for a vanguard party, and applied for recognition to the United Secretariat. It continued to support the SWP's 1984 candidates — it was still claiming to be legitimately within the SWP — Mel Mason for president and Andrea Gonzales for vice-president. Socialist Action has more recently split into two, with Evans moving over to the new group, Socialist Unity.

At the same time that the SWP was experiencing these internal splits, it was being isolated internationally. Camejo's positions found a sympathetic hearing in the Australian SWP, which attacked the U.S. party for being undemocratic. The Australian party also took on the United Secretariat, which it quit in 1985. It levied a particularly heavy attack on the majority of the United Secretariat, essentially the European sections, for ignoring the positive role being played by Cuba in aiding revolutionary regimes and movements.[46] On this point, however, it was in agreement with both Camejo and the majority within the U.S. SWP.

On the other hand, Evans' critique of the SWP found a sympathetic hearing among the European sections of the United Secretariat, which viewed the expulsions from the SWP as undemocratic. They also have criticized the "uncritical" support that the SWP has extended to Cuba, the Sandinistas, the FDR/FMLN in El Salvador, and the African National Congress in South Africa. For the European sections, there is a difference between "unconditional support" and "uncritical support." One can unconditionally support a movement or a regime but offer friendly criticism based on the insights of the theory of permament revolution. Uncritical support logically precludes this and, from their point of view, undercuts the theoretical viability of Trotskyism. This writer must confess that he found not a little irony in listening to Alain Krivine criticize the SWP for exactly the same thing for which the LO and the Lambertists criticize the *Ligue*.[47] It is also ironic that the *Ligue's* criticism of the SWP in the 1980s so closely resembles the SWP's criticism of the *Ligue* for its position on the Vietnamese Communist Party in 1974 (a debate discussed at length in Chapter 4).

Clearly, revolution in the Third World is no easier a phenomenon for Trotskyists to deal with in the 1980s than it was in the 1960s or 1970s.

One new and interesting development within the realm of U.S. Trotskyism is the appearance at the national level of an organization that until 1979 was purely regional. The group is called the Freedom Socialist Party. It began as the Seattle branch of the SWP, but established itself as an autonomous party in 1966. Unlike the Spartacist League and the Workers League — which left the SWP over the Cuban Revolution — the Freedom Socialist Party did not break with the SWP because of a revolution in the Third World. Nor did it break with the SWP in order to adopt a different kind of organizational pattern, as Spark had done when it decided to model itself after the French LO's rather unique pattern of organization. Rather, it left the SWP because of a postion that the SWP took on a sensitive political issue in the United States.

This was the issue of race, and Blacks in particular. The Seattle branch of the SWP was part of a minority which rejected the party's position on Black nationalism, a position which went back to 1939. Although the SWP had not advocated the creation of a separate Black nation, it had committed itself to the support of Black national self-determination if Black people should decide that that was what they wanted. At its 1963 Congress, the party still contended that it neither advocated nor opposed a separate nation, but it did come out for the creation of an independent Black political party, and positive things were said about the nationalist Black Muslim movement led by Elijah Muhammed. The delegates of the Seattle branch argued that the party itself had to decide where it stood rather than wait for external signals. That branch had a very clear idea where the party should stand. It took the position that Blacks were an oppressed race within the United States, not a potential nation. Finally, the Seattle delegate who became the national secretary of the Freedom Socialist Party argued that it would be an irreparable error to extend any support to the Black Muslims, given Muhammed's "position on Black women, his red-baiting virulence, and anti-working class stance."[48] After the minority presented its alternative "Revolutionary Integrationist" position, it claimed to have been the victim of insults and vituperation on the part of the majority. Contending that this behavior revealed "the moral corruption, racism, and sexism" of the majority's "bureaucracy," the Seattle branch quit the SWP *en masse* approximately two years later.[49]

For the first ten years of its existence, the Freedom Socialist Party was confined to Seattle. About 1976, the group moved out a bit, but it restricted itself to the West Coast. It established branches in Portland, San Francisco, and Los Angeles. In 1979, it established a branch in New York City, a creation of West Coast people who had moved to New York. They ran the organization out of their residences until 1983, when they opened an office in New York.[50]

This is an interesting organization for a number of reasons. First, as opposed to the SWP and every other organization discussed in this book, women have always predominated in the top leadership positions, including the national secretaryship. Much of its recent criticism of the SWP was directed at what it saw as male predominance in the SWP's leadership, and the SWP's refusal to permit the creation of women's caucuses. The Freedom Socialist Party maintained that even though the SWP was careful to balance sexually its electoral slates, actual power in the SWP remained in male hands. It was not the analyses of the SWP that it called into question; rather it was the internal power distribution, which it saw as incongruent with socialist-feminist analysis. The mast-head of the Freedom Socialist Party's paper announced, on the other hand, that it was the "Voice of Revolutionary Feminism."

Another interesting aspect of the Freedom Socialist Party was its openness and the way it was able to incorporate internally various aspects of what it saw as this larger emancipatory struggle. In regard to the latter, the organization was racialy mixed and the problems of Black, Asian-Pacific, Chicano/Chicana and Native American peoples were given particular consideration and articulation. The organization is sexually mixed and is particularly concerned with the problems of lesbian women and the relationship between lesbian women and heterosexual women and men. Women from the party have attempted to create a broader women's organization called Radical Feminists. While the party is not even a truly national organization yet, it too has an Australian connection in the form of a sympathizing section in Australia.

Dramatic changes have occurred among U.S. Maoists in the 1980s as well. The Communist Party (Marxist-Leninist), which had the official recognition of the Chinese Communist Party and was thus a fraternal party of the French PCML, no longer exists. The strains imposed by having to carry the banner of the Chinese regime at a time when the regime was both rejecting the heritage of Mao himself and following an anti-Soviet foreign policy that often coincided with U.S. foreign policy became enormous. The French PCML had managed to reinterpret Chinese foreign policy, to disavow China as a model for France, while criticizing the internal dynamics in China, and to reach out to other forces on the French Left, and finally to reject both democratic centralism and vanguardism. In France, it was the "mass line" leaning PCR(m-l) which was struck and wounded fatally by internal liquidationist currents. In the United States, the strains of the CP(ML)'s position brought out the contradiction inherent in Maoism over the party even within the very hierarchical structure which continued to be so supportive of the Chinese. A faction arose within the CP(ML) which questioned the appropriateness of continuing the hierarchical Marxist-Leninist vanguard form of organization. The anti-party faction was denounced as ultra-leftist, but it was strong enough to be fatal to the CP(ML). In January of 1981 Michael Klonsky quit as the chairman of the party and several months later the party was simply dissolved.[51]

One group which shed no tears over the passing from the scene of the CP(ML) was its arch-rival Maoist organization, the Revolutionary Communist Party. It will be recalled from Chapter 5 that the RCP experienced a serious split late in 1977, after the majority of the Central Committee supported the Gang of Four. The RCP lost control over most of the Revolutionary Student Brigades in the East and Midwest to the faction which split off. This break-away minority, referred to within the RCP as the Jarvis-Bergman clique, gave itself the name Revolutionary Workers Headquarters. This group, which sent a general letter of support to the post-Mao regime as it moved against the Gang of Four, never did merge with the CP(ML). It did, however, succeed in establishing a working relationship with the Chinese-recognized group, a relationship which it was deprived of when the CP(ML) folded. The 1977 split appeared to have resolved the RCP's internal tensions over loyalty to Mao and his associates during the Cultural Revolution, on the one hand, and supporting the Chinese regime regardless of that regime's assessment of the Cultural Revolution, on the other. The RCP remained internally hierarchical and dedicated to the Great Cultural Revolution.

This is not to imply that the RCP has remained perfectly static. On the contrary, it has undergone significant changes. One of these changes has involved Chairman Bob Avakian. The same contradiction between the very personalized role of Mao as leader and the egalitarianism of the Cultural Revolution has been replicated in the RCP. Bob Avakian has attempted to adopt the very personalistic leadership style of Mao and his followers have accepted this. His charisma has been put to an even greater test than Mao's because the Chairman has been obliged to do his chairing from France.

As indicated in Chapter 5, members of the RCP were charged with misdemeanors after their January 1979 demonstration against the visit of Deng Xiaoping to Washington. The Department of Justice intervened, however, and the charges were changed to felonies. Seventeen members of the RCP were hit with charges that could have caused each of them to be sentenced to 242 years in prison. Ultimately, the government backed off of the felony charges in exchange for guilty pleas to some of the original misdemeanor charges. Avakian and other members of the party had been subjected to surveillance and the party had been infiltrated since the FBI's COINTELPO program was instituted. In August 1979, the *Los Angeles Times* printed what it claimed was an excerpt from a speech that Avakian had given in Los Angeles on August 5. The presentation in the *Times* led one to believe that Avakian had called upon the audience to murder President Carter as well as police officers and other heads of state. The newspaper partially corrected its quote at the insistence of Avakian's lawyer, and the Los Angeles District Attorney's office called off the investigation which it had begun. Nevertheless, according to the RCP, the Secret Service continued to harrass Avakian. The RCP claims that threats were made against his life "directly by Secret Service and other government agents."[52] After a speaking tour of the United States in the summer and fall of 1979, during which his life was threatened on numerous occasions, according to the RCP, Avakian went underground and surfaced in France, where he requested political refugee status.[53]

Avakian arrived in France on December 21, 1980. Although the formal political refugee status was denied, he was able to remain in France a number of years. As the reader of the previous chapters knows, the RCP had not had any ties with Maoist organizations in France. By May 1981, however, the RCP had established contacts with twelve other organizations in foreign countries and had published the first edition of its *International Marxist-Leninst Journal* (entitled "A World to Win") with them. One of the groups was a French group called *Pour l'Internationale Prolétarienne*. Avakian's presence in France, however, was not enough to hold this new grouping together. In the second number, published in May 1982, the French group explained that it was disbanding because it had "dissipated itself in concrete tasks, not knowing how to transform the general orientation into well-articulated activity corresponding to immediate reality."[54] It argued that the old tools of Marxism-Leninism did not permit it to deal adequately with the new crisis of the imperialist system, which had thrown the world into turmoil, and that the changes in the international Marxist-Leninist movement since the death of Mao demonstrated the weakness of revolutionaries today. It maintained that what was needed before there could be social revolutions in the present context were "ideological, theoretical, and philosophical revolutions which would educate revolutionaries and make them fit to face up to the objective situation. We must make such revolutions and rid ourselves of dead weight by resolutely entering the arena of the actual experience of the proletariat."[55] Thus the RCP's French affiliate was struck by the same kind of liquidationism which destroyed the pro-Cultural Revolution *Gauche Prolétarienne* and the mass-line leaning PCR(m-l). Avakian was left in France without a fraternal party; but he was still the Chairman of the RCP back in the United States. His writings continued to hold a prominent if not predominant place in the RCP's numerous publications.

Aside from Avakian's physical absence for a considerable period, a number of other changes have taken place in the RCP. First, the party has reversed itself on the school busing issue which produced so much conflict between the RCP and virtually every other group on the Left in the United States. The party suggests that it was the revisionist Jarvis–Bergman clique within its ranks—the faction that split off in 1977 and founded the Revolutionary Workers Headquarters—that prevented the RCP from understanding the effect of its position. Its attack on busing was an attempt to avoid casting the White working-class Bostonians as bigots who needed to be controlled by the police, and at the same time to support the rights of Blacks. The RCP has come to admit that the effect of this position was to encourage the most regressive and reactionary elements of the U.S. working class.[56]

In fact, the general analysis of the class situation and the appropriate revolutionary strategy within the U.S. context has changed. The RCP's earlier "workerist" position, which led it to ally itself with segments of Boston's White working class that were opposed to busing, reflected an "economism" which the RCP now rejects. Though it invested much in the strike to organize the Farah workers, it has become convinced that the unionized elements of the U.S. working class have been bought off. Relying heavily on Lenin's analysis of the stratification of the proletariats within capitalist societies, the RCP has adopted the position that is the most disadvantaged segments of the working class that would be susceptible to revolutionary ideas and appeals. Taking a position completely contrary to that of the SWP and its basic-industries strategy, the RCP stated its intention of penetrating and establishing base areas in the most exploitative work contexts. It is in these contexts that im-migrants and minorities are disproportionately concentrated.[57]

Consistent with this new turn and its reversal on the busing issue, the RCP has admitted that its past relationship with the Black Workers Congress left much to be desired: "Often we go from sugar to shit in our approach to nationalist forces, from tailing them to attacking them for not being proletarian revolutionaries. The old polemics with the BWC are useful teachers in that regard."[58] It will be recalled that the RCP had even accused the Black Workers Congress of exhibiting Trotskyism or "Trotskyite features" when it dealt with the national question. A more cutting insult from one Maoist to another is difficult to imagine.

The RCP has remained opposed to both feminism and the Equal Rights Amendment. Its tone, however, is very different now. The 1975 program cried out, "Oppose the 'Equal Rights Amendment'—fight to defend protective legislation and extend it to men."[59] The new program did not mention the ERA, despite the fact that it came out approximately one year before the deadline for ERA ratification, when there was considerable mobilization and polarization over the issue. The RCP's polemical tone was softened somewhat, perhaps because its old adversary in polemics, the CP(ML), was dead or dying when the 1981 program was written. A self-critique within the party also convinced its members that behind the shrill tones was a contradiction. If ERA was rejected for being reformist, was it any the less reformist to call instead for the extension of protective legislation to men as well as women? While the attitude toward homosexuality or lesbianism within the party is far from supportive, it is very doubtful that today Avakian or any other member of the party would refer to the capitalists as "faggots." Even where it has not changed its basic positions, the party has "cleaned up" its language to make it more acceptable within the context in which the RCP must work.

Unlike the French PCML, which has reinterpreted the Theory of the Three Worlds, the RCP has decided to resolve the contradictions imposed by the theory by unequivocably rejecting it. It has done this even though Avakian assigns some of the responsibility for the development of the theory to Mao himself, a big admission, since Mao and his Cultural Revolution are the major source of inspiration for the RCP.[60] The admission, however, is limited to the contention that while elements of the theory can be traced back to some of Mao's earlier analysis, "Mao was not only *not* responsible for but fought relentlessly against the reactionary line of capitulating to imperialism and betraying revolution that has been embodied in the 'three-worlds' theory as put forward by the revisionists now ruling China, who have come to power precisely by overthrowing Mao's followers, and his line, after his death."[61]

A final change in the organization is the emphasis placed upon the role of its newspaper. A centrally-produced weekly edition of *Revolutionary Worker* has replaced the monthly *Revolution,* which used to be supplemented with different editions of *The Worker* produced in a number of cities. The RCP believes that the primary task of the party is "to systematically carry out revolutionary agitation and propaganda, with agitation the cutting edge and the Party's newspaper the main weapon now."[62] Since the United States is not now in a revolutionary condition, the RCP—probably more than any other Maoist group—stresses the ideological function of the newspaper. Its major slogan is, "Create Public Opinion...Seize Power!" It is through the paper that the RCP believes it can transform many local spontaneous eruptions occurring in the U. S. into conscious class struggle. Organizationally, this means that "besides the Party itself, the principal and ongoing forms of organization built are the networks of distribution of the newspaper."[63]

Since the liquidation of the CP(ML) in 1981, the organization closest to its positions has been the U.S. League of Revolutionary Struggle (M–L), formed by the 1978 merger of the Chicana and Chicano August Twenty-Ninth Movement and the Asian-American I Wor Kuen. Subsequent to that formation, other groups and individuals, including the revolutionary Communist League led by Amiri Baraka (Leroi Jones) and a few former members of the CP(ML), Carl Davidson among them, have joined it. Approximately 70 per cent of the members are people of Third World heritage.

Unlike the RCP, the League strongly supported the Theory of the Three Worlds through the early 1980s. Only in the mid-1980s, when the Chinese themselves somewhat softened their attitude toward the USSR, did the League soften its position on the USSR and Cuba. It persists in criticizing the USSR's intervention in Afghanistan, the Vietnamese intervention in Kampuchea., and Cuban support for the war effort in Eritrea.[64] Up until the mid-1980s, its journal *Forward* and its newspaper *Unity* contended that their articles were written "from the standpoint of Marxism–Leninism–Mao Zedong Thought."[65] The publications were then formally separated from the League and designated simply as "socialist." While the League itself maintained its Marxist–Leninist initials, its self-conception as a vanguard party, and its democratic-centralist form of internal organization, the newspaper was to be used for broader external organizing and coalition work. Unlike the RCP, which it views as closed and sectarian, the League does indeed engage in broad networking, on the order of the PAC (or former PCML) in France and the less sectarian Trotskyists in the U.S. This includes support for the Rainbow Coalition and Jesse Jackson's primary campaigns. That continues the strain of Amiri Baraka's unique Maoist electoral thrust back in the 1970s, although by the late 1980s the League preferred to leave the designation "Maoist" to the supporters of the Cultural Revolution and the "Gang of Four" in the RCP.

In the early 1980s, probably the most aggressive organization within the Maoist and/or pro-Chinese domain was the Communist Workers Party. This party, it will be recalled from Chapter 5, was an out-growth of a once exclusively Asian-American group formerly called Workers Viewpoint Organization, which was also for a time the name of the CWP's newspaper. The 1979 murder of five members of the CWP brought the organization considerable publicity. The five were murdered when they engaged in protests against the Ku Klux Klan in Greensboro, North Carolina. Klan and American Nazi Party members, who killed the five and wounded seven others, were acquitted in 1980 of murder by an all-White jury in state court. In 1984, they were acquitted of violation of the victims' civil rights by an all-White jury in federal court in Winston-Salem. The party has been active in other areas of the South, and two of it members or ex-members won a large civil suit against government officials for violation of their civil rights when they worked in Kentucky.

The CWP adopted a position which is quite distinct from that of both the RCP and the League of Revolutionary Struggle. Like the RCP, it has always been positively oriented toward the Cultural Revolution in China. Unlike the RCP, however, the CWP has seen positive aspects in China's very recent foreign policy posture. Among the improvements which the CWP has noted on the part of the Chinese are: abandonment of the idea that world war is inevitable; cessation of attacks on the USSR for instigating the struggle in El Salvador; unconditional support for Namibian independence and refusal to side with U.S. insistence that this be tied to withdrawal of Cuban troops from Angola; establishment of diplomatic ties with the government of Angola, which has good relations with the USSR; offers of material support to the front-line states in Southern Africa, and a public salute from the prime minister of China to the Soviet-influenced South West African People's Organization (SWAPO); receptions of both Libyan leader Qadaffi and French Communist Party leader Marchais in China despite the friendly relations of both with the USSR; and the threat to retaliate against the Reagan administration for the imposition of trade quotas.[66]

The CWP has also seen hope in internal dynamics of the USSR which escaped the RCP. It was particularly impressed with the direction taken by the USSR under the former General Secretary of the Soviet Party, Yuri Andropov. It likened Andopov's attempt to get rid of lazy and corrupt bureaucrats who held down productivity to Mao's Cultural Revolution, and suggested that perhaps Andropov learned something from that experience.[67] The RCP remained totally unimpressed by such thinking, and was so concerned that the "real nature" of the USSR was being forgotten in the Marxist-Leninist world that it called an open national meeting in New York devoted exclusively to the discussion of the precise nature of the USSR. The RCP saw the "accomodationist" position of the CWP as wishful thinking, and very dangerous wishful thinking at that. More recently, the CWP has changed its name to the New Democratic Movement.

One initiative at party building which was referred to in Chapter 3 but which has subsequently fallen flat is the 1977 attempt by the *Guardian* to stimulate the formation of a new Marxist-Leninist party. The former co-editor of the paper, Irwin Silber, left feeling that the staff had not really shaken off its infatuation with Mao's Cultural Revolution. Silber, who came to view the Cultural Revolution as being as great a disaster as the Theory of the Three Worlds, quit the *Guardian* and, with more like-minded comrades, formed a "Marxist-Leninist Journal of Rectification," *Line of March*. This journal has published an extensive critique of the whole Maoist and post-Maoist movements in other countries.[68] The editors of *Line of March* also published a bi-weekly paper called *Frontline*. Unlike the *Guardian's* attempt at party-building, *Line of March* succeeded in building an organizational base and engaging in activities that went beyond publishing. *Line of March* was much more favorably oriented toward the USSR and its international behavior than are the Maoist or pro-Chinese groups.

Silber's obituary for U.S. groups with a Maoist orientation may have been a bit too hasty. The RCP, the New Democratic Movement, and the League of Revolutionary Struggle continue actions and publication programs which reflect considerable commitment and discipline on the part of members and supporters. And they maintain themselves as national organizations.

The RCP may no longer have China as a model and the New Democratic Movement may be disappointed once again in its optimistic view of recent currents in both China and the Soviet Union. But the Trotskyists have demonstrated that Marxist–Leninist groups with a critical perspective can survive and can operate at a certain level of practice without having an ongoing regime as a reference model. The same may be true of Maoist groups.

Both Trotskyists and Maoists in the United States, however, will face two problems. The first is increased repression at the hands of governmental agencies. The Reagan administration granted the CIA free rein to operate inside the United States, and lifted restrictions that were imposed on the FBI after the COINTELPRO disclosures. The unleashing of both the CIA and the FBI posed serious problems for Maoists and Trotskyists.

The Reagan administration justified these actions on the grounds that the government needed greater latitude to deal with people engaged in illegal and violent activities. It contended that these agencies would not infringe on "legitimate" political activity in this country, even if it was oppositional. But, as has been pointed out in this book, much of the effort of the FBI in the past has been devoted to attempts to define groups as violent, and thus illegitimate in the eyes of the public. It is then free to disrupt any of their activities it chooses — including electoral activity. That the CIA in the 1980s was able to act against U.S. citizens operating within the United States was particularly ominous for groups with international linkages.

This, of course, is not a new problem for Trotskyists and Maoists — or for radicals generally — in the United States. The atypical period was the one of restraint, between the time that the COINTELPRO documents were made public and Ronald Reagan's first election. But it does raise the costs to people engaged in Trotskyist and Maoist movements in the United States well above those incurred by Trotskyists and Maoists in France.

A different problem which U.S. Trotskyists have not faced for many years, and which Maoists have never faced before, is how to relate to a wide array of non-Marxist-Leninist oppositional groups and movements. For most of the 1970s, Trotskyists and Maoists dominated left-wing campus politics, and the *Guardian* was the major newspaper read within that milieu. That situation has changed. By the early 1980s, the Democratic Socialists of America (DSA), a non-Marxist-Leninist socialist group which works within the Democratic Party, replaced Trotskyists and Maoists as the major left-wing force on a number of U.S. campuses. DSA sometimes filled a void by the split in the Maoist RCP, which was the parent group of the Revolutionary Student Brigade, and by the industrial strategy of the SWP. Aside from its campus activities and work within the Democratic Party, the Democratic Socialists are active in the labor movement and have some members in very high leadership positions. In addition, the *Guardian* is being given considerable competition by the weekly *In These Times,* which is close to, although not a formal organ of, the DSA.

Of even greater significance is the problem of adapting to the variety of groups which have no specific ideological orientation such as the DSA has. Included here (though the list is not exhaustive) would be the anti-interventionist and solidarity movements dealing with Central America and the Middle East, the anti-apartheid movement, racial groupings, feminist groups, peace groups, environmental groups, gay and lesbian rights groups, groups or locals of militant trade-unionists, and the Rainbow Coalition. These groups assumed increased importance in the U.S. political landscape by the mid-1980s, and neither Trotskyist nor Maoist groups have had an easy time relating to them. The SWP, which was in the forefront of the struggle against U.S. intervention in Vietnam, has been quite marginalized in the world of Central American solidarity. This is in contrast to the central position of the French *Ligue* in such solidarity work, as well as in the New Caledonian independence support movement. Indeed, both the Camejo and Evans factions were dissatisfied by the way that the SWP was attempting to balance the industrial strategy and networking with other groups which were not comprised strictly of industrial workers. If the SWP is uncritically supportive of the Nicaraguan government and the Salvadoran FDR/FMLN, it has been much more hesitant about its dealings with other U.S. groups which support them, too.

In sum, Trotskyists and Maoists in both France and the United States are now operating under contextual conditions different from those of the 1960s and 1970s, when Trotskyism was rejuvenated and when Maoism became a distinct current of Marxist–Leninist theory and practice. In France, they have had to contend with a Socialist government, which also included Communist ministers for a while, and which they viewed as a dismal failure resulting in renewed right-wing unity in that country. Under these conditions, Maoism almost disappeared from the scene, while Trotskyist organizations suffered serious but not devastating losses in membership.

In the United States, the SWP fragmented and lost substantial numbers of members, many of them important former members. It still has retained its predominance within the ranks of Trotskyism, although it will be interesting to see if the Freedom Socialist Party will be able to become a viable national organization in the future. Within the ranks of Maoism and post-Maoism, the CP(ML), with its Chinese recognition, passed from the scene, as have most of the nationally or ethnically specific Maoist groups which emerged in the 1970s. The RCP, the League of Revolutionary Struggle, and the New Democratic Movement continue the struggle begun by U.S. Maoists in the 1960s and 1970s. They have had to contend with the repressive implications of the shift to the right in the United States as well as with the existence of a new variety of oppositional social and political movements.

In conclusion, this updating survey of the evolution of Trotskyism and Maoism in France and the United States through most of the 1980s indicates that, regardless of the point in time at which one breaks into the evolution of these movements, the explanation of their dynamism remains the same. Group fragmentation is dictated by the combined effect of contradictions which inhere in the guiding theories and in the peculiar characteristics of the broader political contexts in which these groups must operate. Once this is understood, one can more easily interpret precise lines of development. What would otherwise be scattered and seemingly inexplicable pieces of descriptive information about such groups then become elements of an understandable, if not completely predictable, pattern of dynamics.

The process, of course, will not end with the present decade, or with the last words of this book. One can be sure that it will continue as Trotskyists and Maoists struggle, not only to survive over time while exercising intermittant influence — which I referred to as the "first level of practice" in the Introduction — but to go beyond that first level of practice to the second and third levels, building mass bases of support and instituting socialism.

Appendix 1.
Chronological Development of French Trotskyism

Major Organizations

1924-1928   French Communist Party purges dissidents attracted to
Trotsky's Left Opposition in the USSR.

1929   Creation of *La Ligue Communiste* by unifying various
groupings of purged former Communist Party members.

1934   In August, *La Ligue Communiste* is dissolved and the
Trotskyists enter the SFIO, the French Social Democratic
Party, as *Le Groupe Bolchevik-Léniniste* (GBL).

1935   In October, the GBL is expelled from the SFIO.

1936

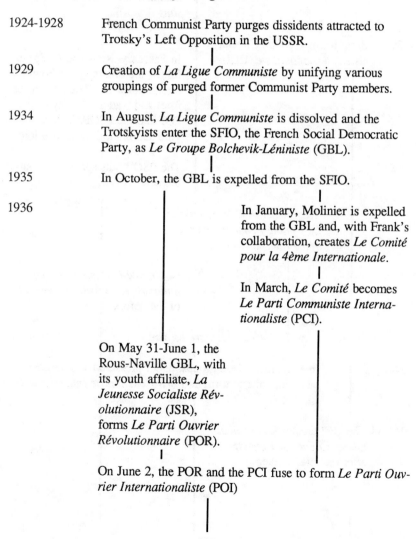

In January, Molinier is expelled
from the GBL and, with Frank's
collaboration, creates *Le Comité
pour la 4ème Internationale*.

In March, *Le Comité* becomes
*Le Parti Communiste Interna-
tionaliste* (PCI).

On May 31-June 1, the
Rous-Naville GBL, with
its youth affiliate, *La
Jeunesse Socialiste Rév-
olutionnaire* (JSR),
forms *Le Parti Ouvrier
Révolutionnaire* (POR).

On June 2, the POR and the PCI fuse to form *Le Parti Ouvrier Internationaliste* (POI)

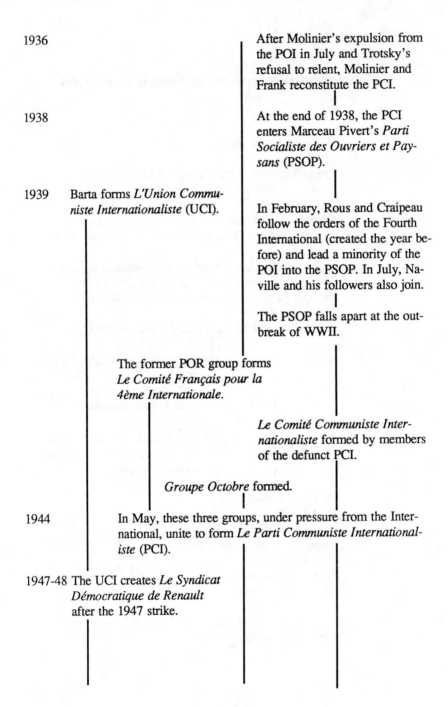

1936 — After Molinier's expulsion from the POI in July and Trotsky's refusal to relent, Molinier and Frank reconstitute the PCI.

1938 — At the end of 1938, the PCI enters Marceau Pivert's *Parti Socialiste des Ouvriers et Paysans* (PSOP).

1939 — Barta forms *L'Union Communiste Internationaliste* (UCI).

In February, Rous and Craipeau follow the orders of the Fourth International (created the year before) and lead a minority of the POI into the PSOP. In July, Naville and his followers also join.

The PSOP falls apart at the outbreak of WWII.

The former POR group forms *Le Comité Français pour la 4ème Internationale*.

Le Comité Communiste Internationaliste formed by members of the defunct PCI.

Groupe Octobre formed.

1944 — In May, these three groups, under pressure from the International, unite to form *Le Parti Communiste Internationaliste* (PCI).

1947-48 The UCI creates *Le Syndicat Démocratique de Renault* after the 1947 strike.

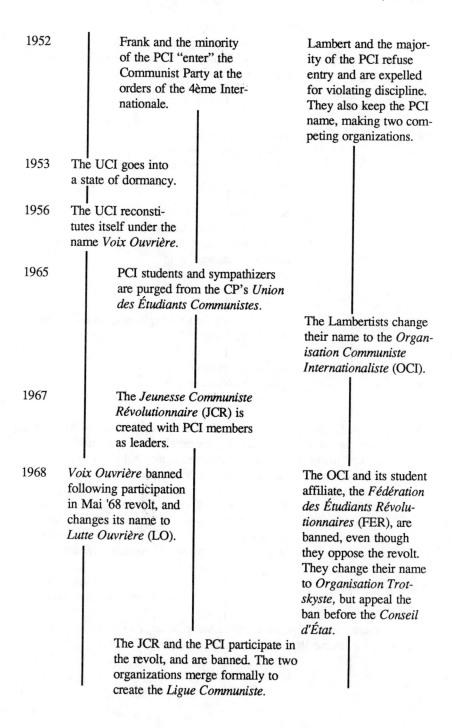

1952	Frank and the minority of the PCI "enter" the Communist Party at the orders of the 4ème Internationale.	Lambert and the majority of the PCI refuse entry and are expelled for violating discipline. They also keep the PCI name, making two competing organizations.
1953	The UCI goes into a state of dormancy.	
1956	The UCI reconstitutes itself under the name *Voix Ouvrière*.	
1965	PCI students and sympathizers are purged from the CP's *Union des Étudiants Communistes*.	The Lambertists change their name to the *Organisation Communiste Internationaliste* (OCI).
1967	The *Jeunesse Communiste Révolutionnaire* (JCR) is created with PCI members as leaders.	
1968	*Voix Ouvrière* banned following participation in Mai '68 revolt, and changes its name to *Lutte Ouvrière* (LO).	The OCI and its student affiliate, the *Fédération des Étudiants Révolutionnaires* (FER), are banned, even though they oppose the revolt. They change their name to *Organisation Trotskyste*, but appeal the ban before the *Conseil d'État*.

The JCR and the PCI participate in the revolt, and are banned. The two organizations merge formally to create the *Ligue Communiste*.

1970	*Lutte Ouvrière* begins negotiating of merger with the *Ligue Communiste*.	The *Ligue* begins negotiations with *Lutte Ouvrière*.	The OCI appeal is won and the name readopted.
1973		The *Ligue Communiste* is banned after a violent clash with a right-wing group.	
1974		Krivine runs in the presidential elections under the designation *Front Communiste Révolutionnaire*. In December, the *Ligue* name is reconstituted.	
1978		The *Ligue* and the OCI begin talks with the hope of a future fusion.	
1979		The *Ligue* creates a youth group, the *Jeunesse Communiste Révolutionnaire*.	
1981	Arlette Laguiller is on the ballot for first round of presidential elections. She comes in sixth out of ten candidates.	The merger talks between the *Ligue* and the OCI fall apart. Approximately 500 Ligue members switch their loyalties to the OCI in a dispute over the Sandinistas in Nicaragua.	
		Krivine is kept off of the ballot. The *Ligue* urges voting for one of the "workers parties."	The OCI changes its name to *Organisation Communiste Internationaliste-Unifiée*.
			OCI urges first-round voting for Mitterrand.

There is no co-operation among the three largest French Trotskyist groups in the 1981 elections. All take different positions.

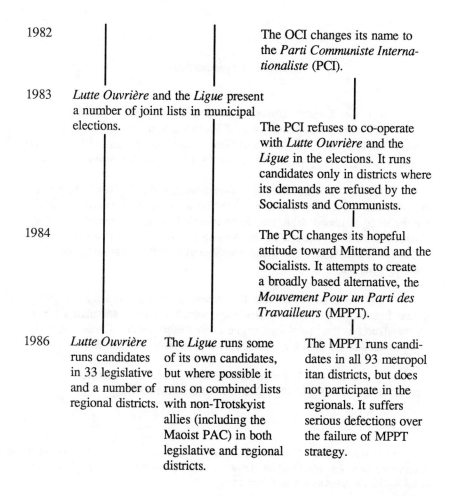

1982

The OCI changes its name to the *Parti Communiste Internationaliste* (PCI).

1983 *Lutte Ouvrière* and the *Ligue* present a number of joint lists in municipal elections.

The PCI refuses to co-operate with *Lutte Ouvrière* and the *Ligue* in the elections. It runs candidates only in districts where its demands are refused by the Socialists and Communists.

1984

The PCI changes its hopeful attitude toward Mitterand and the Socialists. It attempts to create a broadly based alternative, the *Mouvement Pour un Parti des Travailleurs* (MPPT).

1986 *Lutte Ouvrière* runs candidates in 33 legislative and a number of regional districts.

The *Ligue* runs some of its own candidates, but where possible it runs on combined lists with non-Trotskyist allies (including the Maoist PAC) in both legislative and regional districts.

The MPPT runs candidates in all 93 metropol itan districts, but does not participate in the regionals. It suffers serious defections over the failure of MPPT strategy.

Minor Organizations

(1) *Les Comités Communistes pour L'Autogestion* (CCA). Created in 1977 when the French followers of Pablo's International Marxist-Revolutionary Tendency left the *Parti Socialiste Unifié*. Had perhaps 300 members in 1978, but by the end of the 1980s has shrunk to probably fewer than 100.

(2) *Le Parti Communiste Révolutionnaire* (PCR). Not to be mistaken with the *Maoist Parti Communiste Révolutionnaire (marxiste-léniniste)*, the PCR is affiliated with the International Executive Committee of the Fourth International headed by the Argentinian J. Posadas. It was created in 1962, and attempts to work within the Socialist Party. It probably has fewer than sixty members.

(3) *La Ligue Trotskyste de France*. This is a sympathizing section of the International Spartacist Tendency, which has been stimulated largely by the efforts of the Sparticist League in the United States. Created in 1976, it is probably larger than the PCR, but with less than 100 members.

(4) *L'Alliance Marxiste Révolutionnaire* (AMR). Created in 1981 as a result of a split in the CCA. Pablo himself is in the AMR.

The author is grateful to Monsieur Sammy Ketz of the *Centre d'Études et de Recherches sur les Mouvements Trotskystes et Révolutionnaires Internationaux* (CERMTRI) for assistance with this chart.

Appendix 2.
Chronological Development of French Maoism

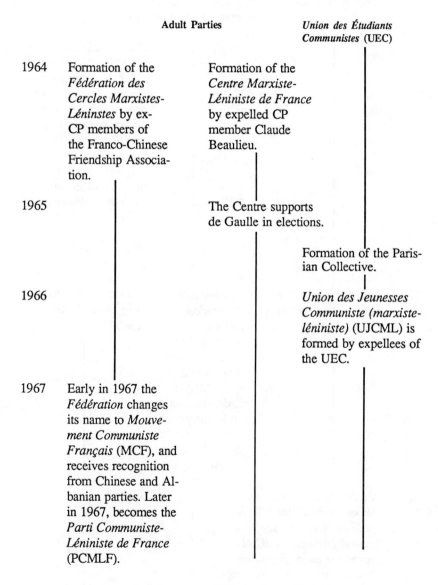

	Adult Parties	Union des Étudiants Communistes (UEC)
1964	Formation of the *Fédération des Cercles Marxistes-Léninstes* by ex-CP members of the Franco-Chinese Friendship Association.	Formation of the *Centre Marxiste-Léniniste de France* by expelled CP member Claude Beaulieu.
1965		The Centre supports de Gaulle in elections.
		Formation of the Parisian Collective.
1966		*Union des Jeunesses Communiste (marxiste-léniniste)* (UJCML) is formed by expellees of the UEC.
1967	Early in 1967 the *Fédération* changes its name to *Mouvement Communiste Français* (MCF), and receives recognition from Chinese and Albanian parties. Later in 1967, becomes the *Parti Communiste-Léniniste de France* (PCMLF).	

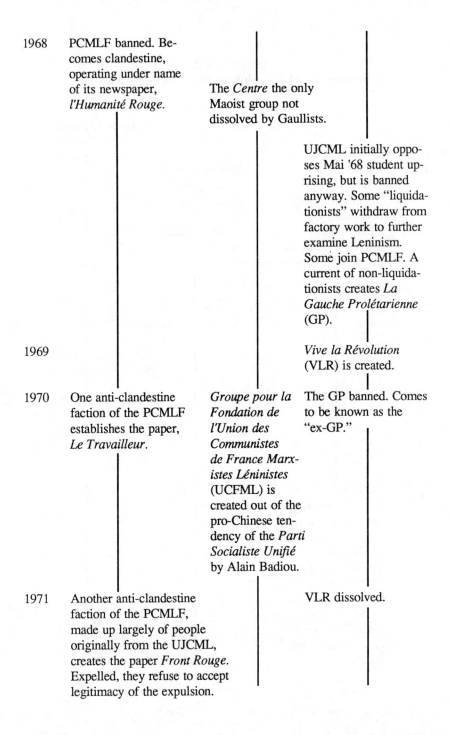

1968   PCMLF banned. Becomes clandestine, operating under name of its newspaper, *l'Humanité Rouge.*

The *Centre* the only Maoist group not dissolved by Gaullists.

UJCML initially opposes Mai '68 student uprising, but is banned anyway. Some "liquidationists" withdraw from factory work to further examine Leninism. Some join PCMLF. A current of non-liquidationists creates *La Gauche Prolétarienne* (GP).

1969

Vive la Révolution (VLR) is created.

1970   One anti-clandestine faction of the PCMLF establishes the paper, *Le Travailleur.*

Groupe pour la Fondation de l'Union des Communistes de France Marxistes Léninistes (UCFML) is created out of the pro-Chinese tendency of the *Parti Socialiste Unifié* by Alain Badiou.

The GP banned. Comes to be known as the "ex-GP."

1971   Another anti-clandestine faction of the PCMLF, made up largely of people originally from the UJCML, creates the paper *Front Rouge.* Expelled, they refuse to accept legitimacy of the expulsion.

VLR dissolved.

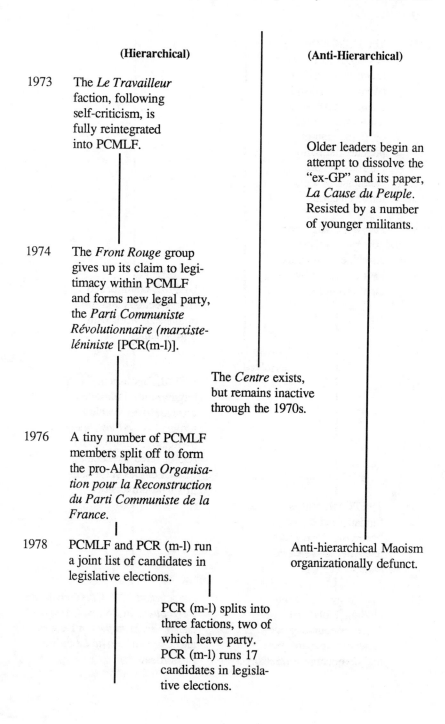

(Hierarchical)

(Anti-Hierarchical)

1973   The *Le Travailleur* faction, following self-criticism, is fully reintegrated into PCMLF.

Older leaders begin an attempt to dissolve the "ex-GP" and its paper, *La Cause du Peuple*. Resisted by a number of younger militants.

1974   The *Front Rouge* group gives up its claim to legitimacy within PCMLF and forms new legal party, the *Parti Communiste Révolutionnaire (marxiste-léniniste* [PCR(m-l)].

The *Centre* exists, but remains inactive through the 1970s.

1976   A tiny number of PCMLF members split off to form the pro-Albanian *Organisation pour la Reconstruction du Parti Communiste de la France.*

1978   PCMLF and PCR (m-l) run a joint list of candidates in legislative elections.

Anti-hierarchical Maoism organizationally defunct.

PCR (m-l) splits into three factions, two of which leave party. PCR (m-l) runs 17 candidates in legislative elections.

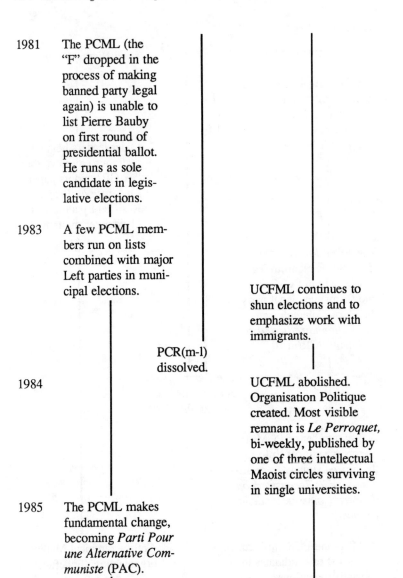

1981   The PCML (the "F" dropped in the process of making banned party legal again) is unable to list Pierre Bauby on first round of presidential ballot. He runs as sole candidate in legislative elections.

1983   A few PCML members run on lists combined with major Left parties in municipal elections.

PCR(m-l) dissolved.

1984

1985   The PCML makes fundamental change, becoming *Parti Pour une Alternative Communiste* (PAC).

1986   PAC runs on lists including Trotskyist *Ligue,* renouncing concepts of vanguard party and democratic centralism.

UCFML continues to shun elections and to emphasize work with immigrants.

UCFML abolished. Organisation Politique created. Most visible remnant is *Le Perroquet,* bi-weekly, published by one of three intellectual Maoist circles surviving in single universities.

Association "Les Conférences du Perroquet" in Reims, *Communistes Démocratiques* in Rennes, and *Union Marxiste-Léniniste* in Bordeau.

Appendix 3.
Chronological Development of U.S. Trotskyism

1928   Cannon, Shachtman, and Abern expelled from Communist Party in October.

1929   In February, they publish a platform for a new group in creation. In May, the Communist League of America, Left Opposition of the Communist Party (CLA) is created in Chicago.

1934   CLA plays a major role in Minneapolis Local 544 Teamsters strike. Merger with A.J. Muste's American Workers' Party to formWorkers Party of the United States.

1936   In March, Workers Party enters Socialist Party.

1937   Trotskyists declare themselves a faction within Socialist Party. In June, separate meeting of this faction is called in New York, leading to expulsion from Socialists and establishment of National Committee of Expelled Branches.

1938   Convention of expelled branches held, with January 1 declaration of new Socialist Workers Party.

1940   In April, Shachtman, Burnham Abern and Bern minority is suspended. They form new Workers Party. In May, Burnham quits, beginning his evolution to the political Right. Shachtman later changes party name to Independent Socialist League, veering Right toward social democracy.

1941   Trotskyists oppose U.S. entry into WWII. Local 544 in receivership, FBI raids offices. On July 15, 28 SWP and Local members indicted for conspiracy, 18 convicted.

295

1944   After appeals, Trotskyist leaders go to prison.

1952   SWP breaks with Pablist International Secretariat
        over policy of entrism. Joins with French Lam-
        bertist Trotskyists in International Committee
        of the Fourth International.

In the heat of anti-communist repression in U.S., a
minority within SWP op-
poses public electoral action
and urges non-electoral effort.
One faction is accused of
"Pablism"—wanting to merge
with Communist Party.
Minority program loses, and
members expelled.

SWP membership in severe decline during heyday of
McCarthyism.

1956   SWP condemns Soviet move into Hungary.

1957   Tim Wohlforth, in break with Shachtman and Independent Socialist
        League, joins with SWP members to found the *Young Socialist*
        newspaper.

1958

Shachtman merges ISL
with Socialist Party.
Shachtman working
with rightist Socialist
Party element, the
League for Industrial
Democracy. A split by
some followers leads to
creation of Independent
Socialist Clubs of Am-
erica.

1959   Sam Marcy leaves SWP and
        forms Workers World Party,
        not publicly a Trotskyist group.

1960   SWP youth group,
Young Socialist
Alliance (YSA),
founded. *Young
Socialist* becomes
its newspaper.

1961   SWP supports Cuban
revolution, breaks with
International Commit-
tee, and moves back
into International Sec-
retariat of the Fourth
International.

1962   Workers World Party
creates youth affiliate,
Youth Against War
and Fascism.

1963   At "Reunification Congress," International
Secretariat changes name
to United Secretariat.

                          Opposition to Cuban
position leads to split,
and expelled faction be-
comes Spartacist League.

1964   Second opposing faction,
including Tim Wohlforth,
expelled from SWP, be-
coming Workers League.
Retains affiliation with
International Committee.

1966   International Committee,
led by Gerry Healy, expels
Spartacist League.

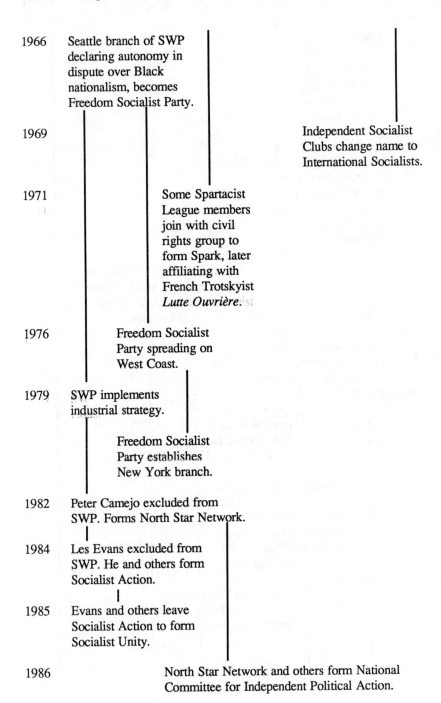

1966   Seattle branch of SWP
        declaring autonomy in
        dispute over Black
        nationalism, becomes
        Freedom Socialist Party.

1969   Independent Socialist
                                                        Clubs change name to
                                                        International Socialists.

1971   Some Spartacist
                League members
                join with civil
                rights group to
                form Spark, later
                affiliating with
                French Trotskyist
                Lutte Ouvrière.

1976   Freedom Socialist
        Party spreading on
        West Coast.

1979   SWP implements
        industrial strategy.

        Freedom Socialist
        Party establishes
        New York branch.

1982   Peter Camejo excluded from
        SWP. Forms North Star Network.

1984   Les Evans excluded from
        SWP. He and others form
        Socialist Action.

1985   Evans and others leave
        Socialist Action to form
        Socialist Unity.

1986   North Star Network and others form National
                Committee for Independent Political Action.

Appendix 4.
Chronological Development of U.S. Maoism

1962   The Progressive Labor Movement (PLM) is founded by members and ex-members of the Communist Party, in June.

1965   PLM becomes a party, the Progressive Labor Party (PLP).

1966   PLP presents its "student power" thesis within Students for a Democratic Society (SDS).

1967   PLP shifts to a "worker-student alliance" position inside SDS.

1968

Bay Area Radical Union (BARU) formed.

PLP opposes confrontations in Chicago because workers not involved, experiences serious defections.

Opposition to PLP within SDS coalesces under the name of Revolutionary Youth Movement (RYM). Opposition includes non-PLP Maoists from Atlanta, Los Angeles and Chicago, as well as BARU.

California Communist League created, mainly by Black and Puerto Rican militants.

1969   At June SDS convention, RYM splits into Weatherman, RYM I, and RYM II. Most Maoists are in RYM II. An SDS move to expel PLP spells demise of SDS.

1970

BARU becomes Revolutionary Union (RU).

1971   October League created by militants from Klonsky's Los Angeles Marxist-Leninst Collective, the Georgia Communist League, and small racial and ethnic groups.

1972   Revolutionary Union joins with Black Workers Congress (BWC) and Puerto Rican Revolutionary Workers Organization(PRRWO) in umbrella group, the National Liaison Committee. Asian-American *I Wor Kuen* (IWK) pulls out soon thereafter.

1973   National Liaison falls apart.

1974   California Communist League creates national Communist Labor Party (CLP).

1975   Revolutionary Union becomes Revolutionary Communist Party (RCP).

"Third-Worldist" Revolutionary Wing created, joining PRRWO to the Mexican-American August Twenty-Ninth Movement, the Black Revolutionary Workers League (RWL), and the former Asian-American Workers Viewpoint Organization (RWO).

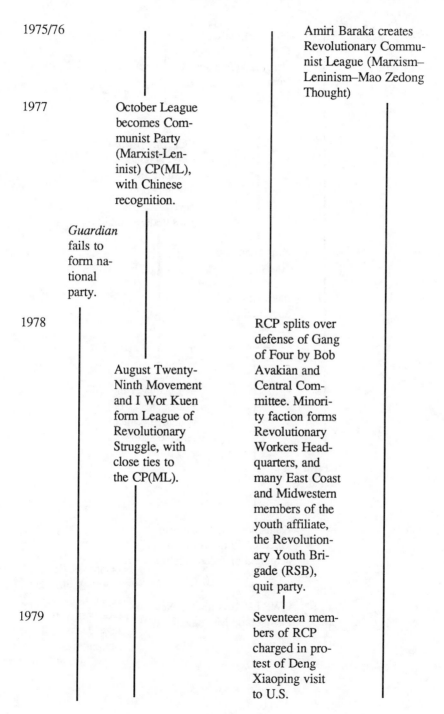

1975/76

Amiri Baraka creates
Revolutionary Commu-
nist League (Marxism–
Leninism–Mao Zedong
Thought)

1977

October League
becomes Com-
munist Party
(Marxist-Len-
inist) CP(ML),
with Chinese
recognition.

Guardian
fails to
form na-
tional
party.

1978

August Twenty-
Ninth Movement
and I Wor Kuen
form League of
Revolutionary
Struggle, with
close ties to
the CP(ML).

RCP splits over
defense of Gang
of Four by Bob
Avakian and
Central Com-
mittee. Minori-
ty faction forms
Revolutionary
Workers Head-
quarters, and
many East Coast
and Midwestern
members of the
youth affiliate,
the Revolution-
ary Youth Bri-
gade (RSB),
quit party.

1979

Seventeen mem-
bers of RCP
charged in pro-
test of Deng
Xiaoping visit
to U.S.

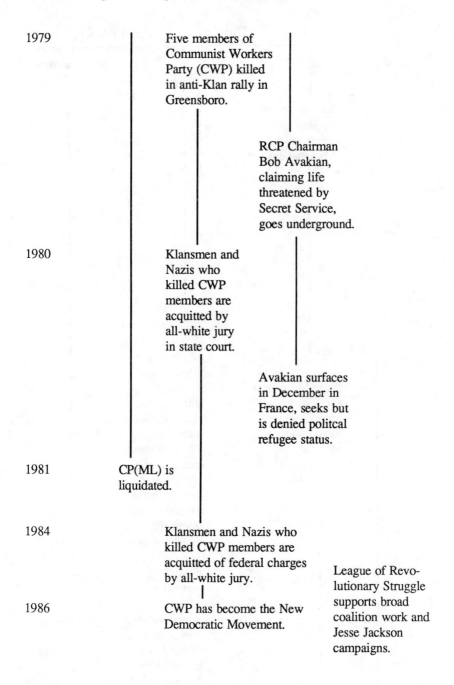

1979   Five members of
                        Communist Workers
                        Party (CWP) killed
                        in anti-Klan rally in
                        Greensboro.

                                                    RCP Chairman
                                                    Bob Avakian,
                                                    claiming life
                                                    threatened by
                                                    Secret Service,
                                                    goes underground.

1980   Klansmen and
                        Nazis who
                        killed CWP
                        members are
                        acquitted by
                        all-white jury
                        in state court.

                                                    Avakian surfaces
                                                    in December in
                                                    France, seeks but
                                                    is denied politcal
                                                    refugee status.

1981   CP(ML) is
          liquidated.

1984   Klansmen and Nazis who
                        killed CWP members are
                        acquitted of federal charges
                        by all-white jury.   League of Revo-
                                                        lutionary Struggle
1986   CWP has become the New   supports broad
                        Democratic Movement.   coalition work and
                                                        Jesse Jackson
                                                        campaigns.

Notes

Introduction

1 Constance Ashton Myers, *The Prophet's Army: Trotskyists in America, 1928-1941* (Westport: Greenwood Press, 1977), p. xi.
2 Jim O'Brien, "American Leninism in the 1970s," *Radical America,* special double issue, 11, no. 6 and 12, no. 1 (Winter 1977-78), pp. 27-62.
3 Robert J. Alexander, *Trotskyism in Latin America* (Stanford: Hoover Institution Press, 1973) and Myers, *Prophet's Army.*
4 Particularly noteworthy are the books by Yvan Craipeau: *Le Mouvement Trotskyste en France* (Paris: Syros, 1971), *Contre Vents et marées: les révolutionnaires pendant la deuxième guerre mondiale* (Paris: Savelli, 1977), and *La Libération confisquée* (Paris: Savelli/Syros, 1978). The French Lambertist Trotskyists have established a documentation center, Le Centre d'Études et de Recherche sur les Mouvements Trotskystes et Révolutionnaires Internationaux, to aid in the study of the history of international Trotskyism.
5 Mario D. Fenyo, "Trotsky and His Heirs: The American Perspective," *Studies in Comparative Communism* 10, nos. 1 and 2 (Spring/Summer 1977), p. 210.
6 That impression preceded but was fortified by this author's experience in presenting a paper on Trotskyism and Maoism at the University of Moscow as part of the proceedings of the Eleventh World Congress of the International Political Science Association held in August 1979.
7 While the author was in Moscow as a participant in the Congress of the International Political Science Association, he was asked for an interview by a correspondent for Radio Moscow. The correspondent was particularly interested in the phenomenon of Maoism. After the responses to some very directive questions about Maoists were not suitably derogatory, he very politely thanked the author, told him that he personally had learned a great deal from it, but said that he doubted very much that his superiors would put it on the air.
8 For a scholarly treatment of Chinese Trotskyism, see Joseph T. Miller, "The Politics of Chinese Trotskyism: The Role of a Permanent Opposition in Chinese Communism" (Ph.D. dissertation, University of Illinois at Urbana-Champaign, 1979).

Chapter One: Theories and Contexts

1 On Trotsky's early years, see the first volume of Isaac Deutscher's fascinating three-volume biography of Trotsky, *The Prophet Armed: Trotsky, 1879-1921* (New York: Vintage Books, 1965).

2 Victor Nee and James Peck, "Introduction," in Victor Nee and James Peck, eds., *China's Uninterrupted Revolution: From 1940 to the Present* (New York: Pantheon Books, 1975), p. 30.

3 Leon Trotsky, *Results and Prospects* in Leon Trotsky, *The Permanent Revolution* and *Results and Prospects* (New York: Pathfinder Press, 1969), p. 77.

4 Ibid., p. 96.

5 Ibid., p. 99.

6 Trotsky, *The Permanent Revolution,* p. 216.

7 Trotsky, *Results and Prospects,* p. 105.

8 Leon Trotsky, "Manifesto of the Communist International to the Workers of the World," in Leon Trotsky, *The First Five Years of the Communist International,* vol. 1 (New York: Pioneer Publishers, 1945), p. 25. Lenin's position, presented to the Congress of the following year (1920), did not include this strong dependency. For an interesting discussion in English of Lenin's position, see Roger E. Kanet, "The Soviet Union and Sub-Saharan Africa," (Ph. D. dissertation, Princeton University, 1966), chapter 2.

9 Trotsky, *The Permanent Revolution,* p. 129.

10 Ibid., p. 279.

11 Ibid., p. 135.

12 Stalin presents a clear picture of his concept of revolutionary stages in his *The National Question and Leninism* (Moscow: Foreign Languages Publishing House, 1952), chapter 3.

13 See Leon Trotsky, *The Revolution Betrayed* (New York: Pathfinder Press, 1972).

14 Leon Trotsky, *The Transitional Program,* in Leon Trotsky, *The Transitional Program for Socialist Revolution,* 2nd ed. (New York: Pathfinder Press, 1974), pp. 74-75.

15 Ibid., pp. 82-84.

16 Ibid., pp. 96-97.

17 Ibid., p. 95.

18 See Georg Lukacs, *History and Class Consciousness: Studies in Marxist Dialectics,* trans. Rodney Livingston (Cambridge: MIT Press, 1971) and Karl Korsch, *Marxism and Philosophy,* trans. Fred Halliday (New York: Monthly Review Press, 1970).

19 Trotsky did write on Marxist ethics and epistemology, but by counterposing them to non-Marxist ethics and epistemology rather than by attempting to develop the Marxian theoretical framework further. See Leon Trotsky, *Their Morals and Ours* (New York: Pioneer Publishers 1942) and "An Open Letter to Comrade Burnham," in Leon Trotsky, *In Defense of Marxism* (New York: Pathfinder Press, 1973), pp. 72-94.

20 Mao Tse-Tung, *On Contradiction* (Peking: Foreign Languages Press, 1967), pp. 36-37.
21 Mao Tse-tung, *On Practice,* in Arthur P. Mandel, ed., *Essential Works of Marxism* (New York: Bantam Books, 1961), p. 508.
22 Mao Tse-tung in a directive of the Central Committee of the Chinese Communist Party dated 1 June 1943, which was originally published anonymously but was attributed to Mao in the current edition of the *Selected Works.* Excerpts appear in Stuart R. Schram, *The Political Thought of Mao Tse-tung* (New York: Praeger, 1963), pp. 316-317.
23 James Peck, "Revolution versus Modernization and Revisionism: A Two-Front Struggle," in Nee and Peck, *China's Uninterrupted Revolution,* p. 97. This essay is the only one known to this writer which attempts to compare Trotsky's theory of permanent revolution and Mao's theory of uninterrupted revolution in nonpolemical fashion.
24 Mao Tse-tung, "Speech at the Supreme State Conference, 28 January 1958," excerpts in Stuart R. Schram, ed., *Chairman Mao Talks to the People: Talks and Letters, 1956-1971,* trans. John Chinnery and Tieyun (New York: Pantheon Books, 1974), p. 94.
25 Mao Tse-tung, "On the Historical Experience of the Dictatorship of the Proletariat," an editorial in the *Jen-min Jih-pao* of 5 April 1956 and excerpted in Schram, *Political Thought,* pp. 432-433.
26 Mao Tse-tung, "Talk on Questions of Philosophy, 18 August 1964," in Schram, *Chairman Mao,* p. 217.
27 See Lin Piao, "Mao Tse-tung's Theory of People's War," in Franz Schurmann and Orville Schell, eds., *Communist China: Revolutionary Reconstruction and International Confrontation, 1949 to the Present,* vol. 3 of *The China Reader* (New York: Random House, 1967), pp. 347-359 and Lin Piao, "Long Live the Victory of People's War," in A. Doak Barnett, ed., *China after Mao* (Princeton: Princeton University Press, 1967), pp. 196-262.
28 Lin Piao, "Mao Tse-tung's Theory of People's War," p. 353.
29 Renmin Ribao, Editorial Department, "Chairman Mao's Theory of the Differentiation of the Three Worlds Is a Major Contribution to Marxism-Leninism," *Peking Review,* no. 45 (November 4 1977) pp 11 and 16. On the Theory of the Three Worlds, see also Hua Kuo-feng "Political Report to the 11th National Congress of the Communist Party of China," *Peking Review,* no. 35 (August 26, 1977), pp. 39-43.
30 Renmin Ribao, "Chairman Mao's Theory," p. 19.
31 Ibid., p. 24.
32 Ibid., p. 22.
33 Ibid., p. 22-23.
34 Ibid., p. 20.
35 Ibid., p. 19.
36 Ibid., p. 22.
37 Chung Lien, "The 'Gang of Four' and the Trotskyites," *Peking Review,* no. 7 (February 11, 1977), pp. 10-15 and *Renmin Ribao,* "Chairman Mao's

Theory," p. 18.

38 "The Theory and Practice of Revolution," press release of the Party of Labor of Albania which appeared first as an editorial in the July 7, 1977 issue of *Zeri i Popullit,* the organ of the party's Central Committee. The portion in double quotes appeared also in Enver Hoxha's report to the party in November 1976.

39 Trotsky, *The Revolution Betrayed,* pp. 245-256.

40 For income inequality rankings, see Frank Parkin, *Class, Inequality and Political Order* (New York: Praeger, 1971), p. 118 and Irving B. Kravis, "A World of Unequal Incomes," *The Annals of the American Academy of Political and Social Science* 409 (September 1973), p. 69.

41 The *Le Canard Enchaîné* break-in, however, took place during Giscard's presidency.

42 Philip Green, "Decentralization, Community Control, and Revolution: Reflections on Ocean Hill-Brownsville," in Philip Green and Sanford Levinson, eds., *Power and Community* (New York: Vintage Books, 1970), p. 254.

43 While the Americans used draftees to fight in both Korea and Indochina, the French used them in Algeria but not in the earlier Indochinese War.

44 Alain Jaubert et al., *Guide de la France des luttes* (Paris: Stock, 1974).

45 For a more detailed and systematic comparison of the stages of radicalization in France and the United States, see my "The Effects of Student Activism in Industrialized Countries: Some Comparative Reflections on France and the United States," in Harvey A. Farberman and Erich Goode, eds., *Social Reality* (Englewood Cliffs: Prentice-Hall, 1973), pp. 287-307 and in Robert Perrucci and Marc Pilisuk, eds., *The Triple Revolution: Social Problems in Depth* (Boston: Little, Brown, 1971), pp. 585-603.

46 Hal Draper, "The Student Movement of the Thirties: A Political History," in Rita James Simon, ed., *As We Saw the Thirties* (Urbana: University of Illinois Press, 1967), pp. 155-156.

47 *Le Monde,* 21 Mars 1972, p. 11.

Chapter Two: Trotskyism in France

1 Leon Trotsky, *The Crisis of the French Section (1935-36),* ed. Naomi Allen and George Breitman (New York: Pathfinder Press, 1977), p. 16.

2 Yvan Craipeau, *Le Mouvement Trotskyste en France* (Paris: Syros, 1971), p. 38.

3 Trotsky, *The Crisis of the French Section,* pp. 18-19.

4 Ibid.

5 Ibid., p. 20.

6 Ibid. p. 91.

7 Ibid., p. 22.

8 This was the same tactic which would later be used by the League for Industrial Democracy to try to bring the SDS back into line in the United States.

9 Trotsky, *The Crisis of the French Section*, pp. 88-89.

10 Ibid. p. 91.

11 It is interesting that a brave and dedicated anti-Nazi Resistance leader like Georges Bidault would later become a major defender of French imperialism and Nazi-like torturing practices in Algeria.

12 Yvan Craipeau, *La Libération confisquée* (Paris: Savelli/Syros, 1978), p. 10.

13 Craipeau, *Le Mouvement Trotskyste en France*, p. 198. See also *Fac-simlé: La Verité 1940/1944, Journal Trotskyste Clandestin sous l'Occupation Nazie* (Paris: Etudes et Documentation Internationales, 1978).

14 Craipeau, *Le Mouvement Trotskyste en France*, p. 199.

15 OCI, *Quelques Enseignements de notre histoire*, supplement to *La Vérité*, no. 548 (mai 1970), pp.43-45.

16 On the various tendencies, see OCI, *Quelques Enseignements*, pp. 60-62.

17 See OCI, *Quelques Enseignements*, pp. 85-100 and Les Evans, "The Fourth International from Split to Reunification," in *Towards a History of the Fourth International*, Part I, Education for Socialists Series (New York: National Education Department, Socialist Workers Party, June 1973), pp. 9-19.

18 Pablo, himself, insists upon the term "conception" rather than theory. Interview of June 15, 1978.

19 The Americans referred to *entrisme sui generis* as "deep entry."

20 Interview with Alain Krivine, May 31, 1978.

21 The Mouvement du 22 mars was a coalition group on the Nanterre campus. The arrest of its leaders and the closing of the Nanterre campus were the events that originally brought the 1968 conflict into Paris.

22 Cited by Dick Fidler, "The Antimilitarist Battle in France's Armed Forces," *Intercontinental Press* 12, no. 30 (August 5, 1974), p. 1069.

23 *Statuts de la IVe Internationale* (Paris: Rouge, 1970), p. 13.

24 At the Congress of 1974 the Argentinian Partido Socialista de los Trabajadores, then the largest national Trotskyist organization in the world, was admitted as a "sympathizing section." However, the repression in Argentina after the fall of Eva Peron's government made it impossible to estimate the subsequent state or size of the PST.

25 Ligue Communiste Révolutionnaire, *Une Chance historique pour la révolution socialiste* (Paris: Cahier Rouge, n.s., no. 1, 1975).

26 Data courtesy of Alain Krivine, interview of June 5 1975.

27 "Ligue Communiste Révolutionnaire Holds First Congress," *Intercontinentul Press* 13, no. 7 (February 24, 1975), pp. 262-263.

28 This was after a change of format early in 1978 which resulted in a jump in sales from 10,000 to 12,000.

29 Ligue Communiste, *Ce Que Veut la Ligue Communiste* (Paris: Maspero, 1972), p. 32.

30 Ibid., pp. 67-71.

31 Ibid., p. 40.

32 Ibid.

33 Ibid.

34 Ibid. p. 41.

35 Ibid.

36 Henri Weber, *Mouvement ouvrier, Stalinisme, et bureaucratie* (Paris: PCI, 1966), p.18.

37 Ibid., p. 19.

38 One of those participating from the Communist Party was Jean Elleinstein, the leading French theorist of Eurocommunism, who has since been expelled from the Party. Festivals are important yearly events for French left-wing groups. The estimated attendance was 10,000. Of the Trotskyists, only the OCI refused to attend the *Ligues's* 1978 festival.

39 As opposed to *l'Extrême Gauche,* which does not have quite the same connotation.

40 The OCT grew out of a split within the *Ligue* in 1971 over work in the unions and the position to be taken *vis-à-vis* China. The dissident group, initially called *Révolution,* preferred the formation of workers' committees to trade union work and viewed China more positively than the *Ligue.* The OCT, however, was neither Trotskyist nor Maoist.

41 See "Femmes, capitalisme, mouvement ouvrier," *Critique Communiste,* special issue, no. 20/21 (décembre 1977/janvier 1978) and Ligue Communiste Révolutionnaire, *Mouvement des femmes et lutte de classe* (Paris: Edition de la Taupe Rouge, n.d.).

42 Ligue Communiste Révolutionnaire, *Oui, le Socialisme!* (Paris: Maspero, 1978), pp. 113-137.

43 While still in the International Secretariat of the Fourth International, Pablo spent 15 months in a Dutch prison for his FLN support work. From 1962 until the fall of Ben Bella's government in 1965, he was an economic advisor to Ben Bella. He encouraged the development of autogestion in Algerian agriculture.

44 On March 20, 1968, some militants of the *Comité* broke windows and wrote on the walls of the Paris offices of the Chase Manhattan Bank, TWA, and American Express. The arrest of several of the students involved was part of the turmoil that led up to the revolt in May. See my "The French Student Revolt of May-June 1968," in S. M. Lipset and P. G. Altbach, eds., *Students in Revolt* (Boston: Houghton Mifflin, 1969), p. 129.

45 See Pierre Rousset, *Le Parti Communiste Vietnamien* (Paris: Maspero, 1973) and Pierre Rousset, "The Vietnamese Revolution and the Role of the Party," *International Socialist Review* 35, no. 4 (April 1974), pp. 5-25.

46 Rousset, "The Vietnamese Revolution and the Role of the Party," p. 24.

47 Ibid., p. 22.

48 Ibid., p. 17.

49 "Argentina: Political Crisis and Revolutionary Perspectives," *Intercontinentul Press* 12, no. 4 (December 23, 1974), p. 1797.

50 Under the recent miliary dictatorship in Argentina, the question of elections became, of course, moot.

51 Every other European section was in the majority faction.

52 This is the Syndicat National de I'Enseignement Secondaire (the SNES).

53 No one on the Left seemed to doubt that the ratio of police agents to non-police agents among the Autonomes is very high. The group was viewed on the French Left in a similar fashion to the way that the National Caucus of Labor Committees (NCLC), which also launched violent attacks on left-wing groups while claiming to he one, was viewed by the Left in the United States.

54 Alain Krivine, *La Farce électorale* (Paris: Editions du Seuil, 1969), p. 39.

55 The voting age had not yet been reduced to 18, something which certainly worked to the disadvantage of Krivine.

56 Fidler, "The Antimilitarist Battle," p. 1068.

57 Ibid.

58 Ibid., pp. 1068-1069.

59 Dick Fidler, "Krivine Campaigns for Revolutionary Alternative," *Intercontinental Press* 12, no.17 (May 6, 1974), pp. 535-536.

60 "Krivine's Assessment: The 'Allende of France,'" *Intercontinental Press* 12, no. 19 (May 20, 1974), pp. 633-634.

61 The reasons that Pablo, who served as General Secretary of the Fourth International from 1942 to 1961, gives for his expulsion are: (1) he took a harder line on Maoism, arguing that it contained too many Stalinist conceptions, than his comrades in the Fourth International who were considering giving the Chinese regime "critical support" in 1961, (2) he argued that the regime under Khrushchev, while still behaving in a deformed manner, was qualitatively different from that of Stalin's, and (3) he, like Ben Bella, supported the Popular Movement for the Liberation of Angola (MPLA) while his comrades supported Holden Roberto's Front for the National Liberation of Angola (FNLA) back in the early and mid-1960s. Interview with Michel Raptis, June 15, 1978.

62 On June 9 1978 I attended a "mass meeting" called by the OCI in Paris (about 40 per cent of its membership is in the Paris region). I was surprised by the numbers of people in attendance. The OCI tally was 6,000.

63 Jean-Jacques Marie, *Le Trotskysme* (Paris: Flammarion, 1970), p. 89.

64 OCI, *Les Marxistes contre l'autogestion* (Paris: SELIO, 1974), p. 21.

65 Ibid., p. 6.

66 See Marie, *Le Trotskysme,* pp. 80-81 and 91-92, and Stéphane Just, "Defense du Trotskysme," *La Vérité,* nos. 530-531 (septembre 1965), pp. 30-43.

67 Claude Chisserey, "La continuité dans le changement: les zigzags centristes de la Ligue pabliste," *La Vérité,* no. 550 (octobre 1970), p. 49.

68 Krivine, *La Farce,* pp. 68-69.

69 OCI, *Quelques Enseignements,* pp. 76-78; Marie, *Le Trotskysme,* pp. 87-88; and Just, "Défense du Trotskysme," pp. 143-158.

70 Pablo responds to such charges by saying that he never held that the Third World was the ideal revolutionary arena, but that in fact that was where revolutions were being made and Trotskyists could not ignore them. Interview of June 15, 1978.

71 While only the French, German, and Mexican sections were formal members

of the International Committee, the formation of CORQI left Healy's international in very poor shape. With the Greek section being the only solid one left in the International Committee, aside from his own British section, Healy and his followers took up the cause of Colonel Qaddafi's regime in Libya, not a measure totally consistent with the former insistence upon the material prerequisites for a socialist revolution.

72 Craipeau, *Le Mouvement Trotskyste en France,* pp. 203-204 and Roland Biard, *Dictionnaire de l'Extrême Gauche de 1945 à nos jours* (Paris: Belfond, 1978), p. 254.

73 *Quatrième Internationale* 10, nos, 2-4 (fevrier-avril 1952), p. 56.

74 See my *Student Politics in France: A Study of l'Union Nationale des Étudiants de France* (New York: Basic Books, 1970).

75 *Le Monde,* 7 janvier 1971, p. 6. In 1978, *Lutte Ouvrière* was being run off at 25,000 copies per week of which approximately 10,000 were sold.

76 The OCI views the USSR as a "degenerated workers' state." It "degenerated" from an initially hopeful revolutionary start. The other Eastern European states had no such revolution from which to degenerate; hence, they are "deformed workers' states."

77 Jean-Marie Freyssat, Michel Dupré, and François Ollivier, *Ce Qu'est l'OCI* (Paris: Éditions de la Taupe Rouge, 1977), p. 138.

78 Dick Fidler, "In the Aftermath of Round Two," *Intercontinental Press* 12, no. 21 (June 3, 1974), p. 680 and Dick Fidler, "How the Far Left Met Mitterrand's Candidacy," *Intercontinental Press* 12, no. 19 (May 20 1974) p. 632.

79 Fidler, "In The Aftermath of Round Two," p. 681.

80 Fidler, "How the Far Left Met Mitterrand's Candidacy," p. 631.

81 Fidler, "In the Aftermath of Round Two," p. 681.

82 Ibid.

83 The figures are from *Les Élections législatives de mars 1978* (Paris: Le Monde Dossiers et Documents, 1978), p. 76.

94 Georges Marchais was and is the General Secretary of the French Communist Party.

85 François Mitterrand was then the First Secretary of the Socialist Party. He was first elected President of France in 1981 and re-elected in 1988.

86 "Debate in French Left: What Stand to Take Toward the Elections," *Intercontinental Press/Inprecor* 16, no. 19 (March 6, 1978), p. 280. Jacques Chirac, was then the Gaullist Mayor of Paris. He had been premier from May 1974 to August 1976, when he was replaced by Raymond Barre. He became premier again in 1986.

Chapter Three: Maoism in France

1 Bernaid Kouchner and Michel-Antoine Burnier, *La France sauvage* (Paris: Editions Publications Premières, 1970), p. 174.

2 Ibid.

3 Ibid., pp. 174-175.

4 "'La candidature Mitterrand,' extrait de 'Comment est née l'Union des Jeunesses (Marxistes-Léninistes)!,' supplement du no. 8 de *Servir le Peuple,* 15 octobre 1967, (Troisième Partie)," in Patrick Kessel, ed., *Le Mouvement "Maoïste" en France, I: textes et documents, 1963-1968* (Paris: Union Generale d'Éditions, 1972), pp. 143-144.

5 It would be most convenient just to use the initials UJC. However, this would not distinguish between the UJCML and the UJCF, another group of the Communist Party. So the initials unfortunately become long.

6 Kouchner and Burnier, *France sauvage,* p. 176.

7 Ibid., p. 177.

8 Ibid.

9 "'Arborer le drapeau rouge pour lutter contre le drapeau rouge' (juin 1967), texte interne du MCF," in Kessel, *Le Mouvement,* p. 269.

10 "'Édifions en France un Parti communiste de l'epoque de la Révolution Culturelle,' *Garde Rouge,* no. 6, mai 1967," in Kessel, *Le Mouvement,* pp. 250-257.

11 Quoted from the minutes of the Central Committee of the MCF. See "La creation du Parti Communiste Marxiste-Leniniste de France," in Kessel, *Le Mouvement,* pp. 315-316.

12 Jacques Jurquet in a political report presented to the first Congress of the PCMLF in 1968. See "'Créons le Parti Communiste de France, Parti authentiquement marxiste-léniniste, Parti de l'époque de la pensée de Mao Tsé-toung,' extrait du 'Rapport politique du camarade Jacques Jurquet presenté au Ier Congrès du PCMLF,' *l'Humanité Nouvelle,* no. 88, 8 février 1968 et no. 89, 15 février 1968," in Kessel, *Le Mouvement,* p. 328.

13 It is interesting that U.S. decision-makers made allusions to Munich and the Second World War in an attempt to sell their Vietnam war policies to the U.S. public. The younger generations of Americans could relate to this about as well as French youth could relate to the slogan of the PCMLF. Both sides could have benefitted from a lesson in Mannheim's distinction between appropriated and personally acquired memory. See Karl Mannheim, "The Problem of Generations," in his *Essays on the Sociological Problem of Knowledge* (London: Routledge and Kegan Paul, 1952), pp. 276-320.

14 "'Pour la grande alliance avec le PCMLF,' extrait de Contre l'anarchisme petit-bourgeois, édifions dans notre pays un Parti de l'époque de Mao Tsé-toung, Lyon, printemps 1968," in Kessel, *Le Mouvement,* p. 423.

15 Ibid., p. 426.

16 The role of the PCMLF is a matter of some dispute. Roland Biard writes that "During the 'events,' the PCMLF did not involve itself much. The student movement is analyzed [by the PCMLF] as a petit-bourgeois self-interested movement and, as such, only ancillary to the workers' struggles." Roland Biard, *Dictionnaire de l'Éxtrême Gauche de 1945 à nos jours* (Paris: Belfond, 1978), p. 270. Richard Johnson lumps the attitudes of the UJCML and the PCMLF together. "The official Maoist party, the PCMLF was equally displeased with the spontaneous tactics of the students....The UJCML and the PCMLF refused to enter the student struggle because (1) petit-bourgeois

revolts were inevitably 'pseudo-revolutionary;' (2) insurrectionary activity was inappropriate at that particular strategic stage; and (3) when violence is used, it has to be conscious, controlled, and directed." Richard Johnson, *The French Communist Party versus the Students* (New Haven: Yale University Press, 1972), pp. 165-166. While no one would argue that the PCMLF was as integral to the fight on the barricades as JCR students, the PCMLF supported the students before and after that night. On May 6, the PCMLF's Central Committee stated that "the student revolutionaries must resolutely rejoin the combat of the working class and place themselves under its political direction. The students struggling against the monopolies will only be able to win under that condition. That is why the militants of the Parti Communiste Marxiste-Léniniste de France are participating elbow to elbow in the student demonstrations and why they are fighting resolutely at the students' sides against the government of the monopolies." The day after the Night of the Barricades, on May 11, the Central Committee issued a supportive statement which contained the following: "The heroic struggle of the students which unfurled with a violent force demands the admiration of the French people. In the night of the 10th to the 11th of May 1968 in particular, Parisian students joined by numerous workers fought back against the violent repression of the reactionary forces with courage and determination....The Marxists-Leninists of the Parti Communiste Marxiste-Léniniste de France have confidence in the youth and are participating in all its revolutionary actions." Jacques Jurquet, ed., *Arracher la Classe ouvrière au révisionnisme* (Paris: Centenaire, 1976), pp. 273-275. A leader of the PCMLF whom I interviewed told me that, although it was before he had become a formal member, he was on the barricades and there were others that he knew of. The evidence is that while the PCMLF certainly felt that spontaneous activity had its limitations, it did not take the negative attitude toward the students taken by the Communist Party, the Lambertist Trotskyists of the OCI, or the Maoist UJCML.

17 One Maoist group has come up with a count of 21 hierarchical and non-hierarchical Maoist organizations in France as of the summer of 1977. Not all were national groups, some were confined to one city or region, most were tiny. "Les Marxistes-Léninistes en France aujourd'hui," *Le Marxiste-Léniniste,* double issue, no. 18/19 (juillet-août 1977), p. 19. This is a publication of the UCFML which will be discussed shortly.

18 Precise numbers are difficult to come by in the case of the Maoists since they have not divulged current membership figures the way some Trotskyist organizations have. The PCR (m-l), the PCMLF's major hierarchical Maoist rival, which will be discussed shortly, claimed to have brought together 3,000 people at the meetings in which it prepared the transition to a party. Alain Jauber et al., *Guide de la France des luttes* (Paris: Stock, 1974), p. 294. In 1970, Kouchner and Burnier contended that *l'Humanité Rouge* "grouped several thousand sympathizers" (p. 182). Since the party had been banned, there were technically no members—at least none that could be admitted to. Biard places the number at between 2,000 and 3,000 in 1970

and, after the 1971-76 decline, thought that the party regained its 1970 membership level by 1978 (p. 272).

19 The PCMLF's daily was *l'Humanité Rouge* and the PCR(m-l)'s was *Le Quotidien du Peuple* (*The People's Daily*). They were both much thinner and less substantial efforts than the Ligue's *Rouge*. They were also not distributed on newsstands as was *Rouge*. Only approximately 2,000 of the 15,000 *l'Humanité Rouge* run off each day were actually sold.

20 The self-criticism only became "official" at the Third Congress of the PCMLF which was held just before the legislative elections of 1978.

21 This is the position of the French Trotskyist OCI.

22 "Resolutions du 3e congrès du Parti Communiste Marxiste-Léniniste de France: autocritique du PCMLF concernant son 2e congrès," *l'Humanité Rouge,* no. 25 (16 fevrier-2 mars 1978), pp. 13-14. This is a special supplementary issue to the daily paper.

23 A Maoist group based in Brittany, the Organisation Communiste Française (marxiste-léniniste), ran candidates in Rennes during the 1977 municipal elections.

24 "Les voix de l'UOPDP: un potentiel pour l'action," *l'Humanité Rouge,* no. 27 (16 mars-13 avril 1978), p 8. This is also a special supplementary issue to the daily paper.

25 PCR(m-l), "A propos de la Théorie des 3 Mondes," *Front Rouge,* n.s., no. 2 (novembre-décembre1977), pp. 7-8. Very interestingly, this article terminates with a summary defense of the theory, "up to the point that we have examined it" (p. 10). More was promised on the theory, particularly its meaning for the First and Second Worlds. Six months later, as of the end of May 1978, the next number of their theoretical journal, *Front Rouge,* with the promised continuation of the discussion, had not appeared.

26 See PCR(m-l), *Programme et statuts* (Paris: PCR(m-I), 1976), pp. 37-38 and Biard, *Dictionnaire,* pp. 273-274.

27 Interview with a PCMLF leader, June 8, 1978.

28 Ibid.

29 "Les Marxistes-Léninistes en France aujourd'hui," p. 20.

30 Its own account of this year is in UCFML, *Première Année d'existence d'une organisation maoïste* (Paris: Maspero, 1972).

31 UCFML, *Une Étude Maoïste: la situation on Chine et le mouvement dit de "critique de la bande des Quatre,"* (Paris: Éditions Potemkine, 1977).

32 Kouchner and Burnier, *France sauvage,* pp. 187 and 159.

33 Ibid., p. 187.

34 Remi Hess, *Les Maoïstes Français* (Paris: Anthropos, 1974), p. 151. See Henri Lefebvre, *Everyday Life in the Modern World,* trans. Sacha Rabinovitch (New York: Harper and Row, 1971).

35 *Tout* was usually printed at the rate of 50,000 copies per issue. One issue was run off at 80,000. Hess, *Maoïstes,* p. 160.

36 Hess, *Maoïstes,* pp. 163-167. Sartre would later agree to serve as nominal editior of *La Cause du Peuple* and *Libération* as well.

37 Hess, *Maoïstes,* p. 167.

38 Michèle Manceaux, *Les Maos en France* (Paris: Gallimard, 1972), p. 201.

39 Ibid., p. 203.

40 Ibid.

41 *Minutes du procès d'Alain Geismar* (Paris: Éditions Hallier, n.d.), p. 24.

42 See my *Student Politics in France* (New York: Basic Books, 1970), chapter 3.

43 *Minutes du procès d'Alain Geismar,* p. 149.

44 Ibid., p. 150.

45 For much supporting data for this argument in the U.S. experience, see Sidney Lens, *Radicalism in America* (New York: Apollo Editions, 1966).

46 Manceaux, *Les Maos,* pp. 211-212.

47 Ibid., p. 65-66.

48 Kenneth Keniston, *Young Radicals* (New York: Harcourt, Brace, and World, 1968), p. 217.

49 Manceaux, *Les Maos,* p. 94.

50 Julia Lesage, "*Tout Va Bien* and *Coup pour Coup*: Radical French Cinema in Context," *Cinéaste* 5, no. 3 (Summer 1972), p. 45. *Tout Va Bien* stars Jane Fonda and Yvès Montand. Paramount, which had originally contracted for the film, refused to distribute it for obviously political reasons. The attraction which this brand of Maoism held for people involved with the cinema is also attested to by the fact that two French journals of film criticism, *Cahiers du Cinéma* and *Cinéthique,* adopted Maoist perspectives, with *Cahiers* turning itself into a Maoist writing collective (Lesage, p. 43).

51 The number of disputes in industrial settings increased from 2,942 in 1970 to 4,318 in 1971 and the number of working days lost due to industrial conflict increased from 1,742,175 to 4,387,781. *Yearbook of Labour Statistics* (Geneva: International Labor Organization, 1976), p. 831.

52 *Pour l'Union des comités de lutte d'atelier, Renault-Billancourt: 25 règles de travail* (Paris: Éditions Liberté-Presse, supplement à *La Cause du Peuple,* no. 11, 1971), p. 31.

53 UCFML, *A Propos du Meurtre de Pierre Overney* (Paris: Maspero, 1972), pp. 13 and 18.

54 Signoret apparently brought some other prominent people along with her on some of her visits. Someone whom she did not bring was her husband, Yves Montand. At the time Montand was occupied making the Godard and Gorin film *Tout Va Bien* with Jane Fonda. See Jean-Pierre Le Dantec (the former CDP editor who made contact with Signoret), *Les Dangers du soleil* (Paris: Les Presses d'Aujourd'hui, 1978), pp. 239-240.

55 *La Cause du Peuple,* no. 20 (11 mars 1972), p. 4. Only a small portion of the workers who worked near windows which overlooked the gate knew what had happened. The word spread to a limited extent right after the event and the CDP claimed that between 1,000 and 1,500 workers participated in a demonstration of sorrow within the plant.

56 The first demonstration in response to the killing was held on February 28. *Le Monde* estimated the number of participants at 30,000. The same paper estimated that approximately 120,000 people participated in Overney's

funeral procession on March 4. *Le Monde,* 7 mars 1972, p. 8. *La Cause du Peuple* estimated the latter at 250,000. I witnessed all of the major demonstrations in Paris between July 1963 and January 1965 and the second wave of demonstrations from June 10 to July 10 in 1968. The funeral procession was the largest demonstration that I have seen in Paris.

57 *La Cause du Peuple,* no. 20 (11 mars 1972), p. 10.

58 For more on that rent strike, see my "The Battle of SONACOTRA: A Study of an Immigrant Worker Struggle in France," *New Political Science* 3, no. 1/2 (Summer/ Pall 1982), pp. 93-112.

59 Centre d'Action Paysanne, *Où En Sont les Paysans?* (Paris: Éditions Liberté-Presse, 1971), pp. 20-21.

60 "Occitanie: 'des luttes paysannes à la révolte d'un peuple,'" *Les Temps Modernes,* no. 310 Bis (1972), p. 169.

61 Centre d'Action Paysanne, *Où En Sont les Paysans?,* pp. 6-7. (Italics in the text).

62 The figures are from *Le Monde,* 21 mars 1972, p. 32.

63 *Les Prisonniers politiques parlent: le combat des détenus politiques* (Paris: Maspero, 1970), pp. 28-29.

64 Geismar told this author that he spent five of his eighteen months in prison in solitary confinement.

65 *Les Prisonniers politiques parlent,* pp. 12-13.

66 The December 9, 1971 and January 15, 1972 issues of *La Cause du Peuple* carried informational and supportive articles on revolts in the prisons of Toul, Nancy, Nîmes, Amiens, Loos, Fleury, and Ré.

67 Hess, *Maoïstes,* p. 219. Hess reports that the CDP was not as straightforward as VLR's paper *Tout* was in its attack on this policy, and sometimes even tried to justify it. This conforms to Sartre's reflections on his relations with the GP Maoists in 1972. After criticizing Chinese foreign policy in Ceylon, Bangladesh, and Pakistan, as well as China's reception of President Nixon, Sartre remarked that the GP Maoists "would not like what I say about China's foreign policy." See Pierre Bénichou, "What's Jean-Paul Sartre Thinking Lately? An Interview," *Esquire* 68, no. 6 (December 1972), pp. 208 and 280.

68 Interview of May 27, 1975.

69 In fact, Mendes-France did indeed give every appearance that he was available to assume the reins of power by appearing before a massive crowd at the Charléty Stadium on the evening of May 27.

70 At the time, the student group of the Lambertist Trotskyists in the OCI wasattempting to take over UNEF, something which it subsequently succeeded in doing. PSU students controlled the national offices and the JCR allied with them to prevent the Lambertists, who had opposed the barricades in May for the same reasons as the UJCML, from taking control in 1968. It is also interesting to note that Pierre Victor, in a disagreement with Sartre, attempted to defend Geismar's participation in the attempt to convince Lip strike leader Piaget to run as a candidate for the Presidency in 1974 by arguing that it was a farce since Piaget would have had no chance of

winning. It was thus presumably still within the realm of *liberté-révolte* rather than *liberté-pouvoir*. See Philippe Gavi, Jean-Paul Sartre, and Pierre Victor, *On a Raison de se révolter* (Paris: Gallimard, 1974), Conclusion.

71 Alain Geismar, Serge July, and Erlyn Morane, *Vers la Guerre civile* (Paris: Éditions et Publications Premières, 1969), p. 371.

72 For a retrospective self-criticism of this shortcoming by a former male leader, see Le Dantec, *Dangers* pp. 213 and 234-235.

73 It is true that in *The German Ideology* Marx and Engels write: "Division of labor becomes truly such only from the moment when a division of material and mental labor appears." Lewis S. Feuer, ed., *Marx and Engels: Basic Writings on Politics and Philosophy* (Garden City: Anchor Books,1959), p. 252. However, Engels was prompted to push further into a detailed analysis of the sexual dimension in *The Origin of the Family, Private Property and the State*.

74 Geismar, July, and Morane, *Guerre civile,* p. 379.

75 Philippe Olivier, "Après la Bataille de Renault," *Les Temps Modernes* no. 310 Bis (1972) p. 29.

76 Philippe Olivier, "Syndicats, comité de lutte, comités de chaine," *Les Temps Modernes,* no. 310 Bis (1972), p. 46.

77 See Jacques Ellul, *The Technological Society,* trans. John Wilkinson (New York: Vintage, 1964) and Theodore Roszak, *The Making of a Counter Culture* (Garden City: Anchor, 1968).

78 Gavi, Sartre, and Victor, *On a Raison de se révolter,* chapters 14, 15, and 16.

79 *La Cause du Peuple,* no. 15 (mai-juin 1977), p. 3.

80 Former CDP editor Dantec does, however, think that the GP through its writings and actions in the earlier part of the decade had an unfortunate influence upon later German and Italian terrorist groups. He also criticized the killing of Tramoni and the new group of people putting out *La Cause du Peuple* for supporting the act. Le Dantec, *Dangers,* pp. 246-248.

81 In 1971, the year prior to the appearance of *Libération,* ex-GP Maoists worked with others in the production of a publication called *J'Accuse! Libération* grew out of that experiment.

82 Hess, *Maoïstes,* pp. 177-181.

83 See André Glucksmann, *Les Maîtres Penseurs* (Paris: Grasset, 1977) and *La Cuisinière et le mangeur d'hommes* (Paris: Seuil, 1975) and Michel Le Bris, *L'Homme aux semelles de vent* (Paris: Grasset, 1977). Both writers have been heavily influenced by the late French thinker Michel Foucault.

Chapter Four: Trotskyism in the United States

1 See Leon Trotsky, *The Draft Program of the Communist International: A Criticism of Fundamentals in The Third International after Lenin* (New York: Pathfinder Press, 1970).

2 James P. Cannon, *The History of American Trotskyism* (New York: Pathfinder Press, 1972), p. 29.

3 His successor was Meany's son-in-law.

4 Cannon, *American Trotskyism*, p. 78.

5 Ibid., pp. 82-84.

6 See the books by a key actor in the Teamster Strike, Farrell Dobbs: *Teamster Rebellion* (New York: Monad Press, 1972) and *Teamster Power* (New York: Monad Press, 1973).

7 Max Shachtman, "Radicalism in the Thirties: The Trotskyist View," in Rita James Simon, ed., *As We Saw the Thirties* (Urbana: University of Illinois Press, 1967), p. 43.

8 Cannon, *American Trotskyism*, pp. 210-211.

9 Cannon claims that the meeting which Professor Hook arranged between the Trotskyists and Norman Thomas, the leader of the Socialist Party, was "the last progressive act in the life and career of Sidney Hook." Ibid., p. 226. The culmination of the episode was not designed to endear James Cannon to Professor Hook.

10 Ibid., p. 252.

11 Shachtman, "Radicallsm," pp. 22 and 30.

12 Cannon, *American Trotskyism*, pp. 252-253

13 A. J. Muste, "My Experience in the Labor and Radical Struggles of the Thirties," in Simon, *As We Saw the Thirties*, p. 141.

14 Ibid.

15 Ibid., p. 142.

16 Ibid., p. 146.

17 Ibid., p. 140.

18 Ibid., p. 143.

19 "The War and Bureaucratic Conservatism" is reprinted in the Appendix of James P. Cannon, *The Struggle for a Proletarian Party* (New York: Pathfinder Press, 1970), pp. 257-293.

20 Leon Trotsky, "A Petty Bourgeois Opposition in the Socialist Workers Party," in Leon Trotsky, *In Defense of Marxism* (New York: Pathfinder Press, 1973), p. 52.

21 Leon Trotsky, "An Open Letter to Comrade Burnham," in Trotsky, *In Defense of Marxism*, pp. 72-94.

22 James Burnham, "Science and Style: A Reply to Comrade Trotsky," in Trotsky, *In Defense of Marxism*, p. 196.

23 Ibid., p. 203.

24 Ibid., p. 205.

25 Ibid., p. 204.

26 James Burnham, "Letter of Resignation of James Burnham from the Workers Party," in Trotsky, *In Defense of Marxism*, pp. 207-211.

27 George Novack and Joseph Hansen, "Introduction," in Trotsky, *In Defense of Marxism*, p. xix.

28 Ibid., p. xix.

29 International Socialists, "What We Stand For," *Workers' Power*, no. 122 (June 5-18, 1975), p. 14.

30 Independert Socialist Clubs of America, "Program in Brief," *Independent*

Socialist, no. 12 (September 1969), p. 19.

31 Joseph Hansen, *The Abern Clique,* Education for Socialists Series (New York: National Education Department, Socialist Workers Party, September 1972), p. 5.

32 George Novack, "Introduction," in James P Cannon, *Socialism on Trial* (New York: Pathfinder Press, 1970), p. 9. This book contains the entire testimony of Cannon, who was the major defense witness. It is a crucial document for those who wish to fully appreciate the nature of the repression. Cannon's *Letters from Prison* (New York: Pathfinder Press, 1973) is also of interest.

33 Novack, "Introduction," p. 9.

34 Ibid., p. 10.

35 Ibid., p. 9.

36 As we shall see, the first effort proved to be a long-term one, while the latter was fairly well accomplished with the passage and application of the Taft-Hartley Act after the war. Those trade union officers who did not tow the line were forcefully ejected from most unions by a combined alliance of labor leaders tied to the Democratic Party and the political leadership of Democratic national adminstrations. And they did not hesitate to use repressive legislation which they could always rely upon overtly conservative Republicans and Southern Democrats to produce. This may have saved them some embarrassment since, after all, they were liberals.

37 Al Hansen, "Introduction," in James P Cannon, *Speeches to the Party,* (New York: Pathfinder Press, 1973), pp. 15-18.

38 "The Roots of the Party Crisis," reprinted in Cannon, *Speeches to the Party,* p. 351.

39 Ibid., p. 372.

40 Ibid., p. 352.

41 Al Hansen, "Introduction," pp. 19-20.

42 Spartacist League, *Cuba and Marxist Theory,* Marxist Bulletin No. 8 (New York: Spartacist, n.d.), p. 5.

43 See Spartacist League, *Wohlforth Against the R.T,* Marxist Bulletin No. 3, Part 2 (New York: Spartacist, n.d.), p. vi.

44 Ibid. The Spartacist view of the split within the Minority Tendency and their expulsion is presented in Spartacist League, *The Split in the Revolutionary Tendency,* Marxist Bulletin No. 3, Part 1 (New York: Spartacist, n.d.).

45 No relation to the author.

46 For more details on the Wohlforth purging and reentry into the SWP, see Nelson Blackstock, "A New Look at the Socialist Workers Party," *The Militant* 40, no. 18 (May 7, 1976), pp. 16-20. In 1977, Healy and the Workers League were to accuse the SWP's Joseph Hansen and George Novack of being KGB agents. Hansen was also accused of collusion with the FBI.

47 Tim Wohlforth, *Revisionism in Crisis* (New York: Labor Publications, Inc., 1972), p. 49.

48 Spartacist League, *Cuba and Marxist Theory*, p. 2.

49 Wohlforth, *Revisionsim*, pp. 48-49.

50 Robert J. Alexander, *Trotskyism in Latin America* (Stanford: Hoover Institution Press, 1973), p. 30. Alexander contended that, as of his writing, Healy's was the only Trotskyist group in the world able to sustain a daily newspaper.

51 Sam Marcy, *The Class Character of the USSR: An Answer to the False Theory of Soviet Social-Imperialism* (New York: World View Publishers, 1977), p. 26.

52 Ibid., p. 16. Also see Workers World Party, *Czechoslovakia, 1968: The Class Character of the Events* (New York: World View Publishers, 1978), p. 2.

53 Leon Trotsky, *The Transitional Program*, in Leon Trotsky, *The Transitional Program for Socialist Revolution*, 2d ed. (New York: Pathfinder Press, 1974), p. 110.

54 Kirkpatrick Sale, *sds* (New York: Vintage Books, 1974), p. 622. The concept of "membership" here should be viewed with caution. The SMC was a loose structure.

55 In 1974 age data were available for the 1974 Illinois slate of SWP candidates, as well as for national SWP leaders. The ages of the candidates in the state of Illinois were: senatorial candidate, 31 (White, male); 1st congressional district for the House of Representatives, 35 (Black, female); candidate for state treasurer, 27 (White, female); three candidates for the University of Illinois Board of Trustees: 25 (Chicano, male), 22 (White, male), 20 (White, female).

In the brochure describing the speakers which the SWP sent around the country to present its positions in 1974, 21 of the 36 descriptions contained an age or year of birth. Among these 21 activists, the average age was 32 and the median age 28. Broken down further by cohorts: six were from 21 to 25 years old, eight were from 26 to 30 years old, three were from 31 to 34 years old, one was 38, one was 41, one was 61, and one was 70.

At the very top level of the SWP in 1976, Jack Barnes, the National Secretary, was 35 and had been in office for four years; Barry Sheppard, the National Organizational Secretary, was 38; and Betsey Stone, the National Field Secretary, was 36.

56 *International Socialist Review* 35, no. 10 (November 1974), p. 3.

57 See Cathy Perkus, ed., *COINTELPRO: The FBI's Secret War on Political Freedom* (New York: Monad Press, 1975).

58 See Jack Barnes et al., *Prospects for Socialism in America* (New York: Pathfinder Press, 1976), passim.

59 Ibid., pp. 258-259.

60 Ibid., pp. 240-241.

61 Members who receive inheritances are expected to share these with the party as well.

62 See "New Supplement" in *The Militant* 39, no. 12 (April 4, 1975), p. 10.

63 It must he kept in mind that these are differences within the Trotskyist category. The most action-oriented Trotskyist organization is more theoretical than most groups on the Far Left.

64 Trotsky, *The Transitional Program,* pp. 74 i5.

65 Ibid., p. 75.

66 See "Discussons with Leon Trotsky," in Trotsky, *Transitional Program for Socialist Revolution,* pp. 113-161 and Trotsky, "The Problems of the Labor Party," Ibid., pp. 241-243.

67 SWP, "A Strategy for Revolutionary Youth," in Trotsky, *Transitional Program for Socialist Revolution,* p. 182. Also see Ernest Mandel, *The Revolutionary Student Movement: Theory and Practice* (New York: Young Socialist Rablications, 1969) and the essays and reports on the radicalization of youth, women, and minorities in Jack Barnes el al., *Towards an American Socialist Revolution: A Strategy for the 1970s* (New York: Pathfinder Press, 1971).

68 The following "suggestions for students in orienting their actions" are included in the "democratic and transitional demands:" "I) A university education for everyone who wants one, the full expense to be underwritten by the government; 2) No maximum age limit on free education; no limitation on the number of years a person may continue in school, or resume school after dropping out, post-graduate studies included; 3) Decent housing for students; 4) An annual salary for all students adequate to their needs and safeguarded against inflation by automatic compensating increases; 5) Guaranteed jobs for students upon graduation."

In the area of student control over their own education: "I) Abolish government-controlled student organizations. Recognize the rights of students to organize and govern themselves according to their own free choice; 2) Joint control by students and faculty over the hiring and firing of faculty members and administrative officials; 3) Let the students themselves democratically decide what subjects should be taught; 4) Abolish the power of professors and administrators to arbitrarily penalize students; 5) Freedom of political association for students and professors; 6) The right to utilize university facilities to promote educational and cultural activities of direct interest to organizations of the working class, peasants, oppressed nationalities and plebian masses."

These two series of demands are followed by a number of others that link the condition of students and the operations of universities with the society at large. See SWP, "A Strategy for Revolutionary Youth," pp. 195-200.

69 SWP, "A Transitional Program for Black Liberation," in Trotsky, *Transitional Program for Socialist Revolution,* pp. 162-180.

70 Derrick Morrison, "The Combined Character of the Coming American Revolution," in Barnes et al., *Towards an American Socialist Revolution,* pp. 60-61.

71 On the position of the Spartacist League, see *Basic Documents of the Spartacist League:* Part H, Marxist Bulletin No. 9 (New York: Spartacist,

1973), pp. 18-24. On the position of the Workers League, see Tim Wohlforth, *The New Nationalism and the Negro Struggle* (New York: Bulletin Publications, 1969).

72 Spark, "The Black Revolt in the USA: A Hope for All Humanity," mimeographed, n.d., p. 7. While Spark advocates such separatism in the United States, it shares Lutte Ouvrière's characterizations of Third World nationalistic revolutions, as well as French regional struggles, as "petit-bourgeois ideological radicalism."

73 Joseph Hansen, *Cuban Question: Report for the Political Committee,* Education for Socialists Series (New York: National Education Department, Socialist Workers Party, April 1968), p. 16.

74 Ibid., p. 12-13.

75 "Draft Theses on the Cuban Revolution" in Hansen, *Cuban,* p. 3.

76 Harry Ring, *Cuba and Problems of Workers' Democracy* (New York: Pathfinder Press, 1972), p. 14.

77 Ibid., p. 15.

78 Ibid.

79 "The World Situation and the Immediate Tasks of the Fourth International," *Intercontinental Press* 12, no. 46 (December 23, 1974), p. 1753.

80 See Chapter 2.

81 George Johnson and Fred Feldman, "Vietnam, Stalinism, and the Postwar Socialist Revolutions," *International Socialist Review* 35, no. 4 (April 1974), p. 40.

82 Ibid p 35

83 Ibid. p. 31.

84 Ibid.

85 Louis Couturier, "The Vietnamese Communist Party and Its Leadership," *International Socialist Review* 36, no. 2 (February 1975), p. 30.

86 Ibid., p. 34.

87 Cannon, *Socialism on Trial,* p. 37.

88 Ibid., p. 40

89 Ibid. p. 41.

90 "Vote Returns for SWP, Raza Unida Party," *The Militant* 38, no. 44 (November 22, 1974), p. 4.

91 It also initially refused to permit the Communist Party to appear on the ballot. In 1972, the SWP was kept off of the ballot because Jenness was not old enough to be president and without her the SWP did not meet the full slate requirement. After litigation, the Communist Party succeeded in gaining ballot status in Illinois.

92 *Vote Socialist Workers in '74,* electoral platform of the Illinois SWP.

93 Ibid., p. 3.

94 Ibid.

95 Ibid.

96 SWP, *The Socialist Workers Party Proposes: A Bill of Rights for Working People* (New York: Socialist Workers 1976 National Campaign Committee, 1976).

97 Lucy Burton, "Committee Puts SWP on Ballot in 28 States," *The Militant* 40, no. 41 (October 29, 1976), p.19.

98 Ibid.

99 Cindy Jacquith, "Massive Illegal Campaign: FBI 'Disruption' Files Made Public," *The Militant* 39, no. 11 (March 28, 1975), p. 3. It is in this issue that the SWP began printing the FBI documents.

100 The phrasing, of course, is ridiculous. The SWP obviously does not direct or support such causes as "integration problems arising in the South." It supports school integration and the respecting of civil rights of people, regardless of their race.

101 This is also inaccurate. The SWP, like any other Trotskyist group, has international contacts with Trotskyists of the same tendency. An accurate statement is that it does not formally join any international organization as this is forbidden by U.S. law.

102 Nelson Blackstock, "The COINTELPRO Papers (Part III): Sabotage of Socialist Election Campaigns," *The Militant* 39, no. 13 (April 11, 1975), p. 16.

103 Ibid., p. 17.

104 Ibid.

105 In 1974, the YSA attempted to get a court injunction against FBI surveillance of its National Convention in St. Louis. The Justice Department defended surveillance on the basis of "national security." The Federal Court refused the injunction so the Convention was convened with the knowledge that there were FBI agents in the midst of the participants.

106 Blackstock, "The COINTELPRO Papers (Part III)," p. 17.

107 Ibid.

108 Ibid.

109 This affair originally began when two little Black boys, aged 8 and 10, were convicted of "assault upon a white female" after they had kissed a playmate. A number of people defending the boys were then themselves charged with kidnapping a white couple. It was a result of this charge that one of the boy's defenders, Robert Williams, fled to Cuba. See Nelson Blackstock, "The COINTELPRO Papers (Part II): FBI's Attempt to Destroy Black Mov't," *The Militant* 39, no.12 (April 4, 1975), p. 25.

110 Ibid.

111 Cindy Jaquith, "Drive to Sabotage De Barry Campaign, FBI Target: Black Presidential Nominee," *The Militant* 39, no. II (March 28, 1975), p. 4.

112 Nelson Blackstock, "The COINTELPRO Papers (Part I): Red-Baiting and Disruption in the Left," *The Militant* 39, no. II (March 28, 1975), p. 6.

113 From a photocopy of the original FBI document.

114 From a photocopy of the original FBI document.

115 The author has seen photocopies of the originals of both of these communications.

116 Taken from a photocopy of the original letter submitted by FBI Phoenix to Washington for approval.

117 Blackstock, "The COINTELPRO Papers (Part III)," p. 17.

118 Blackstock, "The COINTELPRO Papers (Part I)," p. 6. For the uninitiated, "balling" means to have sexual intercourse.

119 Ibid.

120 Larry Green and Rob Warren, "Socialist Office Here Was Looted," *The Chicago Daily News*, 24 March 1975, pp. 1, 12.

121 "Charge Army Aided Illinois Terror Group," *The Chicago Daily News*, 14 April 1975, pp. 1, 2.

122 Ibid.

123 Stu Singer, "Peter Camejo Arrested and Threatened by Houston Cops," *The Militant* 39, no. 10 (March 21, 1975), p. II.

124 Ibid.

125 These two incidents were related to the author by Camejo himself in August 1975.

126 These tactics used against the Left and antiwar groups were even devouring members of the establishment at the local levels of government. Mayor Daley apparently decided, like Nixon, that if these tactics work against the Left and anti-war groups, they should also work against his opponents in the city council and elsewhere in government. Seven aldermen were thus spied upon by Chicago police. Ironically, States Attorney Bernard Carey, who presented much of the information revealed by *The Chicago Daily News* to a grand jury, was also one of those kept under surveillance. See *The Chicago Daily News*, 27 March 1975, pp. 1, 12; 29 March 1975, p. 1; 9 April 1975, pp. 1, 23. Later, of course, it was revealed that the FBI itself was breaking into SWP offices and that the Central Intelligence Agency was also conducting a surveillance program against the SWP.

Chapter Five: Maoism in the United States

1 Kirkpatrick Sale, *sds* (New York: Vintage Books, 1974), p. 64.

2 For an SWP criticism of Progressive Labor, see Mary-Alice Waters, *Maoism in the U.S.: A Critical History of the Progressive Labor Party* (New York: Young Socialist Publications, 1969).

3 Sale, *sds*, pp. 218-219.

4 Ibid., p. 292.

5 After this was written, Davidson confided to the author that he had gotten the idea from the Quebec student movement.

6 Both this and the revised "Road to Revolution–II" have been published in Progressive Labor Party, *Revolution Today: U.S.A., A Look at the Progressive Labor Movement and the Progressive Labor Party* (New York: Exposition Press, 1970).

7 Sale, *sds*, p. 332.

8 "Improve Our Base Building," cited in *Revolution Today*, p. 72.

9 "Black Workers: Key Revolutionary Force, February 1969," in *Revolution Today*, pp. 268-278 and "U.S. Workers: Key to Revolution, August 1969," Ibid., pp. 322-325 and 343.

10 "The Future is Bright, June 1970," in *Revolution Today*, p. 347.

11 The breakdown given by the PLP of purchasers of a single issue of *Challenge-Desafío* in 1970 is as follows: "workers on the job"—53,000; "in working-class neighhorhoods"—14,000; "students"—12,000; "GI's"— 2,000; "high schools"—3,000; "professionals"—2,000; "subscriptions"— 1,000; "at rallies"—4,000; "in Puerto Rico"—5,000; "Canada and other foreign"—4,000. Total: 100,000. Printed on the last page of *Revolution Today.* If these figures are correct, they must represent the world record for a Far Left publication. A 20,000 to 30,000 circulation is quite good.

12 Sale, *sds,* p. 358.

13 Ibid., p. 397.

14 Ibid.

15 Ibid., p. 465.

16 Ibid pp 450-451.

17 Ibid., pp. 475-476.

18 The NCLC was extremely anti-Soviet; it denounced the Black Panthers; and it supported Albert Shanker's New York chapter of the American Federation of Teachers against community control of the schools. In 1973, it announced a campaign to physically annihilate the Communist Party of the United States. In fact, it conducted violent raids against other groups on the Left as well, including the SWP. At this point suspicion began to develop on the Left that it was a government or business-supported group. After a couple of months, it announced that it had succeeded in annihilating the American Communist Party and it attempted to make contact with groups in Europe (including the French OCI) to accomplish the same there. On August 15, 1973, it held a meeting of the "International Caucus of Labor Committees" in Stockholm. In 1976, it created an electoral arm, the U.S. Labor Party. It was able to afford prime national television time for its presidential candidate, Lyndon LaRouche. It has also been able to afford to publish its newspaper, New Solidarity, in nine different languages and to distribute it abroad. It is scientific and technological in orientation and is a staunch opponent of the anti-nuclear power movement. The SWP has accused its members of acting as police informants and provocateurs against that movement.

19 Sale, *sds,* p. 486.

20 "Report Opening the PLP Pre-Convention Discussion, March 1968," in *Revolution Today,* pp. 18-19.

21 "Program for Black Liberation, February 1969," in *Revolution Today,* p. 265.

22 "Revolutionaries Must Fight Nationalism, August 1969," in *Revolution Today,* pp. 288-289.

23 Ibid. pp. 293-294.

24 Sale, *sds,* pp. 508-510.

25 The best source known to this writer on the 1969 convention is Sale's *sds.* All of the material on the convention prior to RYM's walking out is based on chapter 24 of Sale's book. This writer got to the convention only after the walk-out had taken place. It should also be noted that Carl Davidson is

now in the process of writing a book on the SDS experience which will differ in some important respects from Sale's interpretation.

26 Sale, *sds,* p. 567.

27 Cited in Sale, *sds,* pp. 568-569.

28 Sale, *sds,* p. 570.

29 Ibid.

30 See Chapter 4, on the International Socialists.

31 Sale, *sds,* pp. 571-572.

32 Ibid.

33 Cited in Sale, *sds,* p. 573.

34 Pauline Mak, "Some Maoist Groups in America: Experiences of the First Decade," unpublished paper written at the University of Illinois at Urbana-Champaign, December 1973.

35 This phenomenon is absent in Trotskyism both because of its highly theoretical nature and the absence of any regimes and living or recently living who could capture the imagination of people in a variety of decentralized contexts.

36 D.B., "Marxism, Nationalism and the Task of Party Building: History and Lessons of the National Liaison Committee," *The Communist* 2, no. 1 (Fall/Winter 1977), p. 124.

37 Ibid.

38 Amiri Baraka, "Radical Forum," *Guardian* 27, no. 21 (March 5, 1975), p. 17.

39 Sherman Miller, "'Revolutionary Wing' or Anti-Party Bloc?," *Class Struggle,* nos. 4-5 (Spring/Summer 1976), p. 7.

40 Ibid.

41 See I Wor Kuen, "Criticisms of Workers Viewpoint Organization on Party Building," *I.W.K. Journal,* no. 3 (January 1976), pp. 38-78. Workers Viewpoint Organization later changed its name to the Communist Workers Party. It conducted a militant anti-Ku Klux Klan campaign in the South. On November 3, 1979 national attention was focused on the organization when five of its members were shot to death during an anti-Klan rally in a low income housing project in Greensboro, North Carolina. A number of Klansmen and U.S. Nazis were arrested and charged with the crime.

42 The Next 25: Yesterday, Today, and Tomorrow," *Guardian* 26, no. 7 (November 28, 1973), p. 10.

43 Ibid.

44 Irwin Silber, " 'Revolution' Polemic Deceives No One," *Guardian* 27, no. 23 (March 10, 1975), p. 9.

45 See pp. 218-22.

46 *Guardian* Staff, "On Building a New Communist Party," *Guardian,* special supplement, 29, no. 34 (June 1, 1977), pp. S1-8.

47 Jim O'Brien, "American Leninism in the 1970s," *Radical America,* special double issue, 11, no. 6 and 12, no. I (Winter 1977-78), p. 55.

48 Ibid.

49 From October 1976 through October 1977, the *Guardian* printed an average

of 21,712 copies of each issue and actually distributed an average of 20,562. "Statement of Ownership, Management, and Circulation," *Guardian* 30, no. 1 (October 12, 1977), p. 20.

50 On the history of the National Liaison Committee from the RCP's point of view, see D.B., "Marxism."

51 *The Red Papers #6* atuempts to analyze and self-critique RU's agitation and creation of a counter-workers organization to discredit the union in the new bulk mailing centers in New York City. See RU, *The Red Papers #6: Build the Leadership of the Proletariat and Its Party* (Chicago: Revolutionary Union, 1974), pp. 122-126.

52 Ben Bendell, " 'Revolutionary Student Brigade' Formed in Iowa," *Guardian* 26, no. 38 (July 3, 1974), p. 7.

53 "Attica Brigade Seizes Statue of Liberty," *Revolution* 2, no. 4 (May 1974), p. 1.

54 Ibid.

55 The name proved to be divisive. A faction within the RCP and RSB objected to the woid "Communist" in the title, arguing that this was not the party and that the word would drive away young people whom they hoped to recruit. They argued that the name should simply be the RYB on the order of the RSB. The majority of the RCP's leadership, including Avakian, charged the dissidents with insulting American youth and with reraising a question on which they had been defeated before and during the November convention. See "Arrogant Clique Suffers Defeat: RCYB Consolidates on Correct Line," *Revolution* 3, no. 5 (February 1978), pp. 1, 18-19.

56 Ruth Gifford, "Waging Class Struggle in the Trade Unions," *Class Struggle,* no. 8 (Fall 1977), p. 65.

57 "The October League (M-L): A Cover for Revisionism," *Revolution* 2, no. 7 (August 1974), p. 12.

58 O'Brien, "American Leninism," pp. 44-45.

59 CP(ML), *Documents from the Founding Congress of the Communist Party (Marxist-Leninist)* (Chicago: CP(ML), 1977), p. 156 and RCP, *Programme and Constitation of the Revolutionary Communist Party USA* (Chicago: RCP, 1975), p. 169.

60 CP(ML), *Documents,* p. 142.

61 Ibid.

62 O'Brien estimated the RCP's membership to be "probably around 600" (p. 56) and the Workers Vanguard estimated it to be from 600 to 700 (*Workers Vanguard,* January 27, 1978, p. 1). The latter estimate, however, could have been based upon the former, which strikes this writer as a bit low. It should also be kept in mind that these estimates did not include militant members of student, worker, youth, or veteran's affiliates who were not party members. The fact is that the RCP has been one of the most successful organizations on the American Left, if not the most successful, in turning people out at a national level for its own demonstrations or founding conferences. O'Brien estimated that around 3,000 people attended the RSB national demonstration in Philadelphia in July of 1976 (p. 57), that 1,428

people atended the founding of the United Workers Organization and that approximately 650 attended the Revolutionary Communist Youth Brigade conference the following year. This, coupled with the publication of *The Worker* in approximately twenty cities, is an impressive demonstration of capability for a group on the American Left.

63 "Narrow Nationalism: Main Deviation in the Movement on the National Question," *Revolution* 2, no. 10 (November 1974), p. 22.

64 A more precise break-down of that committee is four Black males, three White males, one Asian-American woman, one Puerto Rican woman, and one White woman. One member of the RCP reported to me that at most of its functions there have been approximately one-third non Whites.

65 In the late 1970s, the CP(ML) began to open its own bookstores in several cities.

66 "The China-Albania Split," *Guardian* 29, no. 42 (July 27, 1977), p. 16.

67 Irwin Silber, "China's View of the Superpowers," *Guardian* 30, no. 10 (February 15, 1978), p. 21.

68 "The China-Albania Split," p. 16.

69 Ibid.

70 Silber, "China's View," p. 21.

71 The Albanian position was that there was "the direct danger that mankind will be hurled into a third world war." Reprint of "The Theory and Practice of Revolution," an editorial appearing in *Zeri i Popullit,* organ of the Central Committee of the Party of Labor of Albania, July 7, 1977, p. 9. The *Guardian's* position was that "While imperialism's drive for war is inexorable . . . it is possible in today's world to transform the liberation struggles of oppressed peoples and the peace sentiments of the masses into a powerful material force capable of preventing war." "On Building a New Communist Party," p. S-6. The RCP was not as direct as Silber in the *Guardian,* but in its publication *War and Revolution* (Chicago: RCP, 1976) such a war was always referred to in a conditional verb tense.

72 CP(ML), *Documents,* p. 103. "The contention and uneven development between the two superpowers is bound to lead to a new world war. . . it is inevitable that there will be a war."

73 "Two Superpowers: Equally Enemies of World's People," *Revolution,* 2, no. 10 (August 1977), p. 5.

74 "The October League (M-L)," p. 22.

75 "On the Three Worlds and the Internationai Situation," *Revolution* 2, no. 9 (July 1977), p. 10.

76 RCP, *War and Revolution,* pp. 17-22.

77 Eileen Klehr, "How RCP's 'Theory of Equality' Serves Soviet Social-Imperialism," *Class Struggle,* no. 8 (Fall 1977), p. 50.

78 Joseph Stalin, *Marxism and the National Question* (New York: Intemational Publishers, 1942), p. 72.

79 Ibid., p. 12.

80 Ibid., p. 25.

81 Ibid., p. 24.

82 Joseph Stalin, *The National Question and Leninism* (Moscow: Foreign Languages Publishing House, 1952), p. 35.

83 Ibid., pp. 27-29.

84 Irwin Silber, ". . . Fan the Flames," *Guardian* 27, no. 36 (June 18, 1975), p. 8. For a reprint of Silber's entire series of articles on the issue and Davidson's criticism of Silber's position, see Carl Davidson, *In Defense of the Right to Self-Determination* (Chicago: Liberator Press, 1976).

85 Irwin Silber, "On the National Question," reprinted from the *Guardian* in Davidson, *In Defense,* pp. 70-85.

86 Documents on the conflict between the BWC and RU can be found in RU's *The Red Papers #6.*

87 Quoted in "The October League (M-L)," p. 16.

88 CP(ML), *Documents,* p. 129.

89 Ibid., pp. 129-130.

90 Ibid., p. 129.

91 RU, *The Red Papers #6,* p. 11.

92 Ibid., p. 110.

93 Ibid.

94 RCP, *Programme and Constitution,* p. 122.

95 Ibid., p. 123.

96 Ibid.

97 Ibid., p. 129.

98 Ibid., p. 133.

99 Ibid., p. 138.

100 D. B., "Marxism," p. 157.

101 Ibid., p. 158.

102 Ibid., pp. 127-169.

103 See Leon Trotsky, *On Black Nationalism and Self-Determination* (New York: Puthfinder Press, 1972).

104 Neither the CP(ML) nor the RCP has been as open to alliances with other groups as have Trotskyists or French Maoist groups, such as the GP or the PCR(m-l). Both CP(ML) and the RCP took part in demonstrations to stop the construction of the gym at Kent State University. But both participated "separately" without acknowledging the participation of the other. The same is true of their work in the U.S–China Friendship Association.

105 "People Must Unite to Smash Boston Busing Plan," *Revolution* 2, no. 9 (October 1974), p. 1. See also "Boston Busing Struggle Sharpens," *Revolution* 2, no. 10 (November 1974), pp. 1, 20-22, and "Narrow Nationalism," Ibid., pp. 14-15, 22. The latter article is primarily an attack on the CP(ML)'s predecessor, the October League. It will be recalled that the Black and Puerto Rican affiliates of the Revolutionary Wing opposed busing while the Mexican-American ATM supported it.

106 The Communist Party made a major investment in the creation of a women's organization, Women for Racial and Economic Equality (WREE). It did not, however, have enough control or influence over WREE to prevent the organization from supporting ERA. It was therefore presented with the

hard choice of pulling out of WREE, opposing WREE on a major issue, or following the lead of WREE. It chose the latter.

107 RCP, *Programme and Constitution*, p. 141.

108 Ibid.

109 Ibid.

110 "The October League (M-L)," p. 18.

111 It will be recalled that the positions of the Black and Puerto Rican affiliates of the Revolutionary Wing were identical to those of the RCP, with which they had a previous relationship, while the Mexican-American ATM, which was not involved with the National Liaison Committee, took the pro-ERA position of the CP(ML) and the *Guardian*.

112 *The Young Communist* 5, no. 3 (March 1978), p. 2.

Chapter Six: Conclusion

1 Baruch Knei-Paz, *The Social and Political Thought of Leon Trotsky* (Oxford: Clarendon Press, 1978), p. 186.

2 Ibid., pp. 228-233.

3 It is interesting that the press of the American SWP has published a large anthology of Luxemburg's works and that they are also available in the *Ligue's* Paris bookstore.

4 Trotsky, *The Revolution Betrayed*, p. 96.

5 Baruch Knei-Paz's ignoring of the Transitional Program on this question of the role of the party is curious. In the index of his book there are three page references to that document. However, this writer is able to locate only one actual reference to the Transitional Program in the text, a footnote on page 598. Perhaps one explanation for the lack of consideration of this work is Isaac Deutscher's dismissal of its theoretical importance. Whatever its intrinsic theoretical merit, it is certainly of importance in understanding the operation of contemporary Trotskyist movements.

6 Trotsky, *The Transitional Program*, pp. 81-82.

7 Ibid., p. 91.

8 V. I. Lenin, *What Is To Be Done?* (New York: International Publishers, 1929), p. 117.

9 Ibid., p. 122. Italics in the original.

10 After this was written a Sinologist colleague, Professor Richard Kraus, brought to my attention a similar interpretation of Mao's thought by Maurice Meisner. See particularly Meisner's "Leninism and Maoism: Some Populist Perspectives on Maoism," *The China Quarterly*, no. 45 (January-March 1971), pp. 2-36.

Epilogue

1 Liliane Delwasse, "L'Extrême Gauche aux enfers," *Le Monde Dimanche*, 23 mai 1982, p. iii, and interview with Alain Krivine, June 26, 1986.

2 Steve Clark, "1979: Year of Crisis for World Imperialism," *The Militant* 44,

no. 1 (January 18, 1980), p. 19.

3 On the history of this factional dispute within the United Secretariat, see *Intercontinental Press/Inprecor* 17, no. 47 (December 24, 1979), pp. 1275-1281.

4 The United Secretariat's statement on the Simón Bolívar Brigade can be found in *Intercontinental Press/Inprecor* 17, no. 38 (October 22, 1979), p. 1023.

5 Will Reisner, "France: Alain Krivine Fights for Presidental Ballot Slot," *Intercontinental Press/Inprecor* 19, no. 12 (April 6, 1981), p. 344.

It should be pointed out that at this point in time there was a serious concern on the Left that no candidate of the Left would make it to the second ballot and that the electorate would be faced with a choice between two right-wing candidates, President Giscard d'Estaing and Jacques Chirac, the Gaullist mayor of Paris. There was, therefore, tremendous pressure on the major parties of the Left, especially the Socialist Purty, to go for every potential vote. The prior presidential election had been won by approximately one per cent of the vote. The minor party candidates were thus troublesome.

6 Will Reisner, "LCR Calls for Vote for Workers Parties," *Intercontinental Press/Inprecor* 19, no. 16 (May 4, 1981), p. 429.

7 Pierre Sylvain, "French Voters Give Giscard a Stinging Rebuff," *Intercontinental Press/Inprecor* 19, no. 16 (May 4, 1981), p. 428.

8 "Interview with Alain Krivine: Mitterrand's First Six Months in Power," *Intercontinental Press/Inprecor* 10, no. 46 (December 14, 1981), p. 1212.

9 *Les Elections législatives de juin 1981* (Paris: Le Monde Dossiers et Documents, 1081), p. 12.

10 *L'Election présidentielle 26 avril-10 mai 1981* (Paris: Le Monde Dossier et Documents, 1081), p. 98.

11 "Mitterrand's First Six Months in Power," p. 1215.

12 Patrick Jarreau, "La campagne de l'Extrême Gauche: le refus de 'l'austérité'," *Le Monde*, 4 mars 1983, p. 10.

Actually, not all of the Trotskyist candidates were eliminated. All of them together, i.e. the candidates of the *Ligue*–LO slate and those of the PCI, received almost five per cent of the vote.

Due to the new modified proportional representational system, the *Ligue* was able to elect two of its members to municipal council seats while the PCI was able to elect four of its members. See "The Lessons of the Municipal Elections: Socialist and Communist Parties Get Warning at Polls," *Intercontinental Press/Inprecor* 21, no. 7 (April 18, 1983), pp. 212-214.

13 I am grateful to François de Massot of the PCI for an interview on June 27, 1986, and for documentation on the MPPT's electoral efforts.

14 "Mitterrand's First Six Months in Power," pp. 1212-1215.

15 Alain Krivine, "For a Government of the Workers Parties in France," *Intercontinental Press/Inprecor* 19, no. 20 (June 1, 1981), pp. 582-583.

16 For LO's 1986 vote totals and electoral materials see its monthly publication *Lutte de Classe,* no. 121 (avril 1986). This is also the best source for

an overview of the votes and electoral materials of the entire Far Left in the 1986 elections.

17 Delwasse, "L'Extrême Gauche," p. iii, and "Some Figures on the LCR," *Intercontinental/Inprecor* 20, no. 2 (January 25, 1982), p. 45.

18 Delwasse, "L'Extrême Gauche," p. iii.

19 *Les Elections législatives de juin 1981*, p. 12.

20 Ibid.

21 "Une délégation du PCML a séjourné en Chine," *PCML Flash,* no. 20 (6 janvier 1983), p. 2.

22 "Préparons la fête pour la paix du 19 juin," *PCML Flash,* no. 35 (21 avril 1983), p. 1.

23 "Parlons-ensemble . . . des choix gouvernmentaux depuis le 10 mai," *Travailleurs,* no. 9 (mai 1983), pp. 26-29.

24 Delwasse, "L'Extrême Gauche," p. iv.

25 Ibid.

26 "Municipales 83 . . .," *Travailleurs,* no. 6 (février 1983), pp. 8-10 and Jarreau, "La campagne," p. 10.

27 "Résolution adoptée par le Congrès du Parti Pour une Alternative Communiste," fin decembre 1985, and "Les Ex-maoîstes français se convertissent a l'autogestion," *Le Monde,* 21 juin 1986, p. 7.

28 I am grateful to Alain Sentier of *Presse d'Aujourd'hui,* associated with PAC, for information on the present state of the organization and French Maoism in general. Interview of June 26, 1986.

29 Jacques-Marie Bourget, "La Guerre jamais finie du dernier des mao," *Paris Match,* no. 1926 (25 avril 1986), unpaged.

30 "Editorial," *The Militant* 47, no. 16 (May 6, 1983), p. 14.

31 "Defend Nicaragua, Complete the Revolution," *Workers Vanguard,* no. 329 (May 6, 1983), pp. 1, 6-8.

32 "Why the White House Fears Negotiations in El Salvador," *The Militant* 47, no. 7 (March 4, 1983), p. 10.

33 "Salvador Leftists on to Victory," *Workers Vanguard,* no. 330 (May 20, 1983), p. 1.

34 David Frankel, "Imperialism and the Khomeini Government," *Intercontinental Press/Inprecor* 19, no. 42 (November 16, 1981), p. 1120.

35 Ernest Harsch, "Iranian Workers Struggle to Rebuild Economy, Defend Democratic Rights," *The Militant* 47, no. 12 (April 8, 1983), pp. 10-11.

36 "SWP Bows to Holy Man Khomeini," *Workers Vanguard,* no. 219 (November 17, 1978), p. 10.

37 Ibid.

38 "Down with the Shah! Down with the Mullahs!," *Workers Vanguard,* no. 219 (November 17, 1978), p. 11.

39 Steve Bride, "What Poland's Workers Want," *The Militant* 45, no. 28 (July 24, 1981), p. 19.

40 Ibid.

41 "Reagan Weeps for Counterrevolutionary Solidarnosc," *Workers Vanguard,* no. 298 (February 5, 1982), p. 6.

42 Pedro Camejo, *Against Sectarianism: The Evolution of the Socialist Workers Party, 1978-83* (Berkeley, 1983).

43 Peter Camejo, "Problems of Vanguardism: In Defense of Leninism," *Discussion Articles #1*, North Star Network Conference, San Francisco, December 7-8, 1984, pp. 3-7.

44 Jack Barnes, "Their Trotsky and Ours," *New International*, 1, no. 1, (Fall 1983), pp. 9-89.

45 Les Evans, "Lenin and the Theory of Democratic Dictatorship," *Socialist Action Information Bulletin*, 1, no. 5, (July 1984), pp. 1-12.

46 "Australian SWP Quits Fourth International," *Intercontinental Press* 23, no. 18 (September 23, 1985), pp. 569-70.

47 Interview with Alain Krivine, June 26, 1986.

48 Tom Boot, "Revolutionary Integration Yesterday and Today," *The Freedom Socialist* 8, no. 2 (Spri ng 1983), p. 14.

49 Ibid.

50 I am grateful to women of the Freedom Socialist Party who attended the conference on "Common Differences: Third World Women and Feminist Perspectives," held at the University of Illinois in Urbana from April 9 to 13, 1983, for their willingness to talk about their organization with this author.

51 An article on the split appeared in the party's newspaper right after Klonsky's resignation. See *The Call* 10, no. 2 (March 1981), p. 2.

52 "Battle Sharpens around Bob Avakian's Demand for Refugee Status," *Revolutionary Worker*, no. 157 (May 28, 1982), p. 12.

53 Avakian would have some reason to take death threats seriously. He, of course, knew Black Panther members Mark Clark and Fred Hampton, who were killed in their Chicago apartment by Illinois States Attorney's police. On November 3, 1979, close to the time that Avakian terminated his speaking tour, five members of the Maoist Communist Workers Party were shot to death at an anti-Klan rally in Greensboro, North Carolina. Members of the Klan and the American Nazi Party were brought to trial and acquitted by a state and then a federal court. It was no secret to people on the Left that the FBI had infiltrators and paid informers in these right-wing organizations. The Liuzzo case has established for the public record that people in the pay of the FBI were not above participating in the literally murderous activities of the Klan.

54 *A World to Win: International Marxist-Leninist Journal*, no. 2 (May 1982), p. 18.

55 Ibid

56 "Advance through Criticism of Past Errors: Busing and the Fight Against National Oppression and For Revolution," *Revolution* 4, no. 6 (June 1979), pp. 9-15.

57 See RCP, *Charting the Uncharted Course* (Chicago: RCP Publications, n.d.) and "Report from the Central Committee," *Revolutionary Worker*, no. 194 (February 25, 1983), p. 10.

58 "Report from the Central Committee," p. 8.

59 RCP, *Programme and Constitution of the Revolationary Communist Party USA* (Chicago: RCP Publications, 1975), p. 141.

60 Bob Avakian, *Conquer the World?*, special issue of *Revolution*, no. 50 (December 1981), pp. 30-34.

61 Ibid., p. 34.

62 "Report from the Central Committee," p. 9. See also RCP, *Create Public Opinion . . . Seize Power!* (Chicago: RCP Publications, 1979).

63 RCP, *New Programme and New Constitution of the Revolutionary Communist Party USA* (Chicago: RCP Publications, 1981), p. 44.

64 For a succinct overview of the League's positions see "U.S. Foreign Policy and the World Today: Interview with Mae Ngai of the League of Revolutionary Struggle (ML)," *Forward*, no. 5 (Spring 1986), pp. 65-79.

65 *Unity* 6 no. 3 (February 25-March 10, 1983), p. 2.

66 Cynthia Lai, "China Charts Independent Course: Major Shift in Foreign Policy," *Workers Viewpoint* 8 no. 3 (February 9-15, 1983), p. 10.

67 William Nishimura, "Arousing a Socialist Giant," *Workers Viewpoint* 8 no. 4 (February 16-22, 1983), pp. 7, 15.

68 Editorial Board, "The Trial of the Gang of Four and the Crisis of Maoism," *Line of March* 1, no. 6 (May-June 1981), pp. 7-65.

Bibliography

This bibliography is organized in a manner that is congruent with the major hypothesis and progression of the book. The first section contains theoretical works. Its also includes some biographical material on Trotsky and Mao. The second section contains works that are largely contextual in nature. The remaining four sections contain works that have been useful in the examination of attempts to apply Trotskyist and Maoist theory to practice within the specific contexts of France and the United States. Although some items overlap these categories, they are noted only once, in the section which best indicates their utility for this study. I have donated some of the French documentation which might be difficult or impossible to secure elsewhere in the United States to the Library of the University of Illinois in Urbana.

Theory and Biography

Barnett, A. Doak, ed. *China after Mao*. Princeton: Princeton University Press, 1967.

Basmanov, M. *Contemporary Trotskyism: Its Anti-Revolutionary Nature*. Moscow: Institute of Marxism-Leninism of the Central Committee of the Communist Party of the Soviet Union, Progress Publishers, 1972.

Ch'en, Jerome. *Mao and the Chinese Revolution*. London: Oxford University Press, 1965.

Deutscher, Isaac. *The Prophet Armed: Trotsky, 1879-1921*. New York: Vintage Books, 1965.

—. *The Prophet Outcast: Trotsky, 1929-1940*. New York: Vintage Books, 1965.

—. *The Prophet Unarmed. Trotsky, 1921-1929*. New York: Vintage Books, 1965.

Ellul, Jacques. *The Technological Society*. Translated by John Wilkinson. New York: Vintage Books, 1964.

Engels, Friedrich. *The Origin of the Family, Private Property and the State in the Light of the Researches of Lewis H. Morgan*. New York: International Publishers, 1942.

Feuer, Lewis S., ed. *Marx and Engels: Basic Writings on Politics and Philosophy*. Garden City: Anchor Books, 1959.

Fourier, Charles. *Oeuvres complètes de Ch. Fourier*. 2d ed. Paris: La Société pour la Propagation et la Réalisation de la Théorie de Fourier, 1841-1846.

Howe, Irving. *Leon Trotsky*. New York: Viking Press, 1978.

Hua Kuo-feng. "Political Report to the 11th National Congress of the Communist Party of China." *Peking Review*, no. 35 (August 26, 1977), pp. 39-43.

Keniston, Kenneth. *Young Radicals*. New York: Harcourt, Brace, and World, 1968.

Knei-Paz, Baruch. *The Social and Political Thought of Leon Trotsky*. Oxford: Clarendon Press, 1978.

Korsch, Karl. *Marxism and Philosophy.* Translated by Fred Halliday. New York: Monthly Review Press, 1970.

Lefebvre, Henri. *Everyday Life in the Modern World.* Translated by Sacha Rabinovitch. New York: Harper and Row, 1971.

Lenin, V. I. *What Is To Be Done?* New York: International Publishers, 1929.

Lin Piao. "Long Live the Victory of People's War." In A. Doak Barnett, ed., *China after Mao.* Princeton: Princeton University Press, 1967, pp. 196-262.

—. "Mao Tse-tung's Theory of People's War." In Franz Schurmann and Orville Schell, eds., *Communist China: Revolutionary Reconstruction and International Confrontation, 1949 to the Present.* Vol. 3 of *The China Reader.* New York: Random House, 1967.

Lukacs, Georg. *History and Class Consciousness: Studies in Marxist Dialectics.* Translated by Rodney Livingston. Cambridge: MIT Press, 1971.

Mandel, Arthur P., ed. *Essential Works of Marxism.* New York: Bantam Books, 1961.

Mandel, Ernest. *Trotsky: A Study in the Dynamic of His Thought.* London: New Left Books, 1979.

Mannheim, Karl. "The Problem of Generations." In Karl Mannheim, *Essays on the Sociological Problem of Knowledge.* London: Routledge and Kegan Paul, 1952, pp. 276-320.

Mao Tse-tung. "A Directive of the Central Committee of the Chinese Communist Party of 1 June 1943." In Stuart R. Schram, *The Political Thought of Mao Tse-tung.* New York: Praeger, 1963, pp. 315-317.

—. *On Contradiction.* Peking: Foreign Languages Press, 1967.

—. "On the Historical Experience of the Dictatorship of the Proletariat." In Schram, *The Political Thought of Mao Tse-tung,* pp. 431-434.

—. *On Practice.* In Arthur P. Mandel, ed., *Essential Works of Marxism.* New York: Bantam Books, 1961, pp. 499-513.

—. "Speech at the Supreme State Conference, 28 January 1958." In Stuart R. Schram, ed., *Chairman Mao Talks to the People.* New York: Pantheon Books, 1974, pp. 91-95.

—. "Talk on Questions of Philosophy, 18 August 1964." In Schram, *Chairman Mao Talks to the People,* pp. 212-230.

Marx, Karl. *The Class Struggles in France (1848-50).* London: Martin Lawrence, n.d.

Marx, Karl, and Friedrich Engels. "Excerpts from *The German Ideology.*" In Lewis S. Feuer, ed., *Marx and Engels: Basic Writings on Politics and Philosophy.* Garden City: Anchor Books, 1959, pp. 246-260.

Marx, Karl, and V. I. Lenin. *The Civil War in France: The Paris Commune (The Complete Edition of Marx's Three Addresses on the Franco-Prussian War of 1870-71 and the Commune, and Lenin's Writings on the Commune).* New York: International Publishers, 1968.

Meisner, Maurice. "Leninism and Maoism: Some Populist Perspectives on Maoism." *The China Quarterly,* no. 45 (January-March 1971), pp. 2-36.

Proudhon, Pierre-Joseph. *What Is Property? An Enquiry into the Principle of Right and of Government.* Translated by Benjamin R. Tucker. New York: H. Fertig, 1966.

Renmin Ribao, Editorial Department. "Chairman Mao's Theory of the Differentiation of the Three Worlds Is a Major Contribution to Marxism–Leninism." *Peking Review,* no. 45 (November 4, 1977), pp. 10-41.

Rousseau, Jean-Jacques. *Oeuvres complètes, tome III: du contrat social, écrits politiques.* Paris: Bibliothèque de la Pléiade, 1964.

Schram, Stuart R., ed. *Chairman Mao Talks to the People: Talks and Letters, 1956-1971.* Translated by John Chinnery and Tieyun. New York: Pantheon Books, 1974.

—. *The Political Thought of Mao Tse-tung.* New York: Praeger, 1963.

Sorel, Georges. *Reflections on Violence.* Translated by T. E. Hulme and J. Roth. Glencoe: Free Press, 1950.

Stalin, Joseph. *Marxism and the National Question.* New York: International Publishers, 1942.

—. *The National Question and Leninism.* Moscow: Foreign Languages Publishing House, 1952.

"The Theory and Practice of Revolution." A press release of the Party of Labor of Albania. Appears in the 7 July 1977 issue of *Zeri i Popullit,* organ of the party's Central Committee.

Trotsky, Leon. *In Defense of Marxism.* New York: Pathfinder Press, 1973.

—. *The First Five Years of the Communist International.* Vol. 1. New York: Pioneer Publishers, 1945.

—. *My Life.* New York: Pathfinder Press, 1970.

—. *The Permanent Revolution and Results and Prospects.* New York: Pathfinder Press, 1969.

—. *The Revolution Betrayed.* New York: Pathfinder Press, 1972.

—. *Their Morals and Ours.* New York: Pioneer Publishers, 1942.

—. *The Transitional Program for Socialist Revolution.* 2d ed. New York: Pathfinder Press, 1974.

"Trotsky and Trotskyism in Perspective." *Studies in Comparative Communism,* special issue, 10, nos. 1 and 2 (Spring/Summer 1977).

Waters, Mary-Alice, ed. *Rosa Luxemburg Speaks.* New York: Pathfinder Press, 1970.

Contexts

Alexander, Robert J. *Trotskyism in Latin America.* Stanford: Hoover Institution Press, 1973.

Chung Lien. "The 'Gang of Four' and the Trotskyites." *Peking Review,* no. 7 (February 11, 1977), pp. 10-15.

Clout, Hugh D. *The Geography of Post-War France: A Social and Economic Approach.* Oxford: Pergamon Press, 1972.

Draper, Hal. "The Student Movement of the Thirties: A Political History." In Rita James Simon, ed., *As We Saw the Thirties.* Urbana: University of Illinois Press, 1967, pp. 151-189.

L'Election présidentielle 26 avril-10 mai 1981. Paris: Le Monde Dossiers et Documents, 1981.

Les Elections législatives de juin 1981. Paris: Le Monde Dossiers et Documents, 1981.

Les Elections législatives de mars 1978. Paris: Le Monde Dossiers et Documents, 1978.

Fields, A. Belden. "The Battle of SONACOTRA: A Study of an Immigrant Worker Struggle in France." *New Political Science* 3, no. 1/2 (Summer/ Fall 1982), pp. 93-112.

—. "The Effects of Student Activism in Industrialized Countries: Some Comparative Reflections on France and the United States." In Robert Perrucci and Marc Pilisuk, eds., *The Triple Revolution Emerging: Social Problems in Depth.* Boston: Little, Brown, 1971, pp. 585-606. Reprinted in Harvey A. Farberman and Erich Goode, eds., *Social Reality.* Englewood Cliffs: Prentice-Hall, 1973, pp. 287-307.

—. "The Revolution Betrayed: The French Student Revolt of May-June 1968." In S. M. Lipset and P G. Altbach, eds., *Students in Revolt.* Boston: Houghton Mifflin, 1969, pp. 127-166.

—. *Student Politics in France: A Study of l'Union Nationale des Étudiants de France.* New York: Basic Books, 1970.

Gelman, Harry. "The Sino-Soviet Conflict." In Franz Schurmann and Orville Schell, eds., *Communist China: Revolutionary Reconstruction and International Confrontation, 1949 to the Present.* Vol. 3 of *The China Reader.* New York: Harper and Row, 1973, pp. 262-284.

Green, Philip. "Decentralization, Community Control, and Revolution: Reflections on Ocean Hill–Brownsville." In Philip Green and Sanford Levinson, eds., *Power and Community.* New York: Vintage Books, 1970, pp. 247-275.

Jaubert, Alain et al. *Guide de la France des luttes.* Paris: Stock, 1974.

Johnson, Richard. *The French Communist Party versus the Students.* New Haven: Yale University Press, 1972.

Kanet, Roger E. "The Soviet Union and Sub-Saharan Africa." Ph.D. dissertation, Princeton University, 1966.

Kravis, Irving B. "A World of Unequal Incomes." *The Annals of the American Academy of Political and Social Science* 409 (September 1973), pp. 61-80.

Lens, Sidney. *Radicalism in America.* New York: Apollo Editions, 1966.

Miller, Joseph T. "The Politics of Chinese Trotskyism: The Role of a Permanent Opposition in Chinese Communism." Ph.D. dissertation, University of Illinois at Urbana-Champaign, 1979.

Moulin, Marie-France. *Machines à dormir: les foyers neufs de la SONA-COTRA, de l'ADEF et quelques autres.* Paris: Maspero, 1976.

Nee, Victor, and James Peck, eds. *China's Uninterrupted Revolution: From 1840 to the Present.* New York: Pantheon Books, 1975.

O'Brien, Jim. "American Leninism in the 1970s." *Radical America,* special double issue, II, no. 6 and 12, no. I (Winter 1977 i8), pp. 27-62.

Parkin, Frank. *Class, Inequality and Political Order.* New York: Praeger, 1971.

Peck, James. "Revolution versus Modernization and Revisionism: A Two-Front Struggle." In Victor Nee and James Peck, eds., *China's Uninterrupted Revolution: From 1840 to the Present.* New York: Pantheon Books, 1975, pp. 57-217.

Roszak, Theodore. *The Making of a Counter Culture.* Garden City: Anchor, 1968.

Sale, Kirkpatrick. *sds.* New York: Vintage Books, 1974.

Schurmann, Franz. *Ideology and Organization in Communist China.* 2d ed. Berkeley and Los Angeles: University of California Press, 1968.

Schurmann, Franz, and Orville Schell, eds. *Communist China: Revolutionary*

Reconstruction and International Confrontation, 1949 to the Present. Vol. 3 of *The China Reader.* New York: Random House, 1967.

Simon, Rita James, ed. *As We Saw the Thirties.* Urbana: University of Illlinois Press, 1967.

Snow, Edgar. *Red Star over China.* New York: Random House, 1938.

Sprinzak, Ehud. "Democracy and Illegitimacy: A Study of the American and the French Student Protest Movements and Some Theoretical Implications." Ph. D. dissertation, Yale University, 1971.

Starr, John Bryan. *Ideology and Culture: An Introduction to the Dialectic of Contemporary Chinese Politics.* New York: Harper and Row, 1973.

Vieuguet, André. *Français et immigrés: le combat du PCF.* Paris: Éditions Sociales, 1975.

Williams, Fred L. "The French Democratic Confederation of Labor (CFDT)." Ph. D. dissertation, University of Illinois at Urbana-Champaign, 1973.

Yearbook of Labour Statistics. Geneva: International Labor Organization, 1976.

Trotskyism in France

"Argentina: Political Crisis and Revolutionary Perspectives." *Intercontinental Press* 12, no. 46 (December 23, 1974), p. 1797.

Artous, Antoine, and Michel Dupré. *Pour Débattre avec l'OCT.* Paris: Éditions La Brèche, 1978.

Avenas, Denise. *Maoisme et communisme.* Paris: Éditions Galilée, 1976.

—. *La Pensée de Trotsky.* Paris: Privat, 1976.

Avenas, Denise, and Alain Brossat. *De l'Antitrotskysme.* Paris: Maspero, 1971.

"Background to Split between French CP and SP." *Intercontinental Press* 15, no. 40 (October 31, 1977), pp. 1192-97.

Berg, Charles, and Stéphane Just. *Fronts populaires d'hier et d'aujourd'hui.* Paris: Penser/Stock 2, 1977.

Biard, Roland. *Dictionnaire de l'Extrême Gauche de 1945 à nos jours.* Paris: Belfond, 1978.

Chisserey, Claude. "La continuité dans le changement: les zigzags centristes de la Ligue pabliste." *La Verité,* no. 550 (octobre 1970), p. 49.

Comités Communistes pour l'Autogestion. *Résolution de politique générale du congrès constitutif.* Paris: 1977.

Craipeau, Yvan. *Contre Vents et marées: les révolutionnaires pendant la deuxième guerre mondiale.* Paris: Savelli, 1977.

—. *La Libération confisquée.* Paris: Savelli/Syros, 1978.

—. *Le Mouvement Trotskyste en France.* Paris: Syros, 1971.

"Debate in French Left: What Stand to Take Toward the Elections." *Intercontinental Press/Inprecor* 16, no. 9 (March 6, 1978), pp. 276-287.

"Debate in French Left: What Stand to Take Toward 'Union of the Left'." *Intercontinental Press* 15, no. 1 (January 17, 1977), pp. 20-29.

Delwasse, Liliane. "L'Extrême Gauche aux enfers." *Le Monde Dimanche,* 23 mai 1982, pp. iii-iv.

"Election Platform of the Ligue Communiste Révolutionnaire.' *Intercon-tinental Press*

15, no. 47 (December 19, 1977), pp. 1403-1408.

Fac-simlé: La Verité 1940/1944, Journal Trotskyste Clandestin sous l'Occupation Nazie. Paris: Études et Documentation Internationales, 1978.

"Femmes, capitalisme, mouvement ouvrier," *Critique Communiste,* special issue, no. 20/21 (décembre 1977/janvier 1978).

Fidler, Dick. "The Antimilitarist Battle in France's Armed Forces." *Intercontinentul Press* 12, no. 30 (August 5, 1974), pp. 1068-1070.

——. "How the Far Left Met Mitterrand's Candidacy." *Intercontinental Press* 12, no. 19 (May 20, 1974), pp. 628-637.

——. "In the Aftermath of Round Two." *Intercontinental Press* 12 no 21 (June 3 1974), pp. 680-681.

——. "Krivine Campaigns for Revolutionary Alternative." *Intercontinental Press* 12, no. 17 (May 6, 1974), pp. 535-536.

Forgue, François. " 'Eurocommunisme' ou Stalinisme?" *La Verité,* no. 582 (juin 1978), pp. 133-144.

The Fourth International. "The Split by Leninist–Trotskyist Tendency and Bolshevik Faction." *Intercontinental Press/Inprecor* 17, no. 47 (December 24, 1979), pp. 1275-1277.

Freyssat, Jean-Marie, Michel Dupré, and François Ollivier. Ce Qu'est l'OCI. Paris. Éditions de la Taupe Rouge, 1977.

"From Ligue Communiste Révolutionnaire: Open Letter to the French Communist Party." *Intercontinental Press/Inprecor* 16, no. 4 (January 30, 1978), pp. 111-112.

"Interview with Alain Krivine: Mitterrand's First Six Months in Power." *Intercontinental Press/Inprecor* 19, no. 46 (December 14, 1981). pp. 1212-1215.

Jarreau, Patrick. "La campagne de l'Extrême Gauche: le refus de 'l'austerité';" *Le Monde,* 4 mars 1983, p. 10.

"Joint Electoral Platform of the OCT–LCR–CCA." *Intercontinental Press/ Inprecor* 16, no. 2 (January 16, 1978), pp. 59-63.

Julien, Pierre. "Growing Dissent in French Communist Party." *Intercontinental Press/Inprecor* 16, no. 19 (May 15, 1978), pp. 564-566.

Just, Stéphane. A Propos de la Brochure "Ce Qu'est l'OCI." Paris: SELIO, Documents de l'OCI, 1978.

——. "Defense du Trotskysme." *La Verité,* nos. 530-531 (septembre 1965), pp. 1-256.

——. *Revisionnisme liquidateur contre Trotskysme: défense du Trotskysme 2.* Paris: SELIO, 1971.

Krivine, Alain. "For a Government of the Workers Parties in France." *Intercontinental Press/Inprecor* 19, no. 20 (June 1, 1981), pp. 582-583.

——. *La Farce électorale.* Paris: Éditions du Seuil, 1969.

——. *Questions sur le révolution.* Paris: Stock, 1973.

"Krivine's Assessment: The 'Allende of France'." *Intercontinental Press* 12, no. 19 (May 20, 1974), pp. 633-634.

Lambert, Pierre. *Actualité du Programme de Transition.* Paris: SELIO, Cahiers du Marxisme, no. 2, 1969.

"The Lessons of the Municipal Elections: Socialist and Communist Parties Get Warning at Polls." *Intercontinental Press/Inprecor* 21, no. 7 (April 18, 1983), pp. 212-214.

Ligue Communiste. *Ce Que Veut la Ligue Communiste.* Paris: Maspero, 1972.
——. *Pour une CFDT de "lutte de classe."* Paris: 1970.
Ligue Communiste Révolutionnaire. *Une Chance historique pour la révolution socialiste.* Paris: Cahier Rouge, n.s., no. 1, 1975.
——. *Coup pour coup: aprés le 22e Congrés, questions au PCF* Paris: 1977.
——. *Coup pour coup '78: le débat dans l'Extrême Gauche.* Paris: 1977.
——. *Mouvement des femmes et lutte de classe.* Paris: Édition de la Taupe Rouge, n.d.
——. *Oui, le Socialisme!* Paris: Maspero, 1978.
"Ligue Communiste Révolutionnarie Holds First Congress." *Intercontinental Press* 13, no. 7 (February 24, 1975), pp. 262-263.
Marie, Jean-Jacques. *Le Trotskysme.* Paris: Flammarion, 1970.
de Massot, F. *La Grève Générale* (mai-juin 1968). Paris: Organisation Communiste Internationaliste, n.d.
Mavrakis, Kostas. *Du Trotskysme.* Paris: Maspero, 1971.
Organisation Communiste des Traveilleurs. *Thèses du congrès de fondation de l'OCT.* Paris: 1976.
Organisation Communiste Internationaliste. *De la Crise politique de la bourgeoisie à la crise révolutionnaire: resolution politique adoptée par le IXe congres de l'OCI.* Paris: SELIO, 1974.
——. *L'État, le bonapartisme, la république parlementaire, situation révolutionnaire.* Paris: 1977.
——. *Le Front Populaire.* Paris: SELIO, Cahier de GER no. 7, n.d.
——. *Le Front unique ouvrier et la construction du parti révolutionnaire.* Paris: SELIO, 1974.
——. *Les Marxistes contre l'autagestion.* Paris: SELIO, 1974.
——. *Quelques Enseignements de notre histoire,* supplement to *La Verité,* no. 548 (mai 1970).
Pablo, Michel. *Socialisme et autogestion et La Nouvelle Opposition Marxiste dans les pays de l'Est et le phénomène bureaucratique.* Paris: Lettre Politique No. Special, Sous le Drapeau du Socialisme, 1978.
Pelletier, Robert, and Serge Rave. *Le Mouvement des soldats.* Paris: Maspero, 1976.
"The Political Situation in France after the Elections." *Intercontinental Press/Inprecor* 16, no. 17 (May 1, 1978), pp. 520-526.
Quatrième Internationale 10, nos. 2-4 (fevrier-avril 1952).
Reisner, Will. "France: Alain Krivine Fights for Presidential Ballot Slot." *Intercontinental Press/Inprecor* 19, no. 12 (April 6, 1981), p. 344.
——. "LCR Calls for Vote for Workers Parties." *Intercontinental Press/Inprecor* 19, no. 16 (May 4, 1981), p. 429.
"Rocard: de la S.F.I.O. au Parti socialiste de Mitterrand." *Lutte Ouvrière,* no. 325 (31 mai 1975), p. 8
" 'Rouge' Urges United Far-Left Candidacy." *Intercontinental Press* 12, no. 15 (April 22, 1974), pp. 469-471.
Rousset, Pierre. *Le Parti Communiste Vietnamien.* Paris: Maspero, 1973.
——. "The Vietnamese Revolution and the Role of the Party." *International Socialist Review* 35, no. 4 (April 1974), pp. 5-25.
Sheppard, Barry. "Sectarians Split on Eve of World Congress." *Intercontinental*

Press/Inprecor 17, no. 47 (December 24, 1979), pp. 1277-1281.

"Some Figures on the LCR." *Intercontinental Press/Inprecor* 20, no. 2 (January 25, 1982), p. 45.

"Statement on the Simón Bolívar Brigade." *Intercontinental Press/Inprecor* 17, no. 38 (October 22, 1979), p. 1023.

Statuts de la IVe Internationale. Paris: Rouge, 1970.

Sylvain, Pierre. "French Voters Give Giscard a Stinging Rebuff." *Intercontinental Press/Inprecor* 19, no. 16 (May 4, 1981), p. 428.

Tendance Marxiste Révolutionnaire Internationale. *La Lutte pour l'autogestion et la révolution.* Paris: Sous le Drapeau du Socialisme, 1972.

Trotsky, Leon. *The Crisis of the French Section (1935-36).* Edited by Naomi Allen and George Breitman. New York: Pathfinder Press, 1977.

Weber, Henri. *Mouvement ouvrier, Stalinisme, et bureaucratie.* Paris: PCI, 1966.

In addition to the above sources, *Lutte Ouvrière* was kind enough to supply the author with some of its factory bulletins.

Maoism in France

Barou, Jean-Pierre. "Renault-Billancourt: quatre actes de controle ouvrier." *Les Temps Modernes,* no. 310 Bis (1972), pp. 57-79.

Bénichou, Pierre. "What's Jean-Paul Sartre Thinking Lately? An Interview." *Esquire* 68, no. 6 (December 1972), pp. 204-208, 280-286.

Le Bris, Michel. *L'Homme aux semelles de vent.* Paris: Grasset 1977

La Cause du Peuple, 17 mai 1971; 9 decembre 1971; 15 janvier 1972; 11 mars 1972; mai-juin 1977.

Centre d"Action Paysanne. *Où En Sont les Paysans?* Paris: Éditions Liberté-Presse, 1971.

——. *Le Mouvement de la jeunesse et les paysans de l'uest.* Paris: Éditions Hallier, 1970.

"Le Courant, ni droit ni gauche." *L'Humanité Rouge,* no. 27 (16 mars-13 avril 1978), pp. 26-28. Includes vote totals for Maoist candidates.

Le Dantec, Jean-Pierre. *Les Dangers du soleil.* Paris: Les Presses d'Aujourd'hui, 1978.

"Une délégation du PCML a séjourné en Chine." *PCML Flash,* no. 20 (6 janvier 1983), pp. 1-2.

Drapeau Rouge, *La Classe ouvrière et la revolution: luttes revendicatives, syndicats, groupes rouges.* Rennes: 1974.

Gavi, Philippe, Jean-Paul Sartre, and Pierre Victor. *On a Raison de se révolter.* Paris: Gallimard, 1974.

Geismar, Alain. *Pourquoi Nous Combattons.* Paris: Maspero, 1970.

Geismar, Alain, Serge July, and Erlyn Morane. *Vers la Guerre civile.* Paris: Éditions et Publications Premiéres, 1969.

Glucksmann, André. *La Cuisinière et le mangeur d'hommes.* Paris: Seuil, 1975.

——. *Les Maîtres Penseurs.* Paris: Grasset, 1977.

Un Groupe de militants de l'Humanité Rouge (Collectif "François Marty"). "La Mystification de la 'Théorie des Trois Mondes' et le parti." 2d ed. Paris:

mimeographed, 1978.

Groupe pour la Fondation de l'Union des Communistes de France Marxiste-Léniniste. "Français-Immigrés: égalité des droits politiques." Mimeographed, 1976.

—. *Le Maoïsme, Marxisme de notre temps.* Marseilles: Éditions Potemkine, 1976.

—. *Aujourd'hui, participer aux élections, c'est soutenir l'impérialisme.* Marseille: Éditions Potemkine, 1978.

—. *Les Comités Populaires Anti-Capitalistes, CPAC.* Marseilles: Éditions Potemkine, 1978.

—. *Une Étude Maoïste: la situation en Chine et le mouvement dit de "critique de la bande des Quatre."* Marseilles: Éditions Potemkine, 1977.

—. *Face aux Elections vive la politique révolutionnaire du peuple des campagnes.* Marseilles: Éditions Potemkine, 1977.

—. *L'Internationalisme prolétarien aujourd'hui.* Marseilles: Éditions Potemkine, 1978.

—. *Les Noyaux Communistes Ouvriers: forme actuelle de l'avant-garde, piliers de l'édification du Parti de type nouveau.* Marseilles: Éditions Potemkine, 1978.

—. *Nucléaire, écologie, et politique révolutionnaire.* Marseilles: Éditions Potemkine, 1978.

—. *La Politique Maoïste, affiches et panneaux.* Marseilles: Éditions Potemkin, 1978.

Groupe pour la Foundation de l'Union des Communistes Français (marxiste-léniniste). *A Propos du Meurtre de Pierre Overney.* Paris: Maspero, 1972.

—. *Première Année d'existence d'une organisation Maoïste.* Paris: Maspero, 1972.

Hess, Remi. *Les Maoïstes Français.* Paris: Anthropos, 1974.

Jurquet, Jacques, ed. *Arracher la Classe ouvrière au révisionnisme.* Paris: Centenaire, 1976.

—. "Rapport politique au premier congrès du Parti Communiste Marxiste-Léniniste de France 1968." In Patrick Kessel, ed., *Le Mouvement "Maoïste" en France, I,* pp. 325-350.

Kessel, Patrick, ed. *Le Mouvement "Maoïste" en France, I: textes et documents 1963-1968.* Paris: Union Générale d'Éditions, 1972.

—. *Le Mouvement "Maoïste" en France, II: textes et documents 1968-1969.* Paris: Union Générale d'Éditions, 1978.

Kouchner, Bernard, and Michel-Antoine Burnier. *La France sauvage.* Paris: Éditions Publications Premières, 1970.

Lesage, Julia. "*Tout Va Bien* and *Coup pour Coup*: Radical French Cinema in Context." *Cineaste* 5, no. 3 (Summer 1972), pp. 42-48.

Linhart, Robert. *L'Établi.* Paris: Minuit, 1978.

Manceaux, Michèle. *Les Maos en France.* Paris: Gallimard, 1972.

"Les Marxistes-Léninistes en France aujonrd'hui." *Le Marxiste-Léniniste,* double issue, no. 18/19 (juillet-août 1977), pp. 19-22.

Minutes du procès d'Alain Geismar. Paris: Editions Hallier, n.d.

"Municipales 83. ..." *Travailleur,* no. 6 (février 1983), pp. 8-10.

"1978: C'est décidé! une seule campagne des Marxistes-Léninistes!" *L'Humanité Rouge,* no. 23 (19 janvier-2 février 1978), pp. 6-12.

"Nouveau Fascisme, nouvelle democratie." *Les Temps Modernes,* no. 310 Bis (1972). Special issue written and edited by Maoists working on *La Cause du Peuple.*

"Occitanie: 'des luttes paysannes à la révolte d'un peuple'." *Les Temps Modernes,* no.

310 Bis (1972), pp. 141-170.

Olivier, Philippe. "Aprés la Bataille de Renault." *Les Temps Modernes,* no. 310 Bis (1972), pp. 3-33.

——. "Syndicats, comité de lutte, comités de chaine." *Les Temps Modernes,* no. 310 Bis (1972), pp. 34-56.

Parlons-ensemble...des choix gouvernmentaux depuis le 10 mai." *Travailleurs,* no. 9 (mai 1983), pp. 26-29.

Parti Communiste Marxiste-Léniniste de France. *La Question de l'énergie nucléaire.* Paris: 1978.

Parti Communiste Révolutionnaire (marxiste-léniniste). "A propos de la Théorie des 3 Mondes." *Front Rouge,* n.s., no. 2 (novembre-décembre 1977), pp. 5-10.

——. *Manifeste pour le socialisme.* Paris: PCR(m-l), 1977.

——. *Programme et statuts.* Paris: PCR(m-l), 1976.

"Plein succès du 3e congres du PCMLF: communiqué de presse." *L'Humanité Rouge,* no. 24 (2-19 février 1978), p. 5.

Pour l'Union des comités de lutte d'atelier, Renault-Billancourt: 25 règles de travail. Paris: Éditions Liberté-Presse, supplement à *La Cause du Peuple,* no. 11, 1971.

"Préparons la fête pour la paix du 19 juin." *PCML Flash,* no. 35 (21 avril 1983), p. 1.

Les Prisonniers politiques parlent: le combat des détenus politiques. Paris: Maspero, 1970.

"Rapport du 3e congrès du PCMLF." *L'Humanité Rouge,* no. 24 (2-19 février 1978), insert.

"Resolutions du 3e congrès du Parti Communiste Marxiste-Léniniste de France: autocritique du PCMLF concernant son 2e congrès." *L'Humanité Rouge,* no. 25 (16 février-2 mars 1978), pp. 13-14.

"L'Unification des Marxistes-Léninistes: notre volonté." *L'Humanité Rouge,* no. 22 (5-19 janvier 1978), p. 27.

"Les voix de l'UOPDP: un potential pour l'action." *L'Humanité Rouge,* no. 27 (16 mars-13 avril 1978), p. 8.

"Votez Union Ouvrière et Paysanne: pour la démocratie prolétaricnne!" *L'Humanité Rouge,* special election issue, no. 26 (2-16 mars 1978).

Trotskyism in the United States

Abern, M. et al. "The War and Bureaucratic Conservatism." In James P. Cannon, *The Struggle for a Proletarian Party.* New York: Pathfinder Press, 1970, pp. 257-293.

Barnes, Jack et al. *Prospects for Socialism in America.* New York: Pathfinder Press, 1976.

——. *Towards an American Socialist Revolution: A Strategy for the 1970s.* New York: Pathfinder Press, 1971.

Blackstock, Nelson. "The COINTELPRO Papers, Part I: Red-Baiting and Disruption in the Left." *The Militant* 39, no. 11 (March 28, 1975), pp. 5-8.

——. "The COINTELPRO Papers, Part II: FBI's Attempt to Destroy Black Mov't." *The Militant* 39, no. 12 (April 4, 1975), pp. 25-27, 30.

——. "The COINTELPRo Papers, Part II: Sabotage of Socialist Election Campaigns." *The Militant* 39, no. 13 (April 11, 1975), pp. 15-17, 26.

—. "A New Look at the Socialist Workers Party." *The Militant* 40, no. 18 (May 7, 1976), pp. 16-20.

Boot, Tom. "Revolutionary Integration Yesterday and Today." *The Freedom Socialist* 8, no. 2 (Spring 1983), pp. 1-26.

Breitman, George. *How a Minority Can Change Society: The Real Potential of the Afro-American Struggle.* New York: Pathfinder Press, 1965.

—. "The National Question and the Black Liberation Struggle in the United States." In Ernest Mandel, ed., *50 Years of World Revolution.* New York: Merit Publishers, 1968, pp. 205-219.

Bride, Steve. "What Poland's Workers Want." *The Militant* 45, no. 28 (July 24, 1981), pp. 19-20.

Burnett, James Thomas. "American Trotskyism and the Russian Question." Ph.D. dissertation, University of California at Berkeley, 1968.

Burnham, James. "Letter of Resignation from the Workers Party." In Leon Trotsky, *In Defense of Marxism.* New York: Pathfinder Press, 1973, pp. 207-211.

—. "Science and Style: A Reply to Comrade Trotsky." In Trotsky, *In Defense of Marxism,* pp. 187-206.

Burton, Lucy. "Campaign Puts SWP on Ballot in 28 States." *The Militant* 40, no. 41 (October 29, 1976), p. 19.

Camejo, Peter. *Allende's Chile: Is It Going Socialist?* New York: Pathfinder Press, 1971.

Cannon, James P. *The First Ten Years of American Communism.* New York: Pathfinder Press, 1962.

—. *The History of American Trotskyism.* New York: Pathfinder Press, 1972.

—. *Letters from Prison.* New York: Pathfinder Press, 1973.

—. "The Roots of the Party Crisis." In James P. Cannon, *Speeches to the Party.* New York: Pathfinder Press, 1973, pp. 338-411.

—. *Socialism on Trial.* New York: Pathfinder Press, 1970.

—. *The Struggle for a Proletarian Party.* New York: Pathfinder Press, 1970.

"Charge Army Aided Illinois Terror Group." *The Chicago Daily News,* 14 April 1975, pp. 1-2.

Clark, Steve. "1979: Year of Crisis for World Imperialism." *The Militant* 44, no. 1 (January 18, 1980), pp. 17-19.

Coontz, Stephanie. *What Socialists Stand For.* New York: Pathfinder Press, 1973.

Couturier, Louis. "The Vietnamese Communist Party and Its Leadership." *International Socialist Review* 36, no. 2 (February 1975), pp. 28-35.

"Defend Nicaragua, Complete the Revolution." *Workers Vanguard,* no. 329 (May 6, 1983), pp. 1, 6-8.

Dobbs, Farrell. *Teamster Power.* New York: Monad Press, 1973.

—. *Teamster Rebellion.* New York: Monad Press, 1972.

"Documents: World Congress of the Fourth International." *Intercontinental Press* 12, no. 46 (December 23, 1974), pp. 1715-1840.

"Down with the Shah! Down with the Mullahs!" *Workers Vanguard,* no. 219 (November 17, 1978), p. 11.

"Editorial." *The Militant* 47, no. 16 (May 6 1983), p. 14.

Evans, Les. "The Fourth International from Split to Reunification." In Socialist

Workers Party, *Towards a History of the Fourth International, Part 1*. Education for Socialists Series. New York: National Education Department, Socialist Workers Party, June 1973, pp. 9-19.

Fenyo, Mario. "Trotsky and His Heirs: The American Perspective." *Studies in Comparative Communism* 10, nos. 1 and 2 (Spring/Summer 1977), pp. 204-215.

Foley, Gerry, and Malik Miah. *Tragedy in Chile: Lessons of the Revolutionary Upsurge and Its Defeat*. New York: Pathfinder Press, 1973.

Frankel, David. "Imperialism and the Khomeini Government." *Intercontinental Press/Inprecor* 19, no. 42 (November 16, 1981), pp. 1116-1122.

Green, Larry, and Rob Warren. "Socialist Office Here Was Looted." *The Chicago Daily News,* 24 March 1975, pp. 1, 12.

Hansen, Al. "Introduction." In James P. Cannon, *Speeches to the Party*. New York: Pathfinder Press, 1973, pp. 5-23.

Hansen, Joseph. *The Abern Clique*. Education for Socialists Series. New York: National Education Department, Socialist Workers Party, September 1972.

—. *Cuban Question: Report for the Political Committee*. Education for Socialists Series. New York: National Education Department, Socialist Workers Party, April 1968.

—. "Grounds for Revolutionary Optimism." *Intercontinental Press* 12, no. 46 (December 23, 1974) pp. 1716-1720.

—. ed. *Marxism vs Ultraleftism. The Record of Healy's Break with Trotskyism*. New York: National Education Department, Socialist Workers Party, 1974.

Hansen, Joseph, and Caroline Lund. *Nixon's Moscow and Peking Summits: Their Meaning for Vietnam*. New York: Pathfinder Press, 1972.

"Hard Times for the SWP: Barnestown, USA." *Workers Vanguard,* no. 320 (December 31, 1982), pp. 6-10.

Harsch, Ernest. "Iranian Workers Struggle to Rebuild Economy, Defend Democratic Rights." *The Militant* 47, no. 12 (April 8, 1983), pp. 10-11.

Healy, Gerry. *Problems of the Fourth International*. New York: Labor Publications, Inc., 1972.

Independent Socialist Clubs of America. "Program in Brief." *Independent Socialist,* no.12 (September 1969), p. 19.

International Socialists. "What We Stand For." *Workers' Power,* no. 122 (June 5-8, 1975), p. 14.

Jaquith, Cindy. "Drive to Sabotage De Berry Campaign, FBI Target: Black Presidential Nominee." *The Militant* 39, no. 11 (March 28, 1975), p. 4.

—. "Massive Illegal Campaign: FBI 'Disruption' Files Made Public." *The Militant* 39, no. 11 (March 28, 1975), p. 3.

Jenness, Linda, ed. *Feminism and Socialism*. New York: Pathfinder Press, 1972.

Johnson, George, and Fred Feldman. "Vietnam, Stalinism, and the Postwar Socialist Revolutions." *International Socialist Review* 35, no. 4 (April 1974), pp. 26-61.

Kerry, Tom. *The Mao Myth*. New York: Pathfinder Press, 1977.

Mandel, Ernest, ed. *50 Years of World Revolution: An International Symposium*. New York: Merit Publishers, 1968.

—. *The Revolutionary Student Movement: Theory and Practice*. New York: Young Socialist Publications, 1969.

Marcy, Sam. *The Class Character of the USSR: An Answer to the False Theory of Soviet Social-Imperialism.* New York: World View Publishers, 1977.

Morrison, Derrick. "The Combined Character of the Coming American Revolution." In Jack Barnes et al., *Towards an American Revolution: A Strategy for the 1970s.* New York: Pathflnder Press, 1971, pp. 43-61.

Mueller, Fred. *SWP: Reform or Revolution.* New York: Labor Publications, Inc., 1972.

Muste, A. J. "My Experience in the Labor and Radical Struggles of the Thirties." In Rita James Simon, ed., *As We Saw the Thirties.* Urbana: University of Illinois Press, 1967, pp. 123-150.

Myers, Constance Ashton. "American Trotskyists: The First Years." *Studies in Comparative Communism* 10, nos. 1 and 2 (Spring/Summer 1977), pp. 133-151.

——. *The Prophet's Army: Trotskyists in America, 1928-1941.* Westport: Greenwood Press, 1977.

Novack, George. "Introduction." In James P. Cannon, *Socialism on Trial.* New York: Pathfinder Press, 1970, pp. 7-14.

Novack, George, and Joseph Hansen. "Introduction." In Leon Trotsky, *In Defense of Marxism.* New York: Pathfinder Press, 1973 pp. vii-xxii

O'Casey, Dennis. *Ernest Mandel: The Fraud of Neo-Capitalism.* New York: Labor Publications, Inc., 1971.

Perkus, Cathy, ed. *COINTELPRO: The FBI's Secret War on Political Freedom.* New York: Monad Press, 1975.

"Reagan Weeps for Counterrevolutionary Solidarnosc." *Workers Vanguard,* no. 298 (February 5, 1982), pp. 1, 6.

Ring, Harry. *Cuba and Problems of Workers' Democracy.* New York: Pathflnder Press, 1972.

——. *How Cuba Uprooted Race Discrimination.* New York: Pathfinder Press, 1961.

"Salvador Leftists on to Victory." *Workers Vanguard,* no. 330 (May 20, 1983), pp. 1, 4.

Shachtman, Max. "Radicalism in the Thirties: The Trotskyist View." In Rita James Simon, ed., *As We Saw the Thirties.* Urbana: University of Illinois Press, 1967, pp. 8-45.

Singer, Stu. "Peter Camejo Arrested and Threatened by Houston Cops." *The Militant* 39, no. 10 (March 21, 1975), p. 11.

Socialist Workers Party. "Discussion with Leon Trotsky on the Transitional Program. In Leon Trotsky, *The Transitional Program for Socialist Revolution.* 2d ed. New York: Pathflnder Press, 1974, pp. 113-161.

——. *The Nature of the Cuban Revolution: Record of a Controversy, 1960-1963.* Education for Socialists Series. New York: National Education Department, Socialist Workers Party, April 1968.

——. *The Socialist Workers Party Proposes: A Bill of Rights for Working People.* New York: Socialist Workers 1976 National Campaign Committee, 1976.

——. "A Strategy for Revolutionary Youth." In Trotsky, *The Transitional Program for Socialist Revolution,* pp. 181-203.

——. *Towards a History of the Fourth International: Part I.* Education for Socialists Series. New York: National Education Department, Socialist Workers Party, June 1973.

—. *Towards a History of the Fourth International: Part II.* Education for Socialists Series. New York: National Education Department, Socialist Workers Party, November 1973.

—. *Towards a History of the Fourth International: Part III.* Education for Socialists Series. New York: National Education Department, Socialist Workers Party, March 1974.

—. *Towards a History of the Fourth International: Part IV.* Education for Socialists Series. New York: National Education Department, Socialist Workers Party, March 1974.

—. *Towards a History of the Fourth International: Part V.* Education for Socialists Series. New York: National Education Department, Socialist Workers Party, April 1974.

—. "A Transitional Program for Black Liberation." In Trotsky, *The Transitional Program for Socialist Revolation,* pp. 162-180.

—. *Vote Socialist Workers in '74.* Electoral Platform of the Illinois SWP.

Spark. "The Black Revolt in the USA: A Hope for All Humanity." Mimeographed, n.d.

—. "Peaceful Coexistence: The Shortest Path to World War III." Mimeographed, n.d.

—. "The 'Rebuilding' of the IVth International." Mimeographed, n.d.

—. "The Trotskyist Movement and the Problem of the People's Democracies." Mimeographed, n.d.

Spartacist League. *Basic Documents of the Spartacist League.* Marxist Bulletin No. 9, Part 1, 2, and 3. New York: Spartacist, 1973.

—. *Cuba and Marxist Theory.* Marxist Bulletin No. 8. New York: Spartacist, n.d.

—. *Expulsion from the Socialist Workers Party.* Marxist Bulletin No. 4, Part 1 and 2. New York: Spartacist, n.d.

—. *From Maoism to Trotskyism.* Marxist Bulletin No. 10. New York: Spartacist, n.d.

—. *The Nature of the Socialist Workers Party — Revolutionary or Centrist?* Marxist Bulletin No. 2. New York: Spartacist, n.d,

—. *The Split in the Revolutionary Tendency.* Marxist Bulletin No. 3, Part 1. New York: Spartacist, n.d.

—. "Why We Support the ERA." *Women and Revolution,* no. 4 (Fall 1973), pp. 24, 20.

—. *Wohiforth Against the R.T.* Marxist Bulletin No. 3, Part 2. New York: Spartacist, n.d.

Spartacus Youth League. *China's Alliance with US Imperialism.* New York: Spartacus Youth Publishing Co., 1976.

"SWP Bows to Holy Man Khomeini." *Workers Vanguard,* no. 219 (November 17, 1978), p. 10.

Thomas, Tony, ed. *Black Liberation and Socialism.* New York: Pathfinder Press, 1974.

—. *Marxism versus Maoism: A Reply to the "Guardian."* New York: Pathfinder Press, 1974.

Trotsky, Leon. *On Black Nationalism and Self-Determination.* New York: Pathfinder Press, 1972.

—. "An Open Letter to Comrade Burnham." In Leon Trotsky, *In Defense of Marxism.*

New York: Pathfinder Press, 1973, pp. 72-94.

—. "A Petty Bourgeois Opposition in the Socialist Workers Party." In Trotsky, *In Defense of Marxism*, pp. 43-62.

—. "The Problem of the Labor Party." In Leon Trotsky, *The Transitional Program for Socialist Revolation*. 2d ed. New York: Pathfinder Press, 1974, pp. 241-243.

—. *The Third International after Lenin*. New York: Pathfinder Press, 1970.

"Vote Returns for SWP, Raza Unida Party." *The Militant* 38, no. 44 (November 22, 1974), p. 4.

"Why the White House Fears Negotiations in El Salvador." *The Militant* 47, no. 7 (March 4, 1983), p. 10.

Wohlforth, Tim. *Marxism and American Pragmatism*. New York: Labor Publications, Inc., 1971.

—. *The New Nationalism and the Negro Struggle*. New York: Bulletin Publications, 1969.

—. *Revisionism in Crisis*. New York: Labor Publications, Inc., 1972.

—. *The Struggle for Marxism in the United States: A History of American Trotskyism*. New York: Labor Publications, Inc., 1971.

Workers World Party. *Czechoslovakia, 1968: The Class Character of the Events*. New York: World View Publishers, 1978.

"The World Situation and the Immediate Tasks of the Fourth International." *Intercontinental Press* 12, no. 46 (December 23, 1974), pp. 1748-1774.

Maoism in the United States

"Advance through Criticism of Past Errors: Busing and the Fight Against National Oppression and For Revolution." *Revolution* 4, no. 6 (June 1979), pp. 9-15.

"Arrogant Clique Suffers Defeat: RCYB Consolidates on Correct Line." *Revolution* 3, no. 5 (February 1978), pp. 1, 18-19.

"Article by the BWC for the *Guardian* and RU Reply to the BWC." *Revolution* 2, no. 4 (May 1974), pp. 6-7, 16.

"Attica Brigade Seizes Statue of Liberty." *Revolution* 2, no. 4 (May 1974), p. 1.

Avakian, Bob. *Conquer the World?* Special issue of *Revolution,* no. 50 (December 1981).

Baraka, Amiri. "Radical Forum." *Guardian* 27, no. 21 (March 5, 1975), p. 17.

"Battle Sharpens around Bob Avakian's Demand for Refugee Status." *Revolutionary Worker,* no. 157 (May 28, 1982), pp. 1, 12-13.

Bendell, Ben. " 'Revolutionary Student Brigade' Formed in Iowa." *Guardian* 26, no. 38 (July 3, 1974), p. 7.

Black Workers Congress. "Criticism of 'National Bulletin 13' and the Right Line in the RU." Reprinted in Revolutionary Union, *The Red Papers #6.* Chicago: Revolutionary Union, 1974, pp. 23-34.

"Boston Busing Struggle Sharpens." *Revolution* 2, no. 10 (November 1974), pp. 1, 20-22.

"BWC Pamphlet: Taking the Wrong Path." *Revolution* 2, no. 5 (June 1974), pp. 5, 22-23.

The Call 10, no. 2 (March 1981).

"The China-Albania Split." *Guardian* 29, no. 42 (July 27, 1977), p. 16.

Communist Party (Marxist-Leninist). Documents from the Founding Congress of the Communist Party (Marxist-Leninist). Chicago: CP(M-L), 1977.

Davidson, Carl. "Angola: The *Guardian's* Treachery." *Class Struggle,* nos. 4-5 (Spring/Summer 1976), pp. 26-40. This is the journal of the Communist Party (Marxist-Leninist).

—. *In Defense of the Right to Self-Determination.* Chicago: Liberator Press, 1976.

—. *Left in Form, Right in Essence: A Critique of Contemporary Trotskyism.* New York: Guardian, 1973.

—. "Which Side Are You On?" *Guardian* 26, no. 17 (February 6, 1974), p. 9; 26, no. 23 (March 20, 1974), p. 8; 27, no. 9 (December II, 1974), p. 8; 27, no. 11 (December 25, 1974), p. 9; 27, no. 12 (January 8, 1975), p. 7.

D. B. "Marxism, Nationalism and the Task of Party Building: History and Lessons of the National Liaison Committee." *The Communist* 2, no. 1 (Fall/Winter 1977), pp. 123-170. This is the journal of the Revolutionary Communist Party.

Gifford, Ruth. "Waging Class Struggle in the Trade Unions." *Class Struggle,* no. 8 (Fall 1977), pp. 55-71.

Guardian Staff. "On Building the New Communist Party." *Guardian,* special supplement, 29, no. 34 (June 1, 1977), pp. SI-S8.

—. "The State of the Party-Building Movement." *Guardian* 31, no. 2 (October 18, 1978), pp. 11-14.

I Wor Kuen. "Criticisms of Workers Viewpoint Organization on Party Building." *I. W. K. Journal,* no. 3 (January 1976), pp. 38-78.

—. "Opportunism in the Asian Movement: Wei Min She/Revolutionary Union." *I. W. K. Journal,* no. 2 (May 1975), pp. 1-30.

Klehr, Eileen. "How RCP's 'Theory of Equality' Serves Soviet Social-Imperialism." *Class Struggle,* no. 8 (Fall 1977), pp. 33-52.

—. "Whitewashing Enemies and Slandering Friends: An Exposure of the RCP's Revisionist Line on the International Situation." *Class Struggle,* no. 7 (spring 1977), pp. 19-38.

Lai, Cynthia. "China Charts Independent Course: Major Shift in Foreign Policy." *Workers Viewpoint* 8, no. 3 (February 9-15, 1983), p. 10.

Line of March Editorial Board. "The Trial of the Gang of Four and the Crisis of Maoism." *Line of March* 1, no. 6 (May-June 1981), pp. 7-65.

Litt, Barry. "Nationalist Reformism Disguised as Marxism: A Polemic Against the Political Line of the August 29th Movement." *Class Struggle,* no. 7 (Spring 1977), pp. 67-87.

Mak, Pauline. "Some Maoist Groups in America: Experiences of the First Decade." Unpublished paper written at the University of Illinois at Urbana-Champaign, December 1973.

Marxist-Leninist Group of ex-RU Cadres. "Radical Forum." *Guardian* 26, no. 37 (June 26, 1974), p. 8.

Miller, Sherman. " 'Revolutionary Wing' or Anti-Party Bloc?" *Class Struggle,* nos. 4-5 (Spring/Summer 1976), pp. 4-24.

"Narrow Nationalism: Main Deviation in the Movement on the National Question." *Revolution* 2, no. 10 (November 1974), pp. 14-15, 22.

"The Next 25: Yesterday, Today, and Tommorrow." *Guardian* 26, no. 7 (November 28, 1973) p. 10.

Nishimura, William. "Arousing a Socialist Giant." *Workers Viewpoint* 8, no. 4 (February 16-22, 1983), pp. 7, 15.

"The October League (M-L): A Cover for Revisionism." *Revolution* 2, no. 7 (August 1974), pp. 11-22.

"On the Three Worlds and the International Situation." *Revolution* 2, no. 9 (July 1977), pp. 5, 18-19.

"People Must Unite to Smash Boston Busing Plan." *Revolution* 2, no. 9 (October 1974), pp. 1, 18-19.

Progressive Labor Party. *Revolution Today: U S. A., A Look at the Progressive Labor Movement and the Progressive Labor Party.* New York: Exposition Press, 1970.

"Report from the Central Committee." *Revolutionary Worker,* no. 194 (February 25, 1983), pp. 5-12.

Revolutionary Communist Party, USA. *Charting the Uncharted Course.* Chicago: RCP Publications, n.d.

—. *Communism and Revolution vs. Revisionism and Reformism in the Struggle to Build the Revolutionary Communist Youth Brigade.* Chicago: RCP Publications, 1978.

—. *Create Public Opinion... Seize Power!* Chicago: RCP Publications, 1979.

—. *CUBA: The Evaporation of a Myth.* Chicago: RCP Publications, 1977.

—. *A National Workers Organization: A Powerful Weapon for Our Class.* Chicago: RCP
Publications, 1977.

—. *New Programme and New Constitution of the Revolutionary Communist Party USA.* Chicago: RCP Publications, 1981.

—. *Programme and Constitution of the Revolutionary Communist Party USA.* Chicago: RCP Publications, 1975.

—. *The Task of Party Branches, The Task of Revolution.* Chicago: RCP Publications, 1977.

—. *War and Revolution.* Chicago: RCP Publications, 1976.

Revolutionary Student Brigade. *The Future Is Ours if We Dare to Take It: Documents from '77 Founding Convention of a Young Communist Organization (RSB).* Chicago: RSB, 1977.

Revolutionary Union. *The Red Papers #6: Build the Leadership of the Proletariat and Its Party.* Chicago: Revolutionary Union, 1974.

—. *The Red Papers #7. How Capitalism Has Been Restored in the Soviet Union and What This Means for the World Struggle.* Chicago: Revolutionary Union, 1974.

Silber, Irwin. "China and the Three Worlds." *Guardian* 30, no. 17 (February 1, 1978), p. 21.

—. "China's View of the Superpowers." *Guardian* 30, no. 19 (February 15, 1978), p. 21.

—. "...Fan the Flames." *Guardian* 27, no. 36 (June 18, 1975), p. 8.

—. "On the National Question." Reprinted from the *Guardian* in Carl Davidson, *In Defense of the Right to Self-Determination.* Chicago: Liberator Press, 1976, pp. 70-85.

—. " 'Revolution' Polemic Deceives No One." *Guardian* 27, no. 23 (March 19, 1975), p. 9.

Spartacist League. "RCP Splits!" *Workers Vanguard* (January 27, 1978).

"Students: Important Revolutionary Force." *Revolution* 2, no. 4 (May 1974), p. 18.

"Two Superpowers: Equally Enemies of World's People." *Revolution* 2, no. 10 (August 1977), pp. 5, 14.

Tyler, John B. "WVO's [Workers Viewpoint Organization's] Opportunism in Theory and Practice." *The Communist* 1, no. 2 (May 1, 1977), pp. 88-108.

Unity 6, no. 3 (February 25-March 10, 1983).

Waters, Mary-Alice. *Maoism in the U S.: A Critical History of the Progressive Labor Party*. New York: Young Socialist Publications, 1969.

A World to Win: International Marxist-Leninist Journal, no. 2 (May 1982).

The Young Communist, formerly *Fight Back!, The Revolutionary Student Brigade National Newspaper*, 5 no. 3, March 1978.

Index